Multinational Corporations
and the Control of Culture

Multinational Corporations and the Control of Culture

The Ideological Apparatuses of Imperialism

ARMAND MATTELART

Translated from the French by
MICHAEL CHANAN

HARVESTER PRESS·SUSSEX

HUMANITIES PRESS·NEW JERSEY

First published in Great Britain in 1979 by
THE HARVESTER PRESS LIMITED
Publisher: John Spiers
16, Ship Street
Brighton, Sussex

and in the USA by
HUMANITIES PRESS INC.
Atlantic Highlands, N.J. 07716

Reprinted in hardback 1982
First paperback edition 1982

Harvester Press   ISBN 0-85527-851-X   Hardback
                            0-7108-0348-2   Paperback

Humanities Press   ISBN 0-391-00978-8   Hardback
                            0-391-02553-8   Paperback

Manufactured in the United States of America

CONTENTS

LIST OF TABLES

LIST OF FIGURES

TRANSLATOR'S FOREWORD

A book is not like a computerised information system which can be updated continuously. Since this book was first published in France in 1976 there have, of course, been various changes in the companies discussed in it, including changes in the ownership of certain subsidiaries, and developments such as the awarding of important new contracts, which affect the state of competition between rival concerns. For example, as the finishing touches were being put to the translation, the news was announced that Cable and Wireless, the British State-owned telecommunications contractor, had won a contract in Saudi Arabia worth more than £300 m.—by far the biggest deal ever signed by the company, covering the supply and installation of a complete telecommunications system for the Saudi National Guard. (The Guard, whose current budget was £405 m., is entirely separate from the rest of the Saudi armed forces, with its own logistics and training systems; it operates as an internal security force.) However, we have not made any general attempt to incorporate such fresh information into the English edition. Some modifications to the original text have been made in the form of additions dealing with features of the operations of multinational companies in Britain, which were not detailed in the original but which are obviously of particular interest to a British readership. Otherwise alterations have only been made where they deal with developments which materially affect the book's argument. In both cases, many of the amendments are contained in new notes. Tables and Figures have not been updated.

None of this implies any kind of unfavourable judgement about the usefulness of books as against the electronic information systems which are discussed in the present work. On the contrary, what is important about books generally, and about this book in particular, is not so much the data contained therein as the analysis presented. For example, the analysis presented here of the connections between the development of communications systems and security forces. In this respect the present study is a pioneering work. There has been very little work done so far on the evolution of what is now the fastest growing sector of production in contemporary capitalism: the electronics-based multinationals involved in communications and the media, the companies responsible for the ideological apparatus of imperialism which this book analyses. Mattelart explores new aspects of the concentration and centralisation of capital, new patterns of production and consumption, new ways in which cultural production and the media are subordinated to capital, new forms of State practice in partnership with capital in the era of the multinationals. This is vital if we are to comprehend the ways in which the relations of capital have imposed themselves on cultural production and the mass media, indeed the way in which the media are *formed* by the relations of capital—as well as the correspondence between this process and the development of other new forms of social control which are more indirect and may be even more treacherous.

In fact, so little work of political economy of this kind has yet been done that the author of a recent article on the subject called his piece 'Communications: Blindspot of Western Marxism'; and two English mass media analysts a short while ago included the present work in a brief list of four or five books which, they said, were unfortunately ignored by writers concerned with the mass media and 'mass culture'.* If this is true of marxists, it's even truer of non-marxists. Of course the fact is that in spite of the development of sophisticated electronic information systems, the data which this book collects and analyses is outside general knowledge precisely because these systems are not intended to serve general knowledge, but form part of the arsenal of social control and subjugation developed by multinational companies and US imperialism for their own purposes. But again, that's exactly why this book is so important, because it tells us what is really going on behind the closed doors of the multinationals.

I am grateful to Armand Mattelart for his thorough co-operation during the job of translation. I have of course gone back to the original English sources for quotations translated by him into French. (Quotations originally in Spanish have been translated directly from the Spanish edition.) In one or two cases, however, passages originally in English have had to be retranslated from the French because the original sources were among papers belonging to the author which were destroyed by agents of the Chilean Junta when he was expelled from Chile after the coup d'état in 1973.

---

* Smythe, 'Communications: Blindspot of Western Marxism', *Canadian Journal of Political and Social Theory,* I, 3, Fall 1977; remarks by P. Golding and G. Murdoch in a paper presented to the Conference of the British Sociological Association, University of Sussex, April 1978.

FOREWORD

When it comes to standing back from slogans born in the heat of indignation stirred up by brutal interventions, tortures and genocide, when it comes to giving imperialism a content which no longer depends on its spectacular dramatisation but brings it off stage to mix with the public, then it is difficult to find agreement even among the most virulent of the placard-carriers, chanting 'Yankees, Go Home!' in front of US embassies around the world.

Imperialism doesn't only live in the exotic moments of its most brilliant coups, its coups d'état. It has its own normality, a daily timetable which unfolds in the margins of its unpublished confessions. We can only speculate about it: the flood of scandalous revelations often allows us to put off the moment of analysing this normality or stops us from pursuing it further. There is nothing more convenient than the way we let the traits of the enemy congeal when it comes to covering up our own errors in the choice of arms to be made for the fight. If, when we engage in concrete analysis of the machinery of imperialism, we no longer achieve the hallowed unanimity of the placards, this is above all because every definition, every approach towards the class enemy, is intimately connected with a definition of the strategy to be adopted to defeat this enemy. Thus, paradoxically, the profile certain sectors of the left often give to the picture of their adversary more often traces their own ghosts and zones of darkness than the enemy's reality.

To tackle the problem of the ideological apparatuses of imperialism is already to take sides. It is to recognise as a field of class struggle a domain which many of the actors in this struggle cover up with an inevitable show of neutrality. When someone decrees that it's enough to invert the relations of the forces to transform the bourgeois State apparatus, every questioning of the class character of this State becomes useless. It was the purpose of a previous work, devoted to the analysis of ideological struggle in Chile during the Popular Unity period, to demonstrate how the media function within the system as a whole; how, in the event of class confrontation, the truly class

character of this apparatus reveals itself in opposition to the revolutionary forces.*

The object of the present study is to specify the contours of the
ideological offensive of the ruling classes at the present stage of the
international accumulation of capital, to discern the mobility of its
agents, and to determine the transfers of power which the present phase
exacts. What type of ideological apparatus accompanies the phenomenon of multinationalisation? To each phase of the process of
accumulation of capital there corresponds a citizen made to the
measure of a certain set of social practices which gives life to the
legitimate and natural character of this process of accumulation. To
each phase there corresponds mechanisms of conditioning which
guarantee what the strategists of the Vietnam War denoted without
precautionary oratorical deceits as 'the conquest of hearts and minds'.

It is this necessary character which accompanies the expansion of
Empire at each moment of its history that gives whoever traces the
thread of imperialist penetration and undertakes the analysis of the
way it functions the impression of being faced with an implacable
machine. Nevertheless one should not confuse necessity with infallibility, and assimilate the logic of expansion and the survival of the
system to its supposedly invincible character. Behind the myth of the
invincible Superman there is always the reality of disarray of a paper
tiger, the reality of a threatened Empire. Rosa Luxemburg put it in
simple terms: history is made of two necessities in struggle, the
necessity which calls for continuous capitalist accumulation, and that
of the reply to this mounting oppression, the necessity of revolution.

In the last fifteen years, the apparatus of cultural production of the
North American Empire has suffered profound mutations. No sector,
be it press, radio, television, cinema or advertising, has escaped. In the
course of the process of industrial concentration, the owners of high
technology have increasingly become the ones who determine not only
the manufacture of hardware and the installation of systems, but also
the development of programmes, the content of messages. A field such
as education which had not previously been affected by massive
industrialisation has begun to be colonised by the newcomers. The
internationalisation of production has posed the problem of the
internationalisation of cultural merchandise.

* See Armand Mattelart, *Mass Media, Idéologies et Mouvement Révolutionnaire*,
Paris, 1974, Editions Anthropos, English translation forthcoming, Harvester Press;
also 'Chili 1970–1973: appareils idéologiques d'Etat et lutte de classe' (Interview with
Mattelart by S. Daney & S. Toubiana), *Cahiers du Cinéma*, Nos. 254–255, translated
as 'Interview with Armand Mattelart' in Michael Chanan, ed., *Chilean Cinema*, BFI,
1976.

Cultural production also reflects the character of the new political and military stakes in North American society. It is impossible to ignore that the rise of advanced communications technologies is associated with the rise of a high technology looming up in the shadow of a war economy. It cannot be dissociated from this context of State monopoly capitalism which leads to the tightening of bonds between the Pentagon and the big industrialists. It is within the framework of this increasingly close cooperation that the traditional partitions between the economic, the political, the cultural and the military have collapsed, the tangle of interests has been institutionalised and new forms of State practice have appeared. The post-Vietnam era, which also coincides with the end of the first phase of the conquest of Space, has seen the large US electronics and aerospace multinationals engaging in the 'civilisation' of the advanced techniques of 'electronic warfare'. Thanks to the social application of these techniques 'in the service of mankind', the computerisation of civil society is under way. But the introduction of new communications systems takes place within the already established relations of forces.

On the other hand, 'low profile' strategies, more subtle as forms of intervention against popular initiatives, have given the ideological level an importance of the first order within the international class struggle. In the politics of destabilisation conceived by Kissinger, these new forms of psycho-political warfare contribute by making space for chaos. Methods of approaching different sectors of the public are marked by a growing rationalisation of social control. The producers of so-called mass culture are bringing their mode of operation up to date. Destined to become the universal culture which encourages the expansion of Empire and by the same stroke contributes to the enslavement of each country's national consciousness, this is a culture which is beginning to take account of the specific needs and interests of each age group, each social category. The economic profitability of such a process is doubled by its ideological profitability. The new communications technologies open the way for this ever more intensive technification for which the present phase of accumulation of capital claims the need. In the same way that the structural crisis of the years 1880–93 gave birth to a new mode of circulation and of the exchange of commodities, persons and information, so the structural crisis which the world capitalist economy is now passing through signifies and demands a remodelling of the modes of communication.

Fifteen years passed between the time of Kennedy's exhortation to the officers of the Military Academy to read the classics of Mao Tse-tung and Che Guevara, the better to arm themselves against National Liberation Movements, and that other exhortation which in 1975 such a multinational as IBM lavished on its employees, to read the works of Marighela on the urban guerilla in order to protect its subsidiaries against revolutionary violence. This very strikingly epitomises the entire trajectory of the North American Empire which this book tries to elucidate.

The reinforcement of the technology of repression within the capitalist State—and its totalitarian character—poses the revolutionary movement, whether in clandestinity or in its legal forms, with new problems of organisation, and inevitably opens new fronts of struggle. This growth of technification and the changes in the organisation of the ruling classes which it supposes are themselves the product of class struggle. Behind the computer facilities offered to the intelligence services of the Chilean dictatorship by the Pentagon, to file their information on workers' and peasants' leaders and militants, there is the defeat of electronic warfare in South East Asia. Under the modernisation of the neocolonial State apparatus, equipped with the most sophisticated satellite communication systems, and the new underthrust represented by Brazilian imperialism, lies the victory in Angola. Beneath the triumphalist aggressiveness of the US aerospace firms selling thousands of missiles and planes to the countries of the Third World, is the economic and political crisis of imperialism searching uncertain markets.

Armand Mattelart
March 1976

CHAPTER I

HARDWARE AND THE MULTINATIONALS

BEFORE analysing the concrete forms which are taken in the course of setting up new communications technologies—satellites, cable television, video and all the other products which one way or another belong to computer telecommunications—it is appropriate to examine the evolution of the big electronics and aerospace manufacturers: the firms which develop the new technologies and which, in organising the way they enter into society are in the process of determining new modes of production and distribution of information and of mass culture.

Ancestors and newcomers in US electronics

In the course of the last two decades, the monopoly character of North American capitalism has become remarkably accentuated. In 1954, the top 500 firms in the United States represented half the sales of the country's industry and gathered two-thirds of the profits. Twenty years later, the 500 top firms produced two-thirds of the industrial turnover, received three-quarters of the profits and provided employment for more than three-quarters of the national labour-force. The differences which can be observed between the 1954 and the 1974 lists constitute another index of the movement of concentration. Of the 500 firms in the 1954 list, 159 have disappeared from view as a result of mergers with other more important enterprises.[1] From such absorption at the level of the big firms we can gather what has happened at the level of the small- and medium-size enterprises.

The big producers of electronic hardware nearly all figure in the top 100 American firms. Five or six of them, for the last few years, invariably turn up in the cluster of the top twenty: General Electric, IBM, ITT, Western Electric (which is only a division of the telecommunications giant American Telegraph and Telephone —ATT—whose turnover has reached more than $26 billion and which employs almost a million workers), Westinghouse, General

Telephone and Electronics (GTE-Sylvania) and Radio Corporation of America (RCA). The leap achieved by certain electronics enterprises explains the dynamism of this sector. Between 1966 and 1970, ITT moved from 28th position to 8th. In 1962, Xerox occupied 423rd place; in 1965, 171st, and in 1974, 41st. In the course of the last twenty years, the profits of this last company have grown at an average rate of 34% per year, one of the five highest rates of growth in the United States. It was only in 1975 that this progress suffered a small setback as a result of the economic crisis. Firms like the specialist in giant computers, Control Data, and the leader in mini-computers, Digital Equipment, which now figure in the club of the 500, didn't exist twenty years ago.

Table 1

Main Electronics Companies in the US (1974)

Company	Sales	Net income	Employees
	(in millions of dollars)		
General Electric	13,413	608	404,000
IBM	12,675	1,838	292,000
ITT	11,154	451	409,000
Western Electric*	7,382	310	190,000
Westinghouse	6,466	28	199,000
GTE-Sylvania	5,662	—	198,000
RCA	4,594	113	116,000
Xerox	3,576	331	101.000
Litton	3,082	40	107,000
Singer	2,662	10	111,000
Honeywell	2,626	76	92,000
Sperry Rand	2,615	113	99,000
TRW	2,486	101	88,000
Bendix	2,481	76	82,000
NCR	1,979	87	81,000
Raytheon	1,929	58	54,000
CBS	1,751	109	30,000
Texas Instruments	1,572	90	66,000
Burroughs	1,510	143	52,000
Motorola	1,367	71	51,000
Control Data	1,081	4	45,000
Zenith Radio	911	13	28,000
Hewlett-Packard	884	84	29,000
Digital Equipment	422	44	18,000

Source: 'The Fortune Directory of the 500 Largest Industrial Corporations', *Fortune*, May 1975. For GTE-Sylvania, see *Fortune*, July 1975.

* Western Electric is a subsidiary of American Telegraph & Telephone, whose total sales exceed $26 billion.

But the power of North American electronics is far from homogeneous. The firms involved present different characteristics, a diversity which has only been revealed and accentuated over the years.

The pioneers of electrical and electronics manufacture like General Electric, ATT and IBM, were all founded at the end of last century or the beginning of this, and their growth has been steady.[2] Between 1962 and 1972, for example, General Electric doubled its turnover, from $5 billion to $10 billion. This was achieved without the need to acquire enterprises outside their original field of activity, while for ATT and IBM, even the annexation of electronics firms has been pretty rare. The last time IBM purchased an electronics enterprise was before the Second World War. But this cannot be said for General Electric which, over the last ten years has colonised more than 30 enterprises in its own sector in the most diverse countries. Other veterans who, like Singer, National Cash Register (NCR) and Burroughs, have attached their names to sewing machines, cash registers and office equipment respectively, have also diversified without going outside the electronics field, but rather by laying hands on unlucky competitors. Singer bought up the firm of Frieden, in order to gain access to the market for calculators, long dominated by NCR. All these firms have started manufacturing computers, and each has succeeded in capturing 2 or 3% of the market. Since the end of the 60s, the audio-visual field has also interested them. Honeywell, world number two in computers after IBM, although far behind it, was only a modest manufacturer of temperature control systems in 1885. A pioneer of automation systems, it remains uncontested master of this field, from which to this day it draws half its turnover. Information processing provides the rest.

A second group of firms, as old as the first, can be distinguished by the fact that they have moved into other sectors. This policy of diversification was developed from the mid-60s on. Westinghouse and RCA are the clearest prototypes. In less than four years, the first of these bought up a car-hire firm, a hotel chain, construction companies and cement factories, several well-known fizzy drinks bottling plants and a watch manufacturer (Longines-Wittnauer). These acquisitions together soon came to constitute 15–20% of the corporation's turnover. Proceeding from the reorganisation of some of its previously established divisions, it launched out into what the company itself called 'the field of social problems': cheap housing, public transport, pollution control and education. In this way it has managed to triple its sales and quadruple its profits in the course of the last six years. RCA has also diversified rapidly. In 1972, the new properties acquired since 1966 already constituted a quarter of its turnover. Among the firms which thus came under its control were the famous car-hire firm Hertz, the no less famous publishers Random House, a construction company, a carpet factory and a frozen foods company. Well satisfied with this first step towards the formation of a diversified conglomerate, the Chairman of RCA declared in 1972: 'More than 70% of the company business is still in electronics, but RCA is now considerably more than an electronics company'.[3] Another significant index is the evolution of the services/industry relationship. In 1962, 64% of RCA's income came from industrial production, 36% from services. Ten years later, services represented 46%.

A third type of electronics enterprise—that of mushroom conglomerates—is particularly indicative of the speculative process of mergers and acquisitions of an indiscriminate kind which certain firms have followed during the last decade. The examples of ITT and Litton are among the most eloquent. In 1960, Litton's income was only $250 m. Ten years later, this figure was ten times larger. During the same period, the chemicals complex Dupont of Nemours had only advanced from $2.2 billion to $3.6 billion. The different divisions within Litton now manufacture dental instruments, warships, teaching materials, typewriters and office equipment (the Royal range of products), television set components and cash registers (Sweda). Towards the end of the 60s, anticipating the 'energy crisis', they set up a division for geophysical exploration (Western Geophysical Company). The case of ITT (another of this group) is much better known. In less than ten years, it has acquired more than 100 enterprises and its turnover has gone from $800 million to $8 billion. In 1975, the production of telecommunications equipment now counted for no more than 27% of the turnover of this supposedly telephone manufacturing company. The rest came from the most varied enterprises which they had acquired: bakeries, spare parts manufacture, construction firms, insurance companies, hotel chains . . . but in the last few years they have had to dispose of some of their most recent acquisitions, such as Avis car-hire, in response to anti-trust charges.

Finally, the last category is that of newcomers, which includes companies with an often spectacular growth based on a particular sector of electronics. This is the case with firms devoted to reprographics and to miniaturised information processing. In 1960, the moment when Xerox launched its 914 copier on the market, its turnover was only $33 m.; in 1975, this small and obscure Rochester firm had increased its sales one-hundredfold. Likewise only a short while ago, an important development in the technology of information processing—the micro-miniaturisation of electronic components—promoted a number of old-established firms to the top level, like Texas Instruments, founded in 1930, Fairchild, and

Motorola. In 1965, Texas Instruments did not exceed $500 m. Between 1971 and 1974, this firm, which invented integrated circuits, doubled its turnover. From still less than $800 m. it rose to almost $1.6 billion, thus overtaking such firms as the mining companies Anaconda and Kenecott which supply the raw materials for its micro-components. The big names in miniaturised information processing and other inventors of pocket calculators like Hewlett-Packard and Digital Equipment are further examples of this irresistible ascent. (In 1973, more than 6.5 million pocket calculators were sold in the US alone.)

These electronics companies are in their turn embedded within the

Some of the relationships between
banking groups, electronics companies and the mass media

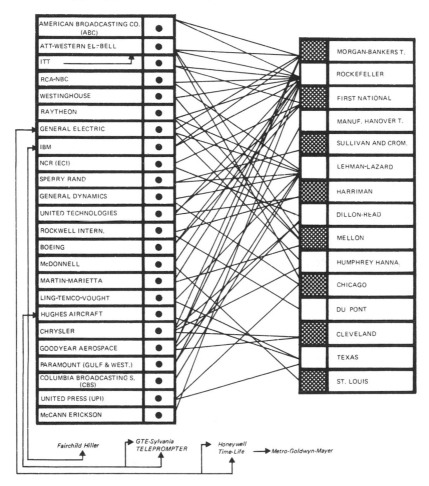

large financial groups which polarise the economy of the United States.[4] This structure is a classic one and is already sufficiently well-known that a detailed description is unnecessary here. We need only remember that the Rockefeller group is in dispute with Morgan Bankers over the most important part of the North American electronics industry. Chase Manhatten Bank and the Chemical Bank, both members of the Rockefeller Group, are in fact proprietors of a third of IBM's assets, a quarter of those of ATT, ITT and Westinghouse, and a fifth of those of RCA. Furthermore, Rockefeller possesses large interests in two airplane construction companies (McDonnell Douglas and Martin-Marietta). Morgan, which excercises total or partial control over such firms as Coca-Cola, General Motors, Procter and Gamble, Gillette, Anaconda and Kenecott, owns two-thirds of the assets of General Electric, half those of IBM, and a quarter of the assets of ATT. The First National City Bank is one of the biggest shareholders in NCR, holds the remaining shares in ITT and controls two-thirds of those of the big aeronautics firms Boeing and United Technologies. The Mellon-First National Boston group holds the other two-thirds of Westinghouse and has a majority holding in Raytheon. Lehman-Goldman-Sachs controls half the assets of Sperry Rand and RCA and shares control of the aeronautics firm General Dynamics with the Chicago Crown-Hilton group (proprietors of the famous hotel chain). A good many things reveal themselves when you have the patience to study the consequences of these inter-relationships within each banking group. Without doubt the most striking recent development is the direction which has been taken in following a policy of diversification by the petroleum company Gulf Oil, the main property of the Mellon group: they have followed the route mapped out by Westinghouse, which is a member of the Mellon group, and the biggest constructor of nuclear power stations in the world. The relations between General Electric and the big mining companies Anaconda and Kenecott are of the same type.[5]

A quick examination of the Board of Directors of these firms is a good way to discover the layers of interest groups which govern the progress of the electronics industry. Let us take the case of General Electric and set out the affiliations of the 21 members who compose its top management:

—13 members of the Board of General Electric are directors of banks. Two of them belong to the Board of Morgan, while the Chase Manhatten Bank, First National City Bank, and the Banks of Cleveland, Chicago and Boston each have one representative.

—6 belong to companies engaged in the exploitation of natural resources in third world countries. Represented in this way through the intermediary of these directors are the mining companies Hanna Mining, Consolidation Coal, Chrysler, National Steel, Kerr-McGee and Utah Construction and Mining. (Hanna Mining Co., for example, owns mines in Guatemala, Colombia and South-East Asia; it controls the richest veins of iron ore in Brazil, where, in addition, together with the Alcoa company, it also exploits the bauxite deposits in the State of Minais Gerais).

—7 have occupied or occupy important posts in the Defense Department or in other institutions connected with the military apparatus. Thus two directors have been Secretaries of Defense.

—12 have occupied or occupy key positions in US economic and foreign policy making. These include an ex-Secretary of the Treasury and Minister of Commerce appointed by Nixon in 1972.

—6 belong to other industrial multinational companies. The Board of General Electric includes the Presidents of Coca-Cola, Procter and Gamble, Campbell Soup and the paper company, Scott Paper. The links could not be more mechanical; Morgan Bank is in effect proprietor of the entire assets of Coca-Cola, Campbell Soup and Scott Paper, and two-thirds of Procter and Gamble.[6]

The boards of other electronics enterprises display in addition the strategy of international expansion adopted by these companies in the last few years. In 1972, for example, the chairman of the Société générale de Belgique was invited to sit on the board of Westinghouse, side by side with the Presidents of the International Harvester Co. and of Champion International, one of the directors of Eastman Kodak, the ex-president of the Massachusetts Institute of Technology and the current rector of Brown University. In 1972, Xerox introduced onto its board the ex-President of the airline KLM, and in 1974 came the turn of the current President of the Compagnie financière de Paris et des Pays-Bas, one of the most dynamic economic groups in Europe and one of the strongholds of the modernist wing of the French bourgeoisie.[7]

The process of multinationalisation

Between 1961 and 1970, electronics firms of North American origin set up 1,006 establishments abroad. This was only exceeded by the petrochemicals industry which established 1379 companies, and machine-tools which installed 1,317. Over the same period, North American banks opened 632 offices abroad.[8] The results of this mass invasion are obvious.

In dependent capitalist economies like Brazil, foreign capital —under North American hegemony—controls no less than 70% of the production of electrical equipment and 60% of domestic electrical appliances. The profits of the Brazilian subsidiary of General Electric, the foremost electrical manufacturing company in the country, exceed those of the subsidiaries of Shell and of Texaco and represent three-quarters of the profits of the foremost motor-car manufacturer, a subsidiary of Volkswagen. In the European countries, where American firms are still trying to consolidate their lead, the situation is less settled. In France, the index of foreign penetration in electronics has reached 32.5% of sales and more than a half of investments. These at least are the figures given by those responsible for the National Plan for 1971, which also says that foreign electronics firms employ 26.2% of the work force.[9] In the field of new technologies, this dependence is increased. The manufacturers of semi-conductors, for example, who produce the micro-components that are now incorporated into all sorts of equipment from elevators to air-conditioning plants as well as telecommunications and television sets, are for the most part North American in origin. In 1974, the United States controlled two-thirds of the world market in semi-conductors. The Western European countries consume 23% of worldwide production of semi-conductors, but they manufacture only 14%. The rest is supplied by US companies. In 1973, France imported from the United States $90 m worth of semi-conductors. This figure represents half the total turnover of the French semi-conductor industry. Furthermore, the semi-conductors which aren't imported are manufactured mostly by three firms. Two of them are of foreign origin: Philips and Texas Instruments. The third is a French company, Thomson CSF. A fourth firm joined them in 1975, Motorola, American. According to the projections of the Fairchild Company, this unequal balance of forces will grow worse between now and 1980. In that year the Western European countries will be consuming 26% of world semi-conductor production, but manufacturing only 10%. The North American companies will be consuming 42% and producing 64%. Japan, which is now consuming and will continue to consume a quarter, will continue to produce enough to meet its needs.[10]

American hegemony over the production of semi-conductors opens the door to other more unexpected levels of dependence. In 1975, Lip, which operated one of the most extensive distribution networks for watches in France, began the marketing of watches using quartz components, made by the North American firm National Semiconductors, consistently second or third world producer of integrated circuits. In return for the exclusive agreement, Lip provided the North American firm with the cases for its watches. This is the third agreement of this type made between an American group and European watchmakers. Earlier, Hughes Aircraft, which also manufactures microcomponents, made an agreement with a Swiss group, and its models are now hidden in cases made by the house of Jaz. The same with Herma and Yema watches. In this way, American technology comes bit by bit to dominate the promising market for the electronic wristwatch. 'Does this agreement between Lip and National Semiconductors not sound the knell for any effective research by the French in this field?' asked a specialist, expressing doubts that Lip might be able to continue its own research programme in quartz watches. 'Lip is pushing back further and further the production of its own quartz watches with digital display. Its boss claims that the project has not been abandoned, but one does not very well see any more how it can undertake the marketing of two models within the same distribution network. Besides, the development plan for the quartz watch in France directed by Montrelec, the company created in 1971 by the 15 major watch manufacturers and Thomson CSF to study the electronic watch, has broken down. The French watchmakers, it is being said, are incapable of reaching agreement among themselves'.[11]

In the Federal Republic of Germany, subsidiaries of foreign companies control no less than 40% of electronics production. Great Britain suffers a similar degree of dependence. In 1970, there were roughly 250 foreign companies operating in the British electronics industry: 150 American, 25 Dutch, 15 German and a dozen French. Among the six leading companies, which accounted for 70% of British production, three were of foreign origin (IBM, ITT and Philips); and yet Great Britain is the only European country where a national company acting independently has achieved decisive importance in the field of information processing. In 1974, the firm International Computers Ltd. (ICL), with nearly 35% of the computer fleet in Great Britain, continued to challenge IBM, with 38.4%. One may well ask how long it will take for them to increase this. In order to escape IBM's lead, the British company has already considered forming an alliance with another American firm, Control Data. In Italy, IBM has more than 70% of the field, in France and Germany around 57%. Although, as far as pocket calculators go, the situation could be more favourable, the North American firms control no less than 60% of the European market. Digital Equipment, the pioneer of miniaturised systems, alone controls 30% of the sales of pocket calculators in Europe.[12]

The electronics firms are therefore participating today in a new international mode of accumulation of capital. They are the protagonists in a process of internationalisation of production which characterises the phenomenon of multinationalisation. The capital they export serves not only to widen the process of circulation but

Table 2

Value of Computer Fleets Installed in Various Countries
(in billion of dollars)

Country/Region	1975		1980	
	Value	% of Machines of North American origin	Value	% of Machines of North American origin
USA	38.6	100	59 −65	98
Canada	1.9	95	3 − 4.5	95
W. Europe	19	84	31 −37	75
Socialist countries	2.5	5	5 − 7.5	10
Japan	6.1	47	12.5−16	40
Others	1.9	84	3 − 5.5	75
Total	**70**	**87**	**115 − 130**	**81**

Source: A.D. Little (Le SICOB, *Le Monde*, 18–9–1975).

is invested directly in productive activity. Like most other sectors of industry, these firms first introduced the substitution of imports and in their place the production by their subsidiaries of commodities which were previously exported. In certain countries this process of import substitution began before the great wave of multinational-isation was launched in the 60s. For example, during the 1930s depression, and above all during the course of the Second World War, it was this process of substitution which initiated the industrialisation of a number of Latin American countries. RCA's network of factories in Brazil and in the southern cone of Latin America dates from the 1940s. This was the platform from which RCA launched its monopoli-sation of numerous sectors of cultural production, which has increased as the years passed. Witness the record industry, where it was one of the first to begin recording the music of these countries, and the radio industry, where it imposed the North American model of broadcasting network. The Standard Electric division of ITT began to manufacture radio and telecommunications equipment in Santiago de Chile from 1942 and its Brazilian production began around the same time. The same phenomenon of substitution explains why most of the sub-sidiaries of General Electric were Latin American up to the beginning of the 60s. For a long time this firm has operated in Chile (where it has been installed since 1945), Venezuela, Mexico and Brazil. Not until the 60s was General Electric fully to install itself in countries such as

Malaysia, and in Hong Kong, where it operates not just with a view to production for the country itself but for the purpose of export. In so doing, it only follows the general movement which characterises this new phase of multinationalisation; a movement which was wonderfully well described in an advertisement for ITT which appeared in an Argentinian weekly in 1972, which also displays the mythology which this international penetration is clothed in:

> We are in the process of making Argentina a country equally famous for its telecommunications. When experts talk about the best meat in the world, they speak of Argentinian beafsteak. No other country is capable of creating the qualities of our excellent livestock. We will certainly always be famous for our meat. But Argentina is in the process of becoming equally famous for other exports. . . In the course of the last few years we have exported more than 8,000 telecommunications links to Chile, radio transmitters to Paraguay and Venezuela, 500,000 telephone dials to Brazil, 30,000 telephone receivers to Peru, vhf transreceivers to Zaïre (ex-Belgian Congo), Colombia and Brazil. We have carried off these contracts in spite of competition by the most important international telecommunications companies.

At the same moment, the staff and workers' union of the ITT subsidiary in Argentina accused the company of having invested more than 2 billion pesos in the construction of the Sheraton Hotel, an investment exempt from taxes, instead of reinvesting these profits in the modernisation of machines and in improving the working conditions of the personnel.

Most of the American electronics firms receive more than 40% of their revenues from abroad. Some indicators: in 1974 Xerox received 42% of its revenue and 52% of its profits from foreign subsidiaries. The same year, it undertook the construction of three new factories, in France, in Spain, and in its home territory. Equally in 1974 Sperry Rand's international turnover comprised 43% of its total. Approximately $800 m. out of a total of $3 billion came from the company's activities on the European continent. And also in 1974 Honeywell for the first time exceeded $1 m. from abroad, which made up 40% of its revenue. ITT took the sum of $6.2 billion from more than 50 countries where it operated; its total turnover was $11.2 billion. The previous year NCR and Burroughs had extracted 41% and 53% of their profits respectively from abroad. The amazing growth of firms like Texas Instruments shows the speed which the process of internationalisation can take in certain instances. In 1965 it included 14 factories in 6 countries. At the beginning of 1974 it operated in 19 countries and ran a network of 45 factories. It was only in 1973 that it established operations in San Salvador, Oporto, Kuala Lumpur and Japan, at the same time that it built two more factories in the United States.[13]

Table 3

US Direct Investment Abroad (1966–1973)
(in billion of dollars)

Country/Region	Investment*		Earnings	Reinvested earnings
	1966	1973	1973	1973
Canada	17.0	28.1	2.8	1.8
Europe	16.3	37.2	5.9	3.5
G.B.	*5.7*	*11.1*	*1.5*	*0.7*
E.E.C.**	*7.6*	*19.3*	*3.2*	*1.9*
Others	*3.0*	*6.8*	*1.2*	*0.8*
Japan	0.8	2.7	0.5	0.3
Australia, N. Zealand, S. Africa	2.7	6.1	1.0	0.5
Latin America	11.5	18.5	2.6	1.0
Africa		2.8	0.6	0.2
Middle East	6.6	2.7	2.3	0.1
Asia and Pacific		3.9	1.0	0.2
International or non-situated		5.3	0.6	0.5
Total***	54.8	107.3	17.5	8.1

Source: *Survey of Current Business*, August 1974.
    * Book value at year'end.
   ** Belgium, France, Federal Germany, Italy, Luxemburg, Netherlands.
  *** Detailed figures may not add up to total because of rounding.

But as the policy followed by General Electric and Westinghouse within the European Common Market customs union towards the end of the 60s shows, this process of international expansion could take on a much more diffuse form.[14] In 1968, the year that Westinghouse intensified its offensive in Europe, this firm's international turnover represented barely 8% of its global revenue. Four years later its international turnover had already grown to 20%. During this period it acquired control of the largest electrical engineering firm in Belgium (ACEC), and of a Spanish firm, Constructora nacional de maquinarias electricas (CENEME). At the same time it was involved in negotiations with two Italian firms and suffered the belated objection of the French Government which finally prevented it laying hands on the Jeumont-Schneider group. But, on the other hand, Westinghouse succeeded in stealing a march over General Electric in the market for nuclear power stations in France, by its 45% participation in Framatome (Creusot-Loire, controlled by the Belgian trust of Baron Empain), the biggest so-called French nuclear company, with whom it manufactures pressure-cooled generators. It was not until August 1975 that the French Government contemplated proposing to the American company to purchase some of its interests in Framatome under conditions extremely advantageous to the Americans.

The experience of General Electric on international markets is almost a century old. Lenin wrote about it in *Imperialism, The Highest Stage of Capitalism*. He described the process of concentration which created the General Electric Co. (GEC) in the US and the General Electric Co. (AEG) in Germany. Quoting Heinig's comment, 'there are no other electric companies in the world *completely* independent of them', he continued

> . . . in 1907, the German and American trusts concluded an agreement by which they divided the world between themselves. Competition between them ceased. The American General Electric Company (GEC) 'got' the United States and Canada. The German General Electric Company (AEG) 'got' Germany, Austria, Russia, Holland, Denmark, Switzerland, Turkey and the Balkans. Special agreements, naturally secret, were concluded regarding the penetration of 'daughter companies' into new branches of industry, into 'new' countries formally not yet allotted. The two trusts were to exchange inventions and experiments. The difficulty of competing against this trust, which is practically world-wide, controls a capital of several billion, and has its 'branches', agencies, representatives, connections, etc., in every corner of the world, is self-evident. But the division of the world between two powerful trusts does not preclude *redivision* if the relation of forces changes as a result of uneven development, war, bankruptcy, etc.

It was still the epoch when imperialism and the international mode of accumulation of capital proceeded principally by means of portfolio investments (the 'fleecing' of dividends in Lenin's expression). The strategy which General Electric has adopted towards European countries since 1965 proceeds through the most diverse agreements with national enterprises. In 1964, General Electric, profiting from the French Government's non-intervention policy, took control of 66% of the machine company Bull, up till then belonging exclusively to French capital. It would resell its shares in Bull to Honeywell, in 1970, a company of which it is also the principal shareholder. In the same period, thanks to a special dispensation from the American Senate, GEC began to make civil aviation engines with the French firm SNECMA which enlisted the technology of the future North American B–1 super-bomber. In order to worm their way into the French market for nuclear power stations (they controlled 38% of world production in 1973) and directly to counter their rivals Westinghouse (who controlled the same proportion), General Electric in 1972 granted licences for steam heated nuclear plants to the Compagnie générale d'électricité (CGE) after forming associations with others in Holland, Spain and Italy. At the same time they also reinforced their position in Germany by increasing their capital participation in AEG-Telefunken. In 1975, their French ally CGE brought about a merger between the Compagnie internationale pour l'informatique (CII) and Honeywell, a merger which consecrated the progressive alignment of French data-processing with American technology. However, after this resounding success, the CGE-General Electric tandem suffered a reverse: in deciding that there was room only for one manufacturer of nuclear power stations, the plan for the restructuring of the French nuclear industry excluded CGE—at least for the moment—from the market for nuclear generators which it had just squeezed into on the back of General Electric. The Westinghouse licences exploited by Framatome were given preference.[15]

Like most of the huge North American multinationals, the electronics companies have also used the pretext of the present crisis to re-examine their policy of expansion. Far from disengaging themselves from their foreign investments—even if these are occasionally slackening off—they are trying to adapt. Tactical retreats are married with strategic advances. A period of re-arrangement of subsidiaries is following the wave of wide-ranging acquisitions of the late 60s. They are already disentangling themselves from those which have not come up to scratch, and other forms of diversification are beginning to suggest themselves. For example, in 1975, General Electric got rid of a Belgian subsidiary which manufactured medical equipment, and of some of its properties in the field of teaching materials, and resolutely planted itself in the field of natural resources. Moreover, the interest manifested by General Electric in raw materials and energy expresses a basic trend in the comings and goings of diversification by the big North American companies. Initiated during the Arab oil embargo, this phenomenon continued to expand with the increase in oil prices. According to Wall Street experts, more than half the forty largest mergers carried out in the US in the last six months of 1975 had mining companies or energy producers as their object. Thus, into the snares of public bidding fell the copper mines of Anaconda and the Cerro Corporation, those companies so well known for their front seat role in the invisible blockade operated by the multinationals and the North American State against the economy of Popular Chile. Following the trend, the electronics giant laid claims to Utah International. The purchase of this mining company has constituted one of the largest company mergers in the economic history of the US—General Electric now controls directly the uranium, coal and iron mines which Utah International owned practically everywhere in the world, and which the electronics company needed to extend its nuclear expansion. As for Westinghouse, it relinquished a French subsidiary which made

Table 4

**Sales by Majority Owned Foreign Affiliates of US Companies by Destination
(in billions of dollars) 1966–1972**

Country/Region	Total Sales		Exports—%of total (1972)*	
	1966	**1972**	**to USA**	**to other countries**
Canada	23.9	48.7	17	6
Europe	40.5	97.0	2	24
G.B.	*13.4*	*24.4*	*2*	*20*
E.E.C.	*20.2*	*56.2*	*2*	*24*
Others	*6.9*	*16.4*	*2*	*32*
Japan	2.1	7.7	—	4
Australia, N. Zealand, S. Africa	5.2	10.8	1	12
Latin America	14.3	26.3	9	16
Africa	1.9	5.1	3	37
Middle East	4.0	11.3	4	78
Asia and Pacific	3.3	8.7	8	35
International or non-situated	2.7	5.5	6	45
Total**	**97.8**	**221.0**	**7**	**22**

Source: *Survey of Current Business*, August 1974.
  * Balance therefore represents sales on the local market.
 ** Details may not add up to totals because of rounding.

elevators to the profit of a Scandinavian group, and negotiated the sale of its majority holding in the Belgian company ACEC to Baron Empain, who had sold it to the company himself some years earlier. Both of them, General Electric and Westinghouse, are trying to draw closer to the stable financial resources provided by the State. Since Honeywell, thanks to its association with the French State, saw a market open up in the field of public administration and the research funds allocated to it, Westinghouse followed suit and agreed to sell some its interests in Framatome—but in return, the research capacities of the Atomic Energy Commission were surrendered to it, and some of the French uranium. For its part, General Electric, excluded from the French market for nuclear power stations, nevertheless succeeded elsewhere in Europe, as the North American empire launched its second offensive, and thanks to its Italian licence acquired a presence in the national commission (Nuclital) responsible for putting Italy's nuclear policy into shape. Meanwhile ITT, following other US firms, has begun to dispossess itself of some of its French subsidiaries. This becomes a way of maintaining its presence indirectly, since at all events the companies which are bought back by the local bourgeoisie need ITT's technology in order to progress. It is a kind of remote control which insures ITT against nationalisation in the event of the realisation of the *programme commun* (common programme) of the left.

There are very few North American electronics companies which do not have a network of production abroad. Nevertheless, however pradoxical it may seem, this is the case with the biggest of them, ATT. This is a decision which goes back to 1925. At that time, Western Electric, a division of ATT, ceded in its entirety to the newly born ITT, its subsidiary, International Western Electric, which owned a pre-cociously multinational network of factories manufacturing telephone equipment in England, Belgium, Spain, France, Holland, Italy, Norway, Poland, Australia, China and Japan. A premonition of its multinational destiny, ITT was founded in 1920, by two brothers who came from a small island in the Antilles, for the intention of uniting Cuba and the United States by telephone cable! Through purchasing the entire shareholding of the Western Electric subsidiary for thirty million dollars, ITT began its international expansion.[16] Despite this premature rupture, ATT is present everywhere today, thanks to its patents (in telephone equipment as well as movie sound systems, since together with RCA, ATT was the pioneer of the film industry) and its licences and experts.

Runaway production

The diverse forms which the internationalisation of production takes are clearly tightly bound up with the conditions of production in the host countries. Two relatively recent examples demonstrate this. In 1973, Honeywell, which six years earlier had timidly opened a simple sales office for computers in Madrid together with a servicing centre for its equipment, thought up the idea of converting them into a production centre with the double purpose of supplying the Spanish market without having to import, and of exporting to the Common Market countries from this Spanish base. The company even an-nounced that it would reduce its activities in other European countries—which amounted to closing offices—in order to transfer them to the Iberian peninsula. Other factors entering into this action? The fact is that around the same time Honeywell sacked 1,150 workers in its Scottish factory, which had needed British Government subsidies in setting it up. And these are the motives Honeywell's director gave to explain the flight towards Spain: 'Spain could be the Japan of Europe'. A summit meeting of Honeywell representatives in Europe was held to thrash out the following table: a machine operator in Britain cost 100 dollars per week, 152 in the German Federal Republic, while in Spain it was necessary to pay only 53 dollars for a job at the same level of skill. We can add that at this time Spain was beginning to benefit from the preferential agreements stipulated by the Common Market, which enabled it to export its products under highly advantageous conditions (75% on customs tariffs). The same year, another data processing company, Univac (a division of Sperry Rand) also decided to turn this difference in wages to its advantage and installed itself in Spain; it was rapidly followed by Westinghouse, who soon began producing transformers there. Their first customers were the Argentinians.[17]

The other example is at the same time older and more recent. Since 1965, North American industrialists have begun flowing towards the Mexican frontier cities bordering the United States, such as Tijuana, Mexicali and Nuevo Laredo. After looking around in Puerto Rico, Jamaica, Honk Kong, Taiwan and South Korea, the North American based multinationals went to Mexico in search of the cheap and abundant labour power which they needed. The restrictions imposed by the US Government on the entry of *braceros*—agricultural day-labourers authorised to cross the frontier to go to work—only succeeded in aggravating unemployment in the border region, and the Mexican Government regarded these new possibilities of employment favourably. A decree allowed the companies establishing themselves in these towns to bring in machines, equipment and raw materials free of tax. In return they undertook to re-export their produce directly. South of the frontier, as denounced in a slogan of the local section of the AFL-CIO—the most powerful trade union organisation in the United States—a worker was paid $1.60 per day; in Texas, $1.60 per hour. The North American executives were able to carry on living in the United States although they worked in Mexican territory. But there was another advantage, rather more seductive: 'Mexico is a politically stable country—there are no big anti-US demonstrations in the streets or war clouds in the sky. Harassment and terrorist tactics by Chinese Communists in Hong Kong have caused some worries about the future of US business in that British colony, and seem to have given impetus to the industrial buildup in northern Mexico'.[18] During the 70s, these enterprises, baptised with the name *maquiladoras*— border plants—reached a level of employment of 80,000 people, mostly women. All the large North American electronics firms profited from the opportunity. General Electric, Fairchild, RCA, Zenith, Litton, and Motorola installed factories for the assembly of television and radio sets, record players, tape recorders and semiconductors. Between 1965 and 1974, their investment in the zone rose to more than 55% of the global investment by the North American firms. Merely through assembling the various components imported from the United States, the workers in all the industries established in this zone added an annual value of $140 m. to North American products.

But with time, the situation deteriorated. Between October 1974 and April 1975, some 25,000 employees were sacked. The motives alleged to justify this withdrawal: the economic recession, the increase in minimum wages, and the protectionist campaigns of the AFL-CIO who, armed with the figures, had stood up forcefully to these companies who were exporting employment.[19] In 1971, United States imports coming from Japan, Korea, Taiwan, Singapore, Mexico and other factories in the exterior, comprised 54% of black and white television sets sold in the U.S., 18% of colour sets, 32% of record players, 91% of radios and 96% of tape recorders. 'Imports came both from foreign companies and from American subsidiaries abroad. In no other industry have U.S. corporations moved so much of their manufacturing overseas for the purpose of exporting back to the U.S. market. Many of the big electronics companies—Admiral, Motorola, Philco, RCA, Zenith—bring in the foreign-made product under their American brand names. (Only a close examination of the chassis may reveal a Made in Taiwan label). To the unions, this offshore move is the ultimate betrayal; it is viewed as another variant of the 'runaway shop'. From 1966 through the first eleven months of 1972, employment among workers making domestic radios and TV sets fell 18.5%—from 128,600 to 104,800. An additional 64,000 production jobs were lost in the manufacture of electronic components and accessories'.[20] In 1970, RCA closed its colour TV factory in Memphis established six years earlier, in order to transfer the bulk of its production to Taiwan. In so doing, 4,000 workers were sacked.

The return of electronics production to the metropolis must be explained by a technological reason. Manufacturing a colour television set demands a great deal of manual labour. The electronics companies operating in Mexico reckon that three quarters of the work necessary to construct a set is represented by the sum of manual operations (assembly of components). The total cost of this semi-skilled manual work necessarily increases everywhere, and so the companies try to develop the automation of this work. The director of Motorola has put the matter clearly: 'Up until now cost-cutting efforts have been concentrated on going overseas for hand labor. But that is getting less advantageous. Labor rates overseas have been increasing much faster than in the United States . . . semiconductor firms at least will have to automate.'[21] Up till now the rapid progress of colour television technology has paradoxically impeded automation of production lines. Almost as soon as they become operational they are outmoded by the discovery of new components. In the space of a few years, valves have been replaced by transistors and soon these will see themselves replaced by integrated circuits. And the application to television of the technology of the integrated circuit—a silicon chip the size of a finger-nail, with the power of about a hundred transistors—this is only just beginning in the United States. (On the other hand, almost 70% of colour sets in Federal Germany are already made with 'fully integrated circuits'. In the United States the figure is no more than 20%. And only the Zenith Corporation, the largest North American manufacturer of radios and television sets, is beginning to establish itself as a serious competitor). One can foresee that automation will become easier to the extent that the application of these components which so greatly simplify the electronic part of the television set, is increased. A considerable part of the assembly work will thus be superceded and the manual labour needs which the North American firms prefer to find abroad will be considerably reduced. The projections produced by the research departments of the North American electronics firms seem explicit enough. '. . . the circuits could reduce the total part count of a color TV from about 1,400 to possibly 100,' says Donald F. Johnstone, who heads General Electric Co.'s Television Receiver Dept. And he figures that this would mean 'a gradual return of TV assembly from overseas'. Motorola's prognosis follows the same line with even more optimism: 'By 1980 television sets will be built with 15 or 16 integrated circuits and then TV assembly will return to the US "just as ICs brought back calculator production"'. This is the appropriate context to interpret the words of Zenith's director when he opened the firm's second automated production line, in Chicago: 'We decided that the most self-defeating business strategy is chasing cheap labor around the world.'[22] One hardly knows whether to congratulate him for this statement, or on the contrary, to deplore it!

However, one shouldn't jump to conclusions and declare en-thusiastically that the period of runaway production of mass produced consumer electronics is coming to an end. The very recent evolution of Mexican subsidiaries of North American firms colours most of these hasty confessions, if it does not invalidate them. In February 1976, the Mexican Chamber of Industry announced that during the next 15 months, 200 to 250 factories for the assembly of all sorts of products would be set up in the new 'free zones' situated in the interior of the country. Other regions would therefore be opened up to North American firms, who continue to take advantage of the imbalances of internal colonialism. In the narrow peninsula of Yucatán, in Durango, San Luis de Potosí, in Jalisco, which Motorola has already moved away from, manual labour is half as expensive as in Tijuana (in the frontier zone the minimum hourly wage has reached $1.50). Some weeks before, apparently by coincidence, Stanford Research Institute had sent in a study in which it said in black and white that the unemployment which affects the interior regions en masse runs the risk of provoking serious social disorders if no remedy is found.

One sees in their schemes of expansion the role of planners of world production which the companies are called upon to play and in which nothing opposes them. The specialisation of subsidiaries which they set up abroad is another of the traits which defines this role. Each factory, each laboratory, is only one piece among many, dispersed around the world. The example of IBM is indicative of the interdependence of subsidiaries: 'One product per factory is always the slogan of internationalised manufacture . . . Thus, the Italian factory of Vinercate which makes central processors for the Series 3 and card input/output units, and obtains other system elements from other factories: keyboards, disc units and card-readers from Britain; memories, cables and panels from Germany; printed circuit logic boards from France, printers from Sweden and Holland, screening units from Argentina.'[23] This division of labour—in addition to fragmenting technical knowledge with the aim of control and preventing any country from nationalising an IBM factory—leads to a real discrimination in production according to the levels of development in the host country. A general tendency can be noted to concentrate manufacture of more sophisticated products in the more strongly industrialised countries; the rest is left to the periphery.

Multinationals of European origin

Only recently have certain European-based electronics companies begun to approach the trans-Atlantic multinational model, this *corporatum americanum* which, in the final analysis, seems to constitute the highest paradigm for the concept of multinationality. The most notable case is that of the Dutch firm Philips, the world's fourth largest electronics company. The leaders of electronics in the United States can only envy its size and the rhythm of its growth. In 1959, it had a turnover of $1.3 billion; in 1974, with factories in 40 countries and sales companies in 60 others, turnover had exceeded ten billion. Out of 412,000 workers in its employment, scarcely a quarter were based in the Netherlands. (We can note in comparison that out of 292,000 persons employed by IBM, about 140,000 worked outside the United States.) But it was only around 1972 that the Dutch company—in spite of the age of its international installations which date from before the First World War—started massively to reorganise its foreign subsidiaries. In two years, in the words of its North American competitors, Philips became a model of its type, 'a textbook example of how a multinational can optimise production'.[24] Fourteen years after the creation of the Common Market, Philips, in spite of its geographical dispersion, did not yet exploit the advantages of economies of scale. The firm was still traditionally organised so as to extract the largest profit from each national market on the basis of a network of factories set up in each country producing for local consumption. As the directors of the company realised before adopting the 'concept of centralised control' of the North American giants, all these units led to inconvenience although they did help to reduce the chance of people identifying Philips as a foreign firm, and make it easier to respond to local needs and tastes. In the new era, under the sign of North American management, the number of factories making radio sets was reduced from 14 to 9, the number making turntables from 8 to 3. Each was produced for the entire company and not only for the national market. Production of tape recorders was centralised in two factories, in Austria and Belgium; the Netherlands now provides electric shavers and other personal care appliances and sends them out to all European countries and to the US. Washing machines come from Britain, Italy and France. Dish-washers are made in Germany. To appreciate the rearrangement of these European subsidiaries in the overall policy of the multinational Dutch firm, one should know that these European centres of production furnish the company with the largest part of its turnover (69% in 1974). Its Latin American and US subsidiaries provide 17%; the rest comes mostly from Asiatic markets. It goes without saying that the reorganisation of the European subsidiaries was marked by numerous conflicts. Thanks to the concerted action of the unions in all the affected countries, grouped together under the Fédération européenne de la métallurgie, the Dutch firm had to accept the principle of trade union rights to information. But in return, it denied them the right to negotiation over the outcome of investment programmes. In spite of these limitations, it remains a unique example. No other multinational company has followed it along the same path. On the international scale, the 'prerogatives of the company director' are not therefore subject to any compensatory mechanism.[25]

In developing two world production centres in Rio de Janeiro and in Singapore, long before proceeding to the restructuring of its European bases of production, Philips had benefited from the difference which existed between the costs of manual labour in the European countries and the countries of the third world. The most complex equipment and systems, for example those used in road traffic control, are made by the

Table 5

Principal Electronics Companies in Europe (1974)

Company	Sales	Net income	Employees
	(in millions of dollars)		
Philips	10,118	294	412,000
Siemens	6,506	184	309,000
ITT-Europe	5,540	–	243,000*
AEG-Telefunken	4,975	–	170,000
C.G.E.	4,069	23	132,000
General Electric (G.B.)	2,739	171	200,000
Groupe Thomson	2,497	37	88,000
IBM-Germany	1,869	156	25,000
Thorn Electrical	1,514	85	87,000
Ericsson	1,474	49	81,000
IBM-France	1,309	81	20,000
Olivetti	1,223	6	72,000
Rank-Xerox	1,130	206	34,000
Plessey	965	53	75,000
EMI	953	33	47,000
IBM-Great Britain	807	54	13,000
Grundig	695	34	33,000
IBM-Italy**	581	–	8,400
Honeywell-Bull	533	25	16,000
ICL-Computers	460	3	29,000

Source: 'Annual Survey of international corporate performance: 1974', *Business Week*, 14. VII. 1975; 'The largest corporations outside the US', *Fortune*, August 1975; 'Le classement des premières sociétés françaises et européenes', *Les dossiers d'entreprise*, November 1974; 'Les 500 premières entreprises européennes', *Vision*, October 1975.

* ITT employs 71,000 persons in Federal Germany, 45,000 in GB, 31,000 in France, 27,000 in Spain, 22,000 in Italy and 16,000 in Belgium.

** IBM's fifth largest European subsidiary, IBM–Netherlands, declared sales of $324 m. and employs 5,900 persons.

Hilversum workshops and that of the French subsidiary Télécommunications radioélectriques et téléphoniques (TRT). The investment projects to be carried out over the course of the next few years show the growing decentralisation towards the countries of the periphery. According to these plans, the main investments in the production of electronic components will be directed towards South Korea, Hong Kong and India. The components will then be sent to the production centres situated in the industrialised countries. This division of labour is duly acknowledged in the company's annual reports, where it is explained in its own way: 'The trend already noted in preceding reports, according to which production capacity, like the evolution of markets for our products, grows proportionately faster in the less industrialised countries than in the others, has continued in 1974. In the industrialised countries, the nature of the tasks will be more and more in harmony with the level of training existing in these countries. One can observe, moreover, in many Western European countries, a permanent necessity to improve the direct conditions of labour, a growing tendency towards the establishment of concrete and institutionalised formulae of internal agreement. This evolution manifests itself on the part of employees equally as a need for the extension of their responsibilities as for a greater desire for influence over their own conditions of work . . . Within this perspective, it is essential to take into consideration such modifications as the development of new products and new methods of production'.[26]

The physiognomy of the electronics industry has suffered profound modifications in all the European countries. It has passed through a very active phase of regroupment, mergers and reorganisation. In Great Britain, the mergers effected between 1967 and 1970 created a vast movement of concentration of companies in this field. The General Electric Co. Ltd. (GEC)—which has nothing to do with its North American namesake—has been the principle protagonist and beneficiary. It absorbed two large enterprises one after the other, Associated Electrical Industries (AEI) and the English Electric Co. (EE), not long after the latter had just acquired another British firm, Elliott Automation.[27] This new industrial holding company which employs more than 250,000 people is today one of the three most important complexes not only in electronics but also in the aerospace industry. The Marconi division of the new company, for example, manufactures the whole range of aeronautics products, military and civil, from satellites to radar. (GEC also had a 40% holding in one of the principle British airplane manufacturers, the British Aircraft Corp). With English Electric it acquired 18% of the British computer company ICL [see footnote 27—trans.]. Without taking into account its innumerable minority holdings in the cables industry in South Africa, India, Iran, Australia, New Zealand and Sweden, GEC owns more than 35 foreign subsidiaries ranging from English Electric Marconi Argentina to the Société d'équipement industriel électro-mécanique in France and Marconi Italiana Spa. Its international network of factories provides it with more than a quarter of its turnover. Electronics is one of the branches of the British economy deeply involved in the international penetration of the country's direct investments. It is worthwhile remembering that British industry occupies second place in this field after the USA. Between 1970 and

1974 total direct investments by private British companies abroad rose from $21 billion to $35 billion (those of the United States from a little less than 80 billion to almost 120 billion). During the same period, international investments by German companies went up from $6 billion to $14 billion.[28]

A rapprochement, strongly encouraged by Bonn, between the two largest German electronics companies, Siemens and AEG-Telefunken, made consolidation of their penetration of foreign markets easier. In 1968, the two firms decided to establish two joint subsidiaries in the area of turbines, electricity power stations and transformers. The companies thus established were Kraftwerk Union AG and Transformatoren Union AG. It was thanks to this base in energy production that in 1975, Siemens, which had become a producer of nuclear power stations, was able to confront Westinghouse on the international market and in particular to wrest from it the custom of the Brazilian Government. This first stage of regrouping will be followed by plenty more. Among the most important one notices the concentration of activity by the firms of Siemens and Bosch in the field of domestic appliances in a new company whose shares are held in equal measure by the two of them; the merger of Siemens Bauunion with another German company, Dyckerhoff and Widmann AG; and the setting up of the Unidata association with Philips and the French CII in the attempt to form a 'Europe of computers'. This attempt to lay the foundations of a European capitalism with distinct interests from those of North American companies and giving preference to the products of European firms, was arrested by decision of the French Government. Under suspicion of seeking hegemony, Siemens did not inspire the confidence of the French industrialists. 'The company from across the Rhine', explained the propagandists of rapprochement between French data processing and Honeywell, 'which has just absorbed Telefunken, will simply gobble up little CII. It doesn't play fair. It refuses to market French materials in the Federal German Republic'. According to these same spokesmen, the strengthening of a supposedly French computer industry could only proceed 'by means of an alliance with an American manufacturer, because the idea of an all-European data processing industry is no more than a castle in the air. The Governments of Bonn and the Hague have no political will in this domain; they have neither the desire nor the means to take the place of Siemens and Philips. The Unidata agreement cannot last'.[29] After this wave of understandings and of collaboration, Siemens has launched a new offensive, with the aim this time of acquiring control of companies in partnership. In 1975, AEG-Telefunken entered negotiations with Siemens to cede to them the parts they held in the joint subsidiary

Kraftwerk Union. At the same time, Siemens announced that it was buying the entire holdings which AEG-Telefunken and another German firm Nixodorf owned in the data processing company Telefunken Computer Gmbh. On the level of international alliances, with Philips withdrawing from Unidata, Siemens preferred to resolve the problem of its data processing production by turning towards the Japanese. In making an agreement with the Japanese firm Fujitsu, the German company seemed to wish to escape from the technical dependence on the United States which its previous French partner in Unidata had been reduced to. This was the second time the German had escaped the vigilance of the North American owners of high technology in the strategic domain of electrical and electronic construction. Sometime earlier, Siemens had already 'Germanised' water-pressurised nuclear power stations and produced its first big international contracts in 1975 in masterly style. (France, through its agreements with Westinghouse, is subject to North American technology at least until 1982.)

In the last three years, Siemens has seen production by its foreign subsidiaries representing 20 and then 26% of its revenue, while the percentage of persons employed outside German territory rose from 19 to 29%. In 1974, Siemens business abroad constituted 51% of new orders, as against 40% four years earlier. It has production plants in 57 countries. Five years earlier it had them in only 47. In 1974, almost a quarter of the firm's investments went abroad, a figure which is well beyond the average for German industry, whose foreign investments generally do not reach half this level. Indicative of its decentralisation, its last factory has been built in Malacca, in Malaysia. It manufactures electronic components.[30]

The makers of Atlantic data-processing policy confess more and more loudly: in this field, French firms cannot compete with the big German companies. And yet French electronics has tried to remodel itself in the 70s. In spite of this effort, the French groups remain weaker than their German counterparts. The size of the workforce in the Siemens factories (300,000 workers) is more than twice that of Thomson, and the German company's turnover exceeds that of the French group by the same proportion. In 1974, production by electronics firms within German territory reached more than $8 billion, while in France this figure was only $4.5 billion. But the structure of production in the two countries is very different; Germany is far superior to France in the production of large-scale equipment for the public sector, while on the other hand, France produces much more communications equipment than its neighbour. Here, French firms reached a production level of $920 m., as against $637 m. on the part of

German firms.³¹ In various sector of electronics, therefore, French firms do not appear to have overcome the handicap which affects the French bourgeoisie in the face of other monopolist bourgeoisies in the big capitalist countries.

Three important facts have marked this alteration in the electronics industry. After having absorbed several companies and reorganised its subsidiaries, the firm of Thomson-Brandt, thanks to a packet investment by the Bank of Paris and the Netherlands, became the majority shareholder (51%) in its namesake Thomson-CSF. The second item to be noted is the agreement which was concluded between the Thomson group and its competitors the CGE group, itself right in the middle of a phase of acquisition and reorganisation. This agreement provided for the rationalisation of the ensemble of activities of the two groups, and organised their cooperation in common areas so as to avoid unnecessary competition, and in this way strengthen the position of the French electrical and electronics industry on the international level. Out of the this 'treaty of good feeling' (often subjected to difficult tests, for example in respect to the CII-Honeywell merger) the economic interest group Telespace was born, which allowed the group to establish their position in the international market for ground stations for satellite communications in competition with Philips' French subsidiary, TRT, which specialised in this type of production. Telespace is well situated for, and has serious chances of carrying off, the conquest of its first major contract for the construction of ground stations in Africa, in Zaire, where a project to install twelve stations was announced on the occasion of a trip by the French head of state. The third step sealed the rapprochement between the two big French electronics companies and the North American owners of high technology. Bit by bit, CGE and Thomson-CSF have drawn closer to the big US companies in order to enter the markets and the sectors which they have coveted for some time. The alliance between CGE and General Electric which would be bound to allow the French partner to capture a portion of the market for nuclear power stations, and of which the direct repercussions can be seen in the Honeywell case, was the starting signal. It has been followed by many other developments. Among the most recent: Thomson-CSF entered the market for telecommunications and switchgear by joining up with the Canadian firm Northern Electric, which itself already had a close relationship with the North American monopoly American Telegraph & Telephone; in order to strengthen its chances in tele-data-processing, it also signed an agreement of general cooperation with the North American company Computer Sciences Corporation, one of the most important companies in the world specialising in information systems and services. In every branch of new communications technology (video-disc, cable television, satellite) Thomson-CSF has assured its presence on the Americans' flank. We shall come back to this in due course.

However, the two French companies have reached very different levels of internationalisation of production; even though they have both followed to the letter the injunctions of the experts of the 1970 plan who declared that the problem 'is not the high rise of foreign investment in France, but the fundamental disequilibrium attached to the weakness of the implantation of French electronics industries abroad'.[32] More than 60% of French telecommunications production, at that time, was provided by subsidiaries of foreign groups. In this sector, foreign investment in France went from 200 million francs in 1970 to 360 millions in 1972. In parallel to this, investments abroad by genuinely French companies reached 75 million francs in 1972, against 30 million in 1970. Between 1968 and 1972, foreign production by CGE increased from 2 to 10% of its turnover. The five year plan adopted by the company projected the establishment of bases for international expansion which would stretch the foreign contribution to 55% of turnover, producing 25% through subsidiaries situated outside France and 30% from export sales. Following this oracle, CGE decided on a train of acquisitions unprecedented in the company's history. In 1972 alone, the French firm took control of a German electrical appliance company, purchased 49% of a Spanish construction company, took over a Canadian battery manufacturer and created a centre for the production of communications materials in Portugal. In 1971, ITT-Europe had ceded to it its French data-processing services subsidiary.[33] The Thomson group is far more advanced in its multinationalisation programme. In 1974, the level of foreign activity by Thomson-CSF was of the order of 48% of total sales with 54% envisaged for 1975. A new subsidiary Thomson-CSF International, was set up at this time for the purpose of strengthening and co-ordinating more tightly the network of foreign subsidiaries. Installed practically throughout the world, it can be found in Germany, where the adoption recently by the US army general staff of the French-German Roland armaments system has contributed powerfully to the consolidation of one of its two factories; in Argentina, where it has specialised in rural telephone systems; in Morocco, where apart from radio communications materials for the local market it also produces components—memories, relays, transistors—destined for export; in Brazil, where it is in process of constructing a third factory (one devoted to export of components); in Spain, where the company Equipos electrónicos—of which it owns

39%—has just started manufacturing naval equipment.[34]

The second wave of the Japanese invasion

In Japan, the majority of electronics firms are contained within some six large interest groups (Zaibatsu) which form the base of modern monopoly capitalism in that country. Thus Mitsubishi Electric—of which Philips controls one third—is enclosed within the group of the same name with activities right across the board: banks, brewing, mines, planes, construction, textiles, paper, petrochemicals, cement, fisheries, transport, etc. The firms Hitachi and Sharp are attached to the Fujo group which controls Canon cameras as well as the car manufacturers Nissan Motors. Nippon Electric belongs to the Sumimoto group. Fuji Electric and Fujitsu are held by the Furukawa-Daiichi group.[35] When one of these enterprises moves abroad, you can be sure to see it followed by a swarm of its colleagues from the same group.

Although Japan has the appearance of a giant on the international market, it is only recently that it's begun to increase the number of its factories abroad. A number of factors have obliged Japanese enterprises to emigrate. Among them, an international climate of protectionism, hostile to massive exports; the revaluation of the yen which took place in December 1971, which increased the price of exports and reduced the rate of profit; inflation and the rise in the cost of labour power. At the end of 1972, direct investments by Japanese firms abroad were equivalent to only one nineteenth of total investment by the United States (90 billion dollars) and a quarter of British investments. But then in the space of a year they doubled. In March 1974, direct Japanese investments were $12 billion; the Tokyo Ministry of Industry and International Trade envisages 45 billion at the end of the decade reaching 94 billion in 1985.[36] Japanese industrialists leaving the country obtain benefit from measures taken by the Japanese Government to encourage them. As early as 1972 the Ministry of Industry proposed to the Diet a law for the protection of Japanese investments abroad, which increased from 10 to 30% the sum which companies could reclaim by way of tax deductions in respect of losses which their foreign investments suffered.

Beginning around 1968, when the Japanese balance of payments revealed a surplus, the invasion of Japanese factories was particularly accelerated during the course of 1973.[37] At this date, the electronics firm Sony announced its intention of producing 25% of its exports (exports constituted half its total sales) through subsidiaries which it was beginning to establish abroad. Among the regions chosen were

Table 6

Principal Japanese Electronics Firms (1974)

Company	Sales	Net income	Employees
	(in million of dollars)		
Hitachi (1)	6,183	120	145,000
Matsushita Electric	4,838	179	88,000
Tokyo Shibaura	4,117	49	119,000
Mitsubishi Electric (2)	2,261	29	70,000
Nippon Electric	1,624	4	58,000
Sony	1,378	87	22,000
Sanyo	1,373	31	17,000
Fujitsu (3)	856	21	31,000
Fuji Electric	771	6	23,000
Sharp	651	9	10,000

Source: 'The largest corporations outside the US', *Fortune*, August 1975.

(1) Production figures for the whole group. Hitachi electrical/electronics announced sales for 1974 of $3,739 (*Business Week*, 14.VII.1975).

(2) Includes only the group's electrical division. Sales for all Mitsubishi enterprises (including chemicals, petrol, textiles, metals, etc.) exceeds $15 billion.

(3) In computers, Fujitsu is aligned with Hitachi, Nippon Electric with Toshiba, and Mitsubishi Electric with Oki Electric Industry Co.

Brazil, South Korea, Puerto Rico and California. Crown, makers of television sets and tape recorders, the victim of serious difficulties in the metropolis, removed the greater part of its production to Seoul, where the wages of Korean workers did not amount even to one fifth those of Tokyo. Sanyo installed itself in Saigon to produce black and white television sets. Hitachi established itself in the United States by buying in from General Electric one of its factories for magnetic materials; it began to make television sets and transistors in Singapore and opened a factory for semi-conductors in Malaysia. Among the job advertisements which it published in the Malaysian newspapers, an indication was let slip—to which those who can read between the lines cannot remain indifferent—of the reasons which had been pushed for its establishment in this country: 'Newly established Semiconductor Company Hitachi Semiconductor (Malaysia) SDN.BHD. located in Bayan Lepos, Penang, commencing factory operations shortly, invites suitable applicants to work as FEMALE PRODUCTION OPERATORS'.

Far too concentrated at first in South East Asia (in 1973, 37% of investment in Thai industry was Japanese and 90% of new industrial investments in South Korea came from Tokyo) Japanese firms have undertaken to extend their branches through other continents. After the defeat of the North American army in South-East Asia, Washington's decision to withdraw to the large Pacific archipelagos will undoubtedly provoke increased competition with Japanese firms in this part of the world. The Japanese seem to have foreseen this, and their policy of diversification of investments, which coincides with research into primary materials, has taken the Latin American countries and most particularly Brazil as its target. In 1969, Japanese investments in this country were no greater than $55 m. In 1974 they were eight times as much. One can predict, given the rhythm of these things, that soon the Japanese industrialists will be able to overtake the German investors (whose investments during the same period went from 177 million to almost 600 million).[38] After Mitsubishi's entry into mining, and the optical instruments industry, after that of Toyota into the automobile industry, the firms of Sony, Toshiba, Matsushita, Sanyo and Sharp have fully launched themselves into the manufacture of electronic appliances for the general public. For the first time in 1974, in spite of a relative fall of investment due to the economic recession, Tokyo invested in the Latin American countries the same amount as in the Asiatic countries. Total direct investments at this time by Japanese enterprises in Latin America reached $2.5 billion, while the figure in Asia was 3 billion: 20 and 24% respectively of capitals exported by Japanese industry. Naturally the Americans did not approve of Japanese expansion in the southern part of the continent. Numerous incidents indicate the pressures which they tried to exercise over their competitors. Among these incidents, the delay suffered by the construction of a port on the west coast of Mexico, which continues to depend for its trade in this part of the world on North American ports; the obstacles raised to impede the Japanese industrialists increasing their penetration in the copper mines of Bolivia; and —rather more well known—the veto imposed until very recently on Cuban access to loans granted by the Japanese Import Export Bank.

The installation of a base for production in the United States has equally become an objective of the first order (European firms also have this preoccupation, and Philips' recent acquisition of Magnavox is an index). Sony took the first shot. Three arguments in the company reports justified their establishment at San Diego in California: the questions of pre-empting the wave of protectionism arising in the USA, of avoiding the increased costs of shipment across the seas, and also the numerous dock strikes which had already handicapped Japanese exports. There was a fourth motive, but it was never publicly admitted. By producing television sets in the United States, Sony was finally able to escape accusations that it had been involved in the practice of dumping on the North American market; and, paradoxically, at the same time it was able to resort to other more subtle forms of dumping not considered by the law. 'When Sony exported television sets from Japan, it was vulnerable to the charge of selling them more cheaply in the US than at home. Now Sony assembles television sets in San Diego, using components imported from Japan. If it chooses, it could lower its US costs by cutting prices on the imported items. It is relatively easy to decide what the price of a television set should be by comparing Sony's US prices with its Japanese prices. But it is much more difficult to determine a so-called arm's-length price for a component, since many are proprietary and are not sold on the open market. As a result, the US Treasury, which administers our recently toughened anti-dumping laws, will have trouble preventing violations.'[39] After Sony, Hitachi and so many others, Matsushita (which lurks behind the most diverse labels and trade marks, Seiko, National Panasonic) found no better way of increasing the production of its colour televisions and other types of audio-visual apparatus than to acquire in 1974 the subsidiary of the North American company Motorola which specialised in this area. This acquisition has just been added to 28 other production centres which the Japanese company owns throughout the world and which make up 22% of its turnover. The geographical distribution of these subsidiaries is a faithful reflection of the successive priorities adopted in the course of expansion. Nine installations in Asia (South Korea, Taiwan, Philippines, Thailand, Malaysia, Singapore, Indonesia, Vietnam, India), five in Latin America (Mexico, Costa Rica, Venezuela, Peru, Brazil; one should add Puerto Rico here), one each in Iran, Tanzania, Australia and Canada and three in Europe (Belgium, Spain and Great Britain, the last European creation, which dates from 1974).[40] Japanese data processing has recently aligned itself with international norms. It has recourse to the most diverse formulae for this. In Spain, an agreement concluded at the beginning of 1975 provided for the construction of a Spanish-Japanese computer factory. Fujitsu, one of the three largest Japanese data processing companies, set up the Sociedad española de communicaciones e informática in which it has a 30% shareholding, the rest owned by Spanish banks, the national telephone company and a Madrid industrial holding company. The alliance with Siemens is the second European step. To understand the importance of this new development in Japanese industry one should note that in 1973 Japanese data processing companies already provided 53% of home computer needs.[41]

This leap by Japanese industry into multinational production is not lacking in repercussions on the way the Japanese firms manage themselves. They have set about learning from their North American elders, established in the international field since the 50s. This at least is what proposals by those responsible for Mitsubishi, the largest of them, suggest. 'For the past two years, we have been in a process of Americanisation, changing to the American management system . . . Until two years ago . . . Mitsubishi International's basic mission was to promote the interests of the parent company through its transactions. It bought minority shareholdings in, for example, raw materials producers mainly to obtain exclusive trading rights in the products. Now we are more independent as a profit centre . . . we are interested in direct profits and capital gains, not just the profits from buying and selling. And instead of sending the profits back to Japan . . . we now are ready to reinvest and increase employment in the country. That is quite a drastic change in our philosophy.' According to the same person, the Americanisation of an enterprise manifests itself above all in decision making and in personnel policies. 'In Japanese companies, plans typically are drafted by middle management, sent up to the managing directors for a decision by "consensus", and adopted by the president. The system avoids personal responsibility or credit. . . . Now there is more decision-making at the top. Also, we are changing the wage system. We had the Japanese system of giving annual wage increases to people whether they work or not. Now those who work hard will get the wage increases.'[42]

Two sorts of aerospace companies

The North American aerospace companies constitute a much narrower range of types than the electronics firms.[43] In the first type, you have the big airplane manufacturers who, at one time or another in their existence tied in their social justification with a celebrated civil or military prototype: McDonnell Douglas and its Phantoms, the DC–9, the DC–10; Boeing and the B–52 and the 700 series; General Dynamics and the F–16 (which the Norwegian, Dutch, Danish and Belgian air forces preferred to the French Mirage, when the renewal of their fleets took place in 1975 in what seemed like the 'sale of the century'); Northrop, another pretender to the same market, and its Cobras; Rockwell International and its Super-Sabers (in anticipation of its future B–1 super-bomber); Lockheed and its Hercules, and its triple-jet Tristar; United Technologies and its Pratt & Whitney engines which already equip a large number of European planes, and its Sikorsky helicopters. Less well known publicly is another aspect of their identity; these big names are also the ones involved in space conquest. McDonnel Douglas made the capsules for the Mercury and Gemini projects, and the third stage of the Apollo/Saturn rockets.

Table 7

Principal US Aerospace Companies (1974)

Company*	Sates	Net income	Employees
	(in million of dollars)		
Ling-Temco-Vought	4,769	112	66,000
Rockwell Internat.	4,409	130	137,000
Boeing	3,731	72	74,000
United Technologies	3,321	105	95,000
Lockheed	3,222	–	–
McDonnell Douglas	3,075	106	71,000
Textron	2,114	106	68,000
General Dynamics	1,968	52	64,000
Martin-Marietta	1,157	81	25,000
Grumman	1,113	33	30,000
Northrop	854	18	26,000
Avco	628	20	27,000

Source: 'The Fortune directory of the 500 largest industrial corporation'. *Fortune*, May 1975.
 * Hughes Aircraft not included. According to another source, Hughes Aircraft has sales of more than $1 billion.

Table 8

Proportion of North American Military Aeronautics Materials in European Countries (1975)

Country	Material of European origin		Material of North American origin		Total millions of EUR*
	Value in millions of EUR*	%	Value in millions of EUR*	%	
Federal Germany	1,347.6	39.3	2,077.4	60.7	3,425
Belgium	154.9	33.6	305.8	66.4	460.7
Denmark	49.2	32.9	100.5	67.1	149.7
France	1,661.3	93.1	122.2	6.9	1,783.5
Ireland	1.4	100	–	–	1.4
Italy	690	63	405.2	37	1,095.2
Netherlands	87.2	23.6	282.3	76.4	369.5
United Kingdom	1,680.5	69.4	740.1	30.6	2,420.6
EEC	5,672.1	58.5	4,033.5	41.5	9,705.6

Source: *Industrie et Société* No. 14, Paris 1975.
 * EUR = Eurodollar, EEC unit of currency, equivalent to 1.2 North American dollars.

Rockwell has had more than 80% of rocket launchers. Boeing made the lunar exploration vehicles. General Dynamics made the Atlas and Centaur rockets. The list could be extended until finally you reach the grand specialist in civil and military satellites, none other than Hughes Aircraft.

Some of these firms, traditionally identified with aeronautics, have launched themselves into a process of diversification which centres most particularly on electronics and machine-tools. General Dynamics, for instance, broadly diversified into shipbuilding, electronics, telecommunications, building materials and mining, drew 30.4% of sales and 37.8% of net income from aerospace in 1975. Rockwell International represents the optimum example of a policy of accelerated diversification and multinationalisation. Its change of name—at the beginning of the 70s it was still called North American Rockwell—is a sort of symbolic ratification of its new strategy. Rockwell manufactures offset printing equipment, automobile components, machines for the textile industry, and—evidence of its recent penetration in the field of micro-electronics from which it was effectively absent in 1969—pocket calculators and integrated circuits. In 1973 it took over one of the big specialists in military telecommunications, the North American Collins Radio Company, which carried with it ten centres of production abroad (Australia, Brazil, Canada, Great Britain, France, Germany, Hong Kong, Italy, Japan and Mexico). In 1974, through the purchase of the television manufacturers, Admiral, it inherited three other large centres of production, in Taiwan, Mexico and Canada, as well as a network of licences granted in 16 other countries. On other fronts and in 1974 alone, Rockwell formed a joint company with a British firm specialising in the manufacture of equipment for oil prospecting; acquired 75% participation in a French automobile component firm (Herwaythorn S.A.); and in Brazil, the largest manufacturer of industrial machinery for lumber working. The results were not long waited for; in 1974, Rockwell's international sales increased by 72% and went roughly from $500 m. to $900 m. Foreign subsidiaries supplied more than 15% of its turnover and the rest came from exports. Before 1970, Rockwell's aeronautic operations represented more than 60% of the firm's revenue; in 1973 they represented 30% and in 1974, 26%.

The second type of aeronautics manufacturers takes the form of odd conglomerates. This is the case with the world's largest manufacturer of civil and military helicopters, the Textron company, which draws 40% of its turnover from its Bell Helicopter division. In the last twelve years, Textron has acquired, apart from its base in textiles which gives it its name, 70 of the most varied companies ranging from watchstraps to carbon paper by way of Shaeffer pens. Between 1952 and 1974 its sales increased from $71 m. to more than 2.1 billion. Other manufacturers who equally belong to this club of diversified companies, have also attached their names to space conquest: Ling-Temco-Vought which at the same time encompasses the manufacture of rocket launchers, and insurance houses, also produces food, steel, carpets, tennis rackets, and pharmaceutical goods, not forgetting the control it exercises over the *Times Mirror* newspaper chain. A little less eccentric, Martin-Marietta, which draws half its turnover from missile construction, notably Pershing ground-to-ground rockets, and from space vehicles, also manufactures Portland cement, Sinclair and Valentine inks and paints; nor should one disparage its exploitation of bauxite beds in Africa. Goodyear Aerospace and Aerojet General, which belong to General Tire & Rubber, demonstrate that the giants of the pneumatic and rubber industry can also have interests in aeronautics. As for Chrysler, which is much better known for its cars, it manufactures no less than the Saturn rockets.

The aerospace industry is the branch of the economy which contributes most to keeping the US trade balance in equilibrium. In 1964, its international sales represented 8% ($1.6 billion) of total turnover. In 1975, in all likelihood, this international revenue will reach almost $8 billion and will constitute a third of sales. This sum represents about 8% of all exports achieved by the whole of North American industry.[44] The aggressiveness of the aerospace companies abroad becomes clearer and clearer. In 1974, the three principle manufacturers of commercial aircraft, Boeing, McDonnell Douglas and Lockheed received orders for 564 civil aircraft of all models, 356 of them for export. With 188 civil aircraft ordered in 1974 and 189 sold, Boeing alone covered 56% of the Western market. It can be estimated that in the same year, 99% of the civil market in the non-socialist countries and 80% of the military market belonged to the North American companies; the rest was supplied by European industrialists who only managed to achieve a quarter of the European market. The level of dependence of countries in the European Community (Such as the Netherlands, Denmark, Belgium and to a lesser extent, the German Federal Republic) in respect of North American military aeronautic supplies varied between 60 and 70%.[45]

The structure of aeronautics companies in other capitalist countries is closer to the first type of North American enterprise. Hardly diversified, they possess only a few centres of production abroad. Dassault, for example, whose international turnover represents more than 60% of its total turnover, possesses factories in Spain, Switzerland and Italy. But mutual co-operation agreements tend to grow up in the civil as well as the military domain. However, the French failure in the 'sale of the century' indicates the difficulties encountered in creating an all-European aeronautics industry. It showed above all that most of the European partners did not conceive the building of a Western aeronautics community without the participation of the United States. 'The Common Market should look resolutely towards the exterior, because in the long term we shall have problems, together or alone. The American market is very important. We should ally with the United States if we want to maintain our market or have access to the American market.'[46] One cannot fail to notice a sense of bitterness in this statement by Sir Kenneth Keith, the chairman of Rolls Royce—the British firm which makes aircraft engines as well as motor cars for millionaires—when one knows that the development of the North American jet engine industry stems from the concession of licences to Pratt & Whitney by the British manufacturers thirty years ago, for example, for Nene engines, and to General Electric for the Whittle patents. [Keith was previously chief executive of the merchant bankers Hill Samuel, who advised GEC on the merger with AEI—see footnote 27—Trans.]

Co-operation between the North American aeronautics companies and their foreign colleagues reveals increasingly a form of coproduction which really often only allows foreign firms to be sub-contractors to North American industry. Inversely, this formula allows the North American aircraft manufacturers to benefit from the subsidies offered by the Governments of their associates. We can cite by way of example the collaboration between Boeing and Aeritalia (which belongs to Fiat) guaranteed by the Italian State. Recent agreements between Rockwell International and the Japanese firm Fuji to manufacture jointly an 8-seater commercial airplane clearly indicate the limits of these coproduction treaties, which constitute new strategies for invading markets. According to these agreements, the Japanese firm was due to bring in 60% of the finance for the programme. It would be responsible for manufacturing detail work and sub-assemblies, which would be sent directly to the American firm's factory in Oklahoma for final assembly. The American partner would furnish the engines, the landing gear and other important components. Fuji would be able to sell the plane in Japan and the Far East. Rockwell kept exclusive rights for the rest of the world.[47] Brazil has just given the starting signal to its own aerospace industry by subscribing to similar agreements. Embraer (Empresa Brasileira de Aeronautica) has begun, for instance, to assemble components for Piper Aircraft Navajos for the national market and, when the opportunity arises, for export. A second stage envisages, in the medium term, the progressive replacement of

Table 9

Principal European Aerospace Companies (1974)

Company*	Sales	Net income	Employes
	(in millions of dollars)		
Hawker Siddeley	1,496	64	87,000
SNIAS	1,116	(−82)	40,000
Rolls-Royce	1,102	28	42,000
Dassault-Breguet	822	19	15,000
British Aircraft Crop.	638	28	38,000
MBB-Messerschmitt	599	3	20,000
VFW-Fokker	576	3	18,000
SNECMA	471	6	19,000

Source: 'Les 500 premièns entreprises européennes', *Vision*, October 1975.
* Not included in the list, the Swedish firm Saab-Scania, for which aeronautics is only one of many activities (total sales in 1974: $1,606 m.).

components sent from the United States by components made in Brazil. In a third phase, the North American company would be obliged to develop with its Brazilian counterpart a plane intended for export.[48]

The 'sale of the century' was the last opportunity the North American industry had to find efficient forms of coproduction within the limits of subcontracting. 1500 of General Dynamics' F-16 airplane were coproduced by the aeronautics companies of the four client countries: 350 were ordered by the air forces of these countries; 650 by the American air force and another 500 will be sold off to other countries. In applying the agreement between Washington and the Governments of the four main purchasing countries of the American fighter, the European firms have to produce 40% of the value the aircraft ordered by the European countries, 10% of those ordered by the US Air Force and 15% of those ordered by other countries. The companies of the four countries which make up the consortium are thus each assigned the manufacture of a section of the components. The Belgian firms Fairey and Sabca, for example, will assemble the Pratt and Whitney engine and construct the radar data processor. The Dutch firm Fokker-VFW is responsible for the central fuselage, the fuel counters and the radar aerials, among many other things. Norway—an aluminium exporting country with which General Dynamics has special agreements—will make the fuel tanks and, among many other elements, will coproduce the jet fuel starter with

Denmark. Denmark in its turn will produce the integrated fire control/navigation panel. And so on and so forth to the completion of a European version of the American aircraft. A special team (ESPO–European System Program Office), composed of representatives of the air forces of the four countries and of the USAF, together with engineers from the American firm, will direct the co-ordination, from the Ministry of Defence in Brussels. Each subcontracting company has a strict relationship with the North American companies which manufacture the various components of the North American version. According to calculations made by the US Treasury, this multinational operations will altogether produce a benefit of more than three billion dollars for the United States balance of payments. Moreover, the American fighter made by the Europeans will cost $140,000 dollars less than its counterpart made in the United States. The price of the aircraft has been fixed at $5.6 million.[49]

All these forms of multinational expansion by firms which were mostly content up till now purely and simply to export their aeronautics production have been inaugurated progressively as the imbalance between the US aeronautics industry and that of the rest of the capitalist world becomes accentuated.

Notes

1 *Fortune's Directory of the 500 Largest Industrial Corporations*, May 1975; Linda Grant Martin, *The 500: A Report on Two Decades*, ibid.
2 For the evolution of electronics and aerospace firms, cf. the classic works of reference, *Moddy's Industrial Manual*, and the annual company reports.
3 Radio Corporation of America (RCA) Annual Report 1972.
4 For the power structure in the US, cf. S. Menshikov, *Managers and Millionaires,* Moscow, Progress Publishers, 1969.
5 Jean-Marie Chevalier, Où les compagnies pétroliéres vont-elles placer leurs pions, *Le Monde*, 5.II.1974.
6 This analysis is based on General Electric Annual Reports for the years 1971–2 and on a document prepared by a study group, 'The GE Project', *Behind the corporate image: what General Electric did not say in its annual report*, Cambridge, Mass., 1971.
7 The Westinghouse Corporation, Annual Report 1972; The Xerox Corporation, Annual Report 1974.
8 *Business Abroad*, June 1971.
9 For Brazil, see *O Jornal do Brasil*, December 1975; for France, Datar, *Investissements etrangers et aménagement du territoire, Livre blanc*, Paris, 1974.
10 *Business Week*, 20.IV.1974.
11 André Dessot, 'L'offensive américaine dans la montre à quartz', *Le Monde*, 16.X.1975.

12 Ambassade de France en Grande-Bretange, *Le marché britannique de l'électronique*, London, 1973; *Dun's Review,* January 1975; 'Special informatique', *L'Expansion*, July-August 1974.
13 For the presence of North American firms abroad see the various annual reports of the different companies (1973 & 74).
14 *Business Week*, 2.X.1971, 24.II.1973, 9.VI.1973; *Advertising Age*, 30.IX.1971, 18.IX.1975.
15 For the Honeywell-Bull affair, see *Le Monde*, 14. V. 1975; for the restructuring of the French nuclear power industry, *Le Monde*, 8.IX.1975.
16 Note, however, that the recent rise of telecommunications systems is in the process of provoking a change in ATT's strategy. Its presence in Iran (cf. Ch. III) allows this North American telephone giant to initiate a new approach towards international markets.
17 *Business Week*, 7.IV.1973.
18 *Business Week*, 2.XII.1967.
19 Harold Burton, M., 'That incredible economy south of the border', *Fortune*, September 1975.
20 Irwin Ross, 'Labor's big push for protectionism', *Fortune*, March 1973.
21 *Electronics*, 17.IV.1975.
22 For the declarations by officers of G.E, Motorola and Zenith, see *Business Week*, 18.VIII.1973.
23 On this policy, cf. the document of denunciation written by an ex-IBM director of sales for a European country: 'IBM ou l'emergence d'une nouvelle dictature' *Le Temps Modernes*, October 1975. IBM-France, with exports of more than 2 billion francs annually, is the seventh largest French exporter. It is only exceeded by firms such as Renault, Peugeot, Air-France and leads other such as Michelin, Dassault, Rhône-Poulenc, Creusot-Loire and the principal electronics exporting group Thomson which occupies fifteenth place (*Moci-Moniteur du commerce international*, 'Les leaders de l'exportation française', 15.IX.1975).
24 *Business Week*, 13.1.1973.
25 *Philips Annual Report 1974; Philips global view*, Hilversum, 1975. On the union conflicts, cf. the study produced by J.P. Laviec, in *Syndicats et sociétés multinationals*, Paris, 1975, published by La documentation française.
26 *Philips Annual Report*, 1974.
27 'The General Electric Company Limited', *Informations generales*, Verlag Hoppenstedt & Co., Darmstadt—Société de Documentation et d'Analyses Financières, Paris.

The merger with AEI took place in 1967. AEI was suffering at the time from a bad ten-year run during which its capital had increased by about 60% and its turnover almost doubled, but without improving its rate of profit. Nevertheless its sales were running at £260 m. as against £180 m. for GEC. EE's sales at the same time were the largest of the three, at £411 m. At the time the merger with GEC took place, AEI had just sacked 4,400 workers, closed 4 factories and were trying to decide whether to call in the North American management consultants McKinsey. The merger took place under the watchful eye of the Industrial Reorganisation Corporation (IRC), set up by the Labour Government the previous year to implement rationalisations in the private sector which were considered desirable but were not taking place as a result of market forces. The GEC-EE merger of the following year was the second important merger of 1968. The first was the creation of International Computers (ICL) out of International Computers and Tabulators

(ICT) and EE's own computer interests. It was the result of £17 m. of Government money and the Government's decision to create a large British computer company capable of competing more effectively with the North American giant IBM. Similar thinking lay behind their support for the GEC-EE merger. According to Robert Jones and Oliver Marriott in their book *Anatomy of a Merger, a History of GEC, AEI and English Electric* (Jonathan Cape, 1970), Labour's Minister of Technology Anthony Wedgewood Benn told Lord Nelson of EE that he was in favour of the GEC takeover bid (whereas the Government did not approve of the parallel bid which Plessey was making) and, moreover, that it 'was not one that could be left for the market to decide'. Thus on 13th September 1968 the Government put out a statement saying 'The Government takes the view that the rationalisation which the proposed merger would facilitate would increase the efficiency and productivity of the electrical engineering industries, and in particular the effectiveness of the export effort of these companies, whose overseas sales are of the greatest importance to the balance of payments.' And this in spite of the fact that the two companies had not yet even got so far as to decide the financial terms they would put before their shareholders. As Jones and Marriott explained, the merger represented a victory for those members of the Labour Government 'who believed that Britain's industrial strength would be enhanced by the creation of giant companies comparable in size to the leading businesses in America and on the continent. It was a very different Labour Government from the Atlee regime of 1945–51 which had created the Monopolies Commission to curb the activities of giant companies'. (In the event, GEC, through the two mergers, raised its sales from £180 m. to £900 m.). The recent nationalisation of the British aerospace industry was motivated by the same rationale. (Translator's note).

28 *Business Week*, 14.VII.1975.
29 Reported by J.M. Quatrepoint, 'Les Etats-Unis plutôt que l'Europe', *Le Monde*, 14.V.1975.
30 Siemens, *Annual Report 1973–1974; Voilà Siemens,* 1975
31 *Electronics*, 26.XIII.1974, 9.I.1975.
32 cited by J.M. Quatrepoint, 'Des experts du Plan s'inquiètent de la pénétration américaine dans l'industrie électronique francaise', *Le Monde*, 13.IX.1973.
33 On the CGE strategy, apart from annual reports, see *Business Week*, 7.VII.1973; *Dossiers d'Enterprise*, 16–23 November, 1973.
34 Thomson-CSF, *Exercise 1974—Assemblée ordinaire au 12 juin 1975.*
35 For the evolution of monopoly capitalism in Japan, cf. Tasuku Noguchi, 'Japanese monopoly capitalism and the State', *Kapitalistate*, 1973, No. 1.
36 *Business Week*, 7.VII.1975.
37 *Electronics*, 22.XI.1971; *Business Week*, 24.III.1973, 31.III.1973.
38 'Latin America 75: Special Feature', *Far Eastern Economic Review*, 12.IX.1975; by way of comparison, in 1973, North American investments in Brazil were 3.2 billion.
39 Sanford Rose, 'The misguided furor about investments from abroad', *Fortune*, May 1975.
40 Matsushita, *Annual Report 1974.*
41 *Electronics*, 3.IV.1975.
42 *Business Week*, 24.III.1973.
43 cf. the annual company reports and the *World Space Directory* annuals, *New York*, Ziff-Davis Publishing Co.
44 *Aerospace facts and figures 1975–76*, Aerospace Association of American Inc. In 1974, exports by the US aeronautics industry reached $6.3 billion. French aircraft

manufacturers occupied second place with 2.3 billion, British industrialists third place with 1.5 billion.

45 *Industrie et Société*, Paris, 1975, no. 14.
46 *Le Monde*, 29.V.1975.
47 *Aviation Week and Space Technology*, 9.VI.1975. Since the end of the Second World War, the Pentagon has tried to promote the signing of coproduction treaties in aeronautics. Since 1949 the F-86 plane has been made in Canada. In 1953 Fiat began making it in Italy and Mitsubishi in Japan. But the new formulas now being proposed are largely breaking the framework of the earlier experiments.
48. C. Brownlow, 'Brazil presses to build aircraft industry', *Aviation Week & Space Technology*, 6.I.1975.
49 *Aviation Week and Space Technology*, 8.IX.1975.

CHAPTER II

THE PRODUCERS OF ELECTRONIC WARFARE

National security—a clever idea

> But without them, she couldn't see in the dark. She has good reason to fear the dark. She has retinitis pigmentosa. This eye disease usually begins as a kind of night-blindness. But little by little, many of its more than 100,000 victims will go totally blind. The electronic binoculars you see here can help during the night-blindness stage of the illness. They detect light even in near-total darkness—then electronically amplify it so even failing eyes can see. We developed these binoculars with the help of the Government's Night Vision laboratory. Now we're working with the National Retinitis Pigmentosa Foundation, to make a less expensive, pocket-sized model. So that more of the children and adults who become afflicted each day and need them, can have them. To us, there's a particular satisfaction in putting science to work for the benefit of people. Letting some light into darkness, where we can.

This text from an ITT advertisement is accompanied by a photograph of a young woman whose binoculars—rather big ones—make her look like a soldier in the Africa Korps. The advertisement appeared in 1974, in the large circulation business reviews in the United States. It corresponded to a new line of approach to the public which the multinational had adopted in the slogan, 'The best ideas are the ideas that help people. ITT'. A more concrete and personal slogan than the one engraved in golden letters in the hall of the ITT building in New York, at the base of a mosaic which represents a guardian angel embracing the two hemispheres: ITT at the service of men and nations.

Three years earlier, these electronic binoculars were still the exclusive property of the US army, and allowed Thieu's troops and their advisers to fight the revolutionaries of the Popular Revolutionary Government of Vietnam at night. Before they could be put on display in opticians' shop-windows, three intermediate projects were necessary by the Defence Department, entrusted to various ITT divisions: the initiation of infrared electronic binoculars for drivers of land vehicles, STANO (Surveillance-Target-Acquisition-Night-Observation); the development of a radar system for nocturnal helicopter missions; research into an image-intensifier to be mounted on rifles and machine-guns to identify their targets at night. At that time, ITT did less to disguise its belligerant activities:

> We're skilled in providing techniques that help keep tactical and strategic aircraft from becoming sitting ducks. That's one reason we've been picked to design and develop major new systems. These systems are helping to protect military aircraft from a variety of hostile threats. To efforts such as these we bring all our experience as a major supplier of navigation and electronic defence systems for the US Navy and Air Force. Plus a dedication to the subtle arts of confusing those who hunt the hunters. ITT Avionics Division, a member of the Defence-Space Group, International Telephone and Telegraph Corporation.

The fall-out of electronic warfare in the field of civil uses does not always take on the shape of a young American woman whose double fragility, both as a woman and someone suffering from a rare disease, testifies to the philanthropy of a medical research foundation. Other advertisements which claim the conversion to peaceful uses of electronic apparatus originally conceived for combat, effectively leave the repressive intention of their originals transparent: 'What we've learned in meeting the defense and space needs of the nation is now serving to meet the social needs of man . . . The data handling skills that help track a heartbeat on the moon now also help police enforce our laws. IBM Federal Systems Division.' Opposite this text, the photograph of a young FBI agent in front of the illuminated display of the latest tele-data-processing marvel. Similar words of wisdom are offered by other companies. For example, this extract from one of Westinghouse's annual reports: 'Safety wiring devices, plastics and such electronic wonders as low-light-level tubes that see in the dark are produced by 'Components and Materials'. Advanced technologies from 'Defense' are adapted to meet new applications in civilian problems, such as weapon detectors for airport use'. Further passages from the advertisements of US aerospace and electronics firms would only reinforce the impression already given here of an intention to convince the consumer of the social benefits to be drawn from apparatus derived from defense. There is no other way to read such publicity as this, put out by the aerospace group of General Electric, which is headed 'For the benefit of all Mankind':

> Sensors developed for astronaut monitoring are finding many uses. This infant [the reference is to a picture of a little girl in a California hospital] wears around her neck a tiny sensor that sounds an alarm if she experiences breathing difficulty . . . Use of space-developed infrared sensors is proving useful in the early detection of cancer. If an assessment of the total social effect of the benefits [of space technology] were made, we might well be astounded at the resultant improvement in the condition of mankind in only a decade . . .

But the main interest in these new slogans does not reside in their manner of professing civic virtue, especially when you know that these firms continue to maintain the field of armaments as an important proportion of their production. What we should notice is that in order to reach the potential individual consumers of such 'civilised' machines, these companies try to persuade them that their own identity is threatened, just as the identity of the State which orders these war machines is threatened in such conflicts as the opposition of Vietnam to the North American empire. The new motivation which these advertisements deal in presents the user of these new beneficent technologies as another being threatened by an enemy present everywhere: the transposition of the schema of aggression onto a private level. 'Ultrasonic detection is no longer a military secret. Profit from it. The thieves entering your home are professionals, greet them as professionals. Ultrasonic anti-theft detector, conceived by Singer'. This advertisement, published in *Le Monde*, 11th June 1975, shows the transistor radio which serves to disguise the anti-theft detector in the foreground, while in the background appears a warship equipped with the military version of this ultrasonic transmitter. The beams (as illustrated in the advertisement) which these two pieces of apparatus emit, join up in the same configuration.

On one level, these texts trace the path followed by North American electronics and aerospace production; in 1967, businessmen recognised among themselves: 'the majority of our new products find their primary application in the military domain'. Thus spoke the vice-president of Litton, who then became the budget controller for Nixon and Ford. This is the reality which today allows this firm to offer its services as a promoter of all-round development, proclaiming; 'Litton believes that economic development can accelerate if there is access to practices and programmes put forward for planning. Litton also believes that these principles which have allowed the United States to progress militarily and in space can be applied to resolve the problems of every nation. The LIDCO division of Litton offers this to you.'[1]

In 1967 Litton was the first to recognise the regime of the Greek colonels. Eight days after the coup, it proposed an $850 m. investment programme to the putchists, repayable over a 12-year period. The colonels were eager to accept the proposition, and the LIDCO division of Litton was charged with planning the economic development of Crete and the Western Peloponese, including a formal undertaking 'to preserve the historic monuments and the natural aesthetic resources of the region'!

Table 10

Principal Contractors to the Defense Department (1967–1974)
(in millions of dollars)

Company	1967	1970	1972	1974
US total all contracts	**39,219**	**31,315**	**33,362**	**34,357**
General Dynamics Corp.	1,832	1,183	1,289	1,853
Lockheed Aircraft Corp.	1,807	1,848	1,705	1,464
McDonnell Douglas Corp.	2,125	883	1,700	1,309
United Aircraft Corp.*	1,097	874	996	1,212
General Electric Co.	1,290	1,001	1,259	1,211
Boeing Co.	912	475	1,171	1,076
Litton Industries, Inc.	180	543	616	926
Hughes Aircraft Co.	420	497	688	825
Rockwell International Corp.	689	707	703	819
Raytheon Co.	403	380	507	740
American Telephone & Telegraph Co.	673	931	1,122	691
Grumman Corp.	488	661	1,120	687
Northrop Corp.	—	184	370	491
Westinghouse Electric Corp.	453	418	387	461
Textron Inc.	497	431	242	418
Chrysler Corp.	—	92	94	412
Sperry Rand Corp.	484	399	414	393
FMC Corp.	—	141	180	351
EXXON Corp.	235	229	209	340
General Motors Corp.	625	386	256	300
Honeywell Inc.	314	398	334	281
LTV Corp.	535	479	449	268
Standard Oil Co. of California	—	140	146	267
Tenneco Inc.	—	249	505	264
IBM Corp.	195	256	260	252
Martin-Marietta Corp.	290	251	256	246
RCA Corp.	268	263	275	243
Intern'l Telephone & Telegraph Corp.	255	217	258	237
Teledyne Inc.	88	238	180	228
TRW Inc.	121	179	146	203

Source: Dept. of Defense, *100 Companies and Thier Subsidiary Corporations Listed According to Net Value of Military Prime Contract Awards* (annually).
* United Aircraft was renamed United Technologies in 1974.
NB. A dash indicates that the company did not figure that year among the 30 leading companies.

Defense contracts

In 1974, Department of Defense contracts extended to the whole of North American industry increased to $34 billion. This total is close to the average annual budget allocated over the course of the previous eight years, which fluctuated around 30 billion. These contracts reached a maximum of $43 billion when the United States devoted 29 per year to the war in South East Asia.[2] The most surprising result is that the revolutionary government of Saigon unwillingly became the owner of so many helicopters and planes that it was propelled to the position of third biggest client of the US aerospace industry.

As an index of the high degree of concentration in military orders, in 1974, 25 firms shared half the contracts. Only one firm in this list of 25 is not an electronics or an aerospace firm: the Exxon oil company, in 19th place, which received contracts worth $289 m.; seven times less than the Pentagon's biggest client, General Dynamics. And with the funds allocated by NASA (National Aeronautics and Space Administration) the concentration is even greater. In 1972, for example, the space organisation's ten biggest clients shared 50% of the contracts. The first company—McDonnell Douglas—had 16% of the total for itself, that is, nine times the sum awarded to Fairchild in tenth place. The same year McDonnell Douglas occupied second position among the tax-farmers of the Pentagon. NASA funds are very much smaller than those of the Defense Department: $8 billion during the year of space conquest, stabilising to around 2.5 to 3.5 billion after 1972.[3] Another less well-known index of the process of concentration is that of the evolution of certain segments of the defense business in the last few years. For example, there are now only 12 missile builders and 7 shipyards building naval ships; 10 years ago there were 15 of each. The others have been forced to work as subcontractors, to merge, or have been forced out of business.

The dynamicism which defense has given to the electronics and aerospace industry emerges even more clearly when you examine the military contribution to the finance of 'development, research, test and evaluation' programmes by these firms. Each year North American industry devotes the equivalent of $20 billion to research and technological innovation. Electronics and aerospace absorbs more than half this sum. These are the sectors with the highest budgets. In 1971, for example, the chemical industry spent 3.5% of its turnover, or almost $2 billion, in its laboratories and research operations. This proportion increases to 20% in aerospace and 8.1% in electronics, each spending about $5 billion.[4] The course which this technological innovation follows means that 41% of aerospace products and 12% of

Table 11

Principle Contractors to NASA (1967-1974)
(in millions of dollars)

Company	1967	1970	1972	1974
Total Industrial Contracts	**3,864.1**	**2,759.2**	**2,143.3**	**2,118.6**
Rockwell International Corp.	983.8	531.5	175.1	486.5
Martin Marietta Corp.	12.8	108.0	208.4	201.8
McDonnell Douglas Corp.	243.9	236.3	343.1	156.0
Bendix Corp.	120.0	109.8	88.0	79.8
General Dynamics Corp.	61.0	38.0	66.6	79.5
General Electric Co.	179.3	131.7	114.9	65.0
Boeing Co.	273.5	158.6	94.2	60.0
International Business Machines Corp.	186.4	133.4	72.0	47.5
United Aircraft Corp.	40.0	27.1	15.9	39.7
Philco-Ford Corp.	32.1	24.0	36.2	36.0
Lockheed Electronics	—	—	24.4	35.4
RCA Corp.	57.5	54.5	57.2	34.7
Computer Sciences Corp.	11.8	11.0	23.3	27.4
Sperry Rand Corp.	38.7	48.1	33.5	21.7
Federal Electric Corp.	12.3	26.3	23.5	20.9
TRW Inc.	52.6	58.3	33.3	20.8
Hughes Aircraft Co.	19.9	9.0	22.0	18.0
LTV Aerospace Corp.	46.3	17.9	21.9	17.2
Thiokol Corp.	—	2.0	3.0	17.0
American Airlines, Inc.	—	—	—	16.9
Northrop Services, Inc.	8.8	—	4.9	16.3
Chrysler Corp.	76.6	16.7	24.3	16.1
Morrison, Knudsen Co., Inc.	—	—	—	15.6
Fairchild Industries	9.8	1.9	42.0	13.0
Honeywell, Inc.	22.6	11.5	11.1	12.3
Teledyne Industries, Inc.	—	—	6.0	12.3
Litton Systems, Inc.	—	1.8	6.0	11.3
Grumman Aerospace Corp.	481.1	284.4	28.5	11.1
Harris Corp.	—	—	—	10.6
Textron, Inc.	—	4.2	5.4	10.1

Source: National Aeronautics and Space Administration, *NASA Annual Procurement Report.* (Annually).

electronics products on the market in 1975 did not yet exist in 1972; while in fields like maritime and ground transport, this percentage was no greater than 3%, and reached 6% for oil companies.[5] In 1970, 79%

of finance for aerospace research came from government agencies, of which the Pentagon was the most important; the other 21% came from the enterprises themselves. Five years earlier the State pulled even more weight, since it provided 88% of the industry's research funds. The electronics industry presents a similar picture. Every year, those in electronics get 60% of their research budgets from the Defense Department.[6] You just have to glance down the list of beneficiaries of Defense research contracts. Among the first 20, you find 18 aerospace and electronics firms. The other two are university laboratories (Massachusetts Institute of Technology and Johns Hopkins University). Among such firms, like Lockheed, so-called independent research, that is, not financed by the Pentagon, receives funds nine times smaller than the research allied to defense. In 1972, out of $224 m. given over to research by RCA, 60% came from the Defense Department. And RCA was not, that year, one of the Pentagon's largest subscribers. In 1974, spread throughout its 100 laboratories— which produce more than 1,000 patents per year—General Electric spent $800 m. of which 500 m. came from the North American State. Xerox, with 12 m. in official funds, itself financed scarcely one tenth of its research. With IBM, public contributions have represented, during the last three years, 15–20% of its research budget.[7]

But there was a time when military investment in data-processing research was the most important. As a report published by the OECD recognised, it was the financial contribution of the Defense department which in the 50s allowed the data-processing industry to take off. 'In 1959, research and development contracts worth almost a billion dollars were allocated to computer manufacturers [in the United States]. This figure is comparable to the total sales figure for computers on the civil market in the same period, and it certainly exceeds considerably all support given to the computer industry in other countries. Coinciding with these years during which this new and important industry was established, this policy has without doubt had much more effect than any other national policy pursued at the time or since'.[8]

In point of fact, one could make the same observations for most of the products of advanced technology. Moreover, the Pentagon continues to be the most important user of these computers among the various institutions of the North American State. At the beginning of 1973, out of the 6,731 computers installed in various Government agencies, only 2,000 were at the disposal of civil offices; 4,000 came under the rubric 'special management', and were used principally by the organisations of Defense and Intelligence, in so-called classified

Table 12

Principal Research, Development, Test and Evaluation Contracts to the Defense Department, 1973
(in thousands of dollars)

1 McDonell Douglas Corp.	431,313	26 AVCO Corp.	52,514
2 Rockwell International Corp.	405,351	27 Mitre Corp.	41,634
3 Boeing Co.	401,549	28 Texas Instruments, Inc.	36,477
4 Grumman Aerospace Corp.	333,139	29 GTE Sylvania, Inc.	36,005
5 General Electric Co.	330,123	30 Northrop Corp.	34,649
6 Lockheed Missiles & Space Co., Inc.	278,195	31 Aerojet General Corp.	33,883
7 Western Electric Co., Inc.	264,699	32 Textron, Inc.	33,104
8 General Dynamics Corp.	226,514	33 Litton Systems, Inc.	32,905
9 Raytheon Co.	217,676	34 General Motors Corp.	29,919
10 Hughes Aircraft Co.	204,341	35 Teledyne Industries, Inc.	28,779
11 United Aircraft Corp.	175,876	36 International Telephone & Telegraph Corp.	28,536
12 Lockheed Aircraft Corp.	145,405	37 Stanford Research Institute	26,966
13 RCA Corp.	139,424	38 Federal Electric Corp.	26,789
14 International Business Machine Co.	126,627	39 Fairchild Industries, Inc.	26,508
15 Massachusetts Institute of Technology	123,992	40 Global Associates	22,715
16 Westinghouse Electric Corp.	119,361	41 Motorola, Inc.	21,912
17 Philco Ford Corp.	97,364	42 University of California.	21,895
18 TRW, Inc.	84,736	43 Automation Industries, Inc.	20,167
19 Johns Hopkins University	75,901	44 Calspan Corp.	19,440
20 Aerospace Corp.	70,588	45 LTV Aerospace Corp.	18,919
21 Sperry Rand Corp.	69,462	46 Sanders Associates, Inc.	18,585
22 McDonnell Douglas Astronautics Co.	65,877	47 Ketron Hawaii, Ltd.	17,810
23 Martin-Marietta Corp.	60,688	48 System Development Corp.	17,774
24 ARC, Inc.	54,993	49 Bendix Corp.	17,587
25 Honeywell, Inc.	52,657	50 Chrysler Corp.	16,556

Source: *Aviation Week & Space Technology,* 6 May 1974.

Table 13

Federal Expenditure in Research and Development According to Organisations (in million of dollars)

Year	Total	DOD	NASA	AEC	Others
1960	7,738	5,654	401	986	697
1961	9,278	6,618	744	1,111	805
1962	10,379	6,812	1,257	1,284	1,026
1963	12,000	6,849	2,552	1,335	1,264
1964	14,694	7,517	4,171	1,505	1,501
1965	14,875	6,728	5,093	1,520	1,534
1966	16,002	6,735	5,933	1,462	1,872
1967	16,842	7,680	5,426	1,467	2,269
1968	16,865	8,148	4,724	1,593	2,400
1969	16,207	7,858	4,251	1,654	2,444
1970	15,632	7,568	3,753	1,616	2,695
1971	15,050	7,541	3,382	1,303	2,824
1972	16,629	8,275	3,422	1,552	3,380
1973	17,407	8,574	3,315	1,623	3,895
	Total	**DOD**	**NASA**	**ERDA**	**Others**
1974	18,239	8,956	3,256	1,825	4,202
1975*	19,437	9,096	3,207	2,323	4,811
1976*	21,653	10,235	3,498	2,809	5,111

Source: Budget of the United States Government (annually).
* Estimated.
NB. DOD—Department of Defense; AEC—Atomic Energy Commission; ERDA—Energy Research &Developement Administration: set up in 1974, ERDA brings together research activities in energy.

installations (the network of the Defense department, ships, submarines and planes); the other 731 were part of regular Pentagon equipment. Out of the 797 computers purchased by government services in 1972, 753 were assigned to defense usage.[9]

The degree of dependence of each company on military contracts is relatively variable. Such dependence is strictest in the aerospace industry. In 1975, military contracts represented between 60 and 95% of the turnover of North American plane producers. Firms like Hughes Aircraft sell more than nine-tenths of their helicopters, planes and satellites this way. In Europe, by comparison the military production of the aerospace firms is around 65%. In France it reaches more than 70%, while in England it comes to a half. In 1972 with firms like

SCNECMA or SNIAS armaments formed 71% and 62% of turnover respectively. It reached 93% with Dassault. The electronics industry taken as a whole depends less on defense contracts, which represent about a quarter of its work. In France, this proportion was estimated as 20% of electronics production, but for firms like Thomson-CSF, it reached 60%.[10] In 1970, 12% of Westinghouse revenues came from its defense division; General Electric announced sales of 20% under the same heading, Litton 26% and RCA 13%. However, two factors get in the way of extracting the real participation of each firm in the defense industry from these figures contained in their annual reports. General Electric's 20% only refers to finished products delivered to the armed forces. The supply of components to other firms who employ them in the construction of war machines is strictly excluded. Actually, according to estimates produced at the beginning of 1960, two-fifths of the industrial products sold by General Electric to other firms are intended for this use.[11] If this is taken into consideration, the extent of General Electric's dependence takes on a proportion of 40%. Moreover, Pentagon contracts with each firm do not necessarily fall to its defense division. Thus ITT supplies the Pentagon not only through its defense division but also through its educational division and its hotel network.

These proportions also vary over time: 52% of the turnover of Sperry Rand came from government contracts in 1961; in 1974 these contracts represented no more than 18%. Raytheon, which in its early years was linked to the Pentagon as if by an umbilical cord, fell from 83 to 48% in the space of eight years. In 10 years, RCA saw the figure fall from 33 to 10%. The fluctuation of defense contracts has remained relatively stable for others. This explains how certain executives can still rejoice in their defense activities while others pine for times gone by. 'Our defense activities continue to enjoy success in an otherwise depressed market.'[12] Thus Westinghouse. This also seems to be the opinion of the directors of Honeywell, whose participation in the defense industry has stabilised itself at about 15 to 20% during the last three years, and who, as they let it be understood, have known better moments in times of war economy: Honeywell's aerospace and defense revenue volume in 1974 was $417 million, compared to $373 million in 1973. Earnings were up 25.9% from $27 million in 1973 to $34 million in 1974. The group experienced its strongest peace-time year in history, with major contributions coming from aircraft flight controls, marine systems, ordnance and the Space Shuttle program.'[13] Meanwhile RCA wrote less happily: 'Lower sales and earnings from government business in 1972 reflected the continuing decline in expenditures by the Department of Defense and the National Aeronautics and Space

Administration . . . However, activities in this field continue to be a well spring of advanced technology and technical competence.'[14]

Behind these fluctuations there is of course the reality of the expansion and diversification of these firms. Thus, for example, when you notice that sales by Lockheed to the North American Government between 1970 and 1971 fell from 93%, the level at which they had been maintained for more than ten years, to 74%, and on the other hand, foreign sales increased during the same period from 3 to 8%, you can obviously identify a new phase in the international expansion of the North American aerospace industry. But behind these figures are also the crises which shake these industries and which from time to time reduce their military custom in absolute terms; crises, moreover, which are not unexceptional to the extreme dependence on the objectives of a war economy which marks the electronics and aerospace industries.

The crises

Around 1970–when the North American economy entered on a classic crisis of overproduction and prepared itself to export primarily the still healthy capitalist economies in order to resolve its problems—at this time several factors combined to accentuate the malaise in the electronics and aerospace industry. These were, simultaneously or successively, the partial retreat in Vietnam, the end of the buying cycle of space vehicles and commercial aircraft, the cuts made in the military budget by the US Congress and also by the Nixon administration, which at that moment believed that a reduced use of technology could assist its campaign against inflation.

In January 1969, defense activities provided employment to 3.4 million civilians. Eighteen months later this figure had fallen to 2.9 million and the Ministry of Labour expected a further reduction of 600,000 jobs by June 1971 (not counting the effects of the demobilisation of 300,000 military personnel between June 1969 and June 1970, and similarly the laying off of a large number of civil employees of the armed forces). It was the aerospace industry which took the brunt: 1.5 million workers in 1968, 1.2 million in 1970, 969,000 in 1971. This loss of jobs particularly affected the non-diversified companies. Boeing's work force fell by 20% in 1969 and the number of workers in its Seattle factory fell from 101,000 to 38,000 in less than two years. This was the time, according to rumours, when the company requested the last employee to turn out the light after him in the interests of general economies! Rockwell, the great beneficiary of the Apollo programme, finally reached the point where it had to dismiss two-thirds of its aerospace personnel, Lockheed lost a third, and General Dynamics, less well off at that time, got rid of a little less than half: 26,000 of its 56,000 workers.[15]

This wave of dismissals also affected research and executive personnel. 25,000 researchers, engineers and scientists lost their jobs. In estimating the future demand for PhDs on the basis of the trends recorded at this period, it would seem that in 1980 75,000 specialists will be unable to find any outlet. At the beginning of 1971, the Association of Electronics Engineers recognised that they were about to confront 'the longest and most difficult period of specialist unemployment for the last twenty years'.[16] 40% of physicists and a fifth of engineers in the country depended on sources of work created by defence.

Various economists and futurologists elaborated models at the time which would allow them to estimate the effects on the North American industry which an increase or decrease of the defense budget would have—which at that moment stood around $75 billion. According to these calculations, if the military budget were reduced to 59 billion, the aerospace industry would altogether lose 24.4% of its sales, electronics 12.9%, war materials (tanks, guns, munitions, etc.) 32.5% and the iron and steel industry 8%. If the budget were increased to 93 billion, the plane makers would sell 35.5% more, electronics manufacturers 19.2%, manufacturers of tanks and guns, 42.8%, though the steel manufacturers would record a growth of only 1%.[17]

The second alternative in this model was already a temptation. In spite of the numerous amputations to which it was subjected by Congress, the US defense budget for the budgetary year 1976 was increased to $98 billion. For the year 1977, the Defense Department proposed the sum of $112.7 billion, which represented a real increase of more than 7 billion over the preceding year. In order to get a better idea of the significance of this sum to the North American economy, it should be noted that there are only seven other countries in the world whose gross national product exceeds $90 billion (USSR, Japan, Federal Germany, France, Great Britain, China and Italy) and that the national revenues of the African and Latin American countries reach 87 billion and 231 billion respectively.[18] These 98 billion represent a quarter of the whole federal budget. This proportion is of course far from that of the prosperous times of the Korean War—in 1953, when the Pentagon's budget was increased to $47.5 billion, it constituted more than 60% of the federal total. However nothing comparable occurred even with the increase which was achieved during the main period of the wars in South East Asia. Between 1964 and 1968, the military budget increased from 50.8 billion to 78 billion; this represented more than 42% of the Federal budget. The US aerospace companies together sold 60% of their engines to the Government in 1974. Between 1966 and 1970, however, this proportion exceeded 70%.[19]

In order to confront the crisis of the 70s, certain firms decided upon diversifying, and for those who had had the enterprise of doing so since 1965, it was a matter of redoubling their efforts in this direction. Boeing, for example, decided to open up new lines of production alongside its aeronautics construction: radio monitoring apparatus and other electronic gadgets for the police, hydroplanes, building construction and urban dwellings, systems for recycling refuse for the fertilisation of desert regions, desalinisation plants. (This firm took its first timid steps towards diversification at the end of the Korean War, at a time when it sold nearly 98% of its production to the military. But this policy which was followed at the time by a number of other plane makers, generally ended in failure.) We have had the example of diversification by Rockwell International around 1970. In 1967 this firm drew 74% of its income from Government funds; this proportion had fallen to 36% in 1974. McDonnell Douglas, which saw its Government sales fall from 69% to 57% between 1970 and 1972, turned towards its network of computers for hospital use and acquired two electronics companies. The electronics manufacturers among the Pentagon's clients followed the same path. Bendix, whose Government sales were reduced from 72% to 29% over ten years, diversified through the acquisition of 25 companies, mostly associated with the automobile industry and the construction industry. We can also take two firms, which have the most direct contact with the culture industry, Avco and Ampex. In 1963, Avco sold three-quarters of its production to the North American Government, which provided 60% of its profits; in 1971, this was 44% and constituted scarcely 15% of the company's profits. It was over these years that in order to avoid the risks of monoproduction, the company entered the most varied fields of activity: the film industry (Avco Embassy Pictures), cheap housing, credit cards (it owns the White Card), insurance companies and travel agencies. A significant detail: the division named Avco Ordnance (munitions) was retitled Precision Products Division and launched into the production of video-cassettes. Ampex, who invented videotape around 1955 saw its turnover with the Government fall from 50% to 14%. The way it solved its seemingly endless difficulties: it launched itself into the production of computers, a new type of videotape and into geophysical exploration.[20]

At the margins of this pressure towards a much more varied range of products, certain plane manufacturers, like Lockheed, on the edge of bankruptcy, had to be rescued by the Pentagon. In order to complete the manufacture of its giant four engined military transport plane, whose costs proved much greater than envisaged, 24 firms agreed to a loan to the firm, of which one third was guaranteed by the State according to an extremely unusual formula for the United States, and the Pentagon gave a substantial advance. There was no alternative since without the help of Washington, following the bankruptcy of its English associate Rolls Royce, Lockheed would have had to lay off 24,000 people in 25 states, lose $1.4 million investment, upset plans for expansion by TWA who had ordered planes from Lockheed to renew its fleet, and drag down a host of sub-contracting companies (Avco, United Technologies, etc.). This wasn't the first time the North American State had to concern itself with the difficulties of the aerospace companies. Some years earlier, Secretary of Defense McNamara had himself intervened in the signing of a contract with General Dynamics for the manufacture of the famous F-111. This plane which cost a billion dollars more than intended and which had to be withdrawn from Vietnam because of its weak combat capability had been preferred to another plane proposed by Boeing which was much less expensive.[21]

At present, in the general crisis which affects all the capitalist economies, the difficulties are far from being reabsorbed by everyone. But the major new lines (or rather, the logical extensions of activity) by which the electronics and aerospace industries are reorienting themselves, which had scarcely been drawn up around 1970, take time to acquire their shape and to become objects of commercial traffic, and the result is far from being definitely achieved.

The 'civilisation' of electronics

The acceleration of the civil application of those technologies whose exclusively military cycle is over, is confirmed day after day. A considerable extension of the field of application of electronics and aerospace products is going on, and this intensification of the transformation of civil society through electronics can be seen at every level.

We must insist right from the beginning that this phenomenon should not be interpreted (as the propagandists of certain electronics and aerospace firms would have us believe) as a return to a peacetime economy. We have seen and we will see again : the military dynamic has in no way lost its effect. The publicity of other electronics firms belies this optimistic interpretation : 'How Honeywell works with the world's most important computer user. Hand in glove.' The text which follows makes it quite explicit: 'In 1971, Honeywell won the job of providing the computer/communications network that supports the Federal Government's Worldwide Military Command and Control System (WWMCCS) . . . The system is one of the most important projects the Federal Government has today. We're proud of our participation.' The graphic element in this advertisement which appeared in *Business Week* in 1974 takes the shape of an eagle made from electronic micro-components preparing to land on a gloved fist which has the colours of the United States. In Germany, in order to match the national tradition in its advertisements for flying helmets, Honeywell superimposes the image of these helmets over a drawing of the pointed helmet of the Prussian army.

This pretence of an economy of peace, this conversion to civil use, is nothing more than the highest phase in the militarisation of civil society! The master generals of Vietnam cast off their battle-dress in the changing rooms of the big multinationals, and as Litton recognises, propose to plan the development of each nation 'according to the principles which have permitted the military and aerospace progress of the United States'. In this respect, the advertisements by the electronic communications division of NCR (National Cash Registers) are the most faithful to reality, when they talk of their 'revolutionary technology' of 'mini-communications terminals': 'The new militarised mini comm-terminal makes traditional teletypewriters antiques.' There is no place for civil reconversion: the new product which is now at the disposal of the consumer (press agencies etc.) is a military product, a product which satisfies the requirements of the modern world because it satisfies the requirements of defense.

To 'civilise' modern technologies, new state practices appear: the norms which have governed defense contracts between industry and the Pentagon or NASA tend to be generalised and are applied to the most varied sectors. In order to resolve problems of education, public health, housing, transport and general welfare, the State apparatus signs contracts with the companies which transfer to them the planning of important sectors of public services; the administrative methods tested by the military-industrial complex reveal themselves to be more efficient than those of public functionaries. The state is therefore at the point of becoming the arena where major transactions converge, and the private firm is promoted to the position of a technopolitical instrument.

To convice the most sceptical, let the actors themselves speak. Two interventions by high executives of the General Electric company allows us to situate what North American business-men like to call the new 'socio-industrial complex'. 'Private business should play its part in dealing with the problems of housing, education, traffic, health, waste disposal, pollution control . . . We may see the emergence of a 'social industrial complex', a partnership of business and government addressed to the resolution of these major social problems.' This first remark was made by the vice-president of General Electric in May 1971 during a conference which took place at the State University of New York on management and political institutions. The second intervention by a director of this electronics company, which goes back to 1967, is even more explicit:

> The concept of the government contracting with the private sector is as old as our country, but it assumes an urgency at this point in time to solve our urban problems. Many great corporations are already moving into the area of planned communities, one of which already has a fire department owned and operated by an insurance company. And this tendency must accelerate as we become more deeply involved in what may be called the contract state. More and more, government is turning to private business to perform under contract the things we were formerly led to believe that only government could do . . . Although Communists like to think of their way of life as a permanent revolution, in point of fact, that concept better describes the evolution of our own society . . . This emergence of a new social contract between the public and private sectors could be one of the most important and exciting developments in our social history.[22]

Behind such proposals and such practices two necessities stand out: the economic necessity and the ideological necessity. On the one hand, the industrial companies and the State apparatus have the need to deepen their mutual relations in order to apply and to dispose of the new technologies and the new systems in the civil markets. It is indeed no longer possible to begin the 'civilisation' of these technologies without running up against the various institutions responsible for the public services. On the other hand, in proposing the modernisation of the administrative methods of these services, the military-industrial complex begins to create a uniformity in the different ideological apparatuses (education, medicine, town-planning, etc.) which is indispensable in the present phase of accumulation of capital. The force of these two necessities and the requirements of profit-making which accompany them allows us to forecast numerous conflicts which these mutations will be bound to involve.

Alongside the beneficent face which the electronics and aerospace firm displays on entering the school, the hospital and the private dwelling, the other face of 'civil conversion' appears, a face which is openly repressive. The new way forward which Boeing indicates in the manufacture of radio patrol gear, and IBM in delivering its computer systems to the FBI, has not slowed the rhythm of the needs created by the modernisation of the forces of civil repression. The restructuring of the police apparatus undertaken by the Nixon administration has reached an opportune moment. Engaged on supplying what people came to call the 'law and order' market—one of the slogans in the electoral campaign of the Republican candidate in 1968—Boeing Computer Services (BCS) now proposes the most sophisticated products for dealing with delinquents: 'Making policework safer . . . an assignment for BCS. Instant information can often help a policeman more than a gun. Perhaps even save his life. In Wichita, Boeing Computer Services helped develop a system called SPIDER. It gives an officer on the scene all known data after he calls in a fragment of information—an address, a name, a licence number. The computer-assisted report comes back in seconds. Lt. Col. Kenneth M. Duckworth is well aware of the benefits of Wichita's Special Police Information Data Entry Retrieval system: 'SPIDER not only increases an officer's preparedness and safety,' he says, 'but shortens interview time and steps up the entire department's efficiency. Hundreds of hours of paperwork are eliminated, as well as rooms full of "hard copy" storage. And the unit cost of situations handled by our department is reduced considerably.'[23]

In 1966, in order to thwart the infiltration of North Vietnamese troops across the demilitarised zone of the 17th Parallel, the then Secretary of Defense McNamara decided to construct a conventional military barrage along the length of the frontier equipped with electronic warning devices. The idea was favoured, and came to be known as the McNamara Line, and under the direction of the Defense Communication Planning Group, created specially for the purpose, North American aviation interests began to lay a multitude of receptors across the territory of Indo China. Later, battery operated sensors were installed along the Ho Chi Minh Trail, a vital artery for the supply of North Vietnamese troops which crossed Laos. These sensors relayed information to B-52 aircraft flying overhead 24 hours a day.

The pick-ups located in B-52 aircraft over the length of the Ho Chi Minh Trail have become gadgets, and the seismic sensors 'make your home a fortress', while ultrasonic transmitters have been offered by Singer as a defense against undesirables. Special anti-riot police brigades now have at their disposal soft versions of arms which in Vietnam killed and mutilated. The advertisements of the manufacturers of these pieces of equipment now offer them to the police in the third world: 'To take the violence out of men's minds with the least violent means: superior non-lethal weaponry and protective equipment . . . first to achieve familiar "feel" to police handgun joins 4 other popular models.' 'To find a felon . . . when no policeman has seen his face . . . Tools to help you handle one of the world's roughest professions.'[24]

The 'McNamara lines' which tried to bar the way to the Vietnamese revolutionaries began to make their appearance in other continents. In July 1973, the *New York Times* announced that the construction of an electronic wall had been started on the Mexican frontier and would be finished in the course of 1974. This electronic wall, of which the first trials had taken place on a 100 kilometre section of the frontier of the State of California with Mexico around Chulavista three years earlier, would, if one is to believe the authorities, serve to restrain the clandestine entry of immigrants and drug traffickers. More than $1.5 billion was earmarked for this programme in 1974. The *New York Times* cable reported that 'the devices used are sensitive enough—according to the evidence of a military police officer who used them in Vietnam—to detect everything that moves, and indicate the nature, amount and quality of the movement'.

These detectors consist of 'geophones', seismic microphones buried in the earth transmitting seismic movements by radio, their type and their amount; cables sensitive to pressure, buried and transmitting an alarm signal to a receiver station when disturbed by any pressure within a radius of 50 metres; and infrared detectors which respond to the heat of a body. The frontier patrol officers who used these devices on the Chulavista sector for over two years said that they led to the capture of between 20 and 30% of all clandestine immigrants detected the previous year.[25]

The imperative to export

Another direction which the aerospace industry has taken, and electronics following it, is shown in the level of exports by companies such as Lockheed and McDonnell Douglas. The race for the contracts of the century has begun. What happened in the crisis of 1929 is about to repeat itself; in order to combat the present crisis, the big industrial States are throwing themselves into the armaments race. If the North American aeronautics industry succeeds in capturing 90% of the Western market, military and civil, the level of employment could be raised from 930,000 to $1\frac{1}{2}$ million workers. That would mark a return to the better conditions of a war economy. This figure for employment would be doubled if you consider the swarm of sub-contracters which the manufacture of aerospace materials involves. The export of armaments becomes at the same time an economic and a military question.

Between 1950 and 1965, the North American government literally made a present to its allies of a total of $31.7 billion worth of war materials and sold them only $6.5 billion worth. Between 1965 and 1972, US military aid did not go beyond $4.5 billion, but on the other hand, arms sales doubled and the figure reached $11.1 billion.[26] In 1974 the United States received orders from abroad for arms to the value of $8.3 billion; 6.6 billion were cash paid, or about double international sales for the preceding year. In 1975 orders passed considerably beyond 10 billion.[27] The part of the turnover devoted to export among the big armaments companies is markedly greater than the previous year: in the case of Grumman, it went from 3.9 to 26.4%; from 12 to 42.6% with Bell-Textron; from 4 to 13.6% with McDonnell Douglas. Certain senators, scared by this onrush of contracts, have even asked Congress if such arms exports do not indicate that national defense is being put at risk; to which the most frequent reply is that it is precisely the development of exports which allows the activities of most of the electronics and aerospace industries to be sustained and the necessary potential preserved to satisfy the needs of technological renewal by the US army.

On the other hand this is also the point of view of the French industrialists who, in 1974, saw themselves more than triple the sale of arms for export. Faced with this growth, the French Government itself was obliged in 1975 to create an after-sales service, in the ministerial delegation for armaments. 'For the coming years', wrote a high ministerial representative in May 1975, 'the very considerable volume of export orders recorded in 1974 (more than 19 billion francs leading to an order-book that can be valued at present as almost 30 billion francs) and the very favourable forecast for 1975, allow us to consider that exports will assure the maintenance of our industry for the next two or three years'.[28] In 1974 SNIAS exported 74% of its helicopters and 46% of its tactical missiles, while SNECMA exported 57% of its jet engines. In the case of Dassault, 54% of its turnover was given to exports. In the United States, however, after an initial uncontrolled explosion of arms exports, Congress began to keep score at the beginning of 1975 by voting a law which requested the administration to inform it of every arms sale above $25 m., and the first conflict between the White House and the legislative powers broke out in August 1975 over a $350 m. contract with Jordan for the supply of anti-aircraft armaments.

A North American study conducted in 122 countries evaluated the world market in military aircraft at 455 billion francs for the decade 1973–1982, or 29,000 planes, mostly fighter-bombers. As for the sales perspective for civil aircraft, the same study suggested a figure of 215 million francs for a total of about 3,000 planes. The effects of the crisis according to this same report, would be borne almost entirely by civil orders.[29] The first result of the aggressiveness which the armaments industry directs towards the world is already obvious, in those countries which are somewhat distant from being models of democracy. Out of 8 billions in North American arms sales in 1974, 5 billions were bought with the Petrodollars of the Near East. Iran had orders worth 3.8 billion, Saudi Arabia 600 m. The Latin American countries which provided the biggest orders: Chile with 68 m. and Brazil, which spent $220 m. on military aviation alone. When the observers venture to present evidence that the fabulous Middle Eastern orders will dry up rapidly, the officials of the Pentagon rush to reply: 'We don't see an end to it. They'll be wanting the newest weapons, just like we do. And they'll spend as long as their money lasts.'[30]

Many firms with a sagging proportion of military sales in their total turnover during the first period of recession in the aerospace industry have seen the level of these sales appreciably re-established thanks to these spectacular exports. For example, in carrying off the contract for the modernisation of anti-aircraft defense in Saudi Arabia, as well as in the NATO countries (Seasparrow), Raytheon was able to declare in its annual report for 1974: 'Two major new production programs for NATO countries also helped lead the way to an excellent year in government electronics business. An Improved Hawk contract for over $700 million with a six-nation European consortium was won early in the year. About 60 per cent of the contract is to be handled by Raytheon and the rest by the European firms. There was also over $150 million in orders for NATO Seasparrow . . . These programmes, with foreign orders for Improved Hawk and with increasing production orders in other high-priority defense programs, brought the backlog in defense business, both US and international, to a record high of over $1.2 billion at year's end!'[31] Between 1973 and 1974, Raytheon's overseas sales destined mostly for government institutions, went from $318 m. to $517 m., that is, 27% of turnover against 20% beforehand, while sales to the North American government increased only from 769 m. to 792 m.—stagnation, therefore, if one takes account of inflation. Among other indices of the strengthening of military production by these firms, Boeing decided, in August 1975, to equip itself with a new organisation for the purpose of extending its business in the field of military aeronautics. The new unit, which goes under the name Boeing Military Development Organisation, is headed by a general of the USAF reserves, previously at the head of the Government's supersonic transport programme.

The stagnation of commercial aviation can only fan the flame of military exports. The airlines' fall in traffic and their sombre financial situation has reduced civil orders. Lockheed is worried about its Tristars, McDonnell about its DC-9s and DC-10s. And the forecasts provided by the Association of the North American aerospace industry for the year 1976 are scarcely optimistic: the production of civil aircraft would fall from $6.9 billion to $4.9 billion, orders for commercial transport planes from 282 units to 215. On the other hand, production of military aircraft would increase from 8.9 billion to 9.74, missiles from 5 to 6 billion. But these military orders, according to North American industrialists, will scarcely manage to compensate for the civil losses. The United States aeronautics industry is therefore a long way from recovering the level of employment of the years of the wars in South-East Asia: 973,000 persons at the end of 1974, 921,000 at the end of 1975, 900,000 in 1976.[32]

The modernisation of the diplomatic apparatus

The unprecedented offensive of North American exports has been facilitated by a new conception of politico-commercial relations between the multinational firms and government. In 1973 the State Department placed the diplomatic apparatus at the service of the politics of export. In a memorandum sent to all ambassadors, Secretary of State William Rogers explained the reasons for this new practice: 'Our national welfare requires equilibrium in our balance of payments, and a vast improvement in our merchandise trade balance. In full cooperation with the Department of Commerce, which has primary responsibility for domestic activity to encourage exports . . . , we in the State Department want to be sure of the most direct and effective communication with our missions in regard to commercial matters, and we want to render every possible support to what you are doing in the field.'[33] There was indeed something to worry about. In 1972 US exports had been $50 billion, but the commercial balance revealed a deficit of 6.4 billion. In the two preceding years, exports had increased by 15% and imports by 40%.

The State Department therefore set a quarter of its diplomatic personnel stationed abroad to work as touts, and assigned new tasks to each section of the embassies in prospecting for foreign markets. The composition of personnel was subjected to revision and the recruitment of functionaries was required to comply with this new policy. The communication and commercial information services of the embassies was modernised. Beforehand a piece of information took more than 26 days to traverse the labyrinth of slow diplomatic couriers (the *pony express*) and reach the businessman. By turning to the use of tele-data processing, this delay was reduced to less than a week. This is something in which the Japanese long ago overtook the North Americans; their embassies began direct relations with the business concerns of their country from the very first moments of the Japanese export drive.

Listen to a North American functionary speaking of this new constellation of devices installed in US embassies for homing in on markets:

In our Embassies around the world, we are bringing to bear a team spirit on our export expansion drive. All of the elements of the mission are being harnessed in this effort.

* We are sensitising our political and economic reporting officers to be alert to major projects which have export potential.

* We are obtaining through our AID missions more information about internationally-financed projects and technical services which offer opportunities for US business.

* We are seeking, with the full cooperation of our military attachés, to identify commercial trade leads flowing from military sales.

* We are publicising through the United States Information Service our superior technology and the ability of American exporters to satisfy many local development needs.[34]

Never did the articulation of a segment of US foreign policy appear so clearly. And one understands clearly how this technical division of labour inside the embassies can set in motion equally aggressive mechanisms for blocking these same exports in the case of an adverse political climate. Is it necessary to remember that one of the first acts by which the United States indicated their opposition to the Popular Government of Chile was to block the supply of Boeing aircraft which the country needed for the renewal of its commercial airlines. On the other hand, in 1975, the same request by the Pinochet regime met with success.

The State Department selected one country in each major geographical region for a pilot project: Colombia, Zaire, the Netherlands, Iran and Australia. Brazil had the benefit of special treatment and it is no accident that the first public expression of this new form of co-operation between the North American State and its businessmen took this country as its scene. In September 1973 the aeronautics and electronics industries of the United States, under the auspices of the State Department and the Ministry of Commerce, organised the first aeronautics exhibition in Latin America, in Sao Paulo. The following remarks can be found in the report by the North American diplomats: 'Our embassy in Brasilia . . . established seven goals to increase United States exports to Brazil. One of these was to increase our share of the Brazilian market for aircraft, aircraft parts and airport equipment. In pursuit of that objective the Mission undertook to support a US exhibition at the Sao Paulo Aerospace Show—a very successful venture which has just concluded. The Embassy also intends to push the sale of large commercial aircraft to the Brazilian national airline, assist our small plane manufacturers to arrange joint ventures, and promote US equipment and services for the new Sao Paulo International Airport.'[35] In order to prepare this exhibition, an official mission composed of representatives of eight US aeronautics and electronics companies and government functionaries visited Colombia, Venezuela, Brasilia and Sao Paulo in 1972. Among the companies represented: GTE-Sylvania, the electronics division of Boeing, Singer's aerospace group, the international defence products division of Westinghouse.

The programme continues. Between September 1974 and February 1976, the US Department of Commerce organised more than twenty seminars, missions or exhibitions for the aerospace industry throughout the world, from Sweden to Ethiopia to Japan. In September 1975 alone, the joint government-industry mission visited Colombia, Ecuador and, once again, Brazil.[36]

The financial apparatus of the North American State has also contributed and its resources have facilitated the subscription of foreign contracts. Total loans granted in 1974 by Eximbank to purchasers of North American civil materials in 43 countries increased to $917.5 m. in order to finance exports from all sectors of North American industry. Loans granted for the sale of aerospace products allowed the US aeronautics firms to realise exports of the total order of $2.5 billion. It isn't necessary to conduct an extensive examination of the list of firms favoured by Eximbank to discover the weight of the monopoly structure of the North American economy. 83% of loans offered in 1972 and 1973 have financed the exports of 25 big companies; but 60% of the sums awarded to these 25 ended up with 4 of them: Boeing, McDonnell Douglas, Westinghouse and General Electric.[37] Thus it can be explained, for example, how McDonnell Douglas succeeded in 1972 in capturing Greek Government contracts with Dassault and substituting its Phantoms for Mirages. On this occasion the North American Government loaned the colonels in Athens more than $100 m. Pinochet benefited from the same favour to buy his Boeings.

When the multinational firm judges that its own activities and the help of the State apparatus are not sufficient, it takes the initiative itself to force the hand of possible purchasers. This at least is what recent discoveries made by the North American Congress tend to show. In 1971 and 1973, Northrop poured out $450,000 to two Saudi Arabian generals in order to carry off orders for its F-5 aircraft. In Europe, the same firm established a company of Swiss nationality which served as a public relations bureau in its relationships with influential persons in the aeronautics market. In this way, $700,000 was dispensed in the form of tips. Similar manoeuvres were revealed in Iran, Indonesia, and Brazil. It was discovered that with the aid of a Brazilian airforce general, Northrop had employed corrupt practices in order to sell 42 of its fighters in 1973. The Brazilian intermediaries had received a commission of $2.8 m. on an order worth more than 70 m.[38] In July 1975, the North American Congress disclosed the same intrigues in the dealings of Grumman in the Near East. In 1976, it was Lockheed's turn to be accused, before the same authority, of having spent more than 20 millions in clandestine commissions to civil and military personalities in Japan, Colombia, Germany, France, the Netherlands and Turkey.

New roles for old friends, or what's in a name?

In 1972 in Vietnam the United States Air Force began to use a guided bomb which carried a television camera at the front in what can be called its nose. The pilot could follow the missile he had just launched from his cockpit on a small screen and choose its target with the maximum precision. And yet it was the same year that the largest number of bombs fell 'accidentally' on schools, hospitals and, above all, dams! This new war machine was baptised 'Maverick', the name of the indomitable and lucky vagabond who also gave his name to a famous television series produced in the USA and distributed throughout the world. The manufacturer of this warlike version of Maverick is the producer of *Scarface*, which together with *Modern Times* and *I am a Fugitive From a Chain Gang,* disturbed the conformism of Hollywood in the thirties—namely, Howard Hughes, who, trying to remove all traces of the division of labour, placed his aeronautics enterprise at the service of his film production company. During the Korean war he produced a film directed by Sternberg, *Jet Pilot.* Planes made by the Hughes Aircraft Corporation reenacted aerial combats which, in reality, had been conducted by these same infernal machines which the US forces had bought in order to bombard villages beyond the fateful parallel. Today, Hughes has got rid of the shares he owned in the cinema trusts RKO Pictures and has bought a commercial television chain. Since not long ago he has also owned the largest television distribution network, the famous cable television which some people make out to be a force for the democratisation of information and culture.

But our man's megalomania doesn't stop there. In June 1973, the 'Hughes Glomar Explorer', an extraordinary looking floating laboratory, fresh from the naval construction yards on the Delaware River, took to sea; according to a spokesman of the Summa Corporation, this floating umbrella for all the maritime activities of the Hughes enterprise, was given the mission of exploring the ocean depths 'to find an answer to the energy crisis'. Another aim of the operation was unveiled in February 1975 when William Colby, head of the CIA, revealed before the Commission of Inquiry of the North American Senate that the Summa Corporation had been given the ultra-secret mission of fishing out of the Pacific Ocean a Soviet atomic submarine which had foundered several years earlier.

Two months later, Paul Stehlin, ex-European-vice-president of Hughes Aircraft, adviser to Northrop and ex-head of the French aviation General Staff, was forced to offer his resignation for having dared to vaunt the superiority of North American aircraft over the Dassault Mirage and displaying the conviction that only the US had the technical, economic and political means to protect Europe. On the other hand, Hughes' French associates in a Parisian company for researches into cable television showed themselves in no way worried or disturbed although they were in flagrant contradiction with the principle of national sovereignty and the military was bearing all the costs.

One of the detection systems used on the McNamara Line, consisting of receptors both acoustic and seismic which were no bigger than twigs, received the name 'Commando Bolt'. These twigs sent back information about the enemy's activities in the form of luminous spots on a television screen, and the receiver of this information was able constantly to map the progress of enemy convoys and patrols. 'Commando Bolt' is taken from the name of the hero of a comic strip, Big Ben Bolt, boxer, world champion, foolhardy and unruffled at the same time, created by John Cullen Murphy.

After many years, the Defense Department, with the help of a large number of civil, military or para-military research laboratories (such as the National Centre for Atmospheric Research at Monterrey, the Centre for Naval Armaments of California, or the Rand Corporation decided to set up an assualt on geophysics and climatology, studying the possibilities of controlling and diverting cyclones, hurricanes, tidal waves and storms. In 1969, for the first time, North American aviation decided to induce artificial rains in order to block the passage of increasing quantities of materials and ammunition along the Ho Chi Minh Trail. This experiment, which wiped numerous Laotian villages off the map, annihilated their inhabitants and destroyed their crops, is known as 'Operation Popeye', after the little sailor who eats masses of spinach in the cartoon strip created by Elzie Segar in the New York Evening Standard around 1929.

In 1967, the National Security Agency (NSA), the US organisation which makes one largest contribution of the intelligence apparatus, providing 80% of its personnel as well as its information, began to locate Che Guevara's guerillas by intercepting radio communications signals. The radar system which allowed this espionage network to function was known to NSA agents by the name of the 'Mandrake system', after the hero magician created by Lee Phalk and Phil Davis in 1934.

Maverick, Bolt, Popeye, Mandrake, effigies and ceatures with claws! These fantastic monsters, summoned up by the military genie and the planners of electronic warfare, suddenly offer up their hidden meaning; and the generals who shelter behind the mystique of these characters are only diluting their own sarcasm by joking. In fact they play the worst turn possible by playing the role of unearthly beings: bedevilling themselves with the devilry of earthly existence. The migration of the characters of mass culture to the battlefield is no accident. The military here invoke the intercession of these heroes and claim for the reality of their electronic age a mythology which justifies the diabolical direction they impose on the development of technological apparatus.

The presence of these figures in the aggression of Vietnam or the counter-insurrectionary fight in Bolivia doesn't have the same meaning as the coloured Donald Duck stickers on the victorious wings of the flying fortresses with which pilots returning to their bases in England or Guam used to mark the number of German stukas or Japanese fighters shot down. Donald's smiling scowl, under his sailor's beret, plays the role of a graphic mascot, a simple fetish which has nothing to do with the practice of war publicity, even if Donald forms part of the daily arsenal of imperialism and serves to auspiciate battles which are not so explicitly belligerent.* The presence of Popeye and Mandrake has a different character when the air forces of the United States or the intelligence services use them to designate a raid or a machine. Through the intervention of these comic strip heroes, the super-powerful make excuses for the bombardments of schools and hospitals which are no more than smudges made by every powerful technological apparatus. Popeye and his eccentric muscles; Mandrake and his exaltation of a possessed medium turned picturesque screen, the screen which makes us forget that the genocide to which they lend their name is planned in cold blood and allows no margin of error.

Popeye is also the key to the sybilline message, the drug which turns

* Cf. *How To Read Donald Duke* by Mattelart and Ariel Dorfman, International General, New York, 1975 (Translator's note).

on the pilot of a B-52 with a new flight of consciousness in the context of a criminal act. The arsenal made up by the figures of mass culture serve to justify everyday murderous aggression. And in just the same way, Maverick first excuses the technocrats, the bosses and the generals, whose activity is rooted in the war industry, and at the same time allows so-called public opinion to consume the news of the destruction of civil objectives through the phantasmagorical grid of a television series.

This is only one of the many aspects of what can be called the culture of defense, of 'internal security', of the imperial State. The traditional figures of fiction are there to unname a reality which surpasses fiction. And it is not necessary to believe that this use of imaginary supermen is the strict prerogative of a number of militarists, inveterate partisans of punitive expeditions. All the agencies of the system busy themselves under the same flag, in the name of the defense of the Empire.

Popeye, Mandrake, Maverick: logotypes of Pentagon projects; these borrowed names are nothing but a metaphor for the transformation which takes place in the apparatus which produces mass culture. In a world where you hardly know which of two things hides the other, where no-one knows who's who, who makes the television series and who makes the rocket, where in the name of the defense of the empire, the same supposedly private company undertakes the rescue of a strategic wreck, research into bits of cobalt or manganese, and the development of new systems of community television, in such a world it is difficult to continue defining the culture industry as a light industry, just as it is difficult to continue to situate the intelligence apparatus of the North American empire at the simple level of the institutions for which this is their specialised function.

Notes

1 Litton Industries, *International Directory*, Beverly Hills, 1969 (This quotation has been retranslated into English from French since the original was among papers belonging to the author which were destroyed by the Chilean Junta—Trans.)
2 *Aerospace facts and figures, 1975–76.*
3 'Top NASA fiscal 1972 contractors listed', *Aviation Week & Space Technology*, 5.II.1973.
4 *Business Week*, 6.V.1972.
5 US Department of Commerce, *Commercial Newsletter Service*, Washington D.C., August-September 1972.
6 *Aerospace facts and figures, 1972–73.*
7 Annual company reports 1971–1972.
8 OECD (Organisation of Economic Co-operation and Development), *Allocations des ressources dans le domaine de l'informatique et des télécommunications* (IIIème

partie, rapport de base, préparé par S. Gill), OCDE, Paris, 1975.

9 *Business Week*, 24.III.1973.

10 On the participation of the electronics and aerospace industry in the munitions industry, see *Business Week*, 26.V.1973; Jacques Isnard, 'Les ventes d'armes de la France', *Le Monde*, 15.I.1974.

11 Estimate produced by Victor Perlo, *Militarism and Industry*, New York, International Publishers Co., 1963.

12 Westinghouse Corporation, *Annual Report 1972*.

13 Honeywell, *Annual Report 1974*.

14 Radio Corporation of America, *Annual Report 1972*.

15 *Aviation Week and Space Technology*, 12.VII.1973; *Aerospace facts and figures, 1972–73, 1975–76*.

16 *Electronics*, 29.III.1971.

17 Sanford Rose, 'Making the turn to a peacetime economy', *Fortune*, September 1970.

18 *Aviation Week & Space Technology*, 26.I.1976; Jacqueline Grapin, 'L'oncle Sam retourne sa veste', *Le Monde*, 9.IX.1975; *Le Monde Diplomatique*, December 1975.

19 *Aerospace facts and figures, 1975–76*.

20 *Business Week*, 20.VIII.1970, 21.II.1972; *The Electronic Engineer*, February 1971.

21 *Fortune*, June 1970.

22 Cited in J. Woodmansee and the GE Project, *The World of a Giant Corporation*, Washington, 1975, North Country Press.

23 *Business Week*, 14.VII.1975.

24 Advertisement of the Law Enforcement Group of Smith & Wesson. For a recent vision of the police applications of electronics, cf. D. Shapley, 'La police et les techniques de pointe', *La Recherche*, Paris, July-August 1975.

25 NYT cable, *El Mercurio*, Santiago de Chile, 16.VII.1973. For the technology of political control, especially in terms of its application in the U.K., see *The Technology of Political Control* by Ackroyd, Margolis, Rosenhead & Shallice, Penguin 1977 (Translator's note).

26 *US News and World Report*, 22.I.1973.

27 US Department of Defence, Office of the Assistant Secretary for International Security Affairs, *Military Assistance and Foreign Military Sales Facts*, Washington D.C., 1974. For 1975, *Le Monde*, 23–24 November 1975.

28 J.L. Delpech in *Revue de la Dèfense Nationale*, Paris, June 1975.

29 Jacques Isnard, 'Les Etats-Unis et L'Europe se disputent un marché mondial d'avions militaires évalué à 455 milliards de francs d'ici à 1982', *Le Monde*, 20.I.1974.

30 *Business Week*, 11.VIII.1975.

31 Raytheon *Annual Report 1974*.

32 *Aviation Week and Space Technology*, 22.XII.1975.

33 R. Reston, 'US diplomats now promote US business as primary assignment', *Department of State Newletter*, Aug.-Sept. 1973.

34 *Department of State Newsletter*, November 1973.

35 *Ibid.*

36 *Aviation Week & Space Technology*, 2.X.1972; 2.IX.1974.

37 For the list of Eximbank's beneficiaries, cf. NACLA's *Latin American & Empire Report*, New York, 1974, Vol. III, No. 7; *Air et Cosmos*, Paris, 25.I.1975. (Eximbank granted loans for finance of exports up to 30% of the value of the sale, at an interest of 7% over a period of ten years.)

38 A. Shumman, 'Tighter foreign sales controls studied', *Aviation Week & Space Technology*, 16.VI.1975; *Le Monde*, 9.VII.1975.

CHAPTER III
THE DIFFUSION OF SPACE TECHNOLOGIES

THE international diffusion of the new technologies of communication are entangled in the relations of the forces which have just been reviewed. The battle for export has begun. According to a remark by a spokesman for the North American industrialists in June 1975, at the inauguration of the Paris-Le Bourget Air Show, where General Dynamics' F-16 fighters jostled with earth exploration and broadcasting satellites: 'Space technology also has entered the export market on a modest but inevitably expanding scale as the global communications business is experiencing a revolutionary expansion into space systems. The international appetite for earth resources data, weather and navigation space systems has been whetted and will grow during the next decade.'[1]

The forms taken by the implantation of these new communications systems provide faithful evidence of the new practices of multinational companies of North American origin and of the imperialist State.

Space as a terrain of exploitation

'Science will advance—but it will be science with a practical thrust. Today, in the councils between the public, its government, and its government's suppliers in the technology industries, the viewpoint of the pragmatist has superceded that of the patriot and the pure scientist.'[2] Such were the terms in which the general administrator of NASA, in April 1972, traced the new lines of United States space policy in the years to come, and opened what North American scientists have baptised 'the new space era'. There would be no more voyages to the moon. The phase of lunar conquest and exploration was over. It will have cost the North American people something like $50 billion. From now on Earth becomes the principle objective of space activity: 'we are entering an era of the utilisation of space for the benefit of man.'

The manned flights which used to absorb the major part of the funds will no longer represent more than a third of NASA's budget and a fifth of all US space activity, civil and military, national and international. The rare manned flights which are still envisaged will have to be directly profitable. In the course of their three successive missions, the cosmonauts of Skylab, the programme which closed the old era and opened the new one, photographed more than three-quarters of the earth's surface and sub-soil, and took a census of nine-tenths of the population of the globe. Moreover, and above all, the last doubts were resolved: the human being is able to work in a gravityless condition without too many risks. After the space docking experiment between the Soviet (Soyuz) and North American space vehicles in July 1975, we will have to wait till the end of the decade to see other starlit cosmonauts returning to space and living together with their European colleagues in the cabin of the spacelab, a re-usable space laboratory. These two programmes of international rapprochement are also to be located within the terms of the new space policy which, always according to the NASA officials, must try to increase the number of co-operative projects on a 'multinational and transideological' basis, combining the advantages of 'the end of the cold war' with those of 'the extra-territorial neutrality of space'. The application of space technology is the order of the day and the destination of the greatest part of government budgets: national and international communications satellites and their use within the framework of education, weather satellites, satellites for air and sea navigation, space relays for locating and collecting data of all types, from medical records to judicial records, and satellites for the inspection of natural resources.

When the new space era began, scarcely three years had passed since Neil Armstrong's space landing, which collected more than 700 million television viewers and listeners around the North American flag. The last travelling exhibition organised around the world by the cultural services of the US embassies in order to popularise their planetary conquest returned home three years ago. When the third Skylab space laboratory mission returned from a three month gravityless voyage in February 1974, it did not receive the honours of North American television. Space had become a domain given over to the economy, exploitation replaced exploits, technicians substituted for heroes.

During the 60s, the North American Government had accustomed its public to another kind of talk. The information bulletins which reported the results of the Gemini, Mercury and Apollo missions were cast entirely in the special language of sports commentaries: 'The Apollo 17 crew made three sorties on the moon and remained on the selenite surface for 22 hours and 5 minutes, thus beating the record set by Apollo 16 of 20 hours and 13 minutes; they brought back 240 lbs of rocks and specimens of the moon's soil, while the Apollo 16 mission returned with 208 lbs . . .' The choice of this terminology of the sports stadium is not an innocent one. It camouflages the political battle embodied in the lunar stakes. 'The US, its psyche as well as its sense of security shaken by the prestige and military import of Russia's Sputnik, opened wide the fiscal thrusters and spent billions upon billions to catch up to and pass the USSR in space.'[3] In 1961, John Kennedy had asked the North American nation to join forces in order to reach the moon before the end of the decade. This was the point of departure for an unrestricted race which can only be compared to the arms race. (Anyway, the two coincide completely and it's not for nothing that the divisions of the multinational electronics and aerospace firms bring their Defense and Space activities together under the same mark. These two fields of activity are always associated in their publicity.)   At that time, company personnel and senators together made the race for the stars into a primary platform for winning the cold war. The patriots of the space agency didn't hide their political convictions: 'For the first time in the history of mankind the opportunity to leave the earth and explore the solar system is at hand. Only two nations, the United States and the Soviet Union, today have the resources with which to exploit this opportunity. Were we, as the symbol of democratic government, to surrender this opportunity to the leading advocate of the Communist ideology, we could no longer stand large in our own image, or in the image that other nations have of us and of the free society we represent.'[4]

During the course of this competition, space technology remained limited to the accumulating needs engendered by space exploration. The only bridge thrown between the common herd and that whole formidable technological machine was the spectacle and consumption of the cosmonauts' exploits. Hundreds of doctors sharpened their scientific curiosity by dedicating themselves to observing the heartbeats of the three spacemen, while cancer research laboratories saw their already minute budgets put on short allowance. 'The sky above . . . the mud below' became a fashionable expression. Cold war militants were sustained by scientists eager to extend their researches *in vitro*, until the day when they had to accept that they would never tame the enormous growth of information about space until long after the flourishing years of conquest.

In 1972 the situation had developed considerably. Congress displayed more and more reticence in the face of initiatives which did not involve 'an increase in well-being for men living on the earth'. 'The cold war turned more temperate and a more peaceful era converged with a growing awareness of mothholes in the social fabric down here on earth,' said the NASA administrator himself. The opposition expressed in the Senate added another argument: the space projects which responded to the traditional conception and scorned earthly needs could not resolve problems of a deficient commercial balance and of inflation.

One thing is sure. With the new space era—the other face of the process of 'civilisation' of high technology—the United States entered another phase in the politicisation of space, a phase which took on the forms of rivalry implied by 'the epoch of detente'. The cold war patriot gave way to the scientist financed at one and the same time by the North American State and the big multinational companies. This scientist represents the new theorist and the new ideologue, responsible, thanks to science and applied technology, for the materialisation on earth of the universal utopia of the Empire. This new type of proselyte has to adapt the sensibilities of the common herd to the new phase of technological invasion 'for the profit of humanity', so that all should accept it as a decisive step towards their liberation. Here is a sample of the neo-positivist speech of this new personage, the pragmatic, in the politics of space:

> The strengths of science clearly go beyond intellectual enlightenment and adventures of inquiry. Scientific truths are universal and belong to all of us. They extend across national boundaries. They are genuinely international, the possession of all nations. Also, the applications of science to the needs of mankind through technology are enormously varied, essentially infinite in scope. Science can provide all people with useful tools, profitable products, and beneficial services. When the transistor was invented 25 years ago, the concept quickly became the property of all mankind . . . It is sometimes thought that the developing countries, when importing technology, can benefit only from special forms of science particularly designed to match their problems. This is certainly not always the case. We might cite many well-known examples in the fields of health, agriculture, and transportation. Another currently emerging example concerns the transistor and the earth satellite—reflecting very sophisticated technology—which undoubtedly enable many countries to catch up in their communications networks without passing through cumbersome and expensive intermediate stages. In general, then, the most advanced countries often serve the less advanced simply by carrying out their own technical activities and offering their products to the world.[5]

The good samaritan is no longer the peace volunteer who, furnished with a stock of slides provided by the cultural service of the embassy, reveals the grandeurs of the interplanetary race to the peasants of the Andes. He has become a salesman of the latest electronic models produced by the multinationals. It is necessary, said Nixon, 'to offer the spirit of science and North American technology in order to resolve the problems of development'. 'The unprecedented progress of science and technology,' he added, 'the demographic explosion, the explosion of communications and knowledge, demand new forms of international collaboration.'[6]

It is time now to see what concrete forms of co-operation the Empire proposes to 'make its technological resources a common heritage of all humanity'.

A different relationship between state and industry

The way that US space technology enters the international market offers an ominous example going far beyond the telecommunications industry of how the original alliance between the multinationals and the state apparatus can be developed smoothly to achieve what neither partner could achieve on their own. It shows how an enduring partnership between government and industry can be institutionalised so as to alleviate any conflict of interests between the two parties. The few perspicacious economists of this system who have seen in it a schema susceptible of being extended to other sectors of industry are not mistaken.[7]

We may discover in the history of this strict relationship between the organism of the State and the aerospace and electronics firms a dialectical rapport which shows how an industry which is raring to go can pressurise the antiquated bureaucratic apparatus of the imperialist State, forcing it to adopt its own criteria of modernisation; and how the firms of this industry are called upon to exercise officially functions which were previously the exclusive domain of government institutions. Through the analysis of concrete cases of this type it is possible to pluck the thorny question of the new state forms demanded by the present phase of the international accumulation of capital. Furthermore, you can see the import of such a seminal transformation as this in terms of the multinationals' behaviour when you compare it with the process of 'civilisation' which most of these companies have launched themselves into. The canalisation of defense and space technologies into the civil domain tends to precipitate the opening up of the state apparatus to the owners of high technology who become the social planners. There will be occasion to return to these suggestions when it comes to examining the growing importance of the multinational firms in the field of education. For the moment, the question is to trace the trajectory of the government-industrial alliance in the field of application of space technologies.

For this we must go back to 1962, five years after the Soviet success in launching the first Sputnik (1957) to which the North Americans replied with Explorer I (1958). 1962 was the year that the first Telstar satellite was launched, followed in 1963 by Relay and Syncom. These were the satellites which prepared the way for the first commercial telecommunications satellite to be placed in a stationary orbit, Early

Bird, launched in 1965.* Early Bird, which was able simultaneously to transmit 240 telephone circuits or one television channel instead, inaugurated the first generation of satellites which came to comprise the international network of Intelsat (International Telecommunications Satellite Consortium). There were at this time only four earth stations on the entire planet capable of receiving the signals relayed from the satellite. Ten years later there were around 100 and the 7 satellites of the fourth generation (Intelsat IV) had an individual capacity of 4,000 telephone circuits. Intelsat V, the first of them to be launched in 1979, will be made up of satellites with an individual capacity of 12,000 telephone circuits. Meanwhile, six further members of the second series of the fourth generation (Intelsat IV-A) will allow for 6,000 telephone circuits, or 12 television channels. A few years ago, North American aeronautics experts envisaged that it would be possible before 1980 to launch a satellite with 100,000 circuits, but this seems to have been postponed, since even the fifth generation, originally to begin launching in 1977 with satellites of 40,000 circuits, has been considerably checked and reduced.

In 1962 the US set up a body for the exploitation of satellite technology, five years after endowing an organisation for the research and promotion of space exploration projects (NASA). The North American Congress approved the Communication Satellite Act which established Comsat (Communication Satellite Corporation), entrusted to organise and commercially exploit the new discovery. According to a formula proposed by the Federal Commission of Communications (FCC) Comsat took the form of a private company of an unprecedented kind. Half the shares were to be offered to private subscribers, and the other half to 163 agreed companies in the communications industry. American Telegraph and Telephone (ATT) acquired 29% (that is, more than half of those reserved for the industry); ITT,

---

* *Telstar* was a 'low orbit' satellite which could only be tracked from a given point on earth for a short period before disappearing below the horizon. A string of such satellites would be needed to maintain continuous communication. *Relay* was a medium orbit satellite with a longer tracking period. *Syncom*, however, although its first launch failed, was the prototype of the high orbit satellite now used by *Intelsat* (see text below) which, travelling at a height of 35,800 kms. above the equator, had an orbital period that exactly matched the period of the earth's rotation—approximately 24 hours—so that it appeared from below to be fixed in the sky. Only three such satellites in communication with each other are needed to provide communication right around the globe, as the science fiction writer Arthur C. Clarke had suggested to the British Interplanetary Society as early as 1945. (See, for example, Brian Winston, *Dangling Conversations*, Book 2, 'Hardware/Software', Davis-Poynter 1974, Ch. 5, and 'Global Satellite Communications', *Scientific American*, February 1977). (Translator's note).

General Telephone & Electronics (GTE), and Radio Corporation of America (RCA) together took 16.4%, while the other 158 companies divided the remaining 4.6% among themselves. A myriad of 175,000 subscribers acquired the half reserved for private issue. Three government representatives nominated directly by the White House sat on the directors' committee with the delegates of the shareholders. With a third of the action, ATT had the right to three seats. This original formula guaranteed a permanent alliance between the State apparatus and the big manufacturers of the new technologies, an alliance which allowed the elaboration of a common policy of international commercialisation. This in effect constituted the promotion of the big monopolies to the level of the State apparatus. A rebel ex-official of ITT, now a professor at the University of Pennsylvania, wrote that Comsat was without any doubt an institutional mechanism bound to preserve existing power relations. Comsat cannot manufacture equipment, launch satellites or sell services. It serves principally as administrator and intermediary between the established communications industry and the US Government in everything concerning international satellite policy.[8]

With this operational instrument in hand, the United States proposed to the Western countries in 1964 the establishment of bases for an international satellite communication network which would allow all these nations 'to participate in the ownership, administration, construction and conception of the system'. This was the beginning of Intelsat. The proprietors were the non-socialist European countries, Japan, Canada and Australia. The Soviet Union (which launched its first elliptical orbit communications satellite in 1965, less sophisticated than the US stationary orbit satellites) preferred to associate itself with other socialist countries, with whom in 1971 it founded Intersputnik, bringing together the countries of Eastern Europe (apart from Yugoslavia, which joined Intelsat), Cuba and Outer Mongolia. The Soviet Union launched its first stationary satellite, Molnya 1-S, in August 1974. China, which has already launched 5 satellites—mostly for reconnaissance purposes—surely cannot delay much longer before entering the field of communications satellites.

US control over the Intelsat consortium is absolute. With the consent of the organisation's constitutive statutes it owns 61% (Britain holds 8.4%, France and Germany 6.1%, while there wasn't a single third world country among the 19 nations who owned the system). Furthermore, Comsat was chosen as the organisation's manager for a period of 7 years. At the end of 1970, in spite of the entry of a mass of new member countries, the US presence was still marked by a 52.6% holding. As for the supply contracts, the big North American multinational companies had the lion's share. Between 1965 and 1968, out of $122 m. worth of Intelsat contracts, only 18.2% went to European, Australian or Japanese firms. The grievances formulated by such countries as France indicate well enough the malcontent of the European members of Intelsat: industrial returns insufficient in quality (European sub-contractors were often limited to copying North American models) and also in quantity (up to 1973, French industry collected $6.5 m. in contracts, while France's net contribution amounted to roughly 15 millions).[9]

A new regulation was adopted in 1971 after multiple negotiations. Although difficult to apply, it renders North American supremacy less overwhelming. Comsat continues to manage Intelsat, no longer by statute but by contract. The US holds no more than 38.3% of the shares, Britain 10.9% and France 2.98%. After opening up participation to all members (98 countries in 1977) a consultative authority was created where each member was given the right to vote. But the power of decision remained in the hands of a directorate in which participation was proportional to shareholdings. A NASA functionary admitted that 'the control of the organisation continues to be exercised by the advanced nations'. He added, in a paternalistic tone of voice: 'The participation of the less developed countries in an organisation so substantial and so preferential allows them to develop common interests with the great nation of the north and favours the participation of these countries in other important activities on the international level.'[10] North American industry continues to construct the proposed new satellites. The aeronautics firm of Hughes Aircraft has had a monopoly on them since the first generation and they are carried by the North American launch vehicles made by Ling-Temco-Vought and McDonnell Douglas. Since the United States, together with the Soviet Union, are the only ones to possess this kind of vehicle, they instigated a clause to forestall any competition in the Intelsat system, which provides that any member country of the organisation wishing to launch a commercial communications satellite and requiring a US rocket launcher for the purpose would have to demonstrate that the new satellite would do no economic harm to Intelsat. A single exception was allowed: experimental satellites.

Two elements remain from this first supposedly international experiment which have surely weighed heavily on the future evolution of the international expansion of satellite technology.

From its organisationally hybrid platform, Comsat has introduced more and more agile forms of association with the industrial companies of its own country in order to exploit the new applications of satellite technology. The business agreements which give it its real power are innumerable. It stands at the head of one of the four big satellite communications systems which the US will possess by 1977, which it manages by agreement with the telephone monopoly, ATT. Together with Lockheed, which also manufactures satellites, and another marketing and data processing firm, it has set up a mixed company, CML Satellite Corporation, of which it owns one third. The latest Comsat initiative turns on this mixed enterprise. IBM proposed buying 55% of the shares and transforming it into a common subsidiary of IBM-Comsat of which Comsat would hold the other 45%. Through this new company it would marry computers and satellite technology, establishing by 1980 a vast network of computers and tele-information processing equipment, satellite-linked and available for private and public users (SBS—Satellite Business Systems). The Federal Commission of Communications saw in this association between the two giants a danger that they would divide up the world between them, and in June 1975 refused to entertain the project, demanded that the proposed subsidiary be open to other companies and the proprietorship of IBM and Comsat be reduced to 49%. A pretty limited measure to restrain the pretensions of such a monopoly. In October 1975 a third partner, the largest insurance company in the US, and one of the most diversified, Aetna Life and Casualty Co., joined IBM-Comsat in the purchase of a 15% shareholding.[11] The initials of the new consortium—in which Comsat and IBM each retain 42.5%—is something else again: CIA (Comsat, IBM, Aetna). This example allows us to guess the course to be taken by this further application of space technology, that is, tele-computing, which will acquire a leading position in the next fifteen years. To the extent that the functions of satellites are being extended, Comsat is also called upon to organise satellite systems which have little to do with the transmission of commercial or cultural programmes. And in each new segment of the application of space technology, it is always the formula of State-industrial alliance which prevails. When it comes to providing the US with a maritime navigation satellite system (Marisat) —and initiative stimulated by petroleum needs—they will require, merely in order to satisfy their own demands, a fleet equivalent in size to the number of satellites which satisfied the entire world in 1967. In order to facilitate the movement of naval vessels and the North American merchant marine in the Atlantic, the Persian Gulf and the Pacific, Comsat has set up a company with RCA, ITT and the telegraph company Western Union International, of which it retains 80% of the shareholding itself.

With Intelsat, the United States has succeeded in imposing on the field of communications their own particular concept of the international organisation of the new satellite technologies. They are now trying to make this stick as the only possible norm for guiding the further application of this technology. This is the case, for example, with the international air navigation satellite system (Aerosat) and the international maritime navigation system (Inmarsat). But other countries do not wish to repeat the experience of Intelsat. In 1971, the Government of President Nixon categorically refused to accept the terms of an agreement proposed by the European countries which provided for a 50–50 partition of the Aerosat system, at the level of its conception as much as its construction. On the one hand, the North American Government was unwilling to accept the prospect of Europe working with the US on equal terms, and judged this agreement as arbitrary to the extent that what ought to prevail in awarding industrial contracts was the better price, better quality and shortest delivery time. On the other hand, it was not in agreement with the type of organisation envisaged to manage the system, with the European countries asking for agreements between governments and the United States preferring to grant the exploitation of the system to the private or to the mixed sector. The same discussion was repeated with Inmarsat, where the US not only had to face the opposition of the European countries but also that of the Soviet Union, participating in an international system of this type for the first time. In addition to the political stakes, the commercial stakes were considerable. Many countries are now able to furnish this type of application of satellite technology and the exploitation of the system carries dividends: Inmarsat's potential clients number 61,000 vessels of more than 100 tons.[12] Thus a paradoxical situation arises. The United States, which had assumed the leadership in establishing the first international communications system, was marking time in the negotiations while it tried to find other terms for the communal exploitation of the new applications.

The export of national systems

In creating Comsat, the North American Congress had advised itself 'to direct care and attention toward providing such services to economically less developed countries and areas'.[13] Comsat, in its double role as manager of Intelsat and organisation for US foreign policy, had been led to carry out this mission in numerous countries. Where a desire to acquire the new technologies has not been manifest, it has had to induce a need. The countries of Latin America were the first beneficiaries of this tender regard. For the first time, the complementary alliances based on the principle alliance of North

American State and multinational firms, began to take shape and create a common front which combined the supply of hardware and of software. Alongside Comsat and the industry, appeared the educational foundations and the apparatus of higher education of the United States. Let us trace the history of these manoevres.[14]

In June 1967, the University of Stanford published a study under the name ASCEND (Advanced System of Communication and Education for National Development) which contained—although not a single country of the subcontinent had asked for it—a plan for the utilisation of satellites for the purposes of educational television in the countries of Latin America. In April 1969, General Electric and Hughes Aircraft, Comsat and various representatives of North American universities, financed by the Ford Foundation, called a private meeting in Santiago de Chile, in the course of which they proposed that educational programmes by satellite should be developed by 14 universities of the North. It was then decided to create an international audio-visual satellite centre (CAVISAT) with its seat in Colombia, to study the viability of a US-Latin American project, but in place of 14 North American universities, there were ten Latin American universities supported by Foundations of the metropolis, and ten North American universities, which divided among themselves a project addressed to all levels of education, from literacy campaigns to university courses by way of technical courses and manpower training and recycling. There were two further approaches in the same year. The Italian firm Telespazio edited a report on educational television in Latin America, while Page Engineers, the satellite division of the firm of Northrop, carried out a inquiry at the express demand of President Nixon on the future possibilities of a Latin American satellite system.

The nationalist opposition of certain Latin American Governments anxious to preserve their rights of self-determination over cultural and educational matters had good grounds for this sophistry. The insolence of the organisers of the Santiago meeting knew no limits. In their opinion it would soon be unnecessary to seek the agreement of the governments in question since it was already possible to foresee direct transmission satellites, that is, satellites able to transmit directly to the individual home, broadcasting programmes from the United States without needing to go through ground station relays. In any case they left open the possibility that the studies would be recognised and North American titles distributed to the educational population of Latin America for them to follow the miraculous new curriculum. Their effrontery was so overt that the majority of Latin American countries which in 1969 claimed their cultural self-determination against the Comsat-multinationals-universities alliance were not exactly followers of the Cuban Revolution: the Argentina of General Lanusse, the Bolivia of General Ovando, the Venezuela of the Christian Democrat Caldera, the Paraguay of life-dictator Stroessner, Frei's Chile —countries which a few years earlier hadn't been asked for their ministries of public instruction to commence the experiments in educational television financed by the Ford Foundation.

In 1970, these Latin American countries requested the assistance of UNESCO after signing among themselves the Andres Bello agreement, which envisaged their integration in the fields of education, science and culture. Several studies on the viability of educational satellite programmes were undertaken in accord with this agreement. The most recent (SERLA) proposed bringing together Argentina, Bolivia, Chile, Colombia, Ecuador, Paraguay, Peru, Venezuela and Uruguay in a common satellite educational system, technically realisable by the end of the present decade. The main problem remains to be resolved—that of its political viability. One cannot very well see how, for example, the regime of the Peruvian generals, which refused the new educational television series such as *Sesame Street* in the name of the objectives of educational reform, could accommodate the neofascist-like educational directives of Pinochet who, in the first months after coming to power, promised Chileans the luxury of colour television through the agency of the North American multinationals operating in Brazil.*

The political interventions of Comsat are generally more stealthy. It is usually enough for it to insist on its technical competence, which no-one can deny since it is the only organisation able to boast more than ten years' international experience. Now that North American industry has unleashed an offensive for selling national satellite systems, that is, systems which serve, or rather, which would serve, only one country or group of countries, so Comsat has become for the non-socialist countries of the world the best intermediary and councellor. Thus in 1974 and 1975 it found itself in charge of several large projects. In Saudi Arabia it was charged with the construction of ground stations able to receive signals from the Intelsat system, but also from a future local system; Norway suddenly rich from oil, entrusted it with its national satellite system project; Brazil asked it to adapt the three ground stations already installed there to allow the reception of signals from a future national satellite network. Since Comsat does not construct the equipment itself, it chose GTE for the supply of the

---

* This was still true at the beginning of 1976. But political changes have taken place since then. The progressive generals were displaced at the end of 1976 by the right wing of the army. (Translator's Note.)

electronics, the same firm we find again in Iran and which installed the fourteen ground stations in Algeria, which permitted the extension of telephone and television networks to the whole country, thanks to connections with the Intelsat system. Further it built the first audiovisual equipment factory there.

But the most recent and most eloquent case is undoubtedly that of Indonesia. After a visit by Comsat experts, the Indonesian Government signed an agreement with Hughes Aircraft for the construction of two communications satellites and ten earth stations (another thirty are given to other companies). This national system will unite the 5,000 odd islands of the archipelago and will be open to educational television (2,000 television terminals), telephone linking (half a million telephones in a country with only 45,000 at the moment for more than 5 million inhabitants) and data transmission. For a total price of $350 m., Indonesia, has thus become one of the first third world countries to want to possess the same satellite communication system as the one inaugurated in Canada in 1972 with its Anik satellites also manufactured by Hughes Aircraft. It only needed Indonesian oil exports suddenly to reach $6 billion annually for it to be granted such a modernisation of it telecommunications systems. The Djakarta Government had already decided to buy a satellite system in 1970, but the World Bank had refused the request to finance it with the comment that 'it was considered a luxury for a nation with an annual per-capita income of only $70'.[15]

We can therefore presume that the purchasing rhythm for these new communications technologies will be slower and less spectacular in the majority of other proletarian nations which do not benefit from a sudden increase in wealth. The interest of these contracts for the North American firms rests above all in the opening they create for other telecommunications products, telephones, television sets, radios, telephone exchange equipment, computers, audio-visual centres, etc. Among the firms soliciting for these associated markets opened up in Indonesia by the inauguration of a satellite system are the Swedish firm L. M. Ericsson, the Dutch from Philips, the Japanese firm Nippon Electric, and the big North American aerospace and electronics companies, RCA, ITT, TRW, Fairchild, Philco-Ford (which, it may be mentioned in passing, was recently bought up by GTE) and Northrop's Page Communications. The best placed are GTE and ITT, now with Eximbank and World Bank credits. How true it turns out to be that they only lend to those who are rich already!

Within the framework of a contract with the Japanese Government, General Electric, Hughes Aircraft and Philco-Ford, in collaboration with Toshiba and Mitsubishi, should launch the first four satellites in

Japan's national system by 1977. Japan recently voted a budget of $9 billion to launch 65 satellites of all kinds between 1978 and 1987. It will be for Japan that in 1977 General Electric will be launching the first direct broadcast satellite.[16]

A Europe of satellites?

To this armada of equipment contracts collected by the United States should be added the services which NASA supplies as a monopolist. The only one with the rockets, the space organisation is thus the only body able to guarantee the launching of satellites for the other countries of the capitalist world. Each year, NASA collects between $50 m. and $70 m., each launch costing about $9 m. Three missions for the European space agency, two for Indonesia, three for Japan, one for Italy and two for NATO figured in its order books for 1975. The restrictions imposed by the United States on this type of contract have already been indicated. The country concerned has to prove that the communications satellite it is launching will not prejudice the Intelsat system, apart from experimental satellites.

Nevertheless, through such a satellite launch using a McDonnell Douglas Thor-Delta rocket, France and Germany were able to put their first joint communications satellite into orbit in December 1974, followed by a second in August 1975. France had originally envisaged launching these satellites with its own rocket, the Europa-2, but this idea was abandoned in the course of developing the project. The Europa-2 was going to turn out costing five times as much as the NASA rocket. It was truths like that which explain why during the Kissinger exchanges, oaths of allegiance multiplied in number to reassure the United States and persuade them that national satellites did no harm. 'The Symphony programme is essentially an experimental programme in the field of telecommunications. However, if the satellites operate satisfactorily, it is possible that the government of the French Republic or the government of the Federal Republic of Germany will wish to use them for international public or specialised telecommunications service.'[17]

And yet the Symphony satellite, built by a consortium which included the French firms Aérospatiale, Thomson-CSF, Société Anonyme de Télécommunications (SAT), and the German firms of Messerschmitt, Siemens and AEG-Telefunken, was not particularly dangerous for the time being, since it was only able to transmit two colour television programmes and eight sound channels or 1200 telephone channels. Nevertheless it represented the first attempt to create an all-European satellite system. Satellites which are six times more powerful and require much reduced ground stations (Orbital Test Satellite) are being launched in 1977.* This kind of satellite could well constitute the beginnings of a regional European system and, freely adapted, is already on offer to third world countries. The Eurospace association, which groups together the European aerospace firms, has meanwhile developed the Esope project, a project for establishing educational television stations in Black Africa. In December 1974, Eurospace's first clients presented themselves: the Cameroons, wishing to experiment with the distribution of educational television programmes via the Symphony satellite. Meanwhile Rwanda went directly to the Germans.

It is worth nothing that outside the US, the Federal Republic of Germany is the only country substantially to have reorganised the strategy of its educational foundations as a function of the new audiovisual technologies and the need to make them serve as bridgeheads to open up avenues for its electronics industry in third world countries. The cultural services of the West German embassies administer a careful dosage of pilot educational television projects directed by Social Democrat as well as Christian Democrat foundations—several of which, according to North American Senate revelations, have been involved with the CIA—and aid in the export and installation plans of German-based multinationals. So far their preferred target is Latin America—where the political project of Social Democracy is trying to consolidate itself in Venezuela. But more recently Africa has become a new terrain for the hunt. Using Portuguese Social Democracy as its platform, the Social Democrats of Bonn, the left wing of North American Imperialism, are trying to extend their political-commercial offensive to the previous Salazar colonies. Somewhat more discreetly, Great Britain is also trying to bring together the export of hardware and of pilot projects. In Brazil, for example, while the aeronautics firm British Aircraft tried in 1972 to sell telecommunications systems, the

---

* In September 1977, the US Delta 3914 rocket carrying the first European Space Agency experimental communications satellite into orbit blew up only seconds after its launch from Cape Kennedy. This failure under NASA's responsibility carries heavy consequences for Europe's space future. This satellite would have allowed the European countries to affirm their presence in the international market. The explosion has seriously delayed the demonstration of European technology. The original launch had already been delayed owing to an incident with the NASA rocket in June of the same year, while in April a Thor-Delta rocket had failed to put the European scientific satellite, GEOS, into its proposed orbit. Curious coincidences at the moment when the adjudication of satellite systems on the international market is in full swing, although it should be noted that only a few days later an Atlas Centaur 43 carrying an Intelsat 4A also blew up immediately after launch and plunged into the Atlantic off the Florida coast. (Author's note).

British experts of the Centre for Educational Development Overseas—for the same reasons as the North American experts of the omnipresent USAID—developed radio and television programmes for the future satellite network.

Considering the importance which these contracts have in establishing the bases for a European satellite industry, the firms of the old continent have decided for the first time to confront the North American manufacturers on the international market. The first contest deals with a project to install a regional satellite communication network which was agreed by the countries of the Arab League at Beirut in September 1974. Three proposals have been made for this system which would unite some twenty Arab speaking countries (including Mauritania, Morocco, Algeria, Tunisia, Libya, Egypt, Sudan, Jordan, Lebanon, Syria, Iraq, the two Yemens, Saudi Arabia, Somalia, Muscat and Oman) but also extend to countries such as Greece, Turkey, Ethiopia and Cyprus. Two of these proposals have been made by consortia led by European companies, comprising Messershmitt, Selenia (Italy), SNIAS and SAT (France), Marconi and Hawker-Siddeley (Great Britain). The third consortium is directed by the manufacturer of series satellites, Hughes Aircraft, this time in alliance with the Japanese firm Nippon Electric and the French firm Thomson-CSF. Thomson's drawing closer to Hughes for the purpose of strengthening its position on the world satellite market is one more index of the deliberate policy of association with the transatlantic proprietors of advanced technology. After the shattering of the idea of a home grown computer industry for capitalist Europe, and after the upset of the idea of an all-European aeronautics industry (which is confirmed by General Dynamics' success in the renewal of the North European military air fleets) difficulties now emerge to confront the formation of an all-European space applications industry.

And yet this is the mission given to the recently created European Space Agency (ESA) which brings together within a single institution European activity in the field of satellites and rockets that was previously confined to two different organisations. Representing countries such as Germany, Belgium, Denmark, Spain, France, Italy, the Netherlands, Great Britain, Sweden and Switzerland, one of the main aims of this agency is to restructure European industrial groups and rationalise production so as to avoid duplication. According to the calculations of NASA experts less than 20% of the value in orders of the projects of the new agency will go to North American companies. But it will not be until 1980 that Europe will be able to provide its own heavy rocket launchers. Meanwhile it is appropriate to appreciate how the Atlanticist policy of capitalist redeployment in which the ruling classes, especially in France, are resolutely engaged, is able to harmonise with these limited initiatives of a nationalist kind.

The search for natural resources

It is generally recognised that the crisis of energy wastage has provoked certain modification in the relationships between the US oil companies and Washington. The North American Government is strictly dependent on these companies for oil supplies and strategic interests are more than ever mixed up with their own private interests. Furthermore, these companies possess certain information of essential interest to the establishment of a long term energy policy; information which, only a short while ago, was jealously kept secret, to such a degree that you can see why in February 1973, in front of the United States Congress, CIA director Richard Helms was troubled by the reticence these firms displayed in permitting Government organisations access to their data on oil reserves.[18] Since then one can see that under the pressure of repeated threats of nationalisation in the countries where they were installed and the demands of the members of OPEC (Organisation of Petroleum Exporting Countries), the oil companies could only be convinced of the merits of strict co-operation with the government. The recent decision of Chiefs of Staff to rationalise Pentagon operations to protect foreign sources of strategic riches has just confirmed the eminently political character of the resolution of the 'energy crisis'.[19]

But this kind of close association is not the prerogative of the oil companies. It also involves all those firms which, one way or another, are directly concerned with the supply of raw materials. On the one hand this means companies involved in opening up new means of energy production, such as the manufacturers of nuclear power stations, and on the other hand, firms who have devoted themselves to surveying and exploring the natural resources of the planet. And here most of the US electronics and aerospace companies have their say as producers of the relevant technology.

First of all, they dominate the power station industry. Westinghouse and General Electric, the two main manufacturers of nuclear power stations, already monopolised almost 80% of the world market at the beginning on 1973. In 1975 they still controlled 70%. But Westinghouse (with 40% of the market) had overtaken General Electric. The three closest competitors, Babcock and Wilcox (which had suffered serious difficulties), Combustible Engineering, and the atomic division of the oil company Gulf Oil, had scarcely managed in 1973 to gain a quarter of the orders of the two giants. However, in order to follow the internal ramifications of this nuclear power block, one should add that Gulf Oil is an enterprise of the same financial group that controls Westinghouse and accordingly followed an energy policy which fitted in with the production of this nuclear power station manufacturer. On the other hand, General Electric has been associated since 1973 with the nuclear division of Exxon for the installation of the first private uranium enrichment plant in the United States.

In the second place, it is the same electronics and aerospace companies which can be found behind the big geophysical prospecting companies, were they place their latest technologies at the service of teledetection. This interest in natural resources obviously doesn't date from the official inception of the energy crisis. For the most part, as we saw in the case of Litton, the exploration of subterranean resources and of the sea bed constituted a natural development in their policy of diversification. In 1970, Litton's Western Geophysical Company made its first drillings in Brazil and Venezuela, and another of its divisions, the Litton Aerospace Corporation, drew up a map of the Amazon Basin for these two countries. What could be more natural for aerospace giants like Hughes Aircraft possessing such technological potential, than to charter vessels to sound the ocean depths in the search for minerals and, in passing, to carrying out a mission for the CIA! What could be more natural for another aeronautics giant, Lockheed Aircraft, than to establish a division, Lockheed Petroleum Services, and through it to apply the latest teachings of the space race in order to explore the ocean depths with Shell, and at the same time sell its new products for geophysical prospecting to the oil companies. Let us read this extract from the company report, where the logical relationship which exists between the geophysical field and its other activities is explained: 'Petroleum work is a good example of ingenuity in applying aerospace technology to development of new skills and penetration of new markets. Lockheed's capabilities are particularly timely in view of national concern over our growing energy crisis. They include systems that support exploration and offshore production, fuel distribution and storage, and anti-corrosion protection for oil tankers and offshore drilling platforms. Exploration to develop new petroleum supplies is vital. L-100 Hercules airlifters have played major roles in supporting explorations and drilling in Alaska, Canadian Arctic, South America, Africa and elsewhere. Specialised ground vehicles are also needed. One such high mobility vehicle is Lockheed's Twister Dragon Wagon that can move heavy payloads over rough terrain at relatively high speeds.'[20] The same phenomenon can be found among the electronics firms. For some years Texas Instruments has possessed a network of geophysical information processing centres in Canada,

England, Libya, Australia and Holland. In 1963 this company opened up new routes for geophysical exploration through the application of digital technology to the collection and processing of seismic data. And one need only remember that in July 1973, two months before the coup d'état in Chile, another company, ITT Geophysical Incorporated, announced the discovery of copper deposits in the extreme north of the country, seven times the size of Chuquicamata, the biggest open cast mine in the world.

While it is true that the geophysical activities of so many companies were not born yesterday, it is also true that the majority of these firms have considerably increased the volume of their operations in this field in the course of the last three years. Take the case of Raytheon as an example, whose favourite advertising slogan in 1974 centred on the energy crisis: 'Raytheon. Energy is 26% of our business. Raytheon is helping all oil companies find new hot spots in the coldest places.' The director's report to the shareholders made the same point: 'Our energy-related business grew substantially in the past year, and the backlog more than doubled. This rise in business, caused by the world's expanding need for fuel, petrochemical by-products and electric power, had a pronounced effect on our seismic exploration subsidiary, Seismograph Service; our designer and builder of petroleum refineries and petrochemical plants, Badger; and power plant designer and constructor, United Engineers. Seismograph Service continued to expand its worldwide geophysical exploration activity, increasing the number and capability of its crew. By the end of 1974, the number of crews in the field or in preparation was up 40 per cent over the beginning of the year. The Phoenix seismic data-processing system using a Raytheon mini-computer has become widely accepted and, by the end of 1974, some 90 of these systems were in use.'[21] In July 1975, Raytheon announced that one of its subsidiaries had discovered copper deposits in Iran. This is happening all the time. Hughes Aircraft also declared in its advertisements that it had developed a portable antenna which allowed engineers involved in oil exploration in the far north to communicate with their companies at any time by satellite. An advertisement by the firm Bendix in an issue of the *Wall Street Journal* in March 1974 is especially centred on this theme: 'Bendix expects energy related sales to grown in '74', and the firm announced that its oil exploration subsidiary, United Geophysical Corporation, had recently set to work in Peru, Venezuela, Brazil, Nigeria, Alaska and Canada. It added the information in passing that its electronics division manufactured cable systems for nuclear power stations, while its automobile division was searching for the means to economise on petrol through experiments on electronic fuel injection.

Control over raw materials is necessary for the North American firms to maintain their supremacy over their competitors in the race for energy information. Within the framework of the mobilisation to achieve this, we find another application of satellite technology, natural resources exploration satellites. The first of these was launched by the United States in 1972, and the second in 1975. They both carried the name ERTS (Earth Resources Technology Satellites) or LANDSAT. This was an experimental NASA project, whose main vehicle in the private sector was General Electric, who conceived them and centralises the exploitation of the information which the satellites transmit. Nothing astonishing in this when you remember that as a faithful reflection of the circularity of monopolistic power, the Board of Directors of this company is composed a quarter of heads of companies which exploit the natural riches of third world countries. Meanwhile, the projected merger between the Utah Mining company and General Electrical demonstrates the breadth of the electronics firm's interests.[23]

The camera systems of these satellites have photographed 90% of the earth's surface and their precision is great enough to distinguish two points about 585 feet apart. The information provided by the satellites is of multidisciplinary interest, including meteorology, hydrography, oceanography, geography, cartography, demography and agronomy as well as mining. To exploit this information, the US has set up a network of 300 investigators of all nationalities in 37 non-socialist countries. The tele-photos collected by each national team are codified and sent to the United States where they are given the highest priority at NASA's Goddard centre. The data is then sent to foreign governments who ask for it. It is only recently that NASA has entered into agreements with certain countries for processing the data *in situ*. One should add that even then it is generally specialised North American companies who are employed. Thus Brazil, which now has a station of this sort, has to rely on the services of five North American experts. Canada, which has one station, is already thinking of another. Iran has just signed a contract for such a station, and projects are under study for countries such as Germany, Norway, Japan and Zaire. The buyers of this information are extremely varied. For example, the Brazilian station includes among its permanent subscribers the Ministry of Mines, the Ministry of Agriculture, the Interior Ministry and some 300 private companies. Among the most important of these are the North American or mixed-ownership mining companies who hold most of the Amazon Forest concessions. A number of university and other research services gravitate around this project in the United States: they hold NASA contracts for the special exploitation of particular types of information, such as the analysis of crops, or forestry resources, water resources, siting of towns, etc. One can easily see the uses which can be made of such information, from urban planning to agricultural forecasting.

Liberalism in space

After imposing their own norms on the use of the new communications technologies, the United States launched a diplomatic offensive around 1970 at the level of the big international organisations with the purpose of establishing an international consensus on proposed new forms of co-operation, in order to 'naturalise' these forms of co-operation in such as way as to mask their character as new forms of aggression. In 1969, when the Comsat-multinationals-North American universities front encountered the opposition of the South American governments to the idea of setting up a continental satellite communications system, one of the weighty arguments it used in the polemic against the South American thesis of the right to cultural and educational self-determination, rested on the need to respect the free exchange of ideas and the free circulation of information. This was a particularly dangerous argument in the light of the progress already being made towards direct transmission satellites, whose first example, as already mentioned, was due to be launched in Japan by General Electric in 1977. Even if the immediate possibilities for the commercialisation of such a satellite are far from being realised, the legitimation of its indiscriminate usage has disturbed numerous third world countries who fear that they might be inundated by educational and commercial programmes made in the United States. How can the freedom to exchange ideas and information be effectively defined in a situation characterised by such power relations between the metropolis and the rest of the world where the United States controls more than 65% of the flow of ideas and information circulating the world? The thesis of liberalism in space is framed by the principles of commercial freedom: liberalism equals the liberty to dominate.

The need for a treaty which wards off such an invasion was raised by certain third world countries and by the Soviet Union. The United States obviously refused to agree to such an idea, while other countries like France, Canada and Sweden suggested an intermediate position and a moderate recommendation. UNESCO, during its 17th session in July 1972, proposed to its member States to issue a declaration on 'the principles guiding the use of television via satellite, and guaranteeing the free flow of information, the expansion of education and greater cultural exchange'.[23] In anticipation it had already sent all member countries a draft of the resolution. It invited them to subscribe to mutual agreements and reaffirmed the principle of national sovereignty. 'Each country', it read, 'has the right to fix the content of educational programmes transmitted by satellite to its citizens.'

This document is necessarily general in character, even if it represents a step forward and a victory by the proletarian nations. More interesting are the commentaries elaborated in the charmed circles of the White House on the draft proposed by UNESCO. The reader will excuse the following long extract from a confidential memorandum which circulated among the North American UNESCO delegation, since it enables us to appreciate the tactical position of the North American Government in the face of the accumulating resistance which its policies encountered within the international organisations:[24]

The UNESCO proposal has caused a certain disappointment among the largest television companies, in the United States as well as Europe. In fact, at an assembly of regional television associations which took place in Rome last March, North American and European television enterprises declared the proposal unacceptable. In their opinion, what represents the greatest danger of such a declaration is that one day or other it could serve as the basis for regulating, under the pretext of international convention, the conduct of nations and companies in the question of space transmission.

Within the North American Government, opinion is divided. On the one hand, USIA [US Information Agency] and the Office of Telecommunications Policy of the White House, are in favour of totally free flow of information, traffic without any restriction. On the other, institutions which have an educational and cultural mission (AID, HEW, CU) [Agency for International Development, Ministry for Health, Education and Welfare, Council of Universities] reckon that the United States has the moral obligation to respond to the disquiet of underdeveloped countries in this domain. Other government institutions concerned hold an intermediate position.

In order that the point of view of the free traffic in information should prevail, we must ask ourselves if it is possible from a cultural and educational point of view to discuss the concept of the free flow of information without giving the impression of imposing our own political philosophy on other countries, and, if this is possible, how to take it up?

The proposal presented by UNESCO reflects the opinion of a large number of underdeveloped countries that a form of control and regulation is essential for the development of their nation and who wish to arrive at a balance between control and freedom. Less important than whether their opinion on 'economic and cultural imperialism', which, according to them, would result from direct transmission, are correct or not, the problem is how these countries perceive the results of a free flow of information, and the United States must adapt itself to this reality, without giving the impression of imposing its own political philosophy on countries whose television systems and condition of socio-economic development differs from ours.

The UNESCO proposal reveals a fundamentally false conception of satellite functioning. While direct transmission from satellites to individual receivers (equipped with adaptors which cost several hundred dollars each) is technologically possible today, ten to fifteen years may be needed before the adaptors are sufficiently cheap or the programmes sufficiently attractive for a large number of individuals in underdeveloped countries to be able to receive programmes directly via satellites. Before this date, it is not a real problem.

The problem which exists with the underdeveloped countries is essentially a conflict of rights: the right to free flow of information in virtue of which a country must rely on improved means to bring to its people the information needed for its social and economic progress; and on the other hand the right to educate its people and conserve its culture without foreign interference. The first right entails renouncing a certain amount of sovereignty in the face of ideas penetrating the country, the second right entails imposing restrictions on the free flow in information.

The final UNESCO declaration should insist more on the aims of direct satellite transmission which have to do with education, culture and information. The United States should therefore be prepared to speak in a constructive manner about the consequences of the development of new technologies, especially in emerging countries.

National and regional television organisations have a vital role to play in this domain and must be prepared to contribute to the planning of any international arrangement which deals with the utilisation of space communications for educational, cultural and informational ends.

The group of American government councillors is not unanimous on direct transmission of commercial advertising. Commercial advertising often represents the worst aspects of North American culture and we should not continue to insist on imposing a mode of life on others which can frustrate the syndrome of the growing hopes of the underdeveloped countries. But on the other hand, commercial advertising is an integral creation of our system of free enterprise which other countries must recognise.

Recommendations:

(a) from a tactical point of view, given the emotional and political nature of this problem and the present state of the UNESCO declaration, the United States tries only to introduce a small number of changes;

(b) the United States strives to have article 9 of the proposal revised, and if its efforts come to nothing, votes against this particular clause;

(c) the United States adopts a positive attitude towards the formulation of an international declaration and assumes a position of leadership, on the condition that this is a declaration which insists on the beneficial consequences of the new technology for countries on the way to development and which reiterates the willingness of the United States to share its technological resources and its knowledge with other nations, in this sector'.

The only suggestion contributed by the United States to the UNESCO proposal underlines their anxiety to maintain a double field of action, and to favour a private manner of exploitation. In fact, in the original version, the article 9 which the memorandum referred to, restrained the transmission of commercial advertising and, furthermore, delimited the respective roles to be played by regional and national television associations as well as governments in the policies to be adopted over direct transmission. In order properly to appreciate the stakes which the United States were defending, it is only necessary to remember that there are large North American television chains in a number of third world countries which dominate the national and regional associations. The US doesn't see why these private enterprises which had been allowed to install and control commercial television networks in various countries should not also serve as channels for the introduction of educational television. This situation is all the more paradoxical since in the United States itself educational television exists outside the commercial circuit and uses special channels for transmission. This subject will crop up again. In Latin America, the most representative 'regional association' is LATINO (Latin American Television International Network Organisation) established by the American Broadcasting Company (ABC) of New York in 1968 to bring together in the same organisation channels 9 and 13 in Buenos Aires, 9 in Bogota, 7 in San José, Costa Rica, 7 in Santa Domingo, three channels in Ecuador, two in San Salvador, two in the Dutch Antilles, one in Panama, one in Uruguay, channels 2 and 4 in Caracas, Guatamala's channel 3, Mexico's channel 4 and Chile's channels 13 and 4.

However, the UNESCO declaration has not put an end to the debate. In November 1972 the United States found itself alone during the 27th session of the United Nations when member countries voted by 102 to 1 to produce a set of principles to govern satellite transmission.[25] In 1974 the same confrontation occurred within the same arena, but with a new element in evidence: it was no longer only a question of drawing up a treaty to regulate television programme transmission, but of extending the principle to other fields of information. The discussion was carried on around the collection of information on natural resources carried out night and day throughout the world by the ERTS satellites. Several third world countries questioned this new form of spying on primary materials perpetrated without agreement among the nations. More moderately, France and the Soviet Union proposed that information gathered by tele-photography should not be passed on to a third party without the consent of the nation concerned. The United States made the most of the importance of the concept of the free flow of information even in this field. Had they not, six months earlier, released to the press photographs of Soviet rocket launching bases taken by the ERTS satellite![26] It was all further proof—if one is needed—that it is extremely difficult to close off from each other the different sectors of the new technological applications, in this epoch when the struggle between classes is no less all-encompassing, however much more diffuse it may have become on an international scale.

The militarisation of communications

When you analyse the progress of civil applications of satellite technology, it is difficult not to wonder how much some of them must interest the military; for example, satellites which permit study of the state of harvests, weather prediction and the movement of cyclones, are instruments which cannot escape the interest of those planning climatological warfare. But, put this way, the question is posed badly, since, as in the case of the whole group of vanguard techniques, these applications are actually only the fall-out of a technology originally conceived for military purposes. The observations we made on the groupings of the electronics and aerospace industry taken on added point when you examine the origin of this special sector of space technology.

In interesting themselves in the new satellite technologies, the North American military have only renewed the preoccupations they demonstrated after the First World War over the development of the first discoveries in telecommunications. At that time the North American Navy realised the gaps which existed in this field in their national industry. Concrete experience on the battlefield brought them up against the British quasi-monopoly in wireless communications, which lay in the hands of practically only one company, British Marconi. In 1920, at the Navy's instigation, an agreement was signed between the large companies in a position to exploit those technologies of transmission which were classed as strategic materials. Under the aegis of this agreement General Electric purchased Marconi's North American subsidiary, which very quickly became RCA. The agreement stipulated among other things that ATT should have exclusive rights to telephone and radio-telephone services, as well as the right to manufacture transmission apparatus; the exploitation of transatlantic services was reserved exclusively to RCA; General Electric kept wireless telegraphy and the production of all receiving apparatus. This initiative, which succeeded in countering what the Navy feared most—the dispersal of the exploitation of the mostly British patents—established the first foundation of monopoly in telecommunications.[27]

But in an epoch when North American capitalism is developing towards the forms of State monopoly capitalism, the Pentagon has far fewer difficulties in patronising new discoveries. Between 1958 and 1972 the United States successfully launched 115 civil satellites and 700 military satellites for a cost of $27 billion. At the beginning of 1973 it had 55 civil and 282 military satellites in the sky carrying the star-spangled banner.[28] During the course of these fifteen years, the North

American Government spent almost \$65 billion on space programmes, half of what the Vietnam War cost it. Almost 60% of these funds were paid out on the lunar stakes. Almost all the remaining sum was absorbed by Defense Department space protects. From 1962, the Atomic Energy Commission also entered the field, notably in grafting its projects for nuclear propulsion systems onto interplanetary voyages, but it never amounted to more than 2% of the global space budget. An important observation should be made, which specifies the determinant role of the Pentagon in the orientation of space technology: among its numerous attributes we find that of industrial administrator. All NASA acquisitions are handled by the industrial administration apparatus of the Department of Defense.[29] It need hardly be added that NASA itself, apart from its supposedly civil activities, was often charged with specific defense projects. But the

Table 14

Outlays for Space Activities (in millions of dollars)

Year	Total	National Aeronautics and Space Administration	Department of Defense	Atomic Energy Commission	Others
1960	960	401	518	—	41
1961	1,518	744	710	—	64
1962	2,418	1,257	1,029	130	2
1963	4,114	2,552	1,368	161	13
1964	5,970	4,171	1,564	220	15
1965	6,886	5,035	1,592	232	27
1966	7,719	5,858	1,638	188	35
1967	7,237	5,337	1,673	184	43
1968	6,667	4,595	1,890	146	36
1969	6,330	4,083	2,095	116	36
1970	5,453	3,565	1,756	103	29
1971	4,999	3,171	1,693	97	38
1972	4,772	3,195	1,470	60	47
1973	4,719	3,069	1,557	51	42
1974	4,854	2,960	1,777	39	78
1975[e]	4,931	2,903	1,904	44	80
1976[e]	5,446	3,182	2,133	47	84

Source: 1960–1969: *The Budget of the United States* (Annually). *Aeronautics and Space Report of the President* (Annually).

dominion of the Pentagon over the new technologies does not stop there. The first series of supposedly civil satellites—Syncom 1, 2 and 3—were originally built at the request of the Department of Defense, who, since their launching, directed them to use in military communications above the Pacific. Since the early 60s RCA has built a system of meteorological defense satellites for the Pentagon. In 1969, the technical communication satellite, TACSAT I, built by Hughes Aircraft, already had a capacity of 20,000 telephone circuits, and already at this time North American experts estimated that the technologies employed in these satellites would take more than six years to be transferred to the civil domain. For the first three years of its functioning, the Pentagon has reserved 80% of the capacity of the supposedly civil maritime navigation satellite system (MARISAT), launched in 1976.

The Pentagon now wields a triple system of military satellites, one for the USAF, another for the navy, and the last for the Defense Department itself giving global coverage. Thanks to these systems the different wings of the forces are able to communicate with their bases practically throughout the world; but further, the principal problem of communication with mobile units, warships and aircraft, has been resolved. In 1967, the North American army decided to provide its campaign troops in Vietnam with small portable reception antennae which could be installed in any kind of terrain. These experiments, in which reception terminals were simplified as far as possible, led the North American experts to write that before the end of the decade it would be technically possible for an explorer who finds himself in the remotest parts of the Amazon, or a businessman away hunting in the Rocky Mountains, to communicate with anyone who has access to a telephone anywhere in the world, thanks to an apparatus the size of a box.[30] The three military systems carry the following names: AF-Satcom (Air Force), Fleet-Satcom (Navy) and DSCS (Defense Satellite Communication System). Among the long established manufacturers, headed by Hughes Aircraft, are NCR and RCA; among the more recent, Grumman, Honeywell, TRW and IBM.[31]

To complete the defense network in the western world there is a fourth system, that of NATO. The Atlantic defense organisation had already reached the third phase of its communication satellite programme, started in 1967, by 1975. In the earlier phases, 12 ground stations were constructed in the United States, Belgium, England, Canada, Denmark, the Federal Republic of Germany, Greece, Holland, Italy, Norway, Portugal and Turkey. The major beneficiary to these contracts was ITT's German subsidiary, Standard Elektrik Lorenz, AG. Two military satellites conceived by Philco-Ford were

Table 15

US Space Vehicle Systems Sales and Backlog*
(in million of dollars)

	Net Sales			Backlog Dec. 31st		
Year	Total	Military	Non-Military	Total	Military	Non-Military
1961	775	551	224	586	350	236
1962	1,319	712	607	1,435	852	583
1963	1,911	1,061	850	1,612	856	756
1964	2,222	732	1,490	1,611	391	1,220
1965	2,449	602	1,847	2,203	503	1,700
1966	2,710	734	1,976	1,494	428	1,066
1967	2,199	789	1,410	1,974	1,096	878
1968	2,357	899	1,458	1,329	834	495
1969	2,282	1,187	1,095	1,330	869	461
1970	1,956	1,025	931	1,184	786	398
1971	1,725	860	865	916	603	313
1972	1,656	905	751	959	646	313
1973	1,562	902	660	1,177	923	254
1974	1,735	922	813	1,500	1,137	363

Source: Bureau of the Census, *Current Industrial Reports,* Series MQ37D (Quarterly).

* Based on data from about 55 companies engaged in the manufacture of aerospace products. Excludes engines and propulsion units.

launched. The third phase foresees the launching of further satellites while the ground network will comprise stations with more important antennae and a series of mobile stations on earth and at sea. Once completed, the system will allow direct communication with campaign troops in their terrain of operation. Outside the NATO system, the two military satellites launched by Great Britain contribute their assistance. They were built by Marconi and Philco-Ford. Britain became the first European country to construct satellites of this type (Skynet). This development is much more modest in such countries as France. At the beginning of 1975, the technical services of the army announced their next entry into military satellite technology. With operation Sextius in 1977 they proceeded to a military experiment in space telecommunications, via the German-French civil satellite, Symphonie.[32]

The advances made by the North American military in the development of satellite technology pose serious problems for government agencies. When discussion began on the construction programme of the third natural resources satellite, to be launched towards the end of the decade, one of the big arguments against the project, on the part of the White House Management and Budget Office, consisted in pointing out precisely that the envisaged programme would double up on existing ones, and that 'much of the same data could be gathered by Air Force intelligence satellites'.[33] To which the NASA officials replied that 'it would take too long to declassify the Air Force's satellites' data'. Notice, incidentally, the impression here of being submerged in a sea of unexploited information! The project for a new natural resources satellite therefore had difficulty in getting under way. But that wasn't because the 'energy crisis' had been resolved! Quite the contrary. Was it not a measure of rationalisation in the face of the crisis? Didn't the Pentagon already have the information NASA was looking for?

Subimperialism: the Pentagon in Iran

A short while ago, the only official co-operative project between the Washington Government and the Government of a third world country for the purpose of installing a national communication satellite system was the agreement between the US and New Delhi. According to this agreement, signed by NASA and the Indian Atomic Energy Department in 1969, India would transmit educational television programmes, starting at the end of 1975, throughout its entire territory, thanks to the ATS-6 satellite launched by NASA and constructed by Fairchild, although the conception of the system fell to General Electric. For the United States the main objective was clear: to make India a shop window for space technology applied to the needs of so-called backward nations. The agreement made no secret of this: it should 'demonstrate the potential value of satellite technology in the rapid development of effective mass communications in developing countries'.[34] India was the ideal country for this kind of experiment. It had only one transmitter and 10,000 receivers. It was intended to extend the system to 550,000 villages and it had been estimated that the creation of a conventional television distribution system would take 30 years. The launching of a satellite reduced this delay to ten years at an equal annual rate of investment. India itself, accepting the introduction of this new technology, hoped that it would 'improve agricultural practices, contribute to family planning objectives and contribute to national integration'.[35] The agreement between the United States and India synthesised these objectives at the same time that it shed light on the philosophy which animated the North American authorities in such collaboration with a proletarian nation. The United States, it was said, would not be responsible for the programming. Within the framework of this project India will talk to India. But India was to undertake an evaluation of the results of the experiment and place them at the disposal of the whole world. The evaluation would be made as far as possible in quantitive terms. Consequently it was to be expected that the family planning programme would be evaluated by comparing birth rates in villages provided with television and those without. Agricultural productivity and rising income would be the object of a similar evaluation. It would thus be possible to appreciate the value of the experiment, as much for the United States as for India and other nations interested in this type of system.[36]

Other complementary plans for aid came to be incorporated in the project. Indian scientists and engineers were sent to North American universities and sociologists and anthropologists of the Ford Foundation prepared the psycho-social ground in the villages for the arrival of the new technology. Indeed the Foundation had considerable interest in following this first global experiment since its numerous investigators had themselves prepared campaigns for male and female sterilisation financed by USAID and the Population Council. Had they not dreamed up stratagems to persuade reticent peasants to accept vasectomy? By way of recompense, a small transistor set had been given to every candidate for the operation. This wierd dialectical swop between the medical arsenal of sterilisation and the gadgetry of electronic communications becomes a perfect metaphor for the aims of the communications policies which the Empire pursues in its neo-colonies.

But 1975, when the proposed satellite was due to enter into service, was a long way from 1969 when the agreement was signed. Meanwhile India itself had time to enter the game at another table, and signed agreements with the Soviet Union for scientific co-operation in the space field. It was a Soviet rocket which in 1975 launched the first space device built by the Indians. On their side the United States doesn't seem to have waited for the fruits of this huge experiment to begin invading the international markets. While relations between the metropolis and the countries inclined to accommodate imperialist expansion have also needed time to develop a new turn, other actors apart from NASA are now asserting their hegemony. There have been many opportunities for the liaison between the US military apparatus and the multi-nationals to mature, though circumstances, involving resounding failures as well as successes, have constrained them. But the Defense Department has increasingly become one of the bridgeheads for United States foreign policy just to the extent that military objectives occupy a large place in protecting the economy of Empire. The direct role of the Pentagon in the fall of Allende confirmed this in the most brutal way, and CIA agents outbidding each other in their revelations before the North American Congress are hardly going to let us forget the Agency's intrigues, always so discreet. But the priorities of military strategy can also be seen in the dispatch of electronic or aerospace high technology 'made in USA' to countries which have been promoted to the role of policemen installed in watchtowers over their neighbours. In these countries, which become sub-imperialist agents, it is possible to see how a neo-colonial State apparatus is created which is calculated entirely to suit the needs of expansion of the multinationals. The accelerating rhythm of the process of 'electronification' which the Iranian gendarmerie of the Near East and the Brazilian gendarmerie of Latin America have submitted themselves to, clarifies certain aspects of this mutation.

Iran's military contracts with the United States are uncountable. In 1974 and 1975 more than $6 billion was poured out in ready cash for the purchase of arms, which amounts to 40% of total North American arms exports. (By way of comparison, the Federal German Republic, foremost European importer of North American arms, purchased 273 million dollars' worth in 1975.) Thus in 1974, while the rush of petro-dollars led to a 40% increase in gross national revenue, 2,500 Maverick missiles, 80 Grumman fighter-bombers and 489 Bell helicopters of all types were sold to the Iranian forces; in 1975 the purchase of six destroyers made by Litton at a cost of $110 m. each was expected, together with more than 50 F-16s of General Dynamics, not counting the purchase of six French patrol-boats of the 'Combattante' type, and numerous British anti-aircraft radar systems. In addition to these key supplies, the North American companies sponsored the launching of an electronics industry. Hughes Aircraft built an electro-optics factory, whose production will be exported to the countries of the Persian Gulf. ITT set itself up for the production of semi-conductors. Litton Industries will manufacture locally certain components for its navigation systems. Earlier, Northrop set up a joint subsidiary with the Iranian aeronautics industry, repeating the agreement it had reached with Brazil in 1973.

This is the war-mongering environment for the export of a national satellite system to Iran. It is an entirely new but openly acknowledged element that neither NASA nor Comsat are in charge of the installation, but the North American armed forces, and particularly the US Air Force, through the Defense Department. In order to plan this entire modern communications network, the USAF Electronics Systems Division, which has titular responsibility for the operation, asked American Telegraph and Telephone to set up a permanent technical assistance crew mostly made up of experts from the company's various divisions, with others drawn inevitably from Comsat.[37] This system, whose construction is already far advanced, will have four main uses: telephone linking, tele-data-processing of every type, television programme transmission, especially educational television, and military applications. For the first time, the sophisticated trans-receiver equipment installed in all US Air Force and Navy aircraft, will be used to equip the aircraft of a third-world country.

It is only very recently that the real dimensions of this process of huge-scale military electronification have become known. In May 1975, the *New York Times*, following the remarks of a State Department spokesman, announced that the aerospace manufacturers Rockwell would shortly install an intelligence base for the Iranians of prime importance, capable of listening to all civil and military electronic communications in the Gulf region. The State Department spokesman specified that this project, under the code name IBEX, would cost around half a billion dollars.[38] This type of aerospace complex is only installed in countries which are, so to speak, militarily occupied, which become laboratories for the discovery of the limits of strategies directed against the process of liberation. In March 1973 the Puerto Rican daily *Claridad* disclosed that the North American army—which occupies 15% of the arable land on the island—had installed an electronic espionage base at Fort Buchanan, similar to the one proposed for Iran two years later. The Puerto Rican example reveals that in addition to listening to far-off conversations, the interception of telephone and telegraph communications, these bases store up and analyse radio and television programmes, the forums where representatives of progressive forces make their presence felt in the various Latin American countries.

In 1975 the Iranian Government also subscribed to a contract with GTE which was the largest that a private company could ever remember in the telecommunications industry: for the sum of $500 m. and delivery by 28th March 1978, 2 million telephone lines and the associated exchange equipment. The circumstances in which the multi-million dollar contract was signed exhibited aspects of the unbridled competition between North American-based multinational companies that are relatively poorly known. Six companies had responded to a public invitation for tenders: the German firm Siemens, the Japanese firm Nippon Electric, L. M. Ericsson, a Swedish company, the French subsidiaries of ITT, Compagnie Générale de Construction Télé-phonique, Le Matériel Téléphonique, and finally the German subsidiary of the same company, ITT-Standard Elektrik Lorenz. Everyone expected France to carry off the riches through the ITT subsidiaries. The Shah of Iran himself had chosen a French firm of technical counsellors to judge between the various proposals. And in the course of a trip which he made to France the question of this contract was raised in interviews with the French Head of State. Yet, against all expectations, the modernisation of the Iranian telephone system fell into the hands of GTE. It appears that behind the scenes there were two main reasons for this decision. GTE was already there. Earlier on it had signed another contract with the Iranian air force to supply a variety of communications apparatus. This was the trampoline which enabled it to capture the lion-sized contract. But the vexed French officials offered another reason which was surely not without foundation: 'that GTE exploited the recent communist gains in the French elections by warning the Iranians they might wind up dealing with a nationalised manufacturer by accepting the ITT subsidiaries' bid'.[39]

As for the other contract for earth and air surveillance equipment signed with Rockwell, the US ambassador in Tehran, ex-chief of the CIA, Richard Helms, was no stranger, according to the *New York Times*, to the manoeuvres needed to clinch it. His personal participation in the study of Iranian needs was decisive.[40] Rockwell had already sent technical crews to Tehran and had been instructed to engage, in the United States, ex-members of the National Security Agency and the intelligence services of the air force.

This recruitment policy of future instructors to the private firm belongs to a wider training policy. With the country offering itself up to the United States, lock, stock and barrel, as a first class laboratory, the Defense Department began to break new ground in tightening the knots with the private firms which supplied the equipment. Such a sudden flow of arms resulted in the armed forces decentralising their technical assistance operations; the companies were charged directly with guaranteeing the technical training of military personnel. Thus in 1975 the Pentagon supervised no less than five technical assistance contracts in the Near East, with a budget calculated to make just about any polytechnic institute grow pale with envy.

In Iran, 315 million. In Saudi Arabia, 362 million. In Kuwait, 327 million and in Israel 884 million.[41] The programme which the Defense Department confided to Textron's Bell Helicopter Co. in respect of an inter-governmental agreement, which costs $255 m., serves for the training of 1,500 helicopter pilots and 5,000 mechanics, all of them belonging to the Iranian air force. In order to conduct these intensive training programmes successfully, the company had to set up a new subsidiary, in Texas, Bell Helicopter International, which henceforward was responsible for planning the new worldwide services of what was really a parallel technical university. The first external establishment of this new subsidiary reflected the logic of the export trade when the military air base of Isfahan became the site of its first training establishment. Other companies, less in demand, preferred to send Iranian officers to their training centres in the United States. Thus 150 Iranian engineers and specialists were received in the Grumman classrooms. It may be noted that in the last twenty years no less than 10,000 Iranian military personnel have passed through training centres in the United States, or North American foreign bases, under the terms of North American military assistance programmes.[42]

It is obvious that this new practice, born in the shadow of the oil derricks, is a sign of the times and that it develops on a general scale in proportion to increases in arms exports; and that a growing number of companies envisage and are organising training for foreign personnel. The structure of technical assistance set out by the Pentagon in the 60s is now and hencefoward incapable of supporting the rhythms which it is claimed the export boom will impose. It seems that the problem is a general one because the increase in arms exports is also accompanied in countries like France by an reorganisation of so-called after-sales services. Remember the Government decision to create such a service in the ministerial arms delegation. This new stage of militarisation follows that phase which was basically limited to an exchange of specialists between the Pentagon and private industry and vice versa. Between July 1967 and December 1971, the big North American electronics and aerospace companies recruited 1,101 high Pentagon officials, civil and military, in retirement or in the reserves, with the rank of at least major or its equivalent in the heirarchies of public administration. During the same period, the Pentagon engaged 232 high ranking officials from these big companies. Thus, during this period, McDonnell Douglas acquired the services of 70 senior officers and lost 7 members of staff to the Pentagon. Boeing engaged 60, while 8 of its staff went to the Pentagon. Westinghouse, Hughes Aircraft, General Electric, Litton and Grumman, took on between 30 and 40. None of this is surprising, given that out of the ten principal Pentagon officials responsible for the new arms production policy, there are, in company with James R. Schlesinger, five civilians who hail directly from the offices or laboratories of the big aeronautics or electronics firms: the assistant secretary for research is a specialist in laser beams from Hughes Aircraft, the others come from McDonnell Douglas, Ling-Temco-Vought, Philco-Ford and General Motors. They are the ones who have reoriented all the research programmes of the Defense Department, in spite of internal opposition from certain old military leaders. However, this civil-military exchange doesn't stop there. It can be seen on many other levels, for example, in the specialised aeronautics and aerospace press. Ten engineers, 12 civil pilots and 20 ex-air force officials can be found on the editorial board of *Aviation Week & Space Technology*, published by the same commercial firm as *Business Week*.[43]

There is no reason why these tendencies shouldn't also be found in the field of electronics applied to civil repression. Rockwell's recruitment of ex-intelligence officers is exactly the same! And this is indeed the conclusion one reaches, considering the eagerness with which certain North American electronics firms offer their collaboration to the country's police forces. Here is an extract from a report by Northrop's Page Engineers division, produced after the 1972 annual conference of the International Association of Chiefs of Police (IACP) at Salt Lake City:

> THE RESPONSIBILITY OF THE POLICE CONTINUES TO INCREASE EACH DAY THAT PASSES. Our enthusiasm here at PAGE steadily increases also, because PAGE can provide valuable systems and services to meet the communications needs for all police departments in major cities throughout the country. All personnel who are involved in public safety—whether it be country, city or state—recognise that outmoded communications equipments can no longer be tolerated. We lend a helping hand to the criminal when the 'call for help' is unanswered because of the lack of proper equipment. We left our business card with the chiefs; we invited them to use our experience, skill and the application of the total systems approach to meet their specific communications requirements.[44]

The machine necessarily calls its master, and in the process of electronification, it is difficult to say which ideologue is the more effective, the one who continues to dictate courses in McCarthyite propaganda from on high, or the one who teaches the detection of an orderly enemy on a luminous radar screen of the latest model.

The Brazilian police projects

The Brazilian police forces have already answered the question. Between 1969 and 1972 the Public Safety Project directed by USAID allowed 100,000 federal and state police agents to be retrained, and 523 officers to be sent for training in the police academies of the United States. The three favourite institutions were the National Academy of Police, the National Centre of Telecommunications, and the National Institute of Criminology and Identification. One of the main efforts consisted in training technicians in telecommunications, for the construction and equipping of stations to ease communications between each state and the capital, and in the interior of each state. Most of the telecommunications materials, granted by USAID as technical assistance, consisted in mobile equipment. According to the project it was intended to develop the capacity of communication by portable radio in times of civil troubles, and increase the efficiency of operation of police patrols.[45] In 1971 30 US police experts lent assistance to the project while 80 of their Brazilian colleagues attended courses at the International Police Academy in Washington. Plans were developed in parallel by the Communications Group of the US naval mission in Brazil. Rio De Janeiro, in these plans, constituted one of 26 naval communication stations belonging to the US defense communications system, allowing constant contact with Naval vessels in the South Atlantic as well as fishing boats and the North American merchant marine. Finally, through the University of the State of New Mexico, under Navy contract, the US Defense Department conducted the Transit navigation satellite programme in collaboration with the Brazilian air force, which collected information for both governments.

To complete these preliminaries, the Brazilian Government signed a contract with General Electric and Hughes Aircraft for studies to be made for the installation of a national communications satellite. Officially it dealt with an educational system comprising a group of three satellites to be launched from 1976 on, covering 86% of the country's territory, each satellite to carry three television channels and twenty radio chains. The principal transmitter will be situated at the space research institute in Sao Paulo; nine programming stations will supply programmes for children during the first twelve years of education. 150,000 direct receiving stations will provide relays in rural zones. Around the periphery of urban areas, 150 stations will redistribute programmes by land line.

In 1971, before the contract was signed, Stanford University had conducted a group of experiments with Brazilian universities: courses given in Stanford University lecture theatres were transmitted directly to Brazilian engineering students using a NASA ATS-3 satellite. In 1974 another collaborative experiment using a NASA ATS-6 satellite allowed a pilot educational television project to be conducted in the poorest part of Brazil, the North East, reaching 500 schools and 15,000 schoolchildren in the first two years of primary education. More than a thousand teachers had previously been prepared to take charge of reception in the various local communities. The Ministry of Education and the municipalities had also taken care to integrate the children's parents into the experiment, many of whom had never attended school themselves. According to the authorities the results were more than satisfactory. Here is an extract from a report:

> The project organisers were feted and treated as bringers of hope and salvation when they visited the villages and schools involved. For the pupils it is seen as a chance to enter the modern world about which some, though not all, had already heard and

seen so much on their radio and television sets. For the teachers, many of whom are unqualified in any sense, and some of whom left school themselves at only twelve years of age, it is seen as a real chance for betterment, for much of the television teaching is directed at the teachers themselves.[46]

But this entry into the 'modern world' takes place in a precise context. In the present state of satellite technology, and above all in relation to the political, military and economic integration of Brazil with the United States (strengthened by Kissinger's trip to Brazil after the North American defeat in Angola), the future system is evidently not conceived solely as a function of education. In fact, only one of the three space devices will serve for the transmission of educational programmes. The system which General Electric was authorised to design for the Brazilians is a multiple-use system which, it is true, will play a role in the educational field, but it will also be used for direct repression. According to reports prepared by this same company, the

Table 16

The 20 Biggest Private Corporations in Brazil
(Ranked According to Estimated Annual Sellings in 1974)

	Annual sellings (US $1,000)	Liquid assets (US $1,000)
1 Volkswagen (West Germany)	898,601	275,730
2 Shell (UK Netherlands)	572,301	103,079
3 General Motors (US)	546,267	141,504
4 Ford (US)	536,123	164,328
5 Exxon (US)	525,113	66,855
6 Brascan (Canada)	479,905	826,744
7 Sanbra (Bungey Born, Argentina)	414,712	51,277
8 Daimler-Benz (West Germany)	334,002	144,393
9 Atlantic Richfield (US)	283,661	49,300
10 Texaco (US)	282,841	49,540
11 Pirelli (Italy)	260,761	100,110
12 Souza Cruz (Brit-American Tob., UK)	254,926	199,929
13 Rhodia (France)	218,596	133,495
14 Varig Airlines	215,643	96,445
15 Nestle (Switzerland)	197,519	56,584
16 Indústrias Matarazzo	193,423	155,382
17 Electro-Radiobrás	184,471	29,628
18 Anderson Clayton (US)	182,842	38,183
19 Chrysler (US)	173,360	23,133
20 Co-operativa Agrícola de Cotia	166,667	17,050

Source: *Brasil em Exame, Editora Abril*, São Paulo, Sept. 1974 (Quoted in M. Arruda *et al. Multinationals and Brazil*, Toronto, Brazilian Studies—Latin America Research Unit, 1975)

system's 'functions include collection, transmission, switching, reception, recording and display of information' and can be used for 'law enforcement, business, medical, safety, security, control and navigation' purposes. This is only confirmed by the fact that the Ministry of the Interior can be found among the current users of the data transmitted by the ERTS natural resources observation satellite.

What's more, the 'doctrine of national security'[47] which rules the military dictatorship—as in Chile, Uruguay and Bolivia—includes 'not only national defense but everything which concerns economic and social development'. In this respect, education itself is only a part of national security. Is there any better proof that totalitarianism rules the very concept at the heart of the *novus ordo* (new order) in Brazil than the installation of a satellite system, under the cover of the modernisation of education, which actually, through its application in other fields, leads to the modernisation of the State apparatus? After

Table 17

The 20 Largest Foreign Investors in Brazil
(According to the registration issued by the *Banco Central do Brasil* up to December 1972. Companies are Ranked According to their Respective Total Investments.)

	Total Investment (US $ Million)
1 Brascan Ltd. (Canada)	142,038
2 Volkswagenwerke A.G. (West Germany)	118,853
3 British-American Tobacco (UK)	98,881
4 Rhone Poulenc S.A. (France)	80,606
5 Ford Motor Co. (US)	79,849
6 Exxon (US)	71,531
7 Nippon Usiminas Kabushiki Kaisha (Japan)	61,050
8 Shell Overseas Holdings Ltd. (England)	57,194
9 Union Carbide Co. (US)	53,168
10 General Motors Co. (US)	46,764
11 General Electric Co. (US)	46,193
12 Solvay & Cie., S.A. (Belgium)	44,941
13 N.V. Antovido Inc. (Curacao)	43,724
14 N.V. Philips Gloeilampenfabriken (Netherlands)	33,388
15 Daimler-Benz A.G. (West Germany)	30,262
16 Johnson & Johnson (US)	29,731
17 Atlantic Richfield Co. (US)	29,685
18 Anderson Clayton & Co. (US)	29,032
19 Robert Bosch GmbH (West Germany)	28,755
20 Daimler-Benz Holding A.G. (West Germany)	28,332

Source: *Guide to Invest in Brazil,* Brazilian Government Trade Bureau, New York, September 1973. (Quoted in Arruda *et al., op. cit.*)

images of Chilean children, hands on hearts, chanting the national anthem, after this first phase of militarisation which these images indicate, comes the call, used to justify the institutionalisation of an emergency regime, for the unity of national consciousness. Thus the militarisation of the teaching system is being accomplished in countries like Brazil by means of advanced technology, allowing the 'modern' state, devoted to the interests of the multinationals, to endow itself with an educational apparatus which conforms to its neo-colonial conditions.

Brazilian pretensions in aerospace materials too have not waited long to manifest themselves. After coproduction agreements for fighter-bombers with Northrop and General Electric, and for light aircraft designed for use against the 'internal enemy' with Piper Aircraft, the Ministry of Communications announced during the course of a press conference in April 1973 that 'in ten years, Brazil will itself manufacture its own communication satellites'. Walt Rostow, one of J. F. Kennedy's principal counsellors, was quoted in the same AFP dispatch which carried this news, as saying that 'Brazil is on the way to becoming a nuclear power and therefore a potential danger to its neighbours'.[48] This nuclear ambition was crowned with its first success at the end of June 1975. Brazil and the Federal Republic of Germany signed an agreement which laid out a plan for the sale of 8 West German nuclear power stations spread out over 15 years, as well as the installation in Brazil of a factory for reprocessing combustible nuclear waste and a uranium enrichment plant. Brazil thus joined Iran in the desire to become a major nuclear power. By 1990 it will have enough plants and sufficient know-how to make it autonomous in this field. North American pressures have been exerted to try and prevent the sale to Brazil of a reprocessing plant which could be used to manufacture nuclear arms. They have not succeeded. Meanwhile Westinghouse, the North American firm which sold Brazil its first nuclear power station, saw a four and a half billion dollar contract carried off by Kraftwerk Union, a firm controlled by Siemens, which proposed setting up a joint German-Brazilian company. Restrictions brought in by the North American Government itself over the export of technologies for nuclear reprocessing had handicapped the world's foremost manufacturer of nuclear power stations. In requesting the co-operation of Germany, a country it will supply with the uranium which it needs, Brazil seemed to wish to play in a single hand the cards which, on this point and within the limits of a 'tactical autonomy', would enable it to break the strict subjugation which continued to mark most of its coproduction plans with North American firms. This was not the first time Brasilia played on never-ending inter-capitalist rivalry. Some months earlier, ITT had had to sell its production unit, Standard Electrica, to local shareholders. This was the only condition the Brazilian Government would accept in order to award the North American company a contract for the modernisation of its telephone communication system, pointing out that if it didn't agree to sell off its subsidiary, the Swedish firm L. M. Ericsson could easily replace it.

Although Rostow's theoretical writings largely inspired the geopolitics of the 1964 putchists under General Goulbery Couto e Silva, you can understand his disquiet—whether real or simulated—when you know that Brazil has so far refused to sign the nuclear non-proliferation treaty, while control of the entire energy cycle will allow it in the future to manufacture atomic arms. Moreover, it is in conformity with its geopolitical conceptions that Brazil decided to intensify its nuclear potential, so as not to be outflanked militarily by its neighbour Argentina. Argentina, at the time of the signing of the German-Brazilian agreement, had already constructed its first nuclear reactor with the aid of technicians from Siemens and was already on the way to carrying out its first experiments in the reutilisation of nuclear combustibles for military purposes, unlike Brazil which, before the end of the 70s, had made no particular effort to establish a nuclear capacity independent of US leadership, which was hardly inclined to nuclear dissemination. For the German Federal Republic the German-Brazilian contract once more confirmed the renaissance of German imperialism, although it left a certain margin for manoeuvre, corresponding to the essential interests of North American capital. Since 1973, the German Federal Republic, skirting round treaties, has with Washington's encouragement set up armaments factories in Algeria, Burma, Ghana, Indonesia, Nigeria, the Sudan, Singapore and Argentina (where it manufactures tanks). Its latest client, South Africa, has also refused to sign the non-proliferation treaty. By means of contracts such as these with Brasilia and Pretoria, Germany, which is constrained by the Atlantic Pact not to manufacture atomic arms itself, sees a way of manufacturing them abroad. In response to the disquiet of Rostow, the anti-communist sorcerer's apprentice, comes that of the Soviet Marshal Gretchko who, preoccupied with the growing German armaments industry, gave voice to a threat: 'The day the Germans have atomic arms which are not indirectly controlled by the Americans, we will go and look for them.'[49] The speed with which Bonn responded to the North American refusal to sell nuclear power stations to Brazil indicates well enough the ripening of its nuclear policy.

Exporting coup d'états to its neighbours and, it hopes, heavier hardware too, Brazil has begun the business, through delegated multinational companies, of the electronic colonisation of the continent. It already exports colour television sets. In order to reduce the exorbitant production costs of the new sets through the conquest of new markets, Brasilia began to put pressure on Latin American governments around the end of 1972 in order to persuade them to replace their black and white television systems, though these were scarcely amortised, with colour. (At that time only Mexico and Brazil had colour television.)   South Africa and certain Black African countries also figured among the States Brazil wanted to seduce with its young industry. After the investments of Siemens, which got Brazil to choose the German colour television system, slightly modified to produce a hybrid, PAL-NTSC, RCA decided in 1973 to invest $120 m. in the construction of a new plant to manufacture television sets in Rio de Janeiro. Through these operations Brazil is on the way to forcing a process of fresh cultural dependence on its neighbours. A colour receiver obviously supposes programmes in colours, whose costs are far greater than black and white. Latin America will still be far from able to satisfy demand in this field for a long time yet. A recent controversy in Venezuela about colour television exposed the whole irrationality of these policies of adopting new systems in the countries of the Southern Hemisphere. A study produced by the College of Engineers of Venezuela put the technical dimensions of the problem into relief and at the same time indicated the different pressure groups likely to intervene in decisions about this kind of thing: 1) the foreign producers of electronic equipment and their assembly plants. According to this study, the adoption of colour television would entail an expenditure in the next ten years of around 2.4 billion Bolivars (about 8 Bolivars to the pound sterling). A black and white receiver costs an average 1,250 Bolivars, a colour set three times as much. Colour repairs cost twice as much, and a colour set tends to require attention three times a year, against 1.8 on average for a black and white set. 2) Foreign producers and distributors of programme material, who have an accumulated stock of colour programmes from the United States since 1955. Colour programmes cost at least 30% more and direct transmissions in colour are worth ten times current programmes. This would increase the degree of programming dependence on foreign programmes, which already represent 54% of the menu offered to viewers. 3) Advertising agencies, mostly subsidiaries of North American companies, who see colour television as a means of renewing their business and raising tariffs. 4) The Government, itself aligned with the economic groups which control the major television channels, the electronic industries, etc.[50]

But the force of these arguments comes up against the logic of

Communications networks for
education envisaged by General Electric

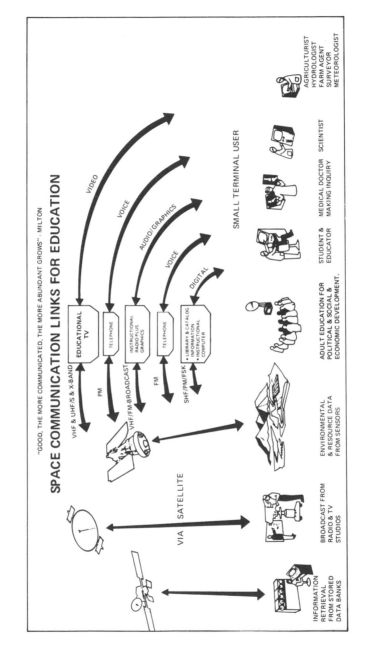

"GOOD, THE MORE COMMUNICATED, THE MORE ABUNDANT GROWS" - MILTON

SPACE COMMUNICATION LINKS FOR EDUCATION

development of the multinational electronics companies. Since this controversy took place, eight Latin American countries have opened new networks. There are even cases where the introduction of colour takes on the symbolic hues of reconciliation: the United States Embassy in Santiago de Chile offered to install colour in the studios of the State Technical University, the university which, on 11th September 1973, after it had offered fierce resistance to the soldiers of the dictatorship, became the slaughter ground of hundreds of students, workers and artists.

Towards computerised institutionalism

When it comes to gauging the promises of technological evolution, opinions differ profoundly. The President of RCA unhesitatingly affirms that we are entering a new era, that of the 'electronic revolution' which offers all inhabitants of the planet, without distinction by race or class, the chance 'to enhance the status of the individual by amplifying the power of the human mind and the precision of human control, just as the industrial revolution amplified the power of human muscle'. Contesting the predictions of Orwell, he adds: 'The industrial revolution was a powerful centralising force . . . The electronic revolution will encourage flexibility and decentralisation of organised activities.'[51] Thus the most optimistic prognostications make us already believe in the arrival of a community sustained by electronics. When the first international agreement for the exploitation of communications satellites was signed, the science fiction writer Arthur C. Clarke declared in front of the signatories, 'Were this its intention or not, you have just signed the first draft of the Constitution of the United States of the Earth'. The mystification which entered into that other revolution, the green revolution, is too well known for us to admit so easily this harmonious vision of the future application of new technology. One can hardly fail to see any longer how existing structures are simply lifted unchanged through these supposed overturnings of society, which in fact clearly fail to change the monopolistic character of the control which the ruling classes exercise over the means of production and distribution.

Others only point up the possible excess of this technical evolution. In this society, sick with a flow of information it cannot control, human beings end up caught in the wires of their electronic networks. The computer and the satellite which record, classify and inform, calculate and number the most everyday actions of our lives.

From both sides, the side of the prophets of doom as well as the side of the prophets of salvation, technology has come to be seen as an autonomous spirit playing a sovereign game, above human and earthly contingencies, above class relations, dispensing benefits or alternatively repressing, saving or damning. Fortunately things are both simpler and more complicated than this theology of the electronic age would have us believe. Looking at it lengthways and breadthways, the new technologies are far from being an extra-terrestrial affair, and they can be assimilated neither to Superman nor to Frankenstein. The forms of their production and the channels of their distribution express the relations of power and domination which really exist, here on this planet.

It is difficult to trace with precision how the ruling classes will organise the social uses of the new technologies of communication, how they will make them follow the dictates of the State apparatus, or, to adopt the terminology of NASA and the White House, how they will be applied to the resolution of the social needs of each community. In their fetishistic language where things acquire a life and soul of their own and human beings are turned into things, the North Americans tell us that 'information has become a factor of production of the same order as capital and labour' and that in their country in 1975 already more than half the active population was engaged in collecting, treating and transmitting information. Speaking of the 'information society'—a concept which they hold to be more precise than the other term, 'post-industrial society', although both terms are equally amorphous socially—they see as the apogee of this society that more than 60% of the workforce will be engaged in the treatment of information, and that this will be achieved around 1980.[52] They promise us a considerable improvement in services provided by various institutions to their users. Some rather more eccentric prophets than most go so far as to suggest that a computer in the home will replace the Cadillac as a status symbol. And new concepts confirm the social extension of electronics: tele-education, tele-medicine, tele-repression, tele-data processing.

Limited projects which lead the advanced capitalist societies towards the constitution of 'global information systems' are already in hand. Projects for information networks have begun to flourish which link up computers in different scientific centres, giving common access to powerful means of calculation for the most diverse uses. For example, in France, the Cyclades network which, since 1975, cross-links twenty computers in research centres, universities and institutes at all points of the compass (Rennes, Grenoble, Lyon, Paris and Toulouse). At the European level, since 1974, the Cost (Comité scientifique et technique) network unites five data processing centres in London, Paris, Milan, Zurich and Ispra (the Euratom research centres). In areas less likely to receive public approval are projects like the well named Operation Safari (Système Automatisé pour les Fichiers Administratifs et la Répertoire Individus-Automatic System of Administrative Indexes and Cataloguing of Individuals), set up by the Ministry of the Interior of the French Government in order to centralise all available information on every individual by computer using a single code.

At the beginning of 1974, following the controversy which was unleashed by revelations about this project, a Commission on Computers and Freedom was given the responsibility of proposing regulations to ensure that the applications of tele-data processing should not be accompanied by a reduction of individual rights. The Report of the Commission was delivered to the Minister of Justice in September 1975.[53] Its general tone was hardly optimistic. Among the most significant phrases, we find: 'It is necessary to take care that the uneven development of computers within the State should not disturb the balances sought by the Constitution and by the Law . . . All things considered, the major threats appear to us to be the encumbrance of social control and an increase in inegalitarian relations within society.' Under the heading 'Computers and Democracy', the report specifies: 'In regard to the public domain, computers are not neutral. The way things are today, they are bound up with an industry where concentration is growing, on a world scale, towards a near-monopoly situation. Expensive and inscrutable, computers primarily serve the powerful . . . It is a matter of a growing carelessness towards the individual . . . It is possible to employ data-processing in such a way that it protects legitimate private secrets, so that it provides decentralised or dispersed bodies with information for decision-making which the authorities have so far left unprovided, or even so as to make computers and their extensions ensure extensive diffusion of information in a democratic spirit. All this is possible, but it has to be demanded. At present, this is not the direction in which the natural course of things inclines.' Forecasting, as it were, the possibility that the new technologies of communication offer multinational companies a way of escaping national regulations, the report takes account of the need to achieve international harmony in legislation. 'The risk is real and the temptation great for certain enterprises to avoid the requirements of the regulatory apparatus by exploiting, through teleprocessing, the data-banks transported or set up abroad, in countries lacking protective statutes or a sufficiently rigorous regulatory system. Just like 'fiscal paradises', there seem to be 'data paradises'. You can appreciate this allusion better when you know that companies like General Electric already have at their disposal an international teleprocessing network which enables them to supply computer and data-bank services to the four corners of the globe without having to shift themselves from their metropolitan centre of operations. Finally the French report proposes a control authority, a permanent committee on 'Computers and Liberty', composed of members of the legislative assemblies, the Council of State, the judiciary, the bar and higher education. This committee 'should possess powers of investigation into the administrative bodies of the State'.

But the tone of the report, which was cast strictly within the limits of liberalism, indicates well enough, through its pessimism, the illusory nature of such regulation, when repressive institutions such as the police and the army seem to be excluded on principle from all control. Concerning the right which all individuals should have to ascertain the contents of the files which are held on them, the report specifies: 'The right of interrogation should be recognised with regard to all files, whose register should be made public, except for those touching national defence, the security of the State and public security.' One may proclaim the 'non-neutrality' of data-processing, but to be really effective it is necessary to go a step further and to question, as the editors of the report seem not to do, 'the neutrality of the State'. It does too much honour to the computer to make it the target of our accusations, when they ought rather to be directed to the policing function of the capitalist State.

Watergate automated

It is in the United States that projects for global information systems are most advanced. In 1970, President Nixon attained what no other president had previously been able to achieve, to wit, the bringing together of US Government activities in communications (from the public television network to civil and military satellites) through the creation of body, the OTP (Office of Telecommunications Policy), directly linked to the White House. He gave the responsibility for this to a technocrat of the famous Rand Corporation, the most well-known of those reservoirs of grey matter, those 'ideas factories', the Think Tanks. In creating this office of co-ordination, Nixon signalled the opening of the era of 'electronic institutionalism'. And if one is to believe the projected curve of technological evolution which this office produced by adopting the implict hypothesis that there would be no important modifications of the institutional framework within which the technology would evolve, one can only foresee the 'network society' of the year 2000. For the first time political power—in accompaniment with the 'civilising' impulse of the electronics and aerospace firms—has foreseen the possibility of combining the audio-visual and computers. The Presidential counsellors who suffered their come-uppance with Watergate were the ones who, in August 1971, in connivance with NASA, proposed a plan for the future utilisation of electronics and satellite technology for social ends. This first project to electronify North American institutions was contained in a report called *Communications for Social Needs: Technological Opportunities*. It was Presidential counsellor John Ehrlichman who coordinated the production of this report, entrusted to NASA and to various US educational institutions. It includes numerous proposals for the reorganisation of the educational system (to be analysed in another chapter) and a group of proposals intended to derestrict the administration of justice, police investigation, national security and the health and postal services. From the very first page of this voluminous report, you can tell the social preoccupations of its editors: 'There is growing recognition in the United States of a family of national problems to which solutions could be provided through telecommunications. Some problems are urgent and immediate; others are still on the horizon. The problem range from the need for distribution of cultural and educational opportunities, through the need for new postal services, to the need for a disaster warning system . . . Accordingly, the overall objective of this study is to define a program of new initiatives to help solve these problems through modern telecommunications. These initiatives could lead to additional opportunities for federal and local agencies to improve their public services and to the creation of new economic opportunities for industry. In this study, emphasis is placed on defining multi-service projects which can clearly demonstrate to the public their social benefits and economic viability'.

Is this to say that before this study the North American authorities had not concerned themselves with the question? Not at all. But the diverse applications of the new telecommunications prototypes had scarcely left the orbit of the Pentagon. In effect, the US aerial defense system set up in 1955, known as SAGE (Semi-Automatic Ground Environment), is the origin of all the big data processing systems, civil and military, in the capitalist countries. The big defense systems currently used in the countries of the non-socialist world have been elaborated on the basis of this model. Among the best-known are the North American Fleet's NTDS (Naval Tactical Data System), 412-L installed by General Electric in Federal Germany, IBM's Strida 2 which serves the French air force, and most recently, NADGE (Nato Air Defense Ground Environment) which covers Western Europe and was produced by an international consortium under the direction of Hughes Aircraft. The three essential characteristics of large-scale data-processing systems were nursed in this military cradle: real time,[54] multiple access and the computer network. In the first place each computer is connected to a radar scanner, which collects data on aircraft flight paths. The transmission of data between computers then permits the simultaneous collection of data from different sources to constitute a base for the continuous monitoring of air space.

The first major supposedly civil network in the United States also saw the light of day, in 1968, under the aegis of the Defense Department: ARPANET (Advanced Research Project Agency Network). Its official mission was to serve projects patronised by the Federal Government. Yet ARPA (Advanced Research Project Agency) was nothing but an arm of the Pentagon. This network, which later came to serve as a reference point for the majority of the networks in the Western countries, relies today on more than thirty computing centres in the principle North American universities and, thanks to a satellite connection, reaches into Europe (London) and the Pacific (Hawaii). From its military origins—experiments were begun in 1958 at the dawn of data-processing—it has kept the example of the initial idea, of a network organised as a chain in such a way that the numerical data can be obtained through a number of different routings so that the whole ensemble would not suffer excessively by the possible destruction of one or more of the computing centres. But this represents, without doubt, only the least of technical bequests, the most important being the kind of social relationship it is intended to maintain. It is also one of the most 'pluralist' systems, since the computers and the terminals it employs differ in style and in kind, built not only by IBM but also by Univac and Digital.

The systems of telecommunications coverage formulated by the NASA specialists for the White House represent a higher level of the social conception of data-processing. Four systems were proposed: not counting tele-education systems these were a public health information system, a system for the electronification of the postal services, a disaster alarm system and a system to facilitate the execution of law and criminal justice. Each system would have its seat of operations in Washington and would form part of the national telecommunications network; it would have a satellite of its own at its disposal, together with a complex of connections and relays which would join the central system to 'institutional terminals' and sometimes even to the homes of particular individuals. Information provided by each of its sources would be collected and stocked up in data banks.

The electronic mail handling system would involve the conversion of each letter into a message transmitted directly by satellite either to a post office or to a terminal in the office of the addressee where it would be printed out automatically. RCA was already, in April 1972, in the process of carrying out experiments in various places in the United States, notably between New York and San Francisco. While this system would considerably reduce the cost of the postal service (an argument which the Federal authorities do not disdain), the system can be considered, as the NASA report underlines, rather as a means of storing up information on citizens. In fact, the FBI communications channel would be permanently linked to the new postal system communications channel in the 65 most important cities of the country. Is it necessary to say that this report was secret, and that its denunciation in front of the US Senate was needed to get it known?[55] As is usually the case, these projects to computerise society are submerged in semi-clandestinity. The public health information system allows the exchange of medical dossiers by satellite, between personnel and institutions specified by the report. The disaster warning system would deal with emergency situations which could be either natural or political. It would allow the immediate and direct access of the central authorities to every North American citizen through radio or television receivers specially constructed so as to be activated by the reception of particular coded signals. The law enforcement and criminal justice system would be the point of convergence of the other three, and would crown the whole citizen surveillance project. Instantaneous communication, at every level—local and national, civil and military—allows every offence and trouble that erupts throughout the States to be systematised. The Federal police were, already in 1970, discussing with NASA the growth of satellite technology and the laser transmission from one end of the country to the other of, among other things, digitalised information. The field of justice is the privileged field for the civil reconversion of the equipment which was used in the anti-guerilla war in Vietnam. We have seen the repercussions which these techniques of war have had in the civil domain, through the intermediary of companies like IBM or Boeing. The White House experts hardly hesitate to suppose that the population will easily agree to these plans for electronification: 'Since the system is dedicated and is accessible only to law enforcement personnel. . . it is not anticipated that there will be barriers to public or business acceptance of the system. . . The overall impact on the public will be that they will benefit from more efficient law enforcement, as implemented by the proposed system. It is implicit that the system itself will be used to disseminate information to the public on these benefits, leading to the conclusion that public acceptance of the system will be achieved by favourable publicity on the system's successful operation'!

On 1st January 1975, following an initiative taken by Congress, the

President of the United States signed a Bill on the protection of individual liberties, to deal with the dangers of files and computers (Records, Computers and the Rights of Citizens). This law required, for example, that the existence and general character of each group of dossiers held by Federal authorities on the subject of individuals be divulged. But, as an expert of the Federal Commission of Communications noted, the possibilities for effective control in this business are progressively more tenuous: 'The text of the law envisages an attitude of non-interference towards organisations charged with law enforcement and the corresponding filing systems. Initítally it was intended that the modes of control over criminal records and filing systems of information related to law enforcement would be dealt with in a separate Bill. However, negotiations between the Congressional Commissions and the Ministry of Justice ran around this autumn, and no such draft bill has seen the light of day. No disposition of a general character can fill the gap which has resulted. On the contrary, the result is that dossiers containing the most sensitive information largely escape verification by the citizens.'[56]

As for the big electronics companies, they continue to base their plans for expansion on these new institutional possibilities. One need only glance at their market reports: 'Law enforcement as a market for electronics—notably telecommunications hardware—continues to expand steadily in fiscal 1975. The Justice Department's Law Enforcement Assistance Administration [set up at the end of the 60s on the initiative of Attorney General Ramsay Clark, with a view to rationalising the whole range of apparatuses involved in civil repression] is planning a $61 m. increase in outlays to $910 m. But the market is spreading, too, as the LEAA grants more and more to state and local government.'[57]

These telecommunications markets have acquired such importance that in 1973 General Electric deemed it advisable to set up a specialist group to study alternative strategies for the company's expansion in the communications field. The principle document produced by the company's engineers and sociologists on the question of communication (Communication Task Force) contains a systematic examination of the possibilities currently opening up in the company's four lines of production in this field: education, the leisure industry, industrial applications and communications networks. Let us take some of its significant points. Among the driving forces which stimulate the development of the production of communications networks, they note the 'increasing communication load; emerging communications needs of lesser developed countries; developing technologies', they say, 'create opportunities and lower costs; law enforcement, business, medical, safety, security, control and navigation all yield increased communications requirements in the future'. Who are General Electric's known competitors in the market? For the electronic mail handling system, General Dynamics, Philco-Ford, TRW, IBM and Xerox. For multiple use satellite systems (which it reckons could account for 20% of a market extending over about 50 countries), Hughes Aircraft, ITT, Nippon. And for the supply of telecommunications equipment, apart from these three main competitors, there are also Ericsson and Siemens. Commenting on these possibilities in somewhat telegraphic language, the experts distinguish five 'key consideration' which the company would have to attend to in order to improve its international penetration: 'Government controls; assumption of system responsibility; local content requirements; must adapt to local business method; financial.'[58]

Notes

1 R. Hotz, 'Editorial: expanding the global market', *Aviation Week & Space Technology*, 2.IV.1975.
2 James Fletcher, 'Toward corporate continuity in space: the case for NASA's future', *Finance*, April 1972.
3 Fletcher, *op. cit.*
4 Declaration by the ex-administrator of NASA, J. E. Webb, in *Space: the new frontier*, Washington, US Government Printing Office, 1967.
5 Declaration by F. Seitz, government representative before the North American Committee on Science and Technology, in *The Department of State Bulletin*, Washington D.C., 1973, No. 1769.
6 *Department of State Newsletter*, February 1971.
7 See for example, E. R. Bagley, *Beyond the Conglomerates*, New York, Amacom, 1975.
8 W. H. Melody, 'The role of advocacy in public policy planning', in *Communications Technology and Social Policy* (G. Gerbner, L. Gross, W. H. Melody, eds.), New York, Wiley Interscience, 1973.
9 M. Bignier, 'Les programmes d'application spaciale et la coopération internationale', *Revue de Défense Nationale*, Paris October 1973.
10 A. Frutkin, 'Space Communication and the developing countries', in *Communications technology and social policy, op. cit.*
11 *Aviation Week & Space Technology*, 2.IX.1974, 4.X.1974, 23.VI.1975, 6.IX.1975.
12 K. Johnsen, 'US to press for private entity Aerosat', *Aviation Week & Space Technology*, 21.II.1972. Same author, 'US in minority on slow Inmarsat pace', *Aviation Week & Space Technology*, 21.V.1975.
13 *Communications Satellite Act of 1962*, Government Printing Office, Washington D.C., 1962.
14 Cf. the dossier on the politics of satellites in Latin America published by the magazine *Communicatión y Cultura*, Buenos Aires, 1975, No. 3.

15 *Business Week*, 24.VIII.1974.

16 For the continuing progress of North American industry contracts for space technology materials, see *Aviation Week & Space Technology* and *Aerospace Facts and Figures*. The Arab countries, too, are now well on the way to acquiring a regional satellite system of their own. Twelve Arab countries are already equipped with satellite earth stations, linked to the Atlantic and Indian Ocean Intelsats, but following the establishment of Arabsat, with headquarters in Riyadh, set up in April 1976 under the aegis of the Arab League, a regional system is now envisaged which, for political and security reasons, will have dual control centres in Saudi Arabia and Upper Egypt. The main contributors to the $100 m. organisation are Saudi Arabia, Libya, Egypt, Kuwait and the United Arab Emirates. Six companies and groups have submitted tenders, including Comsat, Telesat (Canada), Cable & Wireless (UK), a consortium consisting of Telespazio (Italy), Teleconsult (US), two French companies and International Saudi Arabian Consultants, a mixed group called Arab European American, and a German company. (See 'Telecommunications pose problems' in the Arab Cooperation and Development Supplement, Financial Times, 26th September 1977. Translator's note.)

17 Letter in *Aviation Week & Space Technology*, 30.IX.1974.

18 Joseph Collins, 'Etats-Unis et transnationales américaines: retour à l'envoyeur', *Political aujourd'hui*, January-March 1975.

19 *The Elements*, magazine of IPS/Transnational, Washington, May 1975, No. 8.

20 Lockheed Aircraft Corporation, *Annual Report 1972*.

21 Raytheon, *Annual Report 1974*.

22 General Electric Co. and Utah International Inc. finally won Justice Department approval for their merger scheme. The Government had told the two companies it might sue to block the combine because the tie-up with Utah International's uranium mining and milling operations could give GE a competitive edge in nuclear power. The plan now is to put all of Utah International's uranium business into a separate company, which would be owned by GE but would be run until 2000 by independent trustees, and would be barred from selling uranium to GE. (Author's Note).

23 UNESCO, General Conference, 17th Session, Paris, 1972, Document 17c/76, 21.VII.1972.

24 US Government, *Memorandum to Samuel de Palma from John E. Upston*, US National Commission for UNESCO, Advisory recommendations (typewritten copies). (The English version here has been retranslated from French since this is one of the texts, mentioned in the Translator's Preface, whose original was among papers belonging to the author destroyed by the Chilean Junta.—Translator's Note.)

25 On a proposal made by the Soviet Union, see A. Gromyko, *Letter dated 8 August 1972, Preparation of an international convention on principles governing the use by States of artificial earth satellites for direct TV broadcasting*, United Nations, New York, 27th session, doc. no. A/877. On the imperialist origin of the concept of 'free information flow', cf. Herbert Schiller, 'La libre circulation de l'information et la domination mondiale', *Le Monde Diplomatique*, Paris, September 1975.

26 P. J. Klass, 'UN will face broadcast satellite use', *Aviation Week & Space Technology*, 2.IX.1974.

27 The Network Project, *Domestic Communications Satellites*, New York, Notebook No. 1, October 1972.

28 *US News & World Report*, 18.XII.1972.

29 Cf. Seymour Melman, *Pentagon Capitalism*, New York, McGraw-Hill, 1970.

30 *Aviation Week & Space Technology*, 22.VIII.1971.
31 On the technology of military satellites see for example, Philip J. Klass, *Secret Sentries in Space*, Random House, New York, 1971, and the annual reports of Hughes Aircraft, RCA, Northrop (Page Engineers), TRW and NCR. For a critical view, cf. Raimo Vayrynen, 'Military uses of satellite communications', *Instant Research on Peace and Violence*, Tampere, Finland, 1973, No. 1.
32 *Air et Cosmos*, Paris, 7.VI.1975.
33 *Business Week*, 27.I.1975.
34 NASA, *Memorandum of understanding between the Department of Atomic Energy of the Government of India and the United States*, 1969.
35 *ibid.*
36 Cf. A. Frutkin, *op. cit.* This first experiment, known as SITE—Satellite Instructional Television Experiment—covering 24,000 villages, came to an end on July 31st 1975. The following day *The Guardian* reported that 'an assurance was given that 40% of . . . villages covered will continue to receive educational television programmes and moreover a new pogramme will be extended to another 7,000 villages in seven states. This will be done by establishing in each of these states a conventional transmitter with a range of 45 miles at a total cost of £10 million . . . Meanwhile the question whether results of SITE have been such as to justify a major plan to use an Indian satellite—which will be in orbit hopefully before the end of 1978—remains an open one. . . The question of cost effectiveness has to be viewed within the context of a bigger national dilemma over television. Educational television remains a peripheral part of the growing television establishment in the country. Community sets meant for educational purposes are comparatively rare. Most sets are owned by relatively affluent people in major cities who have made no secret about their feeling that they want entertainment not education'. (Translator's note).
37 *Aviation Week & Space Technology*, 25.VIII.1975.
38 *New York Times*, 31st May 1975 (Cable AFP, *Le Monde*, 3.VI.1975). For an analysis of the IBEX project, cf. Barry Miller, 'Contractors sought for Iranian elite net', *Aviation Week & Space Technology*, 10.X.1975.
39 *Business Week*, 28.VII.1975.
40 On November 4th, 1977 Helms was given a 2-year suspended sentence and fined $2,000 for refusing to tell a Congressional hearing about the role of the CIA in Chile before the fall of Allende. *The Guardian* reported (November 5th, 1977) that the outcome of the case was as President Carter had been hoping for, since earlier in the year Carter had authorised his Attorney-General 'to "plea bargain" with Mr Helms on the grounds that prosecution in open court would mean the exposure of sensitive classified documents. . . the compromise. . . was designed to prevent a protracted and embarrassing court battle which would once again bring to the force new evidence about some of the less desirable activities of the CIA'. (Translator's note).
41 *Aviation Week & Space Technology*, 2.VI.1975.
42 Cf. Michael Klare, *War Without End*, New York, Vintage Books, 1972.
43 *Business Week*, 15.I.1972; *Electronics*, 21.II.1974; Aviation Week & Space Technology, 10.III.1975.
44 M. Mancini, 'Hail to the Chiefs', *Page News*, November 1972.
45 US Senate, 'US Policies and Programs in Brazil', Hearings before the subcommittee on Western hemisphere affairs, Committee on Foreign Relations, US Senate (4-5, 11 May 1971), Washington D.C., 1971.
46 Cf. J. J.Sparkes, 'Education by satellite in Brazil', *The Man Made World*, London,

Open University, 1975. Also see Brenda Maddox, 'A Brazilian satellite—for what?', *New Scientist*, 25.IV.1974. On the global project designed by General Electric, cf. General Electric, *Communications Study Advisory Council Briefing April 17, 1973*, New York.

47 On the doctrine of national security, cf. Armand Mattelart, 'Notes on the Ideology of the Military State' in *Communications and Class Struggle* (eds. A. Mattelart and S. Seigelaub), International General, New York, forthcoming, 1978 (Author's Note).

48 *El Mercurio*, Santiago de Chile, 8.V.1973.

49 For an analysis of the German-Brazilian treaty, cf. the report presented to the Russell Tribunal by Peter Lock, Rome, January 1976, *Pseudo-holy Alliance, Comments on the German-Brazilian Nuclear Energy Agreement*. On the strategy of German social democracy, cf. an article by J. P. Vigier, 'Le second souffle de la crise', *Le Monde Diplomatique*, December 1975. Also, A. Fontaine, 'Le dernier quart de siècle', *Le Monde*, 14/15.I.1976.

Shortly after the German-Brazilian contract, the 7 nuclear technology exporting countries, Canada, France, USSR, USA, GB, Japan and W. Germany, agreed to harmonise the export policies for nuclear materials and technology, to prevent purchasers continuing to profit from divergence between them so as to obtain from one what the others refused. (Cf. D. Verguèse, *Le Monde*, 31.I.1975).

50 To develop their network of factories in Latin America, the multinationals operating in Brazil have begun, thanks to the crisis, to purchase companies in other countries. In March 1976, the Chilean Junta sold to an American-Brazilian company the biggest tv-radio-record enterprise in Chile (ex-RCA, nationalised under Allende and renamed IRT).

51 Robert W. Sarnoff, 'The electronic revolution: dawn of a new era', *Economic Impact*, Washington, 1974, No. 7.

52 Cf. M. E. B. Parker, *Incidences sociales des systèmes de télé-informatique*. Conference on the policies of data processing and telecommunications, OECD, Paris, 4–6 February 1975; Ithiel de Sola Pool, *The International Aspects of Computer Telecommunications*, given at the same conference.

For a class analysis of these systems, see Manual Janco and Daniel Furjot, *Informatique et capitalisme*, Paris, Ed. Franço is Maspero, 1972.

53 Report of the Commission *Information et Libertés*, Documentation Française, 1975. On the state of tele-data processing systems and other networks, see the magazine *Interférences* published in Paris.

54 viz., computer simulation which provides an immediate display on the output simultaneously with the setting of the input values—a vital computing advance which permits the monitoring of any kind of continuous flow process (Translator's note).

55 Testimony of the Network Project on the matter of funding for Public Broadcasting before the Committee on Commerce of US Senate, 30th March, 1973; Bill Greeley, 'Public Broadcasting Government Network', *Variety*, 11.IV.73; Henry Smith, Goebbels in Space Government Use of Telecommunications', *Cinéaste, 1973*, vol. 4, no. 4

56 M. W. Sutter, *Dispositions institutionnelles*, Conférence sur les politiques en matière d'informatique et de télécommunications, OECD, Paris, 4–6 Feburary 1975. For the latest developments on this question, see Becky Barna, 'Ford's privacy report', *Computer Decisions*, February 1977.

57 *Electronics*, 21.II.1974.

58 General Electric, *Communications Study Advisory Council. . . op. cit.*

CHAPTER IV

THE NEW EDUCATORS

TOWARDS 1970, at the height of an undisguised offensive, and at a loss to know what else to invent in order to shake off their dependence on institutions which they knew were liable any day to get in their way, the multinationals began to think of creating their own diplomatic system. 'The internationalism of business calls for a new type of embassy. Shouldn't the international giants of industry be represented by their own diplomatic corps in the nations or regions where they operate?'[1] Many of them probably still think this way. But several scandals have broken out since then. And each time a scandal breaks, it threatens to damage an already tarnished image and reinforces a conditioned reflex by which people assimilate these companies, with their head offices in the US, to the image of the 'ugly American'.

According to various statements by their directors for Europe, ITT does not boast about the profile by which the public in the countries of the Common Market identify it, even though its subsidiaries on the European side of the Atlantic continue to bring in more than $5,000 m. a year. In an attempt to modify its reputation and whitewash the image it has of being a malevolent giant, the firm decided in 1974 to launch a publicity campaign costing more than $700 m., beginning in England and then extending to Germany, Belgium, Spain and France. 'Who the devil does ITT think it is?'; 'Does ITT give a damn about Britain's balance of payments?': such were the terms of the publicity campaign in England.[2]

ITT does not bear the costs of disgrace alone. Faced with growing recriminations, the Vice President of the International Division of Pepsi Cola could do no better than latch on to an idea then in vogue among international bodies, and in July 1975 proposed the adoption of a 'code of conduct' to govern the behaviour of multinational firm abroad, which could be established under the aegis of a multilateral organisation such as the OECD. 'Corporations', he claims, 'could become voluntary signatories to this code, and home and host governments would pressure companies to join. In effect, those not signing would be saying that they are not willing to deal ethically'.[3]

Other proposals, just as idealistic, are evidence of even more inordinate ambition, and in the same way that there was talk five years ago of their own embassy, they are beginning to talk now of their own university. Thus, in April 1975, the President of the large North American publicity agency Doyle-Dane-Bernbach asserted before the students of a Canadian University that 'Multinational corporations could solve a part of their image problem through the establishment of global universities'.[4] And he added, going further into a description of his project, that by adopting this formula companies such as Exxon, Texaco or General Electric would have much less need for support by Government, trades union circles and consumers to defend themselves from accusations made against them of violating national sovereignty. The proposal is very simple: the companies would open a university course of two years for students from both industrialised and underdeveloped countries, with the requirement only 'that they spoke perfect English'. These courses could deal with the history of the company, the analysis of concrete examples of marketing, management, international law, the relationships of the enterprise with the community, its social responsibility. Provided with a diploma granted by the company, the students would return to their respective countries and would constitute 'a kind of common denominator of understanding' around the world. In a second stage, third year courses could be offered to the best. The exchange of ideas and experiences between candidates for this new business doctorate, and their professors, would make it possible to advance the practice and science of management.

In putting forward this initially laughable idea, our man was only expressing a latent utopia in multinational circles. What dream more attractive is there for ironing out the conflicts which multinationals continue to provoke, than relying on their own brigades of propagandists and defenders of the doctrine? The expression 'global universities' seems rather pompous for such a project. These dreams of a parallel institution will probably not take the shape which this businessman expects. Is it even necessary that they should take other shapes than those which the current reality allow? The many examples of collusion between the North American State and the multinationals have already amply demonstrated that it wasn't necessary to imagine parallel embassies in order to conquer the problems of expansion in the various different parts of the Empire. Doubtless it will not be necessary to create these so-called global universities as such, since it is equally true that the presence of these firms in the field of knowledge—in what the North Americans call 'the knowledge industry'—is capable of sparing them this detour.

Institutes of advanced technology and school books

> A man who has a sense of effort is capable of great things. Nevertheless, in the Americas, in spite of all their good intentions, many individuals cannot hope to succeed. Because they quite simply lack knowledge, work and the experience which education gives. In order to solve these problems, several educational programmes have been launched in the majority of American countries. ITT is also doing what it can to enable numerous individuals to progress and in this way contribute to the development of the country. Standard Electric, for example, the Argentinian subsidiary of ITT, is sending students to our new advanced study centre with its head office in Buenos Aires. This university, the sole telecommunications institute in Latin America, trains engineers, draughtsmen and maintenance technicians from all the Latin American dependencies. Those who obtain a diploma and demonstrate their abilities are able to continue their studies in ITT's laboratories in Spain, in Madrid. Afterwards they have the choice of working for us or for our customers or setting up on their own. . . Our training programmes in Argentina and in the rest of Latin America are not limited to telecommunications. They also include disciplines such as computer technology, hotel administration, transport, treatment of foodstuff and export-import. Our training mission doesn't date from yesterday. Over the years we have trained more than 55,000 persons of both sexes throughout Latin America.[5]

Like so many other examples this ITT propaganda, published in an American weekly with a Spanish language edition (published in Miami for the entire southern hemisphere), celebrates the philanthropic cult of these firms, a necessary cover for the range of other activities which are more explicitly money-making. But we can read here the growing concern of the multinationals over technical training and see a reflection of the reality created by their recent advances in this field. The most recent of these institutes of further training is the one established by ITT in Santiago de Chile using the indemnity money paid by the military dictatorship for the telephone company nationalised under Allende.

In fact the majority of multinational electronics firms could show the same honours list. General Electric is just as explicit in its own public relations bulletins. It has trained 750 specialists over recent years at its metropolitan engineering centre in the field of nuclear and conventional power stations alone. The courses, which last 30 weeks, relate both to the functioning and maintenance of reactors, and to methods of economic planning and means of solving the energy crisis. The company even tells us that its pupils had an average professional experience of eight years, that they belonged to 53 different firms, and that more than 20 subsequently became at least vice-presidents of the firms where they worked. The 1974 graduates included 58 pupils—27 of them North American, the rest foreigners: Brazilians, Canadians, Ecuadorians, Mexicans, Japanese, Panamanians, Nicaraguans and Vietnamese.[6]

Data processing companies such as Control Data—to take an example other than IBM—have set up institutes of advanced technology where engineers from the company and university professors give seminars to the most varied audience. Every year Control Data's institute, directed by a former Brigadier-General of the North American army, offers 450 seminars in its own classrooms throughout the world, or in borrowed premises. Among its pupils have been people from the Warner Brothers film company, from Kennecott, Chase Manhatten Bank, Sperry Rand, Honeywell, the universities of Wisconsin, New York, Michigan, and Temple—not forgetting the CIA and the various services of the US army. In the introduction to the course programme we read: 'In the age of the "information explosion" when both corporate expansion and government growth call for knowledge-before-the-fact, computer sciences have come into their own, creating both a new language and a new kind of work force. . . A computer without proper programming is a useless piece of equipment. Computers are designed to do only what they are told, and the "telling" is a science in itself.' Summarising why the company has centred its interest on this area of education, the President of Control Data invoked a Chinese proverb: 'If your plan is for one year, plant rice. If your plan is for ten years, plant trees. But if you plan for 100 years, educate men.'[7] Among the themes proposed in the repertoire of the course: communications theory, the organisation of information systems, the application of tele-data processing to bank transactions, to the police, the role of the individual and the place of private life in the face of organisational needs. As for IBM, it has a team of 5,000 instructors in the United States, distributed in 200 centres of formal education, providing three types of courses: training and management, technical up-dating, and professional recycling. Each year these instructors teach 10 million student hours, the equivalent of approximately 40,000 students taking 15 hours per week for 32 weeks.

However, in order to realise the true scope of the activity of these firms in relation to education, you have to abandon the framework of professional training, which is still largely the logical extension of the monopoly they exercise on the knowledge of the technologies which they apply in their factories. In fact, the growing interests of the electronics firms in education manifests itself in a much more global and structural way. These owners of advanced audio-visual technology have now undertaken to complete the range of their products by adding an essential item, the programmes. Thus the majority of these firms now have educational subsidiaries or divisions. Their entry into this field, or the strengthening of their position, is the outcome of a profound restructuring of the apparatus of cultural production. For the moment, it is mainly a question of establishing all the links for their future expansion within the field of education. This is an array which will operate fully only when the installation of the main technologies of communication, such as national satellite and cable television systems, become general.

At the time of their major diversification, the electronics firms absorbed a number of enterprises which brought them in contact with the 'software'.[8] In the first place, publishing houses, RCA became the owner of Random House and its three subsidiaries, Alfred A. Knopf, Pantheon Books and Vintage (which publish fiction, children's books and non-fiction). More recently it added Ballantine Books, specialists in mass circulation paperbacks, and Grove Press, with its progressive reputation. After establishing another publishing house in England under the name Wildwood House in 1972, RCA announced the creation of its 'educational media' division, henceforth to be entrusted with preparing new materials for audio-visual education and, in particular, programmes for primary school teaching, to be contained in a series of video-cassettes.[9] The Columbia Broadcasting System (CBS), owner of one of the three major US television chains, but also the manufacturer of video-cassettes, specialist in laser beams and producer of much electronic equipment, purchased the publishing house of Holt, Rinehart & Winston. Over the course of the last five years it has set up an international education division, acquired in Mexico one of the largest Spanish language publishing houses for school and scientific texts, and organised new companies for the distribution of educational material in Brazil and Ecuador. The objectives of the company are transparent: 'Our company's education and publishing division is one of the world's largest producers of education services and equipment. Its products include study texts, films and other audio-visual media destined for schools, as well as books and magazines for the general public. Its mission is two-fold: to satisfy the demand for services originating in the needs for educational materials in the present decade, and to increase the participation of the company in the supply of materials for leisure-time consumption.'[10] CBS has also reorganised its telecommunications group, creating a new subsidiary, Viacom International Inc., which now groups its activities in cable television, the worldwide distribution of television series and the improvement of its research activities on new systems of video-cassettes and optical communication. As for ITT, it has purchased two publishing houses, Bobbs-Merrill and Howard-Sams, and has thus become the publisher of school textbooks and the famous *Who's Who*. Xerox, which has organised its educational division through the application of its microfilm and xerography techniques, a field which it completely dominates together well with the camera manufacturer Bell & Howell, has acquired the R. R. Bowker Co., a company more than a century old, known in all libraries and by all publishers for its bibliographical reference works. Xerox now offer university teachers and schoolmasters numerous texts which are becoming unobtainable owing to their high reputation on the one hand and their small print run on the other. In its series of educational publications, Xerox is adopting a pioneering policy with an intentionally provocative air: 'We wish to pick out what is at the centre of North American life, understand what young people are feeling, induce them to learn more. The relationships between the races, Vietnam, the women's liberation movement, these are the themes we are taking.'[11] Finally, Raytheon has absorbed D. C. Heath and Co. (and its Lexington Books division), a publisher of school texts specialising in books on elementary mathematics, the applied social sciences, physics, and university French courses.[12]

Parallel with this wave of acquisitions, those electronics companies which already owned media of mass communication, such as Westinghouse and General Electric, have reformulated their policy in the production of programmes in relation to the importance which new markets are acquiring. A report by Westinghouse in 1970 revealed the concern of these large companies in education: 'Group W (Westinghouse Broadcasting), convinced that radio and tv must assume an expanding role and responsibility, particularly in journalism and education, last year sponsored network television programs treating such subjects as black culture, prisons, pollution, mental institutions and welfare.'[13] Together with the publishing group Time-Life, General Electric, which owns six radio stations and three television stations, has established a company specialising in the production of audio-visual educational equipment, the General Learning Corporation. Westinghouse, which also owns seven radio stations and five television stations, is engaged in producing programmes for the youngest age group. In 1972, Westinghouse bought the Linguaphone Institute Ltd., the most important system in the world for language teaching by audio-visual methods. These companies have also converted their own laboratories and educational divisions into classrooms: General Electric has opened a communications school and Westinghouse has been entrusted by the US Government with providing, as from the end of the seventies, for the training of peace corps volunteers leaving for Brazil, Colombia and Morocco, in order to turn them into instructors for the numerous pilot educational television projects to be set up in those countries. In 1973 Westinghouse recruited to the position of Vice President of its tele-education division, Mr Frank Shakespeare, the resigning head of USIS (United States Information Service), the US Government's official information and propaganda agency. In providing his company with an educational division in 1967, the manager of Westinghouse had pointed out the logic behind this development: 'We believe that we are endowed with greater know-how in business affairs and better technical knowledge than the Universities.'[14]

These same companies were equally well placed to apply their technologies by reinforcing the network of technical schools which they owned. ITT has specialised in secretarial and correspondence course schools for all professions. The Pigier courses in France now form part of its network. RCA maintains private institutes which, in the United States at least, secure employment for 90% of its pupils. Ling-Temco-Vought controls 47 technical or professional schools. CBS runs 'Schools of superior quality because public education does not fulfil this need'. Bell & Howell has eight schools in the United States and in Canada with a total strength of 8,500 students who take electronics and accountancy courses. 125,000 others take its correspondence courses. This is a company particularly known for its photographic materials. But it obtains 37% of sales and 54% of its profits from educational services whilst its photographic equipment represents only 20% of its sales and 12% of its profits.[15]

As if to complete this range of transformation, the large publishing houses which had not themselves been merged or taken over by electronics or other multinational giants, have absorbed their unfortunate colleagues and resolutely entered the audio-visual field, setting their hearts on grabbing companies which produce film or television programmes and media systems. This is the case, for instance, with the largest of them, McGraw-Hill. The names of the companies which it has purchased over the last few years are themselves evocative.[16] In 1966, they bought Educational Development Laboratories; in 1967, Medical World Publishing; in 1968, Pathé Contemporary Films, University Films, Data News Inc.; in 1970 Instructo Corp. and in 1972 it was the turn of four television stations belonging to Time-Life. On the international level, to consider only the most important instances, it has acquired, since 1970, an 80% holding in the Paris publishing house Ediscience S.A.; it took over one of the most venerable representatives of Canadian publishing—Ryerson Press; it bought the North American subsidiary of the German publisher Herder and another German firm, Bucher Verlag. In July 1975, it announced that it would assign the 49% share which it held in another French publishing company, the Technic Union, to J. L. Servan Schreiber (*L'Expansion, Architecture Aujourd'hui* and *La lettre de l'Expansion*). Its foreign subsidiaries are innumerable. It has 276 offices in 179 cities from Panama to New Delhi. McGraw-Hill, known particularly for its 57 magazines—including *Business Week* and *Electronics*—now obtains more than half its turnover from educational products, while its periodicals account for only 25%. And the time is not far off when its educational products will account for 90% of its turnover. In 1973, as if to anticipate the march of the future, they introduced onto the board, which mostly consisted of McGraw family members, a man who was a former Director of NASA (James E. Webb—he headed the Space Agency from 1960–8).[17] The two maxims inscribed on the walls, in golden letters, in the first-floor hall of McGraw-Hill's Fifth Avenue building, are indicative: Plato's 'if a man neglects education, he walks lame to the end of his life', and Kennedy's 'Liberty without learning is always in peril; learning without liberty is always in vain'.

The result of this overall restructuring is already tangible: the ten foremost world producers of educational material are, in the following order: McGraw-Hill, Xerox, CBS, Harcourt (a publishing house which absorbed two others, Academic Press and Grune & Stratton), RCA, Prentice-Hall, Scott-Foresman (also a merger of two publishing houses), ITT, Westinghouse, and General Learning Co; not forgetting Litton, which in 1970 declared sales of educational equipment already amounting to $69 m., nearly half of it sold directly to schools, colleges and universities. The turnover of Xerox's educational division in 1974 amounted to $150 m.[18]

Is there an international audio-visual market?

What does this educational equipment consist of? What factors favour the expansion of these markets? What obstacles will they encounter? And where in the world do these companies expect to operate? A straightfoward answer can be given on the basis of the intrinsic simplicity of a market survey carried out by General Electric for internal use, for the purpose of evaluating the strength of its competitors.[19] 'Educom'—the companies' jargon term for the production of educational equipment—includes all products and services fulfilling a role in the transmission of knowledge and information through (*a*) formal educational channels (primary, secondary and higher education) or private educational channels (companies, government, army, professional associations); (*b*) regular or refresher training channels in diverse areas (child development, careers, hobbies, family life, health, ecology, civic education); and (*c*) general publishing channels such as reviews and reference materials. The products include the most varied multi-media programmes, study texts, audio-visual equipment and microfilms. Services: in-site company courses, training contracts, teaching in company schools, educational advice, educational information.

Among the factors said to stimulate commercial activity in the education market, the report mentions the following (in no particular order): the insufficiencies of traditional education; low productivity in the educational sector; the growth of individual dissatisfaction in professional life; the increasingly urgent wish to keep up to date; increased funds owing to government subsidies and the larger share of their budgets individuals are devoting to education; the limitless possibilities which cable and video-cassette technology offers for the resolution of these problems; the importance of the international market. Among the factors said to handicap the companies' activities are the fragmentary nature of the market (the diversity of publics); the resistance of the educational establishment (the teaching body); and the crisis in school budgets.

Endeavouring to investigate the various chances which this programme of expansion has of entering various parts of the world market, the report distinguishes three categories: the developed countries, the semi-developed countries and the under-developed countries. It anticipates that the first of these will open up only for multi-media programmes in permanent education and adult self-improvement (doctors, engineers, technicians). On this point, however, views are, to say the least, divided. On May 1st, 1975, the manager of the Walt Disney Educational Media Co. considered this market to be both the largest and the most limited; the largest because it covered all educational equipment, the most limited because it was concentrated on fewer countries. 'Steady continuing markets exist only in a few countries, such as Sweden, Canada, South Africa, New Zealand and Australia, which have highly developed educational systems that can use US material easily. Other highly developed nations such as France and Germany have the sophistication to use audio-visual materials, but these must be adapted to their needs, demands and language. So far this has not happened on a broad enough scale to generate a continuing business.'[20] So that's the case of the developed countries. The semi-developed countries should open up to products which meet their needs in professional and technical training equipment. As for the under-developed countries—and here everyone seems to agree—they are likely to be customers for the whole range of products and services: technical teaching, primary teaching, literacy campaigns, in-company training, overall modernisation of the national educational system. However, two obstacles may arise: the control exercised by the government of each country on the communications and educational equipment; linguistic barriers. It is simple to say that the multi-nationals' penetration of the educational field runs up against the resistance of a State ideological apparatus, an obstacle they feel less when excercising their prerogatives only within the mass media, much more controlled by economic cliques. The nationalist reaction of certain Latin American Government in the face of satellite policies is only an index of this resistance. The other difficulty is apparently more easily overcome: has McGraw-Hill not already translated its texts and tapes into Afrikaans, Bantu, Chinese, French, German, Malaysian, Portuguese, Spanish, Nyanja and Tonga? They also had an opportunity for solving the first problem. In 1967, an agreement between the Brazilian Ministry of Education, the National Association of Librarians and the ever-present USAID, made texts published by McGraw-Hill obligatory at all levels of Brazilian teaching. But this already goes back over ten years and since then the preoccupations of the North American companies have been sharpened. And it's no accident if, in 1975, Iran provided the occasion to observe how often the question of the export of educational software became the order of the day, both with the North American industrialists and the White House.

In September 1974, the review *Publishers Weekly* (owned by Xerox) spoke of the possibilities which were opened up by the new markets appearing in the Middle East: 'The international market for educational audio-visual materials is another one of those tantalising opportunities which new media publishers have faced so often—the need is huge, the excitement is there, but it remains more potential than reality.

'The excitement, especially, perhaps is more visible at the moment than it has been before, due to the oil-rich Middle East nations seeking new ways to put their immense new revenues to use. One of these uses could be the upgrading of education in these nations. Iran, in particular, has said that it will be buying new educational materials for its population and a special junket to Iran for audio-visual professionals is being planned for later this year by the Educational Media Producers' Council, the National Audio-Visual Association and the US Government.

'Although Iran over the years has been much more progressive than most underdeveloped countries in bringing education to its population, it nevertheless illustrates the need and desire for help from new educational technology. With large masses of illiterate people and all too few teachers and schools, these nations are looking to technology as a means of leapfrogging the evolution of modern school systems such as those in this country. Iran, for example, is very interested in the use of radio and television for conveying lessons from a central point to many thousands of its citizens across the country.'[21]

The penetration by North American firms into the Iranian teaching system isn't just beginning, however. In the early 60s, a small New York company, Franklin Books Programs, which operated in Teheran, was instructed by the Ministry of Education to modernise all the text-books in use in primary schools. After the Minister of Education and 16 senior officials had been sent to Columbia University for five months' intensive study, the Institute of School Texts was set up. Initially, it was a joint subsidiary of the North American firm and the Iranian Ministry of Education. Franklin received a monopoly in primary education text-books, and other publishers shared the texts for secondary education. In the last 12 years, through the Institute of which it became one of the permament consultants, Franklin has assumed responsibility for designing and producing some 400 primary education titles and for releasing some 150 million copies. Around 1965, Franklin launched another important project, again under the aegis of the Iranian authorities, by establishing the Centre for Educational Publications which concerns itself with teachers and parents as well as children.[22]

These first overseas experiments seem to have been conclusive since, in 1974, after joining with the Iranian Government on an educational plan, based on the use of audio-visual techniques, in rural zones, Franklin Books organised a seminar in New York for officials from the Afghan Ministry of Education dealing with the modernisation of school texts. According to the statements of the company, the participants had all qualified at a North American university and had been given the specific task of revising their country's text-books. Among the participating firms at this event, the presence can be noted of McGraw-Hill and of Harcourt.

The problem of language was resolved in somewhat more cavalier fashion in the Indonesia of General Suharto—who also purchased a national satellite system—and the North Americans have been trying to extend their grasp in that direction without showing their hands too much. The 'Berkeley Mafia' (which prepared the Djakarta Coup) made a quick job—in order to complete the purging of the university system—of adjusting Indonesian higher education to its own image and likeness. A report by the USIS, the official body responsible for co-ordinating this reform, prepared for the US Congress in 1972, gives us information on this operation at the same time that it allows us to consider the North American Government's new strategy in this field: the idea of the 'low profile—that is, the indirect strategy which prefers to leave the initiative to non-government bodies and to delegate a major part of the responsibilities to them. 'In Indonesia, we are still mindful of the advantages of maintaining a relatively low official profile. Today the USIS staff level is still far below that of the Sukarno period (in 1961 our total staff was 225: since 1971, 10 years later, it has been 82). Yet, this small staff is involved in some uniquely important programs.

'The Government of Indonesia has made a basic decision to install English as the country's second language, and has invited our assistance in training teachers for several university level language "centers of excellence". USIS has responded by including teachers prominently among our students at two binational centres. Djakarta has 2,000 students, Surabaja has 600, and a new centre will open this year in Medan. In addition, there are Fullbright experts teaching English as a foreign language at nine of the university "centers of excellence".

'The Indonesians have made a second basic decision to revamp the entire social sciences and humanities curriculums at all universities and adopt a modern American model. To assist, we are sending 50 to 60 Indonesian university teachers for graduate study at the East-West Centre and UCLA. As the professors return to Indoneisa, they will convene as a body to rewrite the basic social science curriculum for the entire Indonesian University system. The project is now in its third year.'[23]

Educational aid programmes therefore quite frequently offer a chance of sealing the alliance between North American companies and Government agencies. Indeed a special organisation manages these common interests.[24] Established at the level of the State Department, it has twelve members who represent the interests of the educational production and publishing companies. At their annual meeting in 1974, these representatives requested that Washington let them be more closely associated with the USAID and USIS projects in everything that related to educational plans in third world countries. They particularly expressed a wish to deal with the Indonesian and Nigerian markets. For its part, USAID promised the countries which asked for aid in the educational field a preliminary overall analysis of their situation and needs, so as to stress thereby that it did not intend to provide incidental but all-emcompassing aid, which meant the modernisation of the whole system.

Up to that time one of the only countries to have received such overall aid was the Republic of El Salvador; according to the terms of the agreement, the installation of a new television system constituted the cornerstone of educational reform. The new system was inaugurated in 1974. It covered all levels of primary education. The advisers were experts from the University of Stanford and USAID supplied most of the electronic equipment (cameras, video recorders, tape recorders). The Japan Broadcasting Corporation had tried to approach El Salvador in 1962, but in 1967, at the Punta del Este Conference, in the presence of the General who had just been elected President of the Republic, President Johnson himself undertook to equip El Salvador with a system which would serve as a model for the rest of Central America.[25]

And yet, at the end of the 60s, in the majority of educational assistance plans, USAID was still offering the luxury of part programmes. In 1969 it distributed ten million school texts free of charge throughout Central America. In the reading book intended for children in the third year of primary education, we find the following interpretation of the Spanish Conquest: 'The Indians lived where there was gold but did not know its value. A Spaniard came looking for gold. The Indians showed him where it was. The Spaniard, to show his gratitude, taught the Indians to read and write. He also taught them to believe in one God. The Indians, in turn, were grateful to serve him. Thus, they lived happily in their village mining gold and cultivating the land. Then other Spaniards came and attacked the village. The Indians fled. The son asks, "Why did the Indians not return?" "Because they found a place to live better", answered Mama. They realised that they had found a very beautiful place. The Indians felt grateful to those who had made them flee.'[26] Should one see in this celebration of the Good Spaniards who brought the alphabet and religion a secret attempt to whitewash this further enterprise of cultural colonisation?

A new battle for control of the media

It is the battle for new contracts for audio-visual education which can be seen in the attempts of multinationals to take control of traditional and modern media. During recent years pressures have begun to make themselves felt exerted by such firms as had not yet gained access to major broadcasting channels but had decided to link their electronics and aerospace production with the promise of communications. Two cases call for attention: ITT and Hughes Aircraft.

In 1967, ITT proposed a merger with ABC (American Broadcasting Company), who accepted. ABC is one of the three major television chains in the United States. But it's more than that: its ABC Films and ABC Worldwide Group dominate the world market in television serials, and have direct interests in the television stations of more than 25 countries (South Korea, the Philippines, Japan, Australia and Canada, as well as the majority of Latin American countries). The Federal Communications Commission considered that the proposal called for attention, and after initially approving the merger, changed its mind and had the agreement cancelled. 'We simply cannot find that the public interest of the American citizen is served by turning over a major network to an international enterprise whose fortunes are tied to its political relations with the foreign officials whose actions it will be called upon to interpret to the world.' 'ABC newsmen could not help knowing that ITT had sensitive business relations in various foreign countries and at the highest levels of our Government, and that reporting on any number of industries and economic developments would touch the interests of ITT.'[27]

ITT did everything possible to prevent the announcement of an unfavourable decision. It even resorted to corruption, trying to buy off *New York Times* journalists to publish opinions which favoured the merger. But these manoeuvres, denounced by the journalists themselves, had the effect of putting the members of the Commission even more on the alert, and they finally sank the proposed marriage in 1968. In the same year, Hughes Aircraft—which already owned two television programme production companies—also tried to buy a roughly 50% holding in ABC, and met with the same refusal.

Excluded from the established media, Hughes Aircraft placed its hopes on the new technologies, and sought to enter the information sector and to combine it with education. Not content with manufacturing various series of satellites and cable television systems equipment, it began to enter into the exploitation of tele-distribution systems and the production of programmes for this new form of communal communication. The tele-distribution company, Teleprompter Corp., which it controls, shot up to first place among the owners and operators of cable television.[28] Its organisation is a model of its kind. It foreshadows the kind of company which would control the planning of this marvellous cable institutionalism which electronics experts promise us by the end of the century. Its various departments cover the entire spectrum of possible applications of the new technology. It manages cable television systems which transmit information and education programmes; it produces films for young children and the family public; it offers special services for company surveillance by closed circuit television or by cable alarm systems (the department responsible for developing this apparatus is called National Security Systems); it is already carrying out studies in marketing by television. Its latest creation is a satellite development office which will be especially responsible for programming the medium. Finally, Hughes Aircraft carried off one of four proposals for providing the USA with a national satellite system before the end of the decade.

Table 18

**Principal Proprietors of US Cable
Television Systems (February 1973)**

	No. of Subscribers
1 Teleprompter (Hughes Aircraft)	740,000
2 Television Communications (Warner Communications)	400,000
3 Telecommunications, Inc. (Gulf & Western-Paramount)	326,000
4 American Television and Comm. Corp. (Cox)	300,000
5 Cox Cable (Cox-entreprise journalistique)	230,000
6 Viacom (CBS)	228,000
7 Sammons Communications	221,000
8 Communications Properties	182,000
9 Cablecom General (RKO-General Tire & Rubber)	178,000
10 United Artists-Columbia Cablevision	145,000
11 LVO Cable	118,000
12 Service Electric Cable TV, Inc.	115,000
13 Time-Life Cable Communications	112,000
14 Storer Broadcasting	92,000
15 Vikoa	85,000
16 Liberty Communications	82,000
17 Continental Cablevision (Warner)	70,000
18 Telecable Corporation	68,000
19 General Electric Cablevision	62,000

Source: National Cable Television Association, February 1973

Table 19

Principal Distributors of Cable Pay-tv

1 Gridtronics (Warner Communications)
2 Transworld Communications (Columbia Pictures)
3 Home Theatre Network (J. Paul Getty)
4 Laser Link (Theater Vision)
5 Computer Television (Time-Life Inc.)
6 Theta-Com (Hughes Aircraft)
7 Optical Systems (Pioneer Parachute Corp.)
8 EnDe-Code (Gulf & Western)

Source: The Network Project, *Cable Television*, New York June 1973

Among Hughes Aircraft's immediate competitors in the exploitation of cable television systems are General Electric, Time-Life, CBS and the majority of the large film companies (to whom we shall return later). A 1971 report from Warner clearly stresses the size of the stakes and shows what kind of struggles for influence these new technologies, which are supposed to 'democratise' communications, are involved in: 'Cable television can carry an abundance of programs on an abundance of channels—education, cultural, informational, and of course, entertainment. Principal studies of future cable growth have concluded that one of the major thrusts for growth will be the ability of cable tv to provide on a free basis special entertainment programs such as first run motion pictures. The advantage of our expanding into cable tv were thus apparent.'[29]

It is still too early to determine how far the organisational model of cable television which is now being established in the United States will prove exportable. (There are still only just over seven million homes in North America subscribing to some 3000 systems distributing between ten and twenty programmes. Canada is slightly more advanced, with one third of the country's homes as cable television subscribers.) Nevertheless, Teleprompter is already trying to use its experience in offering services abroad. For this purpose it has set up a joint subsidiary with the Bank of Suez, International Communications Systems. By 1972 it was already to be found in France operating the Multivision company, along with CGE, Thomson, Philips and the Havas and Publicis agencies. In February 1973, to reduce the possibility of competition in international markets, Teleprompter took over one of the only cable television installation companies operating on the international level, International Cablevision Inc., which had already set up shop in Mexico, the only third world country where North American firms have so far begun to try out these new systems. It is possible in Mexico to receive transmissions from Texas, and it is here that the first local try-outs have occurred under these companies' auspices.

European companies in the video era

The approach of the era of video cassettes and tele-distribution networks has provoked a similar drawing together of the European electronics industry and the cultural software industry.

The establishment of these new audio-visual methods has clearly proved slower than their manufacturers envisaged at the beginning of the decade. Sony delayed the introduction of their video-cassette machine on the general market until June 1975. Yet still at that time it decided to make it an experimental offer in three major North American cities. Its Betamax apparatus, using magnetic tape, still costs $785 in Tokyo (1976 prices—trans.), not to mention $1,540 for the appropriate colour television set to go with it. Moreover, it seems that the optimistic forecasts of 1970 somewhat underestimated the problem this last piece of information indicates. Colour television sales have improved relatively slowly in various countries, including industrialised countries, and this has been one of many factors to delay the flowering of large public market for the video cassette. The diversity of the systems offered to the purchaser and the competition between different models, which recalls the early years of cinematography, is no more likely to lead to a reduction in prices and to a popularisation of the medium in this way. Failing a large general public efforts over recent years have been directed towards industrial and institutional customers. The sole exception is Japan where the turnover of the video-cassette industry increased from $37.6 m. in 1973 to $134.9 m. in 1975.[30] At this time Japanese firms were exporting nearly 40% of their production to the US and only 15% to Europe and South Asia.[31]

The road towards general acceptance of the new apparatus has already passed through several crises. In 1973 RCA had to abandon its hologram recorder and adopt the magnetic head system, while CBS, which has promoted the EVR (Electronic Video Recording) system, closed down its cassette production lines after losing $10 m. Avco went through more than $45 m. trying to market Cartrivision. To judge by the recent developments in the various processes, it seems that the future formula for the general public will likely be the video-disc. During the first few months of 1975, the German firm Telefunken introduced the Teldec video-disc system—manufactured in conjunction with the British firm Decca—to the general market. It cost $600 in Europe, twice as cheap as a Sony video tape recorder. The kind of apparatus constructed by Telefunken clearly indicates the markets they are treating as priorities. The system adopted by Teldec is compatible with the NTSC colour television system, which is standard through most of the world but especially in the United States and Japan, and with the French Secam system. The initial range offered by Teldec, in close co-operation with several publishing houses, included 50 titles (Leisure, 'Popular Science', Education, Children's programmes) and the company forecast the availability of 350 titles by the end of 1975.

1976 saw the launching of other video-discs, notably the system developed by Philips and the North American company MCA (Music Company of America). The most serious competitor of this alliance was expected to be RCA. Following setbacks which it suffered in the development of a video-cassette system, RCA decided to try and capture a substantial portion of the new video-disc market, and thus try to repeat the process which, 30 years earlier, took it into the front rank of producers in the record industry. The owner of one of the three major television networks in the United States, NBC (National Broadcasting Company), RCA saw video-disc as a new market for its television scrics. Like the MCA-Philips video-discs, the RCA system was to offer an important advantage over the Anglo-German Teldec: recordings of 30 minutes, against Teldec's 10 minutes. The more expensive equipment manufactured by Sony and other Japanese firms will no doubt continue to be aimed principally at companies and institutions.[32]

Since 1971, the big European publishing houses have combined to face the challenge of the new technologies. In that year they set up the IPA (International Publishers Audio-Visual Association), registered in Zurich and bringing together six of the biggest publishers (Mondadori, Italy; Hachette, France; Editions Rencontres, Switzerland; Bertelsmann, Germany; AB Bonnierfoertagen, Sweden; and VNU, Holland). IPA initially defined itself as a club for international publishing companies for the purpose of promoting audio-visual material and in particular new systems of image-and-sound production: video-discs, video-cassettes, cable television and satellite transmission. The members of the club proposed that contact should be made with the production companies, television networks, and the educational, political and economic institutions, to encourage co-operation with them. Each of these publishers has its own way of doing things. Thus, Tele-Hachette diversified its production by creating a department for industrial and publicity films, and entered the field of training consultancy (Formation-Conseil). One company, Videogrammes, was also created for the preparation of programmes for the new media. Among the shareholders, apart from Hachette, are television networks, certain newspapers, cinema chains and other publishing houses. However, judging by Hachette's first results from this project, it can hardly be said that the experiment has lived up to the enthusiasm of a few years earlier. In 1973, the new Hachette-Formation-Conseil lost 10 m. francs, and 1974 was scarcely any better.

In Europe as in the US, the electronics and aerospace companies have not trailed behind. The reaction of Philips and Siemens—which has closed ranks for the purpose with two leading German publishing companies, Bertelsmann and Axel Springer—has to date produced a joint subsidiary, Polymedia, specialising in audio-visual materials; it offers large companies, stores and distribution chains, video-cassette personnel training programmes. The company reinforces interests which the two firms hold in satellite technology and video-discs. In Italy a national centre of educational technology is being set up which will include the industrial firms of Montedison, IBM-Italy, Pirelli (which manufactures tele-distribution cables), the Italian airline Alitalia and various publishers. CGE and Thomson-CSF in France had already turned towards tele-distribution. The first of them is joint-owner, with the Suez group and La Lyonnaise des Eaux, of Video-City, whose function is the installation and running of cable tv systems. For CGE—one of the major French electronics companies—the application of this new technology has opened up new prospects for its subsidiaries, Câbles de Lyon, Tréfimétaux and CIT-Alcatel. In 1974, Thomson-CSF, to balance out its own activities in tele-distribution, set up two economic interest groups: one with the tele-communications company SAT, called Télé-réseaux, to engineer, sell, install and maintain tele-distribution systems; the other, jointly with SAT, the Compagnie Générale des Eaux and a banking group called Télé-services, to organise and finance tele-distribution installations.

But Thomson-CSF has much more ambitious plans. Since 1970, this electronics company has set up, with Hachette, a study group relating to possible uses of new audio-visual techniques, and has obtained a licence to exploit the CBS video-cassette process. After the failure of the North American firm's system, Thomson turned to another US company. An agreement was signed with one of the largest manufacturers of television sets in the US, the Zenith Corporation, to perfect a Franco-American video-disc. (According to forecasts it should reach the market in about 1979.)

Behind these various technological movements, a mutation of the ideological apparatus is trying to carve a way fowards for itself. In 1970, the French Ministry for Cultural Affairs asked the Thomson forecast study service to determine for it 'what will be the electronic mass-media communications in 1985, and what would should be undertaken in 1970 on that basis, in order that its action may be integrated into what will occur in 1985'. Accepting the task of carrying out this pioneering study, Thomson implicitly declared that it was the best placed 'to draw out the consequences and to define, long in advance of its competitors, a coherent policy of research and production in relation to mass-distribution electronic apparatuses, and that it was not impossible that the public authorities should grant it exclusive rights in the event of large-scale action'.[33] The study related to different levels: transmission, content (information, education, amusement), the mode of reception of the message, the audience (individuals, groups, assemblies, the population). It went as far as posing the problem of the recorder, round which a network of video-clubs could be created.

Since then, the political purpose of the modern bourgeoisie has had time to get beyond the outlines of a sketch, though without successfully imposing itself. With Giscard d'Estaing the restructuring of the ideological apparatuses of communication has become a political necessity. The electoral campaign of the future president, designed according to electoral management models imported from the USA, was an advance warning. We will come back to it. Other initiatives did not take long. The reform of ORTF (the French broadcasting system), by placing the channels in private hands and restoring the strength of advertising pressures, merely returned direct political control of the system to the supremacy of the bourgeoisie. By preaching that competition is necessary in television news, and cannot be achieved without competition between channels, a North American model of broadcasting has automatically been installed. The organisation of local radio has already shown the way.

But this modernisation of the electronic media also has its con-tradictions. The fear demonstrated by those in power towards cable television, whose installation they have delayed for fear of losing political control, contrasts with the growing aggressiveness they show in the business of swallowing up more established media. This fear is only equalled in the educational establishment, where it is more complex, and where, in spite of the pressures exerted by the electronics industry, we find an almost systematic blocking of initiatives aimed at perfecting audio-visual teaching, even within the limits which the established school system allows. This doesn't prevent publishers and electronics experts being among the first to offer their services on the foreign market for the modernisation of school systems and the establishment of tele-education systems, in the African countries and in Brazil.

European multinationals in publishing

These changes are taking place at just the moment when, following other branches of the industry, large European publishing houses have decided to take the offensive in the internationalisation of educational production. Most of them are already solidly planted on foreign soil.

British publishing, with 40% of its business carried out abroad, beats all records. In 1972, Longmans, a firm with 250 years' history, including such past successes as Defoe's *Robinson Crusoe*, obtained 80% of its turnover from abroad.[34] It has a system of subsidiaries from Hong Kong to the Caribbean, which passes through South Africa,

West and East Africa, across the Arab world and into Malaysia, Singapore, Australia and New Zealand. These subsidiaries frequently publish the company's books on the spot. However, an index of the process of concentration in publishing which can be seen almost everywhere in the capitalist world, Longmans is only one of numerous companies in the Pearson publishing empire, which also owns, among other things, the *Financial Times*. In 1972, this group—the most important in Britain—absorbed the world-famous paperback publishers, Penguin. A sign of the dynamism of the group, the management of the *Financial Times* announced in 1975 that this newspaper would be one of the first in the old world to take the leap into the era of computers.

The Hachette company in France has no need to envy its British colleagues. It is in the forefront of European publishing, with an annual turnover of more than three billion francs, as against 1.8 billion for the German Axel Springer group and 800 million for the Italian firm Mondadori.[35] The number of publishing companies it controls is very considerable: Grasset, Stock, Fayard, Tallandier, Albin-Michel, J. J. Pauvert, and Le Livre de Poche, which alone has 35-40 per cent of the market. The newspapers, weeklies and periodicals published by Hachette cover a wide spread of readers. They include *France Soir, France-Dimanche, le Journal du Dimanche, Elle, Le Point, Confidences, Lectures pour tous, Le Journal de Mickey, Réalités, Entreprise, Preuves*, and finally *Télé 7 jours*, in which Hachette has a 50% holding. But the ace in Hachette's hand in this particular game is the hold it has over the distribution system through its delivery services.

The firm's international department includes 50 companies in 33 countries, 13 in the Western hemisphere. Foreign sales represent approximately a third of its turnover. Apart from its many subsidiaries in French-speaking Africa, Hachette owns, for example, an important company in Montreal which publishes school texts (Centre Educatif et Culturel). In Belgium, its presence can be felt in six companies. In Santiago de Chile, Hachette is still at the head of Ediciones Pedagogicas, which took part in the modernisation of text-books under Frei. In Portugal, where the fragmentation of publishing is considerable, the Hachette group is one of the most important Portuguese language publishers. In addition to its local production, Hachette provides international distribution of French newspapers and books (36% of the former pass through its hands). The company is already acquainted with the problems of any multinational. In 1974, the Common Market Assembly accused it of abusing its dominant position and of violating the anti-monopoly regulations of the Treaty of Rome in such countries as Belgium and Luxembourg.[36]

In 1974, this French publisher decided to go a step further in the internationalisation of its production. 'It is necessary,' said Hachette's managing director in September 1974—and he was speaking English at the time—'to "de-Frenchify" Hachette'. By adopting this attitude and following the example of many other European firms of Italian, German and Dutch nationality which have increased their English-language publications, Hachette officially recognised the accent of the so-called Anglo-Saxon transnational language. In fact 40% of Hachette's products are already put out in a language other than French.[37] To avoid accusations of favouring the growth of this transnational culture, Hachette's Chairman insisted on declaring 'We're not traitors to the French language because of that. If we want to support French publications we'll do a better job of it if we have a strong distribution network, and the way to develop and maintain that is to include English—and Spanish—language materials as well.' To achieve production in these languages, 'no form of cooperation is excluded. It can be a majority participation or less, a partnership, association with a big house or a small one'. The company's marketing director, a former employee of the soap multinational Unilever, commented 'we don't expect to become multinational publishers all by ourselves'.[38]

The era of major transatlantic alliances has therefore opened, and it was thus to consolidate its progress that Hachette purchased the North American Regent Publishing Co. of New York from its previous owners, the publishers Simon and Shuster. In the field of periodicals, co-operation with the United States was confirmed in 1970 with the creation of the first pan-European economics journal, *Vision*, pub-lished monthly in English, German, French and Italian. The joint property of Librarie Hachette and the North American group Vision Inc., which is merely the publishing arm of the Rockefeller clan, this magazine appeared in the wake of the offensive in the countries of the Common Market by the Chase Manhatten Bank and other properties of the family of the last Vice-President of the United States. The choice of Hachette as European partner indicated how the North American multinationals valued the contribution of the French group as a privileged representative of their interests. Before setting foot in Europe, the Vision Inc. group had spent more than ten years establishing its publishing empire in Latin America. The financial and general information magazines (*Vision, Visao, Progreso*) which circu-late in all the Latin American countries, have been joined by several specialist magazines for executives and businessmen, in particular in Brazil, and also a network of publishing companies concentrating on university text-books in management and political-economic works recommended by the propaganda agency of the North American Government. The entry of the North American firm into publishing in Latin America was put to good use in the European countries since the Vision-Hachette association began in turn to programme the same titles as the North American group had successfully launched for Latin American businessmen. Thus the books of Peter Drucker, the Pope of North American management, appeared in the European capitals five years after they appeared in Rio de Janeiro and Buenos Aires.

However, other European competitors seemed to want to outstrip the Hachette group by going further in their policy of multinational interlinking. This is the case with the famous Italian group which took shape in 1974, which is dominated by the owners of FIAT, the Agnelli family. In 1972, the North American conglomerate Gulf & Western Industries Inc.—which, as owner of Paramount Pictures, is one of the North American film industry majors—acquired 20% of the shares of the Italian publishing firm, Fratelli Fabbri Editori, a company controlled by FIAT, which publishes medical encyclopaedia and art books but is particularly prominent through its publication of textbooks for Italian education. Gulf & Western's annual report provides us with information on the intentions behind these steps. 'The acquisition of Fabbri is another example of our partnership policy.'[39] In December 1974, through IFI International, FIAT's financial arm operating from Luxembourg, the Agnelli family paid the North Americans back in their own coinage by acquiring Bantam Books—for $70 m.—which was owned by one of the big US insurance companies, National General Corp., which also owns a well-known film production company (National General Pictures). In taking over Bantam Books, the FIAT empire inherited a catalogue of more than 1,500 titles, including such best-sellers as *The Exorcist* (20,000,000 copies sold), and Bantam's British subsidiary, Corgi, one of the leading British paperback houses. The new property, which now forms part of the newly formed Gruppo Editoriale Finanziaria, joins the many Italian publishing and other journalistic companies owned by FIAT, and makes a particular contribution to the group's international dimensions. Apart from Fratelli Fabbri, the motor-car manufacturer controls the publishing houses of Bompiani, Adelphi, Boringhieri, Sonzogno, the Etas-Kompass companies (which publish more than 21 technical magazines and have more than a third of the Italian market), a printing works and two advertising agencies. It also controls Italy's second newspaper, *La Stampa*, holds one third of the shares in *Corriere della Sera*, and 49% of *Espresso*. Abroad, Agnelli shares with the Rothschilds an English subsidiary which specialises in children's books, and controls 20% of Hachette's Livre de Paris. In Germany,

Agnelli has the subsidiary of the North American publisher Praeger and a German publisher (Wissen Verlag).[40] FIAT is of course also involved in all the major initiatives to establish new communications technologies. Its factories produce many telecommunications products and Fabbri Fratelli, in accordance with its owners' policies of alliances, has developed its audio-visual section by making an agreement with the North American firm Bell & Howell. Abroad, Agnelli has a 50% interest in Britain, Fabbri & Partners, for partwork and children's books as well as the Everyman encyclopedia (the Rothschilds have the other 50%).

A year before these new kinds of agreements began to be made, the Italian parties of the left denounced this monopolist wave. 'We must know why all this is taking place and why it is taking place at this moment. There are objective reasons explaining this process: difficulties in distribution encountered by the small and medium size publisher, increases in costs, credit problems, the disproportionate cost of technical rationalisation, the lack of editorial personnel, the old vices of patronage and megalomania which have slowly mounted up, the difficulty of export, etc. But the principle reason must be sought elsewhere: owing to the dynamics of mass culture, owing to the development of education, the enlargement—even relatively—of the market, especially the education market, new prospects have opened up, and industrialists, always looking for new sources of profits and new means of exerting their hegemony on public opinion, quickly understood. The craft and family style which characterised and still largely characterise our publishing industry, relegating it to the rearguard of our national industry, is disappearing. We are obviously giving way to the need for a new and more complex structure.'[41] With variations peculiar to each country, the same phenomenon can be observed throughout Europe.

Notes

1 *Business Abroad*, June 1971.
2 *Business Week*, 30.X.1974; *Advertising Age*, 9.VI.1975.
3 Letter to *Business Week*, 21.VII.1975.
4 *Advertising Age*, 21.V.1975.
5 *Mecanica Popular*, Miami, May 1971.
6 *G. E. International*, New York, June 1974.
7 The Institute for Advanced Technology (IAT), *Seminars for professionals in management and data processing*, Control Data Corporation, Rockville, Mar. To

quote Control Data's advertising in France: 'The Control Data Institute of Paris (there are 35 throughout the world) will attend to your needs for basic computer training in seminars for advanced techniques, and in management training. We use several recognised methods of teaching which have given excellent results, including 'eduvision', using all the resources of multi-media means. We are the only Data Processing Institute whose courses are approved by the Ministry for Industrial and Scientific Development.'

A wider study of the role of multinationals in professional training should deal with the institutes for trade unionist education established with their assistance. See the analysis in A. Mattelart, 'Firmes multinationales et syndicats jaunes dans la contre insurrection' ('Multinational Firms and Yellow Trades Unions in the Counter Insurrection'), *Les Tempes Modernes*, January 1975.

8 In the language of computer technology the term 'software' refers strictly to computer programmes, originally supplied free to customers for a firm's hardware but since recognised as marketable commodities in their own right. More generally, and in this context, software refers to any kind of marketable programme material for any kind of communications or audio-visual equipment, and by extension, includes traditional media such as books. Thus the restructuring of the apparatus of cultural production involves a redefinition of traditional forms to fit the conditions of the new technology. (Translator's note.)

9 RCA *Annual Report 1972*. In 1975, RCA gave up its British publishing subsidiary which succeeded in making a name for itself in the field of so-called 'counterculture'.

10 CBS, *Annual Report 1971*.

11 Xerox, *Annual Report 1972*.

12 Raytheon, *Annual Report 1974*. Although it is true that the majority of publishing houses to change hands were acquired by large electronics firms, nonetheless other conglomerates have also interested themselves in this field. Thus in 1970, W. R. Grace & Co. purchased Baker and Taylor Publishers, a company 150 years old, and used this platform to launch itself into audio-visual teaching. (*Publishers Weekly*, 30.XII.1974)

13 *Advertising Age*, 30.VIII.1971.

14 Westinghouse, *Annual Report 1967 and 1972; Business Week*, 2.V.1970.

15 *Business Week*, 31.VII.1971, 5.V.1973.

16 *Moody's Industrial Manual*; McGraw-Hill Co., *Annual Report 1972*.

17 McGraw-Hill, *News*, 27.V.1973.

18 Litton Industries, *Annual Report 1970*; Xerox, *Annual Report 1974*.

19 General Electric, *Communications Study Advisory Council Briefing April 17, 1973*, New York.

20 in Paul Doebler, 'Is there an overseas market for US audiovisual products?', *Publishers Weekly*, 5.V.1975.

21 *Ibid.*

22 Maya Yates, 'Bringing books to Iran', *Publishers Weekly*, 23.IX.1974.

23 *USIA Appropriations Authorisation Fiscal Year 1973, Hearings Before the Committee on Foreign Relations US Senate*, 22 Congress, 22 Session, 20–21–23 March 1972, Washington, D.C., 1973, US Government Printing Office.

24 Cf. Susan Wagner, 'Flighting illiteracy is at the heart of Washington's book programs', *Publishers Weekly*, 23.IX.1974.

25 Ministerio de Educación (El Salvador), *Historia de la televisión educativa de El Salvador*, 1974. For the global presentation of the plan by a North American expert, the father of communications research, cf. Wilbur Schramm, *Instructional*

television in the educational reform of El Salvador, Washington, 1973, Information Centre in Instructional Technology.

26 Cited in 'Latin America and Empire', *NACLA Report*, February, 1972.

27 Cf. Nicholas Johnson, *How to talk back to your television set*, New York, Bantam Books, 1970.

28 *Moody's Industrial Manual*.

29 Cited in The Network Project, *Cable TV*, New York, 1973, Notebook 5.

30 *Electronics*, 28.XI.1974.

31 Cf. 'L'événement: vidéo-cassettes et vidéo-disques', *Le Monde*, 8.I.1974.

32 On the video-disc industry, see *Electronics*, 6.III.1975, and *Business Week*, 15.IX.1975.

Nothing more has so far been heard of RCA's Selecta Vision video-disc system since its withdrawal for rethinking in the summer of 1977. Meanwhile, however, a full-scale war has developed between the two rival systems, video-cassettes, led by Sony, and video-discs, led by MCA. Sony's introduction of the Betamax system on the US market, offering recording as well as playback, proved extremely provocative. The MCA subsidiary, Universal, together with Walt Disney, filed suit against Sony, various retailers, and the Doyle Dane Bernbach advertising agency, demanding a ban on Betamax recorders and cassettes on the grounds of conspiracy to infringe copyright. They argued that the system has been promoted as a means of pirating their films by off-air recording. Sony defended Betamax with an 'Open Letter to the Entertainment Industry' in *Variety* (15.XII.1976). They countered the charge with the claim that the equipment simply used a 'time-shift' device, and said 'We do not believe that the copyright law was intended to prevent members of the public from deciding how and when they see the television programmes which are beamed into their homes'. Previously scheduled to be heard in Los Angeles Federal Court in January 1978, the case was then put off to be heard in May; it was rumoured that other plaintiffs might join Disney and Universal. The case is obviously extremely significant, since it demonstrates to us the way that new technologies constitute a serious disturbance of those capitalist property relations expressed in the legal superstructure in the form of copyright laws.

Production of the Betamax reached the 100,000 level in 1976 in Japan and the US. But in reaching this level Sony did not achieve control of the market even for cassette systems. Sanyo and Toshiba both brought out competitive versions. To avoid savage and chance-ridden competition, Sony signed a co-production agreement with its two adversaries, with a view to putting a new model on the market, the Beta-format, which was released in 1977. But it met with another competitor, a system developed by Matsushita's subsidiary, Victor. Subsequently Matsushita was joined in this project by another Japanese firm, Nippon Gakki (Yamaha).

The conquest of the mass market was therefore accelerated during the second half of 1977. In Japan, the firms Akai, Sharp, Hitachi and Mitsubishi also decided to adopt the Victor system. In the USA, where the Beta-format/Victor battle also raged, Zenith opted for the Beta-format while RCA, GTE-Sylvania, General Electric and Magnavox (a Philips subsidiary) chose the Victor system. In Japan, production of various recorders went up from 119,000 in 1975, to 286,000 in 1976 and 450,000 in 1977. Meanwhile a new hardware company was formed in collaboration with Pioneer Electronics in Japan for manufacture of MCA/Philips video-disc players, so far handmade by MCA in California.

Concentration in video is therefore very strong. The same is true in the manufacture of magnetic tape: Manufacturers either belong to the chemical industry (like the two world leaders, BASF and 3M) or to the photographic industry (Kodak, Agfa, Fuji) or the electronics industry (Sony, Philips). Certain manufacturers of magnetic tape are also aiming to produce complete systems themselves. Since 1972, BASF, for example, has manufactured recorders, full-scale language laboratories and, thanks to an agreement with Bell & Howell, manufacturers of cinematographic equipment, a new video-recording system. (Translator's Note.)

33 Guy Schwartz, 'Thomson-CSF a l'heure de la prospective', *Le Management*, Paris, January 1971.
34 *Publishers Weekly*, 10.VI.1974, 25.XI.1974.
35 'Le classement des premières sociétés françaises et européennes', *Les Dossiers d'Entreprise*, 16–23 November 1973.
36 On Hachette, cf. the dossiers *Informations Internationales, op. cit.; Hachette la pieuvre, temoignage d'un militant CFDT*, Paris, 1973, Librarie La Commune; *Publishers Weekly*, 3.VI.1974.
37 H. Lottman, 'Hachette defines its worldwide intentions', *Publishers Weekly*, 30.IX.1974.
38 *Ibid.*
39 Gulf & Western Industries, *Annual Report 1972*.
40 H. Lottman, 'A powerful new publishing group rises on the Italian scene', *Publishers Weekly*, 6.V.1974.
41 Roberto Bonchio, 'L'editoria in Italia', in *Radiotelevisione, informazione, democrazia, convegno nazionale del PCI, Roma, 9–31 Marzo 1973*, Rome 1973, Editori Riuniti.

CHAPTER V

THE NORTH AMERICAN TELE-EDUCATION SERIES: A ONE-WAY STREET

THE arrival of new technologies in the field of education has been accompanied by the appearance in the United States of new agents of mass cultural production. Within the field of leisure-time culture, US producers have succeeded in universalising their own particular model of media organisation, imposing certain styles of production, a focus and limits, throughout a large part of the world, a whole way of producing information and consuming free time. Will the coming of the new multinational teachers mean the invasion of the small screen by standardised educational products for the international market, aiming at the same rating on the clapometer as *Mannix* or *The Streets of San Francisco*? The chances are hard to assess. But one thing is certain. A new production system for mass tele-education is being created in the imperialist metropolis in the attempt to respond to the demands of new technology. And the producers are following their natural tendency to impose it as a universal model for the industrialisation of education. We will try to trace the genesis of these new techniques, to explain their particular character and their ecumenical purpose.

The Foundation, the new instrument of the 'television revolution'

In 1968 there were 25,000 Foundations in the United States devoted to the distribution of grants, and the financing of research and experimental projects in the widest possible range of disciplines.[1] There were only 314 in 1940. This spectacular increase is often taken as an index of the growing importance of educational activities, and there are other indices to confirm it. In 1940, the national expenditure on educational materials stood at $3.2 billion. By 1973 it had reached $96.2 billion. In 1940, 3,300 doctorates (the famous Ph.Ds.) were awarded. In 1973,

39,000. The Education Department budget rose from $1.9 billion to $52 billion between 1953 and 1970.[2] But the rising number of Foundations also reveals the increasingly direct interest of the major industries in the education sector. In fact the majority of Foundations are attached to these industries—thus giving Foundations their own role in the era of monopoly capitalism. The Ford Foundation, set up in 1936, heads the list with a capital of over $3 billion. This represents one third of the total capital of the 33 leading North American Foundations and one sixth of the capital controlled by all 25,000 existing Foundations. Among the leaders are those attached to the cereal manufacturers Kelloggs and Ralston Purina, to the chemicals firm Dupont de Nemours, the Mellon banking group, and General Motors, patron of the Alfred P. Sloan Foundation.

A little less than half the fortune of the Ford Foundation is invested in the Ford Motor Company and the rest is divided between shareholdings in major industrial companies and in US Government stock (its fourth line of investment). Every year these holdings bring in an average of $220 million which it uses to maintain its team of 611 professional staff and to finance its various programmes around the world. Although older, its direct competitor, the Rockefeller Foundation, which dates from 1913, has 160 professional staff and only one quarter of the capital of Ford ($830 million). Understandably, the principal investments of the Rockefeller Foundation are in the oil

Table 20

The Ten Leading Foundations in the United States

	Assets	Annual Budget	Origin
	$ Million		
Ford Foundation	3,049	224	Motor Industry
Robert Wood Johnson	1,302	20	Medical Equipment
Lilly Endowment Inc.	1,139	31	Pharmaceutical Industry
Rockefeller Foundation	830	41	Banking Group
Kresge Foundation	658	26	Supermarkets
Andrew Mellon Foundation	636	27	Banking Group
W.K. Kellogg Foundation	577	20	Food Industry
Duke Endowment	367	19	Tobacco Industry
Pew Memorial Trust	580	14	Oil Industry
Carnegie Corp. of N.Y.	338	16	Iron and Steel Industry

Source: *Business Week*, 7.XII.1974. In 1970, the A. P. Sloan Foundation, founded in 1934, occupied eleventh place with assets of $329 m.

companies of the Rockefeller family ($330 million) and the rest generally in companies in which Chase Manhattan has a preferential holding (Xerox, IBM, ITT, ATT). The composition of the boards of these Foundations (in law, the Foundation is its board of directors) is a faithful reflection of the interests that converge on it. On the board of the Rockefeller Foundation, chaired by John Rockefeller and the banker and politician Douglas Dillon, we find the presidents of IBM and Corning Glass Works, the former director of CBS and one of the top men on the Security Council of the US Information Agency, and a Latin American, the former President of Columbia and director of the press group Vision Inc. (see above). The Ford Foundation is chaired by McGeorge Bundy, former counsellor to Kennedy and Johnson on national security matters and well-known for the roles he played in the Bay of Pigs invasion, the landings on San Domingo and the escalation of the Vietnam war. Among his colleagues of long-standing are Robert McNamara, former president of Ford Motor Company and president of the World Bank, the presidents of Levi-Strauss, the denim manufacturers, Shell, Polaroid, and one of the famous Think Tanks, the Brookings Institute.[3] Among recent nominations to the Ford Foundation we find an Indonesian who had earlier been his country's Information Minister, and an executive of ITT, the author of a work entitled *Vietnam Microwave Communications Systems*.

The way in which the US Foundations are embedded in the power structure of their country has been the subject of many analyses. 'The Foundations . . . are the base of the network of organisations through which the nerve centres of wealth impress their will on Washington. This network, the ganglia of foundation intelligence, is composed of a panoply of "independent" research and policy organisations, jointly financed and staffed by the foundations and the corporate community, which as a group set the terms and define the horizon of choice for the long-range policies of the United States government . . .'[4]

The areas of activity where each Foundation has chosen to intervene show contrasting priorities. The name of the Rockefeller Foundation, for example, which has devoted a lot of its resources to agricultural research, is connected with the 'green revolution'. Another of its specialities is the politics of birth control, based on the diagnosis that the Third World is completely overpopulated. Since 1963 its demographic programmes have represented one of its five main items of investment. Remember that the most important organisations in this field, the Population Council, was founded in 1948 by John Rockefeller himself. Most recently the Foundation has latched on to studies and projects for the fight against pollution. But it still lags behind in the cultural field which it continues to approach with very traditional criteria. It assists composers, writers and choreographers, but its sorties into electronic and television experimentation hardly go beyond the teaching of music and the arts. Leaving aside the enterprising activities of one renegade branch (The Rockefeller Brothers Fund) attached to the First National City Bank, which began to get involved with the problems of blacks in the late sixties, the Rockefeller Foundation has few claims to 'activist' status.

The Ford Foundation, on the other hand, which has also ventured into plans for population control, has acquired, at least in certain capitalist circles, the reputation of being more liberal, which earned it a lot of annoying interference during the period of McCarthyite repression. Showing an increasing interest in the problem of ethnic minorities, it has often aroused the wrath of the witch-hunters. Among its 'open-door' policies, the problem of how to put audio-visual resources at the service of the most educationally deprived groups has a central place. Such is the importance of the Ford Foundation's initiatives in this respect that it is difficult to separate its own trajectory from the evolution of educational applications of television.

From 1951, the date when the restructuring of its post-war policy began, the Ford Foundation fought to set up a non-commercial television network in the United States that could eventually compete with the oligarchy of CBS, ABC and NBC. It was a fight against all the blueprints which had brought world-wide success to the US model of commercial television, against all the great soap-operas 'made in the USA'. In doing this, the Ford Foundation gradually gathered together all the disparate and implicit criticisms of certain layers of the North American public who were upset by the overload of violence on traditional television (and especially by the fact that children were subjected to this) and by the situation where the only accepted measure of quality was the ratings bulletin. In the last twenty years the Foundation has spent over $220 million to reach its goal. It established a Fund for Adult Education which in under five years took control of parallel organisations which were trying to set up educational television on a national scale (Educational Television and Radio Center and National Association of Educational Broadcasters). It spent $3.5 million building television transmitters in 35 communities throughout the national territory and obtained a licence from the Federal Communications Commission for part use of 242 non-commercial stations.[5] To complete the project another division, the Fund for Educational Progress, began to produce results that became a model for education through telecommunication, aimed especially at deprived children.

Three major pilot projects were launched, one in Washington

(Hagerstown Project), another in the Latin American ghetto in New York and a third in the US possessions in the Pacific, in particular the island of Samoa. Just as Puerto Rico from 1937 on was converted into a contraceptive testing laboratory where the neo-Malthusian policies reserved by the Empire for the Third World were developed, so Samoa became a guinea pig for the Ford Foundation to study the reactions of an under-educated population to its tele-educational projects. This Pacific area was also used to test plans for satellite education using mobile ground stations.[6] All the conceptions that inspired US research into a model for tele-education for the proletarian nations are revealed by the Samoa project. Here is how the former director of the study describes the situation in Samoa before the development of the project: 'Originally, Samoa's education system rested entirely on ceremony. These ceremonies make them feel very big, very powerful. Their daily life was based on work, not education . . . The original system was based exclusively on the common language, its history and its culture . . . They learned relatively little of the outside world. In fact, no other world existed for them. Samoa was like a ghetto. They lived in an egalitarian fashion. The inhabitant of a Samoan village would give the wages he earned from his work to the head of the village, the *Matai*. All village families lived in the same way; they had equal rights to the same amount of food and clothing.'[7]

After carrying out a number of anthropological studies, the Foundation's experts recommended the following justification for using television: 'to give Samoa a better system of education'. Six television networks were set up with four studios. Every classroom had a television set. Daytime programmes were educational; in the evenings films and serials took over. 'We are trying to set outselves exacting standards in choosing films; it seems to us that *Disney* and *Bonanza* represent the purest kind of programme.' Here's our expert again to tell us the results of the project: 'When we started, they imported nothing, but nowadays the Samoans are beginning to fill their daily menus with foreign food. No one can live on coconuts, papayas and bananas for ever. And they're starting to find there are things which can make life a lot easier—like washing-machines, mopeds and automobiles. They're beginning to appreciate modern comforts and, to an extent, their life-style is changing. Before, they had to give back all their money to the head of the village and didn't get any luxuries in exchange. But now that they find they need money to live comfortably, they're abandoning all their old customs. They say: 'Look, I earn money. And I want money, because then I can buy a car and drive all the way from one end of the island to the other in the same day. We have brought change to Samoa, a higher standard of living . . . a healthier system. The United States has introduced proper drainage and a network of canals which means the population no longer has to depend on rain for its drinking water. There's a hospital now. *In my opinion, the inhabitants of Samoa have become more US oriented than before.* The Samoan system has been hailed as the most successful educational television in the world. Throughout my stay there we were visited by many representatives from different countries and government organisations who wanted to know why it was working so well there and why it isn't working here, in Iowa.'[8]

This cynically pastoral presentation of the age-old act of imperialist aggression as the awakening of the natives to the benefits of a sterile modernity needs no comment.

In 1967, the US government decided to set up a public television service, which became the fourth network (WNET 13/New York). At this time the Ford Foundation was the institution with the widest experience of tele-education as well as the greatest number of experts. Thus its contribution was indispensable and its earlier efforts paid off. It put the national system that it had established in the last few years at the disposal of the US Government and offered the services of its experts. From 1967, the Foundation became the main private moneylender to its former tele-education network, now promoted to the rank of a public channel (which some people called the government channel). A board with 15 members was given control; all of them came from business or government circles. Its first president had been Defense Secretary under Truman and also president of General Dynamics. The second president, appointed in 1973, was the former head of the famous US Government radio station 'The Voice of America'. The public TV network—the only non-commercial alternative to the oligarchy—has two sections: a central unit called the Corporation for Public Broadcasting (CPB) and another body, the Public Broadcasting System (PBS), which administers the various sections and distributes productions. Participating with Ford in the creation of the public network was the Carnegie Foundation which, since 1950, had also been exploring the problems of tele-education particularly with regard to the black population. The Carnegie Foundation, founded in 1911 by the famous steel magnate of the same name, had commissioned the famous Swedish economist Gunnar Myrdal to carry out a study in 1938 on the North American blacks (*An American Dilemma*) which has since become a classic. Ten years later, Carnegie established the Educational Testing Service (ETS) whose job was to advise universities on teaching matters and which was later transformed into one of the most important centres for the evaluation of the effects of tele-education series on children.

The children's television workshop

To consolidate the gains of recent years a new institution was needed, one which could make profitable use of the accumulated experience and regularly produce new programmes. The need was met by the Children's Television Workshop (CTW), a legally independent, non-profit making body. Although it started operating in 1968, its official existence dates from May 1970 when its aims and statutes were approved. These aims were: 'To find the best way of using electronic technology, especially television, as a medium for teaching children'. On the twelve-person board of the Workshop are politicians, directors of US educational television, university professors from Columbia, Duke, Harvard, Washington and Pennsylvania, a director of the Lehman Brothers banking group and the president of Texas Industries.[9] The president of this board, Lloyd N. Morrisett, a former professor at the University of California, was put in charge of the office for training of civilians working with the US Army in the Second World War and later held the post of president of the relatively small John and Mary R. Markle Foundation which until quite recently was almost exclusively involved in financing medical research. It changed course abruptly in 1969 and decided to support projects concerned with 'the educational use of the mass-media and communications technology'. (Founded in 1902, the John and Mary R. Markle Foundation takes its name from a coal magnate who controlled the anthracite industry in Pennsylvania at the end of the last century.)[10]

The presence of government functionaries and businessmen on the board of the Children's Television Workshop expressed for some their support for the programme's aims and for others the necessity of representing the sources of capital that made possible their manufacture. The first two series of US tele-education programmes destined to become models for future productions were developed in this context: *Sesame Street* and *The Electric Company*. The Children's Television Workshop spent about $4.3 million putting together the first 130 episodes of *Sesame Street* between 1968 and 1970 with an additional $2.6 million in support for its research and evaluation sections. During the financial year 1970–71, the Workshop made a further 145 episodes of *Sesame Street* and prepared its new children's series *The Electric Company*. Little by little, production costs rose to $4.75 million and other costs to over $2 million. In 1971–72 it began production of the first 130 episodes of *The Electric Company* and completed another 130 episodes of *Sesame Street*. By 1972 the annual budget of the Workshop had reached approximately $11 million. Where, then, did all this money come from? The bulk of it was from government sources,

Table 21

Sources of Finance for the Children's Television Workshop (1968–72)

Institution	Financial year and amount in $ million		
	1968–70*	1970–1	1971–2
US Dept. of Health, Education and Welfare (HEW)	4,000.0	2,900.0	7,000.0
Ford Foundation	1,538.0	1,000.0	1,000.0
Carnegie Foundation	1,500.0	600.0	1,000.0
J. and M. Markle Foundation	250.0	—	—
Corp. for Public Broadcasting (CPB)	750.0	500.0	2,000.0
Mobil Oil Corporation	—	—	250.0
Revenues from sources outside television	126.3	259.0	165.7
Other TV activities	206.7	84.0	—
Total	**8,371.0**	**5,343.0**	**11,415.7**

Source: *A special report from the Children's Television Workshop*, New York, 1972.
*Covers the two years from the launching of the Workshop.

channelled through the Health, Education and Welfare Department. The rest came from Foundations or big companies.

To interpret the accompanying table correctly, bear in mind the relationship that exists between the CPB (Corporation for Public Broadcasting) and the US Government, which subsidises it to the tune of $23 million to $30 million per annum. Equally important is the relationship of the Ford and Carnegie Foundations to the same CPB, the essential support for the public network. Thus in 1972, the Ford Foundation allocated over $15 million directly or indirectly to public educational television. Another significant index of government involvement in these programmes is the increase in its direct financial contributions from an initial 47% of the total budget to 61% by 1972. The statements of Education Department officials reveal unconditional support for the work done by the educational television workshop: 'When television's ability to draw and to hold an audience's attention is put to educational use, we know that the results can be quite remarkable,' declared the US Education Secretary. 'Overwhelming proof of that is provided by *Sesame Street*, the education programme for pre-school children that the Education Department helped to launch some years ago. *Sesame Street* is fast becoming a national institution and the best possible complement to existing educational programmes for these children. And, in my opinion it's one of the best investments the Education Department has ever made.'[11]

In 1972, the Television Workshop estimated that the cost of the *Sesame Street* series—watched by over 9 million US children out of a possible 12.5 million in its third year—was already 42 cents per viewer per year, that is one third of a cent per programme hour. Included in this figure are production, research and evaluation costs. In the first year the cost was 58 cents per child. The new series, *The Electric Company*, is more expensive. For an estimated audience of around 4 million children, its cost in the first year of transmission was $1.10 per viewer or one penny per viewer/programme.[12] The costs per viewer do not take into account foreign audiences—which have become increasingly important. When the original version of *Sesame Street* was put on the international market in 1968–70, 20 countries bought it. In 1971, 37, in 1972, 48. From this date foreign language versions (which include the adaptation to various 'national realities' as well as translation) went into production. In 1975 *Sesame Street* appeared in nearly 90 countries. What 'independent and non-profit making organisation' could manage to sell a tele-education series in so many countries only five years after its inauguration in New York—unless it used the vast distribution and political-commercial apparatus of the United States?

In fact, the countries that are so happily acquiring the US education series are financing the technological reform of education in the United States (which is thus likely to become the biggest bargain of all time) and handicapping themselves by not searching for alternative tele-education material. *Sesame Street*'s producers make no attempt to conceal their intention to institutionalise their mass line for education from above: 'our aim is to supply the highest quality in technology and education to the greatest number of children, especially in the poorer areas. And at the lowest cost.'[13] According to the projections of the Workshop's accountants, made just before the launching of the Spanish and Potuguese versions, Latin America offers a market of 22 million children of pre-school age for the Spanish version and 11 million for the Potuguese version.

A new patronage

The development of the new tele-education series took place on the margins of the commercial networks, which went as far as to reject any idea of a common project. This is how the president of the Federal Communications Commission described this decision: 'The refusal of television networks to finance *Sesame Street* has been one of the worst commercial decisions in history.' But outside the United States it is a different story. ABC, for example, has become the series' most loyal propagandist among its affiliated companies in Latin America. Once they are away from home, the two poles of US television unite in mutual support. The majority of countries lack an exclusively educational network so programmes like *Sesame Street* have to find a place on the commercial channels. And far from dropping into these channels like a dead weight, the education series plays a useful role in brushing up the image of the major commercial television companies. The clearest example of this comes from Mexican television. All the necessary proof can be found in the propaganda put out by the 'Televisa' monopoly to launch *Plaza Sesamo*: 'A healthy mind on a healthy screen, or rather a healthy mind on . . . *Plaza Sesamo*. A programme that is a part of our daily message—the message that we have developed with such care because it is aimed at children. Children—the most sensitive section of our community and the one on which we pin all our hopes for the future. To capture their attention, give direction to their boundless capacity for wonder and hold their interest, all in a spirit of happiness and entertainment—that's the task we've set ourselves on "Televisa" channels 2, 4, 5 and 8. With *Plaza Sesamo* we are beginning the changes that we've decided on to give more depth, more real content to Mexican television. Televisa. The Sign For Mexico. The Sign For Progress.'[14]

On the other hand, many multinational companies in the metropolis followed the development of the Children's Television Workshop from its inception. 'One of the most significant features of Sesame Street,' wrote an expert from the Federal Communications Commission, 'is that its success is largely due to the tremendous common effort made by the private and public sectors of American society.'[15] Mobil Oil paid for the handbooks distributed to parents so that they could help their children follow the new series. RCA made the Workshop a present of a large number of colour television sets to help them set up viewing centres up and down the country. The children's foods manufacturers, Quaker and General Foods, financed the preparation of a teacher's guide, and Time-Life published without charge a general guide to *Sesame Street* setting out the series' educational aims. So there were a whole range of contributions, of the classical type, based on nothing more than philanthropic concern.

Xerox, however, approached the Workshop with very different intentions, and succeeded in becoming the series' first promoter. As the leading reprographic company, looking for teaching models for its new acquisitions in the educational field, it was quick to see the interest it had in following the Workshop's productions. It wasn't by chance that

Xerox, after paying for most of the translation of *Sesame Street* into Spanish and Portuguese, in 1974 invited the director of the Children's Television Workshop to join its board, giving her the same status as the president of the Compagnie Financiere de Paris et des Pays-Bas.

Taken as a whole, these links have a wider interpretation. They show a change in the attitude of the major companies towards culture and the arts and are undoubtedly inspired by a need to polish up their image. At the same time as ITT was plotting against Allende, it was giving its patronage to the production of twentieth-century ballet in New York. While IBM was being hauled up before the anti-Trust committee, it was sponsoring an excellent documentary on madness on the public television network. The notions of 'quality of life' and 'public responsibility' were behind these new public relations exercises. The president of the oil company Atlantic Richfield[16] who had also become president of the Business Committee for the Arts summed up the nature of this evolution in the preface to the book *The State of the Arts and Corporate Support* published by the Committee in 1971: 'Many corporate executives are beginning to appreciate the importance of the arts and the responsibility of business to help support and expand the nation's cultural resources. However, their appreciation is often qualified by a natural caution about venturing into unfamiliar territory to seek alliances with those whose life style appears, at least on the surface, to be not only different from but even antagonistic to their own. On the other hand, many artists regard the corporation as a monolithic, "soulless" economic structure, dedicated exclusively to profit and, when it employs artists, a ruthless exploiter of talent. They are convinced that the corporate executive is a cultural illiterate who takes a narrowly pragmatic view of business responsibilities to the public. In turn, artists are still regarded by some businessmen as egocentric bohemians, who want a free and prosperous society but appear to be contemptuous of the complex social structures and the individual moral economy needed to achieve and sustain it. Twenty years ago, the attitude of the artist towards the businessman and the corporation might have had some basis in fact. I recall attending a seminar at Aspen then at which someone raised the question whether a corporation had any responsibilities beyond those of its stockholders. Several of those taking part in the seminar did not think it had, although at the time many corporations had begun to contribute regularly to the support of activities in health, education and welfare. Today practically all the business people who attend the Aspen seminars would unequivocally maintain that corporations have broad social responsibilities extending from responsibility for the welfare of their employees and the communities in which they do business to responsibility for help in solving problems that affect society as a whole.'[17] He knew what he was talking about. In 1968, the first eight companies to join this Committee for the Arts, founded in 1967 by the president of the Chase Manhattan Bank, David Rockefeller, poured $91 million into artistic and cultural activities in the United States. This is double the amount that these businessmen had spent on this field three years earlier.[18]

The contribution made to the public television network responded to this new situation. It was the head of public relations of WNET/13 himself who wrote the following: 'The corporate honor roll at WNET/13 and other public television production centers throughout the country includes many of America's most distinguished companies. Why? The desire to perform a public service, in making possible programs which otherwise could not be financed on public tv. To be recognised as socially responsible. To offset the negative corporate image effect of advertising. Many corporate pr conceptualizers understand the public's shoulder-shrugging response to corporate image commercials . . . Advertising has proved to be the greatest medium for creating sales, and commercial television is a most powerful advertising force. Public tv alone, however, offers the corporate underwriter the public perception of performing public service, with all the publicity, awards, community outreach opportunities and social responsibility image which ptv programing generates.'[19]

One of the reasons for the coming together of the worlds of the arts and of business was certainly the intensification of the financial difficulties faced by many organisations in the entertainments industry. Although the problem was not so great for the public network, its own expansion was equally threatened. In 1969, the Ford Foundation launched a major inquiry into the state of the arts and entertainment. The results of this inquiry showed that public and private patrons would have to increase their efforts greatly if they were to keep the US entertainments industries' output of artistic productions on the same level as in 1970–71. Without such supplementary aid the $62 million deficit of this period would increase fivefold.[20] The current contribution of the major US companies to the arts stands at around $100 million. Industrialists who understand these new conditions know they are in a position to bring pressure to bear on life-styles and productions in the arts. 'Business is also learning that much more than money is involved in the financial plight of the arts,' explained a member of the Business Committee for the Arts; 'imprudent handling of finances, last-minute, haphazard fund raising, failure to seek and develop new audiences, inefficient administrative practices, and poor public relations also contribute to annual net deficits. Business reasonably expects efficient administration and financial responsibility from the arts organisations that it helps to support so that the purely artistic functions of the organisations receive the maximum benefit from any financial assistance.'[21] It would be beyond the scope of this study to go more deeply into the new conditions of artistic production that come with the penetration of big business with its need for financial stability and certain profit. But it is certainly an area that would repay attention by anyone concerned with the role and status of the artist in the world of multinationals.

The relationship between the Children's Television Workshop and the major industries goes beyond a simple beneficiary-benefactor framework. It also takes on the character of mutual support, with the Workshop developing not only products for television but also a whole range of spin-offs, comics, puppets and all kinds of gadgets. And these are made thanks to deals with various firms: The Topper Company which produces educational toys; Marvel Comics, which loaned the Workshop a character to launch its series and then re-used it as a TV hero in a new cartoon strip; General Learning which provides audio-visual products. Western Publishing, the famous Walt Disney publishers, congratulates itself in its 1972 Annual Report on the excellent turnover that has enabled it to diversify more and more: 'the growing popularity of Sesame Street and Disney products, together with that of the "Golden Wonders of Growing" of the Sears company which has launched a range of pre-school educational toys has greatly helped the improvement in our trade.'[22] The Workshop's increasingly wide range of products stems from its ever-growing need for financial autonomy as it takes on the dynamic of the education industry. The funds handed over by the Education Department in 1973 only represented 40% of its total budget of $15 million; however, to this must be added the state subsidies to the public network which, in turn, contributes to the support of the Workshop (33%). In 1975 the overall production of the latter enabled it to achieve annual sales that reached $50 million. *Advertising Age* reported in August 1975, that 'New licensees signed since early this year include J. C. Penney Co. for a Sesame Street apparel line (from infants' sleep-wear to pre-teen sportwear); Burlington Domestics for bedding and sleepwear; Fisher-Price for Play Village Sesame Street; Milton Bradley Co. for games, Playskool puzzles and Amsco Sesame Street and Mr Hooper's Store Play-In sets; Knickerbocker Toy Co for Muppets dolls; Bradley Time for Muppets watches and alarm clocks; Owens-Illinois' Lily division for paper cups, plates and napkins. Since last fall Marvel Comics has published a Spidey Super Stories comic book for beginning and poor readers, without ads; Spider-Man has also been featured in segments on the Public Broadcasting Series.'[23]

A challenge to universal success

From its first appearance on the market, *Sesame Street* was hailed as the prototype of 'international television'. UNESCO's *Le Courrier* (February 1971) joined the chorus of praise. Didn't the fact that it had been accepted in so many countries and translated into so many languages confirm that this new teaching model was spreading throughout the world. (Already there was Bonjour Sesame— admittedly a very mutilated version—Sesamstrasse, Sesamstraat, Sesam, Vila Sesamo, Plaza Sesamo.) However, there were still some countries where the series met stubborn resistance and it was precisely on this supposed universality that the opposition based its arguments. Resistance grew in widely differing conditions and came from a variety of viewpoints.

In Britain, *Sesame Street* came up against a categorical rejection from the BBC in 1970 and this position has never been revoked. BBC's Head of Children's Programmes explained why her department had decided that the programme was not going to be the daily television fare for under-fives in Britain in the *Guardian* on 22 December 1970: '(1) It is an American programme which has been built on the television experience of American children, most of whom have until now only watched endless cartoons, commercials, soap operas and crime series. In this country, children have been in the more fortunate position of having a variety of high quality programmes specially made for them. Indeed, the BBC was the first television organisation in the world to recognise the needs of young children when it began *Watch With Mother* specially for them 20 years ago, and more recently when extra broadcasting hours became available they were used for repeats of *Play School* on BBC 1. Do we really have to import commercial hard-selling techniques into our own programmes because Sesame Street researchers tell us that in America children will not watch anything quiet or thoughtful? (2) Sesame Street is an outcome of a philosophy of ever-available "wall-paper" TV programming. American children watch television for hours on end. In all the programmes we make for British children we set out to discourage passive box-watching: our aim is to provide an imaginative and intellectual stimulus and to encourage creativity and activity. Surely it is more valuable to watch with concentration and involvement for the 20 minutes of *Play School* and then to go off and do something suggested by the programme than to be hypnotised into gazing for an hour at a succession of fast-moving images which may often be incomprehensible to a four-year-old. (3) Sesame Street claims to be an educational programme and uses didactic teaching methods which we consider inappropriate for a mass medium. Television can never be a substitute for the actual contact between a child and his mother, his companions or his teacher. Our job is to provide the best possible programmes to enrich and stimulate and entertain.'

The Ministry of Education in Peru, which had undertaken a reform of the education system, rejected the series in 1973. The arguments used to explain this decision centred in particular on the incompatibility of the aims of the reform and the ideological framework of the North American programme. Here are some extracts from the paper presented by a Peruvian psychologist which formed the basis of the government's decision: 'Plaza Sesamo has a concept of strongly directed and vertical participation. The older stars always prompt children to create the learning structure. Our Reform has clearly defined that which is important in the act of participation is the spontaneous desire and creative collaboration capable of generating replies from the bottom upwards (. . .) (moreover) the established system of passing from one scene to another, through short colour segments supported by musical effects, persuades the child to have a concept of order that is totally rigid, invariable and depersonalised . . . to train children through powerful audio-visual means in strict frameworks, is totally contrary to the spirit of the General Law of Education.'[24] It should be noted that, unlike Great Britain, which had been offered the original version, Peru, in common with all the other Latin American countries (which had unanimously accepted it), would have had the series in the adapted version made in Mexico under the sponsorship of Xerox and the Ford Foundation who had taken the trouble to use the services of a team of professors and University researchers from all the interested countries. One example—among many—of the decentralisation process in imperialist culture, in which representatives of the creole ruling classes are delegated to adapt the master-product to meet 'national needs'.

Plaza Sesamo was introduced in Chile on the network belonging to the Catholic University, one of the main bases of the counter-revolution. Its introduction coincided with the launching of an ideological campaign by the right against the education reforms proposed by Popular Unity, a campaign whose main slogan was: 'The new school is not Chilean because it is based on foreign experiments that are incompatible with Chilean idiosyncrasies.' But the same right that rejected supposedly foreign criteria welcomes Plaza Sesamo with open arms. Sheltering behind the so-called neutrality of a series whose intentions were 'to teach children the alphabet and basic arithmetic, to widen their vocabulary and stimulate their powers of region', the right was well aware that the programmes were unlikely to diminish the middle class's fascination with US values and life-styles. The presentation of a social harmony guaranteed by everyone playing their given part (nurse, mechanic, shopkeeper, lorry-driver) joined with the corporatist image of society and allowed certain sectors of the counter-revolution to inflame opposition to the principle of class struggle. At the same time as the strikers, on the pretext of 'defending their strict professional interests' were unleashing violence and terrorism, young Chilean viewers were being taught the justice of a system based on accepting the intangible principle of the social division of labour. While they could see social conflict all around them and the foundations of authority being radically questioned, children were every day learning to keep their eyes glued on a world where all the different interests seemed to dissolve into a series of never-changing roles: mother, father, policeman, farmer, family. Thanks largely to the appeal of its up-to-date technique, *Sesame Street* met with little opposition. Only a few isolated criticisms came from certain sections of the left who pointed out how much the US series clashed with the principles of the United National School. This was the project for democratising teaching that aimed at reconciling manual and intellectual labour, theory and practice, study and production, by breaking down the barriers of narrow specialisation, bringing together the school and other institutions and establishing new relations between teachers, parents and pupils—in other words, at extending the concept of popular power into this traditional bastion of the bourgeois State.

It is quite significant that it is precisely the social framework of the series that is altered in the mutilated French version, *Bonjour Sesame* (cf. footnote 30). The whole social backdrop against which the actions take place in the US series is missing. It is no accident that the French version—which is considerably abridged—is the only one not to mention, in the title, the place, the street, where all the characters, great or small, play out their roles, the microcosm where the archetypes of a whole society are reproduced. The same fear of social specificity, of anything that might suggest the insertion of a determined product into a story, shows itself in the French translations of Walt Disney cartoons, where all the explicitly political terms have been removed—terms like revolution, revolutionary, etc. But then, for the first time in the international TV market, the producers of *Sesame Street* have done everything in their power to make the adaptations as flexible as possible. Two alternatives are open to foreign buyers. The 'co-production' format with about half the material of the new series taken from the North American programme and the other half produced locally in the country in question; or the 'open sesame' format, which consists of a continuous stock of segments usually of 13 to 27 minutes duration, all chosen from the original version. As for English-speaking countries, they are entitled to the complete unrevised original version.

Marketing techniques in education

With the dual objective of instruction and entertainment, the new US tele-education series offer themselves as an alternative as much to traditional teaching as to the equally traditional concept of commercial television in which leisure is brutally separated from 'productive' daily life. The series try to re-unite these two words by providing a more integrated solution. 'A correct use of television should combine education and amusement. If a programme doesn't hold a child's attention, then he won't watch it. And if he doesn't watch it regularly, then he won't profit from it to the full.'[25] So the series attempts to entertain *and* instruct, and to do this by borrowing formulae from traditional mass culture, formulae which in themselves are not explicitly educational. But, in every sense, they pay a high price for this.

In order to unite education and entertainment, the *Sesame Street* experiment relies on the conditioned reflexes created by commercial television on the young audience. According to a study of children in the US, millions aged between two and eleven watch an average of three and a half hours of television per day. By the age of twelve, children will have spent twice as much time in front of the television set as at school. Those who conceived the series do not hesitate to admit to appropriating the whole range of techniques used by the producers of mass culture: 'The techniques developed by commercial television and advertising have proved their ability to entice children into watching all sorts of programmes, even those they do not want to watch. The television workshop has decided to explore these techniques in order to use them for education purposes. Its research has shown that such techniques can be used to great effect in programmes of the Sesame Street format. The first three years of broadcasting of the series has confirmed this.'[26]

It is in this fundamental assumption that the ideological choice of US tele-education producers is revealed. It may seem paradoxical that the series resorts to using techniques that are by definition simply manipulation—which has reached an advanced stage of development in their society—to make attractive an education that is supposed to be liberating. It doesn't seem as if the obviously ideological character of the techniques was ever questioned in the initial studies. Instead the series' controllers see them as a repertoire of tricks and illusions that can catch the public's attention. For them, it seems, these techniques have no values in themselves; their value comes from the product they are advertising or launching on the market. If the object or attitude being promoted is frivolous, then the technique will add to the harm done to the audience. If, on the other hand, the product on offer is a positive one, then the technique will be the instrument for attracting the viewer. Consequently, these premises assumed that 'communications techniques' are intrinsically neutral (and so is the whole apparatus of science and technology as the episodes in the series dealing with science and scientists clearly show). They only take on significance through the purposes to which they are put—positive or negative, good or bad. Through this moralistic conception of the media—good and innocent or bad and guilty according to whether its aims are worthy or unworthy—runs the very simplified myth of technocratic ideology. Its conservative conclusions are obvious: existing cultural forms are the only ones which can communicate reality; all we can change is the content of the messages they carry.

By analysing the ideological struggle which developed in concrete situations—during, for example, the period of Popular Unity in Chile—we were able to demonstrate the impossibility of thinking about 'communications techniques' (where does the definition of a communications technique begin and end?) outside their specific conditions of production.[27] These techniques do not simply represent the means of producing communication, television and education; they correspond to the total reproduction of the life of a particular social system. They are part of a larger structure, and they reproduce the authority relations which inspired their production. In attempting, through 'captivating' techniques, to secure the viewer's attention, the producers of *Sesame Street* inevitably run the risk of achieving their objective (the audience's attention) by confirming the audience's status as passive consumers, trapped in a circle of manipulation. The very techniques which are used cannot escape the accusation levelled against *Sesame Street*—that, contrary to its proclaimed intentions, it is authoritarian. It is authoritarian as much in terms of the 'means' which are used to guarantee teaching success as in terms of the place occupied by the child in the configuration of social relations where the notion of participation is enacted.

Another important, and rather unexpected, indication of an interplay of the world of advertising and *Sesame Street*'s model of tele-education, is the fact that three years after it was launched the model was picked up by advertisers who found certain formulae in the series capable of revitalising their language and increasing their success among certain social groups. An editorial dated 5th February 1973 in *Advertising Age*, the mouthpiece of US advertising agencies, demonstrates this 'boomerang effect': 'When we watch shows like Sesame Street and The Electric Company, we see again what fantastic communications challenges abound on TV. These shows, having borrowed advertising techniques to get their start, are now in a position to teach their teachers . . . We urge advertisers and agencies to learn from Sesame Street and Electric Company. Try harder to produce informative and entertaining commercials, not just spots that sell. Inform the youngsters. Upgrade their lives; don't merely sell to them. Do this, and you will enable your young audience to grow into more productive, more effective persons. And as the children grow and enter the adult world, they become (crass words) better citizens, better consumers . . . We are on the threshold of this right now. Miles Laboratories is distributing ten TV public service commercials that will teach children—and adults who watch them—about nutrition. The spots are to be scheduled on children's programs. Miles is paying for the commercials but there is no "sell" in the accepted sense. Miles, a maker of vitamins, figures the payoff comes later, as youngsters become interested in better nutrition. And Kellog Co. is doing almost the same thing, sending out TV spots that talk to children about better nutrition. The spots close with, "presented in the interest of good nutrition by Kellogg".' In 1974 a major US building materials company used *Sesame Street* methods to boost its sales. *Business Week* gave three full pages to this initiative in the Industrial Marketing section of the 11th May 1974 issue.

The uncritical acceptance of sales methods is revealed in the way the series' producers assess the effects of these methods upon children. Their group of researchers—an army of psychologists, teachers and other specialists—assembled, for the first time ever, a large body of material on the effects of a television series upon a given section of the public.[28] But these 'studies' were in fact conducted along the lines of market research. These are the kinds of questions they asked: '(1) Do children between the ages of 3 and 5 who watch Sesame Street at home or at school learn more than children of similar backgrounds who do not watch Sesame Street? (2) Among those children who do watch the programme, what kind of children learn most/least? (3) Is the programme less effective within certain sub-categories of children between the ages of 3 and 5? For example, does the effectiveness of the series vary according to sex, social class, attentiveness, motivation, etc.? (4) As Sesame Street has opted for a magazine type format, which parts of the programme are best at holding the child's attention and enabling him to learn as much as possible?'[29]

The results of the research show, for example, that after *Sesame Street*'s first season, the total increase in knowledge among 'the most deprived' children had been 9% for those who watched the programmes occasionally, 15% for those who watched it 2 or 3 times a week, 19% for those who watched it 4 or 5 times, and 25% for those who watched it more than 5 times a week. The estimation of children's progress takes into account the specific objectives of the series. The percentage increases in each category and sub-category were based on an ability to locate, name and describe the functions of various parts of the human body: they were also based on an ability to grasp relative concepts (same/different, bigger/smaller, more/less, ideas of time, etc.) and on an ability to recognise shapes, patterns, social entities, inter-relations and so on until all the objectives of the series had been covered.[30]

Research for *The Electric Company* showed that 'the audience from 7 to 10 years of age is more selective and demanding than the pre-school audience of *Sesame Street*. They have different interests, different viewing patterns. Degrees of attentiveness very considerably and this shows that the teaching must be presented more consistently and more precisely . . . Our producers and researchers, working as a team, studied the audience to find out the most appropriate way of teaching children to read in the new series. They discovered, for example, that this age group responds readily to music and that this can be a real stimulus to them'. (That is why *The Electric Company* set up its own pop group, composed of children from the age group at which the series is aimed.) The researchers also discovered that 'action sequences and comedy sketches go down well and that to point a moral directly jars with children of that age'. The series incorporated the results of this research. 'The series conveys instruction under the guise of fun. Cartoons, including letters which move across the screen, were very enthusiastically received by children. We will make the most of this by using a wide variety of electronic and cinematic techniques to make writing more fun. We have also got together a marvellous group of actors and actresses who perform all kinds of roles in sketches linked to the programs' educational objectives. In television parlance this is known as magazine format. That means that the program will consist of short and varied segments, calling on music, cartoons, comedy sketches and electronic effects carefully programmed and assembled to round off the curriculum.'[31]

In the voluminous questionnaires prepared by the Educational Testing Service (ETS) of the Carnegie Foundation and by Ford Foundation specialists, there is not the slightest hint of a question that would allow us to measure, or even suspect, the presence (subconscious or otherwise) of the chosen formats and well-known tricks borrowed from advertising techniques. The producers of the series fail to question the social setting of the characters used to sugar the teaching pill: nor do they question the social framework of the particular medium in which they are working. Their account only slightly modifies the series; it remains within parameters which are those of 'mind-warders' of 'the television revolution'. To study the effects of the new tele-education (in the way study is conceived by the producers) is systematically to confirm the objectives which the producers themselves have established. It is a question merely of administering and planning the contents of the series whose job is to teach children to count, spell and learn the names of things, and neglect everything which does not fit in with things as they are (the acceptance of the adult's domination of the child, of competition, of money, private property, etc.). This 'research' accepts all the assumptions of conventional communications research, that branch of empirical sociology, born in the shadow of market research agencies, which has always been content to ratify the rules of the system.

Bertolt Brecht said: 'In the interests of production, entertainment in capitalist society is condemned to a non-productive roles.' The producers of *Sesame Street* would answer that it is also very much in the interests of production to condemn entertainment to a productive role. The dialectical exchange between tele-education and marketing involves much more than the transfer of new teaching methods to industry and vice-versa, as anyone who takes the trouble to read between the lines can see. It reveals how the norms of 'Taylorism', which governed the industrial practice of US corporations, are invading the educational sphere. Having organised the output of factories, the doctrine and practice of 'Taylorism' now presides over the tightening up of the ideological apparatus to watch over the commercial potential of minds.

The rationalisation of social control

Until recently, US producers of mass culture had not taken the trouble to consider the impact of their television series, magazines and other cultural merchandise upon the public, except through the study of audience ratings. Nor have they been concerned with cataloguing their objectives. Most commercial television writing is left to writers who think within a liberal framework of creativity and inspiration. This approach is ratified throughout television, from commercial reports to script-writers' comments.

One of the creators of *Maverick, 77 Sunset Strip, The Fugitive* and *Run For Your Life* gives his reasons for the mediocrity of most television series. For him, it is firstly a question of deploring the lack of talent: 'There simply isn't enough of it to fit today's needs. Those needs have never been so great in human history. Our civilisation consumes more culture than any other since earliest times—consumes it and demands more. The demand is insatiable . . . But it isn't only talented writers that are needed in the entertainment industry. The shortage also extends to directors, producers, actors, editors, composers—all the creative contributors.' Then, the lack of time. It is impossible to conduct any audience research before the programme is shown. The writer sometimes has to accept a commission for four shows at a time in order to survive slack periods. The question of the budget would come only fourth or fifth in a list of factors preventing the production of good quality commercial television programmes. Finally, there is the restriction on time imposed by television formats. The freedom of the cinema is not enjoyed in television work. However, in the view of this particular script-writer, all these obstacles are relatively insignificant compared to the one central problem: the nature of the audience. 'One of the biggest deterrents to television quality is the nature of the audience itself. The harsh fact is that you cannot, for any length of time, produce television entertainment at a level above the taste of the people for whom it is being made . . . The mass audience resists the new, the provocative, the disturbing, the controversial, the subtle. That audience has demonstrated that it wants continuing characters, preferably ones that are lovable. Hence anthology-shows, which could offer a variety of characters, locales and situations each week, become difficult to sell. Most of all, the mass audience demands a moral universe that is stereotypical. The mass audience will not accept the world as it is but only as it appears through the dark glass of convention. This tends to limit the television series to hackneyed, dishonest material.' Having outlined the difficulties he encountered in trying to introduce into his teleplays another type of requirement, he concluded: 'If I have sounded dissatisfied or unhappy with television it was not my intention. I am inclined to agree with Sir Robert Fraser, who recently said: "Every person of common sense knows that people of superior mental constitutions are bound to find much of television intellectually beneath them. If such innately fortunate people cannot realise this gently and with good manners, if in their hearts they despise popular pleasure and interest, then, of course, they will be angrily dissatisfied with television. But it is not really television with which they are dissatisfied. It is with people".'[32] It is with prejudice of this kind that television's version of the average viewer emerges—just as it does in other mass media. In fact, it is an implicit need to guarantee the reproduction of a particular set of social relations which makes the products of the mass culture empire so uniform. But the producers of the new tele-education series have given more thought to their targets.

At the same time as giving rise to a rationalisation of the message's objectives, *Sesame Street* provided a chance to check out the audience. Interdisciplinary teams, whose task is to monitor the series' effects, maintain a flow of information which helps to manufacture products that are particularly well adapted to the various realities to which they pretend to address themselves. In April 1973, the CTW's international section announced the completion of the first survey of the effects of Plaza Sesamo in Mexico, concentrating on a group of children in working class districts. It was also announced that further surveys were under way in Brazil, Colombia, Chile, and several other countries where the series was being broadcast. They were all financed by the Ford Foundation.[33]

The producers' concern with assessing the reception of the message is not an isolated phenomenon. It fits in with a preoccupation common to US university departments, foundations and official organisations—that of planning the contents of their cultural exports whose sales potential has considerably increased thanks to new technological developments. We read in a report from the John and Mary Markle Foundation that 'People complain a good deal about television and the press, and many suggestions are made for new experiments: but there is an unfortunate lack of empirical knowledge on which to base public discussion, or even discussion among experts working in that field. There are not enough researchers to scientifically investigate the mass media and to try to resolve the methodological problems which those investigations would pose. There is a great need to study the impact of the media'. The same report goes on to say: 'Although it is widely acknowledged that television and the printed word have profound effects upon our lives, little is known about these effects. On reason for the lack of progress in this field is simply its complexity. Many factors intervene: the environment, the state of mind of the viewer, the frequency of exposure to the media. Moreover, the effects are always cumulative, which is to say they are produced only after a certain period of time'.[34] This diagnosis formed the basis for a new research policy for the Foundation which finances not only the CTW but also the most esteemed communications departments in the United States like those at the Universities of Michigan and Stanford, departments which have helped to set up educational television systems throughout the Third World.

Specialised concepts of mass audiences

What characterises mass culture, as the phrase suggests, are the norms it adopts in order to reach the greatest possible number of people. The typical viewer, elevated to the status of representative of the mass by this culture, and to whose hypothetical requirements all its products are tailored, is not explicitly located in a particular social group. In the first place, the choice of this criterion is made for commercial reasons, to attract a wide audience. This is made clear in the policy pursued by Proctor and Gamble when choosing the type of programme which the company should sponsor: 'nothing in the material should directly or indirectly offend any minority group, organisation, inhabitant of a particular state or region, or any commerical organisation. The material should not be critical of political organisations, philanthropic or reform societies, women's group, etc. . .".[35] But the choice of a prototype viewer which determines capitalist models of mass communication does not merely obey commercial ends. It also corresponds to a theory and practice which legitimates all bourgeois institutions. In class society, the organisational model of mass communications is based, in the last resort, on the bourgeoisie's theory of public opinion. Democracy operates above all on the principle of the majority vote. The policies and candidates voted in by the majority are seen as sources of authority. Public opinion becomes confused with the opinion of a majority—supposedly the common expression of a common interest. In keeping with the ways in which the system is reproduced, this theory of public opinion legitimates the decisions of its representative chambers, founded upon the principle of the majority vote, and also the system's ideological apparatus. In the same way that the constitution which established formal democracy tries to embrace each individual citizen, yet is aimed at citizens in general, so the bourgeois apparatus of communication cannot give up the attempt to be commercial unless it also abandons its role as self-appointed representative of the majority. In principle, the media's supposed objectivity and impartiality guarantee their relevance for the entire population—for public opinion—rather than for any particular social class. Gramsci made the point that the bourgeois press unifies its heterogeneous public by 'addressing itself to everyone and to no one'. The common denominator which unifies the audience of the mass media is this average man, this 'common man' who does not in fact exist.

Any paper produced by North American empiricist communications experts will contain a resumé of the interests of this common man. They serve as the platform from which a concensus is proclaimed. Everyone, it seems, shares an interest in '(a) violence, conflict, racial problems, competition and war; (b) love and sex, revealed in our society by a fondness for love stories, family life, children and divorce; (c) the unusual, the exciting, the out-of-the-ordinary; (d) new inventions and other evidence of what is called progress, reflecting general approval of changes in our society; (e) fashion and top people; (f) situations which demand our sympathy and pity; (g) a range of other topics like old people and animals'.[36]

But the model proposed by tele-education pushes aside this generalised and insipid account of the viewer and replaces it with a detailed analysis of the audience drawn up according to the specific interests of specific age-groups. This same approach forms the basis of new research programmes in the field of communications set up by certain university departments and foundations. This area was opened up by technological advances in the field of communications. 'One of the major objectives of the Foundation at the moment is to experiment with forms of communication which distinguish between various kinds of viewers. As currently conceived, the media try to serve a mass audience. As a result, individual needs are not taken into account, and the media's content degenerates to the lowest possible common denominator. This means that in a country where everyone is a member of a minority group, no one is properly catered for. Given that the population is divided by class, profession, education, race, geography, age, etc., the media's critics recognise an urgent need for a greater number of specialised programmes.'[37] Obviously, to take into account the interests and needs of each group is not to call into question the class interests which define the ideological apparatus as a totality. The producers of *Sesame Street* express this in their own terms. 'We must help more deprived children to overcome their social and educational backwardness and allow them to reach the same educational level as their middle-class colleagues.'[38] This is the only place where a concept of class appears. On the other hand, the *Sesame Street* producers clearly display their reticence with regard to the question of class when it comes to describing the young public that their programmes are aimed at: this public is described by all the euphemisms of the politics of integration, 'disadvantaged children', 'deprived children', 'low income groups', 'districts where poverty reigns'.

Community development through television

In 1973, Jack Vaughn was appointed director of the Children's Television Workshop's international section, in charge of promoting and selling the Workshop's productions, and of packaging various foreign language adaptations. During the 1960's, Jack Vaughn had been the Director General of the Peace Corps. He had been instrumental in modernising the work of these groups of well-meaning young Americans in the Third World by giving them access to electronic technology. He was the first person to recognise the need to integrate these agents of US foreign policy into the various branches of tele-education and educational technology. Thanks to Vaughn, the Westinghouse Corporation began to organise volunteers to be sent to Brazil, Colombia, South Korea and Morocco. In Colombia, secondary schools were used as guinea pigs for this process of modernisation. A decree signed by the Colombian Ministry of Education in 1968 raised the Peace Corps 'to the status of an advisory service on education'. 'The Ministry of Education, the Institute of Science, university education departments and Peace Corps volunteers will give every assistance to secondary schools and colleges using the new methods.'[39] The Ford Foundation also chose Colombia as a laboratory. In 1970 and 1971, the Foundation handed out more than $1 million to various Ministry of Education centres and universities in order to research and develop tele-education, and to assess ways of 'bringing up to date science teaching and teacher training' and of 'monitoring the pre-school education of children from the cities'.[40] At the end of President Johnson's term of office, Vaughn was appointed US Ambassador to Colombia.

The appearance of the former head of the Peace Corps in the Children's Television Workshop was no coincidence. The principles which informed the production and distribution of these new series came directly out of a concept of community development which, having been applied in imperialised countries under the auspices of the Alliance for Progress, was then used back in the metropolis to solve urban problems, especially among ethnic minorities. Much of the thinking of Ford Foundation specialists abroad was oriented towards the need to integrate these minorities at home. Here are a few paragraphs from the Ford Foundation's Annual Report for 1971. 'Another phenomenon with decisive educational implications is obviously the deep frustration experienced by minority groups. Blacks, Puerto Ricans, Mexican-Americans and North American Indians have in the 1960's for the first time seen a light at the end of the long tunnel of their segregated lives. Quite understandably they wanted to enjoy society's benefits much sooner than society had made provisions for. So they adopted a new and much more aggressive approach, seeking to use their political power to achieve their ends. The youth, in particular, has opted for new forms of separation, based on a sense of group identity and proud self-assertion. All these movements have had an effect on educational institutions, which had begun to open their doors to an increasing number of students from the ethnic minorities. The result is that, as was the case immediately after World Ward II, there is great pressure on higher education institutions ... The Foundation considers that the most sensitive problem for the United States is that of granting full democratic rights to minority groups and to poorer sections of society. For some time those rights have been both promised and refused. The Foundation's work is aimed essentially at solving this problem.' This ideology—the integration of marginal social groups—informs not only the series' social perspectives, but also the organisation of the community's consumption of those programmes.

Any careful viewer of *Sesame Street* is immediately struck by the obvious presence of this ideological trait. Originally intended to combat 'slow learning and social deprivation' among 'poor children' of the US ghettos, *Sesame Street* could not upset the balance of the system, and had to present an ideal setting of peaceful co-existence inspired both by the dominant class's utopian vision of integration and by its repressive policies, under the cover of a paternalistic concern for the ethnic minorities. In *Sesame Street*, Blacks, Puerto Ricans and Whites cheerfully forget about social and racial barriers. As the UNESCO *Courier* stresses: 'In most countries, young viewers are offered a staple diet of violence. *Sesame Street* is unique in its wit and general good humour. In it we find not a trace of aggression, and it tries to promote the splendid idea that there is no problem in the world that cannot be solved through co-operation.'[41] The violence which is an everyday fact of life for 'small poor children' (and that includes that part of their everyday life spent as passive spectators within the series' own hierarchical teaching situation) is just magicked away by the show. It is here that the phrase 'television revolution' assumes its fullest meaning. The show absolves the system of all its inherent misery.

Another aspect of this participationist ideology can be found in the infrastructure established by the makers of tele-education to organise the programme's reception. 'No commercial network had done sufficient research to be able to assess the educational needs of low-income group communities, and before *Sesame Street*, public television had small audiences ... The Workshop realised from the outset that it had to concentrate on attracting audiences from poorer districts. ...'. From the very first season of *Sesame Street* the producers found a new way of promoting the series: 'At that time we put into operation a plan of community action, without precedent in television history, which aimed to stimulate young viewers and to make their parents participate more fully in their children's pre-school education'.[42] These activities took on such importance that the Workshop set up a community relations department with an even larger budget (almost $1 million in 1972) than the research department.

During the second season of *Sesame Street*, fourteen cities in the most heavily populated regions of the United States were chosen and in each city a co-ordination centre was set up. The function of these centres was to increase audience figures by adapting the business concept of after-sales service to 'electronic education'. This emphasised 'selling programmes by encouraging their use', and had three main aims: (1) to explain the objectives of the series through personal contacts; (2) to improve those facilities which enable people to watch the series, and to make post-viewing activities more thorough, thereby reinforcing the learning process; (3) to distribute more educational material based on the *Sesame Street* curriculum (toys, booklets, magazines, records, puppets, etc.). A further aim was to draw community organisations into the 'active' consumption of the series. It was decided to set up community television centres in poor districts. A network of sales and distribution for magazines and manuals was organised through public libraries, church and other neighbourhood organisations. Seminars for parents, social workers and teachers were organised to allow them to assess the series' teaching methods and to integrate them into these wider activities. All the community development organisations, based on the Peace Corps, were mobilised. In the opinion of the Workshop's experts, these promotional activities in the community allowed them, during the first two years of operation, to maintain close contact with half a million children. But to get closer to the heart of the enterprise, we should read the editorial letter from the director—a young black woman (of course!)—of the magazine *Sesame Street*, which appeared in the Spanish edition, aimed at Puerto Ricans and Chicanos. 'For thousands of children all over the world, Sesame Street doesn't stop when the programme finishes. These children watch the programme in centres specially built for watching Sesame Street (Sesame Street Viewing Centres). And after each programme they spend between half an hour and an hour playing, singing and taking part in activities which help them to understand the lessons which Sesame Street teaches. What is a Sesame Street Viewing Centre? It can be a classroom, an empty shop, a room in a church. Try asking local organisations or local firms to donate the necessary materials. Use your imagination! Pillows or cardboard boxes make fine furniture. You can make toys and building blocks out of plastic bottles, egg-boxes and milk bottles. Take out books and records for the children from the local library. Parents, pensioners and students can make excellent volunteer teachers. Sesame Street magazine's handbook for parents has all kinds of suggestions for helping children to learn. Think up some more! For further information, contact the Viewing Centre, Children's Television Centre, Broadway, New York . . . .'.[43]

The organisation of *Sesame Street*'s reception was a kind of acid test, and was the most difficult aspect of the project, due to the isolation of the pre-school public. *The Electric Company*—the second programme—gained a mass audience more quickly, thanks largely to the availability of community centres used by school-children between the ages of seven and ten. The series became so popular that the US Education Department congratulated the Workshop's experts, pointing out that 'perhaps no other innovation in the history of education had made its presence felt among so many people in so short a time'.[44] (Two months after its first showing the series was being used by 23% of US primary schools.) It was also as a back-up to this second programme that the Children's Television Workshop opened up new experimental fronts in Third World countries, using television-based models of community development. This time it was a Caribbean country which was used as a laboratory. Jamaica, which had been the first foreign country to show *Sesame Street*, was subjected to more pilot schemes when *The Electric Company* was launched as the starting-point of a new adult literacy project. In 1973 this programme had already been broadcast in other Caribbean countries (besides being shown in the United States and Jamaica), like Trinidad and Tobago, Barbados, etc. To help prepare the campaign, a group of students from the University of New York spent four months in Jamaica training hundreds of Jamaican volunteers as monitors for the literacy projects based on *The Electric Company*. Fully supported by the Jamaican government, the campaign's goal was 'to teach more than half a million people to read and write within four years'.[45] Jamaica was also chosen for another CTW experiment. A special study was carried out to assess the impact of television, and its educational potential, for children who had not previously been exposed to the medium. Armed with a videotape system courtesy of Sony, with batteries charged by a Suzuki jeep, a team from Harvard showed *Sesame Street* in mountain villages to find out the reactions of people who had never before seen television. The responses of young viewers were video-taped. The findings from this ground work were used at Harvard by the Children's Television Research Centre, established jointly by the CTW and the Harvard education department, thanks to funding from the Ford and Carnegie Foundations.

Cable TV communities

This type of operation, which makes a television programme the basis of community organisation, was used in an offensive conducted by powerful groups within the system itself to set up a model of communication which makes the 'participation' of the viewing public possible in the transmission of messages. Held back for more than twenty-five years, cable television is now available to the public and is, in principle, a technological medium which could tend to break down the vertical relationship which defines traditional communication. The fact that the nexus of possible broadcasters can suddenly be massively enlarged has already caused the US authorities great anxiety. They issued a number of decrees with the aim of avoiding the 'random' use of this new medium. Since its invention, the problem of how cable television can be institutionalised has been a major concern. As was pointed out in an Alfred P. Sloan Foundation report published in 1970: 'The televised message, like the press, can cause panic and chaos. Who will control its use? And how can we ensure that its power will not be abused?'[46] (It is not only the US government that is afraid of the political consequences of the use of this medium. In France the distribution of cable television is being held up, while discussions on how the Ministry of the Interior can make use of TV information systems are well under way. The fact that no funds were provided in the 'VIIth Plan' seems to confirm that the powers-that-be want to delay the unleashing of cable television as long as possible).[47]

In the United States, the subversive potential of this new technology—whose appearance coincides with a generalised fragmentation of the social order—is neutralised by placing it in the hands of existing institutions. For example, licences are granted to use television stations in different communities to broadcast plays or talks by scientists and other specialists, or to facilitate some degree of community participation in the local council and criticism of representatives. If the use of the new technology follows the line of existing institutions, then the 'democratisation' of mass communications is guaranteed against any transgression of the system's code, while still maintaining the illusion of 'letting people have their say'.

The powers that are organising and institutionalising the development of cable television are the very same 'establishment' institutions which presided over the 'television revolution' when tele-education began. As well as General Motors' Sloan Foundation, they include, as we have seen, the Ford, Carnegie and Markle Foundations. They do not act alone, and their role usually consists of co-ordinating plans and supervising their execution. They work in conjunction with the Think Tanks, like the Rand Corporation. In 1970, the Rand Corporation was assigned by the J. and M. Markle Foundation to analyse the various aspects of controlling the developing cable television industry, and to determine its educational potential. The same Foundation asked MITRE to assess the feasibility of a cable communication system in urban areas. The Ford Foundation helped to set up the national information centre on cable television. All these Think Tanks drew up the plans for the future 'cable community', which promised each cable television user an increase in, and improvement of, the services provided. All citizens would be in direct contact with information banks and would have at their disposal new alarm-systems against theft, short-circuits, fire, etc. They would live in a society without 'liquid' money, as their televisions would be connected to banking facilities; they would be able to receive any document through a reprographic network; they could do their shopping without leaving the house. And in terms of entertainment, there would be a huge choice of programmes. Other services would put them in contact with global news systems. These organisations, Foundations and Think Tanks have all proposed that this new technology be put to educational use. The Ford and Rand Foundations, for example, proposed to the Federal Commission of Communications that two national networks in the television satellite system be reserved exclusively for educational broadcasting. They christened this project, 'the people's dividend'![48]

There is no significant difference between the contests of the various plans. As proof, here are some extracts from the plan outlined by one of these firms and by the Ford Foundation under the direction of Amitai Etzioni of the University of Columbia. With the aim of 'democratising' communication, it suggests that companies which install cable television in urban areas should give over one third of their broadcasting time to non-commercial community organisations. 'Although people can let the producers know their opinions by letters and petitions,' says the report, 'dialogue is not generally possible. Most of the time, communication is one-way. One of the consequences of this is a serious alienation of citizens from social and political processes. A further consequence stems from the fact that, as decisions are made without people's participation and without taking into account their needs and their wishes, those decisions are strongly resisted.' The report goes on to suggest a plan to integrate people into the decision-making process by having them participate in that historic symbol of democracy: the municipal assembly. Having explained, with the aid of graphics, how the cameras and other hardware would be arranged, and having pointed out that 'the danger with this sort of participatory system is that it can be used by groups on the extreme right and extreme left for anti-democratic ends', the plan suggests electronic and legislative counter-measures to deal with this, and then concludes: 'There is no doubt that MINERVA (the proposed organisation), and the relay system, modified in the light of experience, will be an integral part of the social/communications structure of the future societies which are now possible, of the coming era of mass participation!'[49]

When a series becomes a model

'Sesame Street was only the beginning'. So began an article in the magazine *TV Guide* which announced the release of the CTW's second series for children.

Since then the Television Workshop has indeed extended its work into many new areas. In 1974, the American Association for the Advancement of Science launched the first medical series for adults, produced by the Television Workshop. 'The series contains practical information on health and presents it in an amusing and instructive manner.'[50] But more significant than individual examples is the fact that *Sesame Street* and its successors have become permanent points of reference for the education industry and for the various State organisations responsible for the application of electronic methods to teaching. The paper presented to Nixon in 1971, which has already been referred to, is evidence of the burning importance of the new tele-education series.[51] And it provides a good base from which to analyse the ramifications of the *Sesame Street* model. The origins of the ideas and suggestions of Nixon's advisers are clearly revealed: 'The success of Sesame Street in co-ordinating resources of talent, funds and expertise in providing a nationally accepted educationally stimulating program for millions of pre-schoolers, is perhaps among the outstanding examples of the power of telecommunications applied to development needs.' The White House experts suggested that programmes of the *Sesame Street* type be produced for all age groups. Their general aim is obvious: 'it is a matter of laying the foundations for attitudes which can encourage the birth of an adaptable citizen, the kind of citizen, as many have already pointed out, that we will need in the 21st century.'

By examining its various suggestions, the main points contained in the plan can be outlined:

1—A general principle, found throughout the report in various guises according to the age of the young public to which the programmes are addressed, is the need to close the gap between the school and the home. The new communications technology would allow the separation of school and home to be ended. 'Education in the year 2000 is predicted to be largely at-home, electronically delivered and continuous.' School buildings should be no more than distribution centres for educational programmes, community centres or sports centres, laboratories or places for artistic experiment. Outlining these perspectives, the authors of the report were merely repeating the theses expounded at the Conference on Childhood held at the White House. It was said at that Conference that: 'It is possible that advanced technology will return the family to the centre of the stage as the basic learning unit. Each home would become a school, in effect, via an electronic console connected to a central computer system in a learning hub, a video-taped and microfilm library regulated by a computer and a national educational television network.' To achieve this, specific measures are proposed, as in all the sections of the study. For example, let us take the case of pre-school children. To deal with the urgent problems raised by nurseries, which, according to the report, offer 'only deficient services', a three-part strategy is recommended: 'In the first phase, nationally available programs would be developed for utilisation in day-care centers, in schools and homes. They would be of the same nature as Sesame Street but would increase the total amount of high quality early education programming. They would both cover a wider range than does Sesame Street and would have a broad developmental focus (rather than concentrating on pre-reading and pre-academic skills). In addition, the new programs would be designed as a bridge from standard televised services to cassette facilities and two-way transmission. The program might consist of four 30 minute segments distributed each weekday between 10.00 a.m. and 5.00 p.m. In this phase, they might require a one-way system, single channel communication and black-and-white picture. In the second phase, the early education software would be developed in portable cassette form. This would provide for flexible "on-call" use by teachers as needed (frequent indications of this requirement have been expressed in regard to Sesame Street) . . . In the third phase, two-way systems would be developed. Their purpose would be to provide for feedback from instructional systems to children and for interaction between parents at their places of employment and children in day-care facilities.'

2—Ending the separation between school and home would stress the importance of the parents' role as their children's 'electronic monitors'. 'The lack of adequate educational services to aid parents in their role as primary child-rearing agents has become increasingly clear in the last few years. A first major problem in this realm concerns the entire Nation and focuses on insufficient education in the areas of child development, health, nutrition and safety. A second crucial problem concerns the lack of a co-ordinated approach to developing parent-training programs for low-income parents, and adolescents.'

What follows are details of methods to be applied to remove the obstacles blocking the plan for parental involvement. The educational experts suggest three types of approach: (a) broadcasting programmes for the general public; (b) temporary installation of a two-way television circuit for parents showing special learning programmes: (c) access to video-tape libraries. Among the obstacles which might endanger the success of such a programme, the most important is parents' low level of acceptance of electronic interference in home life. To get round this and to ensure parents' co-operation, the report's authors go so far as to suggest 'the production of programmes aimed at reducing the number of child deaths from fire and road accidents'. Once again, the projected programmes would be based on the *Sesame Street* model—*Sesame Street* for adults.

3—The new system of electronic teaching would be central to the child's development from a very early age. No point in the life of the mother and child would escape the influence of audio-visual mass media. Having pointed out that research 'would show that television advertising plays a significant role in the content of the 18 to 36 month old child's vocabulary', the White House experts think it right to emphasise that: 'technology is a supplement to, not a substitute for, loving parents who talk and play with their child, or the opportunity to squeeze, pull, stack, push, bounce, chew and prod; although there are many kinds of supplementary services that could be provided, the field of telecommunications for infants is currently a void'. Among the particular possibilities which telecommunications offer are: (a) the production of a series which, on the basis of appropriate aural stimuli, would encourage language development in children from the age of three to eighteen months; (b) the production of a series for mother and child which would be broadcast every day for a quarter of an hour, and which would encourage experiments in interaction between them, using simple materials found around the house; (c) for children in hospitals or residential schools who could be considered as deprived of varied stimulation (from 0 to 3 years old), the production of video-tapes which develop stimuli appropriate to age, and the installation 'of single station closed circuit television on the child's cot or fixed to the ceiling in his bedroom with an on/off switch controlled by the child'. Finally, repeating their unconditional enthusiasm for the *Sesame Street* model, the psychologists of 'electronic childhood' insist upon the need to produce broadcasts adapted to the most tender age on the one hand and the mother/child relationship on the other.

4—To round off this regimented universe, they found it useful to 'recycle' teachers and to standardise their criteria so that they could judge the models for primary education. 'Telecommunications media can provide enormous help in the alleviation of problems related to the training of day-care staff members via professionally designed curriculum programs'. Systems of pay-video, to which people could be connected by dialling a number and which would transmit world-wide programmes to nursery staff, could broadcast new educational material and new conceptions of teaching, at the same time as ensuring the consistent quality of the staff. This plan would be extremely important in creating a pool of monitors.

5—In the rare references made to the content of these programmes, the experts stress the need to 'educate pre-school children for world citizenship with their fellow-men and protection of their physical environment'. To achieve this end, the aim is to manufacture international programmes, of the *Sesame Street* variety, which seek to promote understanding between different races, cultures and nations, as well as the protection of the environment. It is proposed that there should be a satellite system for children which would broadcast daily worldwide newsbulletins, in a manner appropriate to the young audience.

At this point, however, the report acknowledges possible resistance to the role which federal authorities would be called on to play in the development and orientation of these programmes 'of moral and ethical education for pre-school children'. To neutralise this resistance they argue: 'the Federal role in direct provision of moral and ethical training may be controversial; so, in the 1970's, would a Federal non-role. There already seem to be a consensus that development of attitudes fostering a sense of responsibility for the support and preservation of other men, and for the care and protection of man's physical environment are among the highest national priorities. . . Here perhaps international objectives might be most clearly shared: human relations and issues of conservation and ecology are a common cause among many nations, and could be taught effectively through television programs for pre-school children, who are often most open to new ideas and information, free of indifference, prejudice or hostilities that older people must unlearn. The objectives of such a program could be as specific as those for more academic subjects: the child's acquisition of knowledge himself, others and the world, of the issues confronting men and the ability to use this knowledge in solving problems'.

6—In the plan's execution, the policy of expanding the Public Television Corporation is central. By 1980 that Corporation should have a dozen channels relayed by satellite and a further channel reserved exclusively for the government. 'The University of the air' will have five channels, children's programmes two, educational television two, and the programme 'High School Equivalency' three. Public television services will abandon their present role as experimental laboratories and, by the end of the decade, could have a greater broadcasting capacity than the whole of the official mass communication apparatus has at present.

Notes

1 On the history of the US Foundations, Waldemar Nielsen, *The Big Foundations*, New York, 1972, Columbia University Press.
2 *National Review*, 28.II.1975.
3 The Rockefeller Foundation, *Ten-Year Review and Annual Report 1971*, New York 1972; The Ford Foundation, *Annual Report 1971–72*; for recent nominations: 1973 and 1974 annual reports.
4 David Horowitz and David Kolodney. 'The Foundations: Charity Begins at Home', *Ramparts*, April 1969.
5 On the history of the Ford Foundation's activities in educational TV: The Network Project, *The Fourth Network*, New York, 1971.
6 Cf. Delbert D. Smith, 'Educational Satellite Telecommunication: The Challenge of a New Technology', *Bulletin of Atomic Scientists*, April 1971.
7 Interview with Robert Dahl, *Performance*, New York, September-October 1972.
8 *Ibid.*
9 *A Special report from the Children's Television Workshop*, New York, 1972.
10 The John and Mary Foundation, *Report on program directions*, New York, 1972; *Annual Report 1971–72*.
11 Sidney P. Marland, 'A significant new teaching tool', *The Electric Company*, New York, CTW, 1971.
12 *Memo from the Children's Television Workshop*, New York, 1972; *A special report from the Children's Television Workshop, op. cit.*
13 *A special report . . . op. cit.*
14 Published in *Revista de Revistas*, Mexico, 11 April 1973.
15 Rex Lee in *Memo from the CTW, op. cit.*
16 Atlantic Richfield is the North American oil company which in 1976 acquired 90% ownership of the London *Observer*, established 185 years earlier. It has also purchased a majority holding in the famous copper mining company Anaconda. (Translator's note).
17 *The State of the Arts and Corporate Support* (ed. Gideon Chagy), New York 1971, Paul S. Eriksson, Inc.
18 George Gent, 'The corporation, new patron for the arts', *Economic Impact*, Washington, 1973, N. 3.
19 Elihu Harris, 'Why many of nation's biggest marketers give support to public television shows', *Advertising Age*, 1.IX.1975.
20 Jacqueline Grapin, 'Le financement des spectacles aux Etats-Unis'; 'Show is Business', *Le Monde*, 17–18 August 1975.
21 'Foreword' by Gideon Chagy, *The state of the arts and corporate support, op. cit.*
22 Western Publishing Co. Inc, *Annual Report 1972*.
23 *Sesame Street, playthings, books and records*, New York, CTW.
24 Typed manuscript from the Peruvians Ministry of Education. Many critiques of 'Sesame Street' have appeared in other countries, cf. among others: Horst Holzer, *Kinder und fernsehen*, 1974, Munich, Carl Hanser Verlarg. For an analysis of the Spanish adaptation, cf. A. Mattelart, *El imperialismo en busca de la contra-revolución cultural*, Caracas, 1974, Universidad Central de Venezuela (also published in the review *Communicación y Cultura*, No. 1, Buenos-Aires, 1973).
25 *A special report from the CTW, op. cit.*
26 *Ibid.*

27 For a critique of these techniques, cf. A. Mattelart, *Mass Media, idéologies et mouvement révolutionnaire*, Paris 1974, Editions Anthropos. English translation to be published by the Harvester Press.

28 Among the most important are, Gerry Ann Bogatz and Samuel Ball, *The First Year of Sesame Street: an Evaluation*, Princeton, N.J., 1970, Educational Testing Service, by the same authors, *The Second Year of Sesame Street, a Continuing Evaluation* (2 vols.), 1971; *Reading with Television: an Evaluation of 'The Electric Company'* (2 vols.) 1973; Gerald Lesser, *Children and Television: Lessons from Sesame Street*, New York, 1975, Random House.

29 Samuel Ball and Gerry Ann Bogatz, *The First Year of Sesame Street: an Evaluation, op. cit.*

30 The educational objectives of *Sesame Street* according to the CTW, can be summarised as follows: (1) *Symbolic representation: letters and words* (recognising, linking, picking out letters and about thirty words, reciting the alphabet, understanding the sounds of letters, reading words, grasping spatial and temporal sequence); *numbers* (linking, recognising, picking out and reciting numbers from 1 to 20; learning basic numerical operations, listing, equalising, adding, substracting; recognising and naming geometric forms, circle, square, triangle, rectangle. (2) *Cognitive organisation: discrimination and orientation* (visual discrimination, finding pairs, recognising related shapes, finding the relation between the part and the whole; auditory discrimination, sound association, rhyming, copying a rhythmic pattern, subject/object discrimination); *Relational Concepts* (same/different, differences in size, amount, distance, situation, time); *Classification* (combining, finding the odd one out, matching). (3) *Reasoning and Problem Solving*: inference and causality, generating and evaluating explanations and solutions. (4) The child and the world: *the self* (the mind and its power, the parts of the body and their functions, emotions such as fear, joy, sadness, anger, surprise, pride); *social units* (roles and functions of, for example, a father, a mother, a policeman, a postman, a farmer, a baker, a doctor, a dentist, etc.; roles and functions of social groups and institutions, the family and the home, the neighbourhood, the town or village); *social interactions* (differences in perspective and reaction towards the same situation, cooperation, division of tasks, solution of conflicts, differences in capacities and in results; *the man-made environment* (forms and functions of machines and tools, buildings and other constructions.); *the natural environment* (the sky, land and water, the town and the country), plants and animals, weather and seasons). For more details, cf. bibliography. In the French version it is objectives 3 and 4 that have been most abridged. On the objectives of the second series which teaches reading and writing, cf. Barbara Fowles, 'Building a curriculum for The Electric Company', *The Electric Company*, New York, 1971, CTW.

31 Joan Ganz Cooney, 'Television and the teaching of reading', *The Electric Company*, New York, 1971, CTW.

32 Interview with Roy Huggins, 'What's wrong with the television series', *Action* (Directors Guild of America), September-October 1969. See also Richard Cherry, 'The economics of television series', *ibid.*; Raymond Williams, *Television: technology and cultural form*, London, 1974, Fontana/Collins.

33 Children's Television Workshop, *Editorial backgrounder; Sesame Street overseas*, New York, 1973.

34 The John and Mary R. Markle Foundation, *Annual Report* 1971–1972.

35 Quoted in the Network Project, *Control of Information*, New York, 1973, notebook, No. 3.

36 Cf. Kimball Young, *Social Psychology*, New York, 1956, Appleton Century-Crofts Inc.

37 The John and Mary Markle Foundation, *Report on program directions.*

38 Document presenting *Plaza Sesamo* in Latin America. Also cf. the numerous documents published by CTW in Mexico.

39 'Modernización y Cuerpos de paz', *Operación Cacique*, Bogota, 1972, Ediciones 'Camilo'.

40 The Ford Foundation, *Annual Report 1971–1972.*

41 UNESCO, *Le Courrier*, February 1971.

42 *A special report from the Children's Television Workshop, op. cit.*

43 *Sesame Street Magazine*, New York, December 1970.

44 *The Electric Company in-school utilization study: the 1971–1972 school and teachers survey*, CTW-Florida State University 1972. However, the Workshop's experts point out in these reports that although 23% of schools used the series, 28.5% which also had television rejected it, while the rest (48.7%) either had no television or did not have a sufficient number (and certain schools included in this percentage would have rejected the series if they had had the choice).

45 *Editorial Backgrounder, doc. cit. The Electric Company* series has also been used in adult literacy projects in the United States. (cf. the paper *The Electric Company in 1972–73, a proposal*).

46 Joseph Newman, *Wiring the World*, Washington, 1972, a division of US News & World Report.

47 Cf. Claude Durieux, 'Les retards de la télédistribution', a *Le Monde,* 17–18 August, 1975.

48 Cf. the reports of these Foundations and various studies done by MITRE researchers and the Rand Corporation. As an example, John A. Farquhar, *Education and library services for community information utilities*, Santa Monica, Calif., 1972, Rand Corporation.

49 Amitai Etzoni, Eugène Leonard, 'MINERVA': a participatory technology system', *Bulletin of the atomic scientist*, November 1971.

50 'Scientific meeting to preview progress of new TV series on health for adults by creators of Sesame Street', *News Children's Television Workshop*, 20 February 1974.

51 *Communication for social needs; technological opportunities and educational/cultural*, (Draft/outline), 7 August 1971; *Communications for social needs: technological opportunities*, a study for the President's Domestic Council: final report (NASA), 24 September 1971.

CHAPTER VI

UPSETS IN THE CINEMA AND THE PRESS

On the ashes of Hollywood

The film industry is perhaps the area of cultural production which most sharply shows the pressures which are exercised on the one hand by the new technologies, and on the other, by the all-encompassing strategy of the owners of the new technologies.

In 1969 and 70, most of the major film production companies in the United States entered into crisis. The eight biggest lost $300 m. during these two years.[1] Twentieth Century Fox suffered a deficit of $27.5 m. in 1969 and $76.3 m. the following year. United Artists lost 45 million in 1970 and out of 36 films which it produced that year only one yielded any dividends.

To begin with, the directors of these companies sought the reasons for the depression in their exorbitant budgets. Films like *Tora! Tora! Tora!* produced by Twentieth Century Fox—with the benevolent assistance of the US Army's Green Berets—and *Hello Dolly!*, cost almost 25 million dollars. Both of them were major failures, although the super-production *The Sound of Music*, which in 1966 had established a model for such huge budgets, had cost $7.6 m. and taken 72 millions within the United States alone. As the vice-president of Metro-Goldwyn-Mayer commented a short while later: 'Everybody acted as if there were some God of the movies who would periodically come down and save people from their follies by giving them a big hit. All they had to do was churn out movies and wait for the big smash that would make them well.'[2] At the end of 1968, the list of films not yet released showed their costs of production to have reached a maximum: $1.2 billion worth of films waited immobilised, the equivalent of three normal years' production.

The crisis also displayed changes which had taken place in the structure of the film market. The audience loss relative to the high point of 1946 was 75%. Surveys revealed that about 65% of the population of the United States never went to the cinema. The age-composition of the cinema public had changed considerably. Seventy per cent of the cinema audience was now less than thirty years old. But the disaffection of cinema audiences in no way indicates disaffection with film—it is perfectly obvious that the small screen has played an essential role in this crisis. Apart from that, the cinema industrialists had to accept another cruel piece of evidence. The contraction of foreign markets, which had begun long before, was confirmed, and in this situation, the relative importance of national production in such countries as France, Germany, Britain, Italy and Mexico took some of the terrain away from North American films. In 1972, Hollywood producers drew no more than a third of their revenue from abroad, whereas in more auspicious days this proportion had been a half or more.

Nevertheless, recuperation came fast. In 1973, the profits of the major eight companies reached $168 m. Twentieth Century Fox had absorbed its enormous deficits and declared profits of eight millions for the fiscal year 1972. In 1974, their net profits reached $10.9 m. in spite of a huge loss (more than four million) in the publicity films section. Out of 70 films produced by United Artists in the three years following its big crash, only two were declared unprofitable, and these films had cost, on average, no more than 1.5 million dollars. At the end of 1973, Paramount Pictures announced that its production of *The Godfather*, costing six million dollars, had already brought in $119 m. The cost of this film was an exception among the company's productions which, in the new period, had been fixed at an average of 2 million per film. They spoke of it as 'the biggest financial success in the history of cinema'. MCA-Universal too benefited from this rebirth of North American cinema. In 1975, 45 days after it had been launched in the United States, their production of *Jaws* had already grossed more than 80 million dollars at the box office. For the first time the company announced that revenues from its film division had exceeded those from its television programmes, and that its turnover had doubled during the previous four years. Columbia, where the crisis hit later than elsewhere, with a loss of 28 million in 1971, suffered three successive years of deficit. But by 1975 the cinema industrialists had become more optimistic. The previous year gross box office receipts in the United States amounted to $1.9 billion, the highest since 1946. Even if the value of the dollar had fallen, nonetheless this constituted an increase of more than 25% over the preceding years.

Behind these figures lies the systematic reconversion to which Hollywood has been subjected. For the man or woman in the street, the crisis was condensed into an image of millionaires, museums and the collectors of fetishes outbidding each other for the massive wardrobes and the huge collection of props which had decorated MGM's cast-of-thousands epics. In business circles this was initially translated into a veritable purge of the boards of directors of the film companies. Out of fourteen members of the board of Twentieth Century Fox, only one remained in place. And with reason: he was the owner of the huge newspaper chain of the same name, William Randolph Hearst Jr. The Zanuck dynasty which had presided over the destiny of the company for 36 years suffered expulsion and was replaced by a man of 47 who, six years earlier, had contented himself with being in charge of the purchase of new properties for another major press chain, the Times Mirror Co.

The profile of the film companies has altered greatly. They have come within the grasp of the conglomerates and their lines of production have been diversified. Let us see who the new owners are, and what these companies' activities now consist in.

Before the Second World War there were five major companies and three in the second rank. The five majors were Paramount, Twentieth Century Fox, Metro-Goldwyn-Mayer, Warner Bros., and RKO. The other three were Columbia, Universal and United Artists (which was set up after the First World War by Chaplin, Griffith and Douglas Fairbanks: it did not possess studios but co-ordinated the independent productions of the period). Around 1950, a decision of the US Supreme Court prohibited the five majors from combining the functions of producer and distributor with the function of exhibition. Paramount Pictures Inc. dissolved itself and two new companies were born: Paramount Pictures Corp. (production and distribution) and United Paramount Theatres (exhibition). This second company was promptly bought up by the television company ABC which was just starting up operations at the time and which thus added 400 cinemas to its properties. RKO (Radio-Keith-Orpheum) subdivided itself into RKO Pictures and RKO Theatres. The following year, the 385 theatres belonging to Twentieth Century Fox became the property of a new company, National Theatres. In 1953, Warner Brothers doubled up into Warner Bros. Pictures and the Stanley Warner Corporation (with 340 cinemas). Finally, Metro-Goldwyn-Mayer shook itself off from Loew's Corp., which retained the ownership of 117 cinemas which co-existed within the conglomerate with its hotel chains, construction companies and its cigarette factory, Kent (Lorillard). Since then other modifications have occurred, most of them recently although some are of long standing.

RKO promptly disappeared from the panorama of the major companies. It was eliminated during the 50s by the maladministration of its owner, Howard Hughes. But its social purpose survived and RKO is now a subsidiary of the manufacturer of tyres and aerospace

materials, General Tire and Rubber Co. This subsidiary commands
123 cinemas. It produces television programmes and, through
Cablecom General, figures among the ten major US cable television
enterprises.

The future of MGM was almost completely threatened by its
owner's hazardous investments in the night clubs and casinos of Las
Vegas. In September 1973, it was forced to employ draconian measures
in reducing its film activities, limiting new productions to two 'quality'
films per year. It also announced the sale of its US and foreign film
distribution networks, its foreign-held cinemas and what remained to it
of its studios. During the two preceding years it had already sold its
studios in England at Borehamwood, just outside London, its cinemas
in South Africa, a record company, a large part of its film equipment
and some of its buildings. After all these tribulations, MGM opened
the Grand Hotel Casino in Las Vegas. This operation provided the old
aristocrat of the cinema with 60% of its net profits.

Let us look at the recent history of Warner and of Paramount in
more detail.

From feminism to tourism

Warner Bros-Seven Arts, in July 1969, became part of the Kinney
Services Corp. conglomerate, whose principal business of the beginning of the decade was funeral parlours. Since its beginnings,
Kinney has acquired other properties in the field of cultural production, apart from accumulating supermarket chains, cleaners,
plumbing services and car parks. It set about restructuring its new
subsidiary: the Warner Communications Corporation, as it was
renamed, now has five divisions. Its publishing division (see Table 22)
comprises seven enterprises. Outstanding among them, National
Periodical Publications, acquired by Kinney in March 1968, is one of
the world's largest publishers of comics (including *Superman* and
Batman). The same year Kinney made its first move into the
international book market through buying the London enterprise of
Thorpe and Porter. The concentration in the hands of a single
corporation of publishing, cinema and television, has, as a consequence, the ever narrower integration of these three fields. Movie-
book tie-ins, or a TV series-book package, become highly profitable
consecrated formulas. Movie or tv scripts can easily be turned into
books, reversing the traditional pattern of making books into movies
or serials. More generally, this combination of interests inserts the
norms of spectacle and sensationalism into the book market. The
search for rapid profits stimulates the publication of what we can

Table 22

Paperback Publishing's Corporate Ties

Paperback house	Hardcover affiliate	Parent
Avon	—	Hearst Corp.
Ballantine	Random House	RCA
Bantam	—	IFI International*
Berkley	G.P. Putnam's Sons	MCA
Dell	Doubleday, Delacorte	Doubleday
Fawcett	Holt, Rinehart & Winston	CBS
New American Library	Harry N. Abrams Inc., Times Mirror Book Div.	Times Mirror
Penguin	Viking, Grossman	S. Pearson & co.
Pocket Books	Simon & Schuster	Gulf & Western
Popular Library	Holt, Rinehart & Winston	CBS
Jove (formerly Pyramid)	Harcourt Brace Jovanovich	HBJ
Warner Books (formerly Paperback Library)	—	Warner Communications

Sources: *Business Week*, 4 July 1977.
* Belongs to FIAT (Italy). See Chapter IV.

already call 'phony' books. The book is produced according to the rule of other media which impose their own dynamic on it.

Integrated into a conglomerate, the publishing division has already, more openly than other divisions, displayed the new political practices of the giants of the North American economy. In 1973, Warner gave the order brusquely to suspend publication of Noam Chomsky and E.E. Herman's *Bloodbaths in Fact and Propaganda*, and they fired the personnel who had accepted the manuscript and prepared the publication of this courageous indictment against the Empire's policy of genocide in Vietnam. At the beginning of the same year, Warner successfully supported the launching of a feminist magazine, *Ms.* In May 1975 the Women's Liberation Movement denounced the imposture: 'To many people, *Ms*, appears to be the voice of the Women's Liberation Movement. But in actuality it has substituted itself for the movement, blocking knowledge of the authentic activists and ideas. *Ms* outgrowths proliferate into many other areas—women's studies programs, television shows, feminist organisations—duplicating and many times substituting for the original, authentic activists and groups that sparked the movement. It is widely recognised that one major CIA strategy is to create or support 'parallel' organisations which provide an alternative to radicalism.'[3]

The leisure division brings together the film properties previously belonging to Warner Bros.-Seven Arts, adding to them the numerous record houses bought by Kinney over the last few years. The films made in these studios account for no more than 40% of Warner Communications Corp. turnover. The cable television division was put together in record time. Between 1971 and 1972, the Kinney conglomerate took over four of the largest tele-distribution networks in the United States, with the result that it has been catapulted into second place in this field after Teleprompter. Such speed testifies to the silent struggle which the old producers of mass culture are engaged in, in order to put their mark on the new so-called community systems born in the margins of the monopolies.

In entering the teaching market—another of its divisions—the Warner Communications Group reflects the new developments of the whole of the US culture industry. In 1972, Kinney laid its hands on the Goldmark Communications Corp., founded a short time before by the famous Goldmark, pioneer of colour television and inventor of the CBS video-cassette. Accepting Kinney's control, Goldmark made this declaration to the press: 'I am particularly enthusiastic about devising new ways to use the video tube for education and would like to help make education more palatable—and marketable—by making it more entertaining. What I want to achieve is a lifetime of *Sesame Streets* on every level for every age group from the very youngest to the very oldest.'[4] Incidentally, Kinney also owns one of the manufacturers of audio-visual equipment, Panavision.

Warner Communications Corp.'s last division, Jungle Habitat, is a kind of large zoological park, organised according to the cartoons of the old Warner. In terms of the strategies of diversification of the US film companies, this is far from being exceptional. In 1975, Fox Realty and Development, a division of Twentieth Century Fox, decided to devote $400 m. to the construction of two amusement parks (Movieland) in Southern California, in order to integrate what was left of its old studios. Ten years earlier, Fox had already converted some of its old studios into a residential complex, known as Century City. Such diversification followed the model provided by one of the only film companies to have continued to flourish during the lean years, the Walt Disney Corp. Between 1968 and 1972 Disney's turnover increased from $167 m. to $329 m. Sixty-eight per cent of this figure came from the Disneyland amusement park in California and Disneyworld in Florida (which alone had cost $400 m.). The Corporation is now going to manage a new amusement park in Japan and build a park for adults in Florida. Nor are the major US television networks lagging behind. CBS, which a few years ago managed to buy up the famous Barnum circus, has also decided to return animals to their natural milieu and to present all kinds of spectacles within this framework. ABC owns three large amusement parks where the visitor can admire the natural beauties of lakes, thanks to glass-bottomed boats through which to observe the sub-marine shows of the latest mermaids (Weeki-Wachee Springs, San Francisco, Florida).

All these creations transport the favourite figures of mass culture from the screen to the field developments of the leisure industry, where these archetypes are made to flourish. The 'natural' territories which Scrooge McDuck, Donald and his nephews avidly search for in the course of their incessant travels beyond the metropolis, and which they hold out to their readers as a reward for begging souls, crop up here on all sides in the very heart of a polluted world. This ready-to-hand formula for exoticism, using a lot of already popularised personages, seems like the best way they have to remedy the fall in sales of traditional products, like comics, at the same time that it allows these myths to revitalise themselves in terms of the demands for family consumption which have given birth to tourist society. And this isn't even counting the business which they give to the numerous construction companies and cement factories which many of these companies have annexed in the course of their diversification! After ITT, RCA and Westinghouse, all of them new architects and entrepreneurs, CBS too has taken over a construction company, called Klingbeil.

Mission impossible for Gulf & Western

The most interesting evolution is without doubt that of Paramount Pictures.[6] It began the moment it was incorporated into Gulf & Western Industries Inc. In 1958, Gulf & Western (not to be confused with Gulf Oil!) didn't even exist, and the company with which it began its activities, the Michigan Bumper Co., a manufacturer of chromium plate, had a turnover of only 182 millions. Ten years later, after taking over more than 100 companies, Gulf & Western had achieved a turnover of $2.3 billion. 1966 was the year they acquired Paramount Pictures. Six other companies came within their orbit the same year. The most important was undoubtedly the New Jersey Zinc Co., which from one day to the next gave it a leading position in the mineral and petrochemical industry. Acquisitions made during the previous years had already taken it into the fields of automobile, aerospace and electronics production.

In 1967, Gulf created its new Leisure Time Group, consisting of Paramount and a TV series production house called Desilu Production

Inc. which it bought in the same year. The Famous Players Corp., one of the largest cinema circuits in Canada (with 308 theatres), in which Gulf acquired a majority shareholding, also became part of this new division. Gulf also has theatre interests in Great Britain and France. During the same year, 1967, it announced the manufacture of cable television equipment in its electronics division. As for its other areas of activity, 1967 also saw the creation of an agricultural group. This was made possible by the acquisition of the South Puerto Rico Sugar Co., the largest sugar company in Santo Domingo. In fact, as many people recognise, Gulf was the principal beneficiary of the invasion by North American marines in 1965. And as if fiction did not have to wait upon reality, 1967 was also the year that saw the launching of the famous television series, *Mission Impossible* and *Mannix*, which joined the old *Lucy*.

In 1968 Gulf strongly asserted its position in the field of cable television systems exploitation. It had accumulated by this time the considerable number of 200,000 Canadian and North American subscribers, and considered the potential to be 800,000. The same year that it produced such films as *Romeo & Juliet, Barbarella* and *Rosemary's Baby*, it added a cigar factory (Consolidated Cigar Corp.) and a paper manufacturer (E. W. Bliss Co.) to its properties. 1969 was the apotheosis of its affairs in the Dominican Republic. The Government of this country signed a contract with Gulf to develop the free industrial zone of La Romana. In its Annual Report, Gulf underlined the 'incredible' nature of this privilege: 'This marked one of the few times in the history of international commerce that a nation, by special act of its legislative body, named a private corporation to develop and operate a free zone for the government.

'The free zone will enable US and foreign companies to build and run light industrial plants with such benefits as a 20-year tax exemption, an abundant supply of low-cost labour, low production costs, and good transportation and communications. Work has begun on clearing the site for the free zone, and plant construction is already under way.

'Gulf & Western Americas Corporation has become active in the tourism business with the remodelling of a hotel in La Romana and the planned construction of a hotel in Santo Domingo.'[7]

Still in 1969, Paramount set up its Special Film Projects Division, to produce educational films and series for various government agencies and for business. Through the purchase of a new music publishing house, they seemed to be reminding the consumer that they were also pretty well engaged in the record industry. The Cannes Festival saw the success of another Paramount movie—which almost wasn't made at all until Paramount came up with the money at the last moment—the British production *If* . . . In Canada, Gulf added another 14 premises to its cinema circuit, bringing the number to 368. It approved the construction of 28 new halls, mostly in new shopping centres. More than just a leisure distribution company, its subsidiary Famous Players is above all one of the principal owners of lands and properties in Canada. Apart from cinemas, Famous Players buys and develops real estate. It owns huge stretches of terrain and numerous properties in 136 cities. But luck didn't smile on all its activities in 1969. Canadian legislation limited foreign holdings in the media and put a stop to the development of its cable television networks.

In 1970, foreseeing that many film companies would soon no longer be able themselves to distribute their own production, Paramount together with Universal set up the Cinema International Corporation, a company of Dutch nationality, to distribute the films of the two associates together with those of MGM outside the USA and Canada. Each of the two owns 49% of the shares. Then we move on to 1972. The previous panorama is extended, through the formation of a division specialising in travel and tours, with the evocative names Camino Tours, Fun in the Sun Tours and Hawaian-Polynesia Tours. The cable television subsidiary also takes the prestigious name Athena Communications Corporation. In the sports industry, Gulf increased its investments in the Madison Square Gardens Corporation and increased its hold over two famous hockey and basketball clubs. Within the United States it set up hotel chains. Abroad, it entered the field of the publication of textbooks. 1972 was the year it acquired a holding in the Italian publishing house Fratelli Fabbri, owned by Fiat.

Still in 1972 Paramount inaugurated a new style of management in film production. It announced the formation of a company of film directors which brought together three brilliant young men (Bogdanovich, Friedkin, Coppola) and declared that they would have the benefit of the 'the greatest artistic freedom'. That year, cinema and television furnished the conglomerate with 14% of its total turnover.[8]

In 1973 Gulf completed the conversion of the old Paramount cinema in London's Piccadilly Circus into two auditoria. (Two more cinemas have been added to the complex since then, the fourth of them, opening in 1978, devoted exclusively to the revival of old-time favourites.) It acquired a holding in Bulova watches. In the field of natural resources, its division New Jersey Zinc, by taking up holdings in two companies producing coal, petroleum and natural gas, attempted to deal with the energy crisis after having subscribed co-production agreements with the Belgian company Royale Asturienne des Mines and setting out a programme of geophysical exploration with Brazil.

In February 1975 Gulf & Western announced its decision to purchase one of the last publishing houses in the United States to remain outside the control of the conglomerates: Simon & Schuster. The very same month, before an audience of 500 company chiefs, Charles Bluhdorn, accused the North American Government of entertaining a lame policy towards the countries 'which are seizing the patrimony of the free world, amassed at the cost of so much effort over the last two centuries'. At the end of his intervention he urged an offensive against the 'members of the oil trust of the Arab countries'.[9] A year earlier, almost to the day, the Motion Picture Association of America (MPAA), which represents all US distributors apart from Walt Disney, announced that it was initiating a study to 'evaluate' the payments made by the countries of the Near East for North American films, although claiming that this did not represent any kind of retaliation against the Arab countries. Jack Valenti, MPAA President, declared that the study would result in 'a realistic readjustment of the prices which we obtain for our films in certain countries where funds have now been amassed as a result of the high tariffs which have been established for certain products like oil.' The MPAA made it known that the inspiration for this move came from none other than Gulf & Western President, Charles Bluhdorn.[10]

A new market

United Artists, Universal and Columbia, who were once the little sisters, now belong to conglomerates. And the distance which separated them from their big sisters (the 'majors') is reduced.

In April 1967, United Artists was firmly absorbed by the Transamerica Corporation, a company which operates banks, airlines, insurance agencies, rental and car hire firms, furniture removal companies and credit houses, and possesses more than thirty other branches.

Universal Pictures has become an important division of the Music Company of America (MCA) which, apart from the control it exercises over a number of record companies (Decca Records, with the Kapp, Uni and Coral labels) is engaged in credit and insurance business (Columbia Savings & Loan). One of its latest creations, dating from 1972, MCA Disco-Vision Inc., which is devoted to the research and development of the video-disc, indicates one of its future lines of production. Its first video disc was due to be issued in 1976. But it didn't bring it out alone. In 1974, taking steps towards the world standardisation of the new medium—and again confirming the increasingly close relationship between the manufacturers of hardware and of software—MCA formed an association with the Dutch firm of Philips so that it is finally a joint Philips-MCA video-disc system that is to be launched. Philips will manufacture the television sets and the video-recorder, while the North American company will release its stock of films on video-disc, as well as new programmes which it envisages making according to need. Other rumours are current in Hollywood. MCA is said to be encouraging Philips to launch out into the film industry.

The Columbia Pictures Corp. has lent its name to an enterprise which in the last few years has diversified constantly in the realm of leisure and education: Columbia now covers public opinion polls—which we shall come back to—record companies (Bell Records) and television programme production houses (Transworld Production, acquired around 1970, which joined one of Columbia's oldest subsidiaries, Screen Gems). Together with the latter, the Learning Corporation of America attests to Columbia's pedagogical preoccupations. Another sign of the times, Columbia and Warner decided to pool their equipment and the old Burbank studios for the both of them to use, though each retains its own administration. But in 1973 the two companies invested more than $3.5 m. in the purchase of three studios specialising in videotape production and in television programmes in general. Together with United Artists, Columbia exploits a cable television network, one of the ten most important in the USA.

All these developments indicate a drawing together of cinema and television. The production of television programmes has been a central objective for most of these companies, each with its own bias. In 1972 more than two-thirds of Universal's production was destined for the small screen. Universal is without doubt the company to have pursued this development most resolutely. They had no fewer than twelve series running on North American television companies that year, among them the celebrated *Ironside, Adam 12,* and *Marcus Welby.* In 1976, Universal TV began the season in New York supplying nearly one-quarter of all prime-time network TV programming every week, with series such as *Bionic Woman, Six Million Dollar Man, Barelta, Columbo* and *Kojak.* An indication of the process of concentration, Universal provided fourteen hours of shows each week, against four by its closest competitor. Back in 1972 again, the North American film industry gave birth to a committee for the co-ordination of film and television, and series began to be made which carried over films that had been successful in the cinemas to the small screen; for example, CBS's *Anna and the King,* and *M.A.S.H.*, which was transformed into a series thanks to a co-production between ABC and 20th Century Fox. These initiatives led the companies to declare somewhat eagerly that 'television is in the process of entering a new period, characterised by an increase in quality'.

In parallel with this, the acquisition of teledistribution networks and the perfecting of video-cassette and video-disc systems prepares the ground for a new kind of commercialisation for the stock of films which each of these companies owns. With regard to the possibilities which cable pay-TV opens up, the President of Universal declared: 'Universal Pictures owns 2,000 movies. If only 200 of them are good enough for resale and we collect a $2 royalty for each TV set on which it appears, the sales would be greater than the original gross income for all 2,000 movies. Even if only 10% of the homes buy movies, the figures are still gigantic.' He added that 'If each family buys only three movies a year on cable TV, the sales would equal the 1973 theatre box-office total of $1-billion.'[11]

Undertakings of this kind are growing. Warner began a pilot experiment on its numerous teledistribution networks beginning in 1973, offering subscribers eight films a month for the price of five dollars. Hotel chains became the first choice among clients. Columbia offered its films at 3 dollars apiece in 39 hotels in Canada, Britain and the US. According to their statistics, almost a quarter of the hotel guests asked for the films. The hotel company took 10% of the price. This alliance has developed on the international level where it takes shape in the creation of companies specialising in a new kind of hotel fitting: hotelvision; anyway this is the name that has been adopted by a union between Columbia and the British cinema company, the Rank Organisation, which also owns hotels. And as if this had stimulated a new branch of activity, Rank continued to acquire luxury hotels (in 1973 they bought up one of the largest hotel chains in Europe, Butlin's Ltd.). Hospitals and nurseries constitute another market which have in their turn provoked the formation of joint enterprises for their exploitation, where you find an equipment manufacturer who supplies the materials for the network, a firm specialising in the administration of these systems, and a film company which provides its stock of films. Thus 20th Century Fox has allied itself with the equipment manufacturer Bell & Howell and a company called Primary Medical Communications, which has experience of the hospital milieu. Before joining up with 20th Century Fox, this was a company which was devoted to the supply by means of video-cassettes and cable television of post-university training programmes for the medical and para-medical professions.

At the same time that modifications are developing in the structures of ownership of the big companies, it is also possible to see new smaller interests sprouting up in the film industry. Several companies have equipped themselves with small production houses. The firm of Bristol-Myers, one of largest companies in the field of pharmaceutical products, has transformed Palomar Pictures International, set up by the chief of programming for the TV chain ABC, into one of its subsidiaries and has decided to produce a series of films for the child and family public. Xerox has inaugurated a small production agency, Cinema X. More importantly, Embassy Pictures Corp. was annexed in May 1968 by AVCO, the well-known aerospace firm. The North American leader in toys, Mattel Inc., decided to establish close links between its educational toys industry and film production, and created Radnitz-Mattel Productions for the purpose. Many other companies have invested in film production without going so far as to create special departments for the purpose. *The Assassination of Trotsky* was financed by the North American company Greyhound, a specialist in road transport and food canning. Fleetwood Enterprises, manufacturer of caravans, inaugurated its film activities with *Hammersmith*, starring Elizabeth Taylor and Richard Burton. Reader's Digest produced *Tom Sawyer*, and Playboy Polanski's *Macbeth*. Film investment companies have been created specially to facilitate the participation in film production of individual capital. *The Great Gatsby*, for example, was produced by a company of this type in collaboration with Paramount, Fitz Service Co., set up solely for this purpose, comprised of 18 private investors who each put up $100,000 with another 4.8 million in the form of a loan from the Chemical Bank of New York. The creation of this kind of grouping has become a speciality of certain lawyers and financial counsellors.

European competitors

The film industry in the European countries has also gone through a phase of restructuring. One of the most interesting examples is that of Britain. The crisis there was unleashed with greater ferocity than in other European countries. This ferocity was doubtless not only the result of the higher level of technological development which had been achieved in Britain where commercial television joined the BBC in 1954 and had reached a level of saturation by 1968. It is not for nothing that Britain had already inaugurated satellites which were just as sophisticated as military communications satellites. The level reached by the crisis in Britain can be seen in the figures. In 1946 cinema admissions recorded by box-office figures had reached 1.6 billion. By 1972 this had fallen to 182 million, and the number of cinemas had been reduced from 4,703 to 1,510.[12] In France, the following figures reveal the same crisis: in 1957 there were precisely 5,723 cinemas. In 1973 there were 4,213.[13] In this year, the loss of spectators in relation to the ceiling achieved around 1950 (1946 in Britain) amounted to 58% (90% in Britain). (Compare Italy, where the loss only amounted to 34%, while in Germany and Japan it amounted to 83% and 80% respectively.)[14]

The British film companies became, step by step, minority interests within diversified conglomerates. Take the evolution of the two most important companies, Associated British Pictures Corporation (ABPC) which included the ABC Cinema circuit, and the Rank Organisation. ABPC was taken over by EMI (Electrical and Musical Industries), which already held interests in the company, in 1969[15], the year when investments by the North American film companies which dominated the British film industry were reduced to 40% following the crisis in Hollywood. EMI didn't only inherit a film production company and the very important cinema circuit. They also inherited, with ABPC, a television production company of growing importance, Thames Television, in which it came to hold more than 50% of the interests. In 1970 a further acquisition, Prime Presentations Ltd., was added, and EMI found itself controlling a film complex which was vertically combined: production, distribution and exhibition. But these film industries represented no more than 15% of its turnover. Its main area of production continued to be the record industry (55% of its turnover). It is, in fact, the world's foremost music publishing company. It controls 20% of the world market and its numerous sound and video recording studios both in Great Britain and abroad produce more than 16 labels (Marconi, Pathé, His Masters Voice, Electrola, Capitol, etc.). It outdistances all the big North American companies in music distribution (RCA, CBA, Warner, etc.).[16] From the manufacture of a range of equipment including radios and television sets, record players and household apparatus, EMI has extended its activities in the last few years to include measuring, guidance and detection equipment, and other electronic materials (television cameras and associated apparatus, electronic calculators, control tables, full electronic systems). Among its most recent acquisitions are a restaurant chain, participation in a cable television circuit, and in a tourist complex in Brighton. Abroad, it has taken complete control of the Danish company Fona Radio A/S, which joins an international chain of studios and factories stretching from Karachi to Buenos Aires to Johannesburg, which produced more than 60% of EMI's turnover in 1975.

The Rank Organisation, whose roots go back to the pioneering days of British cinema, has not changed hands, but it now comprises a diversified grouping in which film interests amount to no more than 13% of its business. Apart from the Odeon and Gaumont cinema circuits and Pinewood Studios near London—practically the most modern studios in the world—Rank covers the manufacture of radio and television sets, dance halls, skating rinks, motels, hotels, bowling alleys and bingo clubs, educational, audio visual and photographic equipment, precision instruments and real estate management. Rank-Xerox, controlled as the name suggests by the North American Xerox company and by Rank, manufactures and rents out copying machines and xerographic duplicators as well as computers. It is enough, to guage the relative position of Rank-Xerox in Xerox's international strategy, to observe that it is by the far most important of its foreign holdings. In 1974, the Xerox Corporation drew 52% of its profits from foreign activities. This amounted to $171 m. Out of this, the profits provided by Rank-Xerox amounted to 139 millions.[17] Rank-Xerox in turn set up a new subsidiary in Japan with a local company, Fuji Photo Film Co. Fuji-Xerox is a joint property of Fuji and Rank-Xerox, Collaboration with the Japanese company includes the production of copying machines and computers and also of new audio-visual apparatus. In fact, Fuji is the owner of a video-cassette system. This is the system which is employed in the closed-circuit television installations which Rank exploits with Columbia. Xerox's English spring-board has become an element of the first importance in the multinationalisation of the North American company. It was through the intermediary of Rank-Xerox that Xerox was able to set up its first subsidiary in Black Africa in 1974, with the foundation of a company in Nigeria jointly owned by Rank-Xerox (with 60%) and local industries. It did the same thing the same year in South Korea with Fuji-Xerox.

This association with the big North-American-based multinationals can be found on all levels of the British film industry. In 1972, for example, 16 of the 20 most successful films released in Great Britain were distributed by three principal groupings: 7 by Columbia-Warner, 6 by EMI-MGM, 3 by Fox-Rank.[18] According to another source, six North American distributors accounted for 84% of total distribution receipts in 1970.[19]

In France, dependence on the United States can also be seen most clearly in the sphere of distribution. In 1973 104 distributors shared receipts of 432 million francs. Seven companies distributing primarily North American films collected 184 million; major French distributors, 158 million. (This includes 2 companies with national coverage, 8 regional ones.) Thirty art house distributors shared around 16 million francs, the remaining distribution was in the hands of 57 independents amounting to 74 million francs. Exhibition was also moving towards concentration.[20] Three companies dominated the market, Union

Générale de la Cinématographie (UGC), Gaumont-Pathé and Parafrance (uniting the Paramount circuit and that of the second largest French advertising agency, Publicis). More than 3,000 cinema closures have been recorded and the only explanation for why the number of cinemas is not considerably reduced is that simultaneously, these big companies have created complexes which contain several small cinemas. 255 complexes were created in this way in important urban centres. Even though it's only third after UGC and Gaumont-Pathé (which owns 446 cinemas throughout France),[21] Parafrance is one of the most dynamic companies. In November 1975 its circuit was composed of 100 cinemas, 45 of them in Paris, and it publicised itself thus: 'Because we believe in it! Parafrance, the most progressive force in cinema in France!' Receipts of 1 million new francs in 1954, with 4 cinemas; 55 million in 1972 with 22; 110 million envisaged for 1975.[22]

Even if the development of new audio-visual means is less advanced in France than in Britain and, a fortiori, the United States, nevertheless the presence of the big film companies can be seen in several initiatives in the exploitation of new technologies. Thus UGC has a presence in Vidéogrammes de France and Pathé-Cinéma in the medical audio-visual sector, where the use of video-cassettes has made promising beginnings. As for Gaumont, it has an association with Metromedia in the exploitation of closed circuit systems in hotels.

Concentration and diversification of the press

'Monopoly is less a threat to press excellence than monotony.'[23] This is one of various arguments that the big North American press groups, engaged in a frantic policy of acquiring local newspapers since the end of the 60s, use in opposing their critics who reproach them with annulling the benefits of competition. In effect, the North American press has entered the era of concentration in the last few years. The result of this, expressed in terms of strict capitalist rationality, is that 'Far from cooling off . . . the newspapers industry in general has emerged with renewed vitality, surprising financial strength, and the promise of aggressive growth in the seventies. This remarkable rebirth stems from a combination of circumstances, which have helped to nurture renewed interest in the printed word. These forces include growing affluence, rising education levels, and heightened sensitivity to community, national, and global concerns. It is more so because TV programming at the same time has become increasingly barren. Even more important, however, has been the role played by well-capitalised multi-property publishing companies in acquiring independent or small-chain newspapers around and beyond the country. The acquirers have helped to assure the merged publications' continued viability through the infusion of expertise and professionalism, as well as fresh capital.'[24]

The merger in 1974 between the two big newspaper chains, Knight Newspapers and Ridder Publications, is the most recent expression of the restructuring of the major US press groups. Thanks to this unification, the new enterprise now controls 35 newspapers, whose total daily circulation amounts to more than 3.5 million copies. This operation has allowed Knight—among their newspapers is the *Miami Herald* with its particularly extensive coverage of Latin America—to dispute for supremacy with the country's foremost newspaper proprietors, Gannett. Before reaching this stage, Knight had been accumulating newspaper upon newspaper. In 1969 alone it bought 5 dailies, and by no means unimportant ones: they included the *Philadelphia Inquirer* and the *Philadelphia Daily News*, with a total circulation of more than 600,000 copies in spite of being regional papers. These purchases allowed them to jump, between 1968 and 1972, from $116 m. to $310 m. More modest, its present associate had expanded only from $104 m. to $143 m.[25]

Before the Knight-Ridder merger, the protagonists in the most spectacular business developments were the Gannett Company themselves. In 1975 Gannet had altogether some 54 newspapers, with a circulation of more than two million copies. In 1971 alone they acquired 17 local papers in Michigan and in Hawaii as well as in the island of Guam. Attempting to explain why provincial newspapers succumbed one after the other to the monopolists, often at favourable prices, a Gannett spokesman said that the majority of newspapers sold to the big chains were family enterprises which usually only produced small profits. The family was lacking in ambition and know-how to improve its affairs.[26] Gannett was well placed to make this kind of judgement: in 1972, while engaged on its programme of acquisitions, it equipped several of its newspapers with a new electronic system. Thanks to this process, reporters write their articles on a keyboard connected to a computer and see it appearing instantaneously on a television screen and are then able to make immediate changes. The editor of the newspaper can correct articles in the same way. According to the directors of the company, the gain in time which this process provides in the exploitation of fresh news is considerable: instead of 30 minutes, it takes no longer than 3 minutes to transmit. The installation of these new instruments cannot be achieved without social conflict: a fifth of the employees are laid off.

The struggle which this technological conversion entails in the majority of North American newspapers can be seen in the fight by New York typographers to safeguard their jobs. To avoid the degeneration into crisis which occurred in 1963, when a strike of 114 days in New York closed down four New York papers, the *New York Times* decided in 1972 to conduct experiments in modernisation using video in a small chain of provincial newspapers it owned in Florida, precisely where the unions had been less subjected to these pressures. These conflicts, in their turn, simply prefigure the coming crisis in the press in the majority of capitalist countries. In August 1975, the management of the London *Financial Times*, in the process of going over to the same type of total information systems, announced that it was obliged to reduce personnel by a third. At the end of 1978, the print unions, rather than accede to management's attempt to follow suit, forced *The Times* and *The Sunday Times* to declare a lock-out by announcing the papers' indefinite shut-down. Other countries, such as France, still only on the threshold of such technological conversion, have not yet had to face strikes. Almost all the rotary presses on which the newspapers of the French capital are printed are more than 40 years old. Only *Le Monde*, required by its statutes to reinvest its entire profits for the newspaper's benefit, has undertaken the modernisation of its equipment, without going so far, however, as to abandon classical typographical techniques or employing the new video technologies. The big dailies, *France-Soir* and *Le Figaro* resolved to set up a modern printing plant, but the change in ownership of the latter seems to have postponed the project. The provinces are more advanced in this respect, since papers like *Paris-Normandie* and *La Dauphiné Libéré*—in conditions of quasi-monopoly in the region—have already partly gone over to electronics after reaching satisfactory agreements with the unions.[27] At the moment when the monopolies of information are being reinforced everywhere, in Paris as much as the provinces, the need for the modernisation of printing serves as a pretext for a qualitative jump in the ideological apparatus of the ruling class. In the light of this context, how else can you read the proposals and wishes of the French Government on the 'problem of information': 'The basic problem', the Prime Minister said in January 1976, 'is that of the administration of the organs of the press. The hour of truth must also sound there as well, as quickly as possible. One asks oneself how certain companies can live . . . The solution is to be found in a general effort of re-appraisal of what an enterprise of the press ought to consist in'.

But let us return to the United States. The policy of acquiring small papers has been followed largely by the big papers like the *New York Times*, and if the *New York Times* was successful in its modernisation programme in Florida, this was precisely because around 1970 it had taken over 9 newspapers in the same State. But the majority of the big press groups are not content simply to absorb newspapers. The ramifications of their policies extend throughout the media, in the acquisition of large circulation magazine (*New York Times* now owns *Family Circle*), teledistribution chains, radio and tv stations. All the big press names are now coupled to electronic media. Some have also developed their publishing divisions. The Hearst Corporation, pioneer of the North American mass press, has a powerful publishing house in Avon Paperbacks; the Times Mirror Co. owns several scientific publishing houses (including New American Library). Three publishers come under the aegis of the *New York Times*, Arno Press, Cambridge Books and Quadrangle, 'three specialised publishers of scholarly reprints, textbooks and the like, all packing more potential than present profitability; the three companies are part of an intensive effort by The Times Co. to spreadeagle the informational and educational markets, which also consists of audio-visual aids, microfilm products, library services and a computerised Information Bank now being developed.'[28]

Only rarely have newspaper companies become associated with the manufacturers of hardware. Mention may be made of two relatively isolated cases. Gannett has an association with an electronics company for the development of applications of the laser beam to printing. The other exception is the Dow Jones company, editor and owner of the *Wall Street Journal, Barron's* and *National Observer*. After purchasing almost 15 newspapers, this specialist in the financial press wanted to reinforce its monopoly on stock exchange information and anticipate technical progress. The company set up a subsidiary with the Bunker Ramo Corporation, for the purpose of developing transmission services for its financial news by means of computer, having also invested in another electronics company specialising in equipment used on the stock exchange. This mutation is even stronger in groups which are already engaged in the film market, such as Time-Life. After buying several publishing houses at the end of the 60s, notably the important Little, Brown & Co., more than 130 years old, Time-Life established a video division, in response to the demand for the issue of programmes on video-cassette; it is also powerfully engaged in the exploitation of various teledistribution networks. The leading position which this press group occupies in the application of new audio-visual media was confirmed by an agreement signed in June 1975 between Teleprompter and the Time-Life subsidiary, Home Box Office Inc., to combine transmission by means of future satellite systems with cable television in several of the United States.[29]

An original way of resolving the crisis in supplies

In the course of the restructuring of the press it seems that several newspaper chains have wanted to make provision for themselves against the threat of a paper crisis, which has only a little way to go before taking on the same characteristics as the crisis in the oil market: a significant rise in prices, consumer panic, fear of a money shortage, excessive dependence on a few producing countries.[30]

The *New York Times* has acquired shares—ranging from 35% to 49%—in three large Canadian newsprint companies; with each one it has signed long-term contracts which assure a supply of some 300 million tons of newsprint annually absorbed by the newspaper. Gannett is co-proprietor of a paper company in Quebec. The *Washington Post* owns 49% of the Bowaters Mersey Paper Co. of Liverpool, Novia Scotia, of which it consumes two-thirds of production. The Newhouse group (which publishes 22 newspapers and a number of magazines like *Vogue, Mademoiselle, Glamour*, etc.) made an agreement with the same Bowaters company in 1970 to erect a factory to supply almost half of its paper. Time-Life interests in this sector of industry go back a long way. Since 1955, in association with one of the largest paper producers in the US, Crown Zellerbach, it began producing more than 100 million tons a year in the factories of its subsidiary, Eastex. Since then it has continued to expand its forestry reserves and its re-afforestation programmes, and has intensified production. In 1972 it absorbed another manufacturer whose turnover was equal to that of Eastex, Temple Industries. In 1975 its paper and forestry operations accounted for more than a half of Time-Life's turnover. Paper had only accounted for 18% of company revenue and 31% of profits in 1971.[31]

Vertical integration between producers of primary materials and newspaper publishers is now the order of the day. It can also be found in Great Britain, but the other way round. The famous IPC group (International Press Corporation), owner of the Daily Mirror chain, one of the majors of the London press but also of West Africa, was taken over in 1970 by the powerful British paper enterprise, Reed International Ltd., which has production centres in more than 40 countries.[32]

In other countries like France, the situation of dependence on the principal producing countries has been considerably aggravated during the last few years. Having preferred to rely on imports at a time when the price of wood wasn't high enough to interest landowners, the public authorities encouraged French industrialists to obtain their supplies abroad. But the paper producing countries were less and less content to sell only their wood and increasingly went over to marketing the finished product. The results of this policy of 'massive disinvestment' as the French trade union organisation CGT called it in 1974, are already obvious: 46% of the woodpulp consumed in France in 1973 came from imports (more than half from Scandinavia). For finished products (paper and cardboard) imports have increased from 7.5% in 1960 to 26% in 1973. The extent of dependence is pretty well largest in the case of newsprint: national production fell from 430,000 tons in 1970 to about 280,000 in 1973, while imports increased from 170,000 to about 320,000.[33]

Commerce in paper is also no longer a marginal interest for the press groups dominated by the dependent bourgeoisies in Third World countries. In the countries of Latin America, the vertical integration which is avidly sought in a number of advanced capitalist countries has already been realised to some extent, even before the first indications of a crisis in supply. Popular Chile tried vainly to nationalise the Manufactura de Papeles y Cartones, the locally owned paper monopoly allied with Crown Zellerbach, whose principal shareholder was the press group which published the country's foremost daily, *El Mercurio*. And it was of course in the name of the liberty of the press that the local bourgeoisie was sufficiently incensed to oppose the project of Popular Unity to create a national paper institute charged with establishing the most equitable distribution of primary materials and a corresponding forestry policy. Without a word, this same ruling class accepted the denationalisation of the paper industry which the Pinochet regime effected through selling off the country's largest cellulose factory to a multinational group. In Argentina, scarcely three years ago, when the country's first newsprint factory was set up, the most important publishing group in the country, Abril, representing the interests of Time-Life in the Rio de la Plata, carried off the public contract. Some years earlier, the owner of *La Plata*, one of the capital's biggest newspapers, preferred to pay for imports, but at his own personal profit. Having acquired a share in a Canadian forestry enterprise, he imported paper into Argentina for which, by playing the exchange market, he obtained a price that was three times its value.[34]

But it is in Brazil that it is possible to observe movements which, in the long term, are liable to change the face of the world pulp and paper industry most radically. In 1976, the big US paper trusts, International Paper, Crown-Zellerbach and Continental Group Inc., decided on investment projects reaching almost $2 billion. Three types of factor seem to have motivated this mass operation, which fits in with the multinationals' invasion of the Amazon basin. In the first place, the shorter growing time which the sunny Brazilian climate makes possible. A pine tree that takes 20 years to reach maturity in the Southern US, for example, can be harvested in Brazil only seven years after planting. Secondly, corporate investors in Brazil can cut their tax bills by 35% by investing in cultivation. Finally, environmental constructions that limit expansion in the US and Europe do not exist there. Brazil hopes to export almost 2 million tons to Europe and the USA in 1980—via these multinational companies. In that year the countries of the Common Market will be needing 10 million tons of pulp a year. The Canadian companies, who would like to escape the numerous strikes which break out among Canadian woodsmen and pulp and paper workers, have also taken their first steps towards Brazil. Brascan Ltd. and Macmillan Bloedel Ltd. have acquired more than 250,000 acres of forest and have proposed a newsprint venture with *O Estado de Sao Paulo*, Brazil's largest newspaper.

The consequences of the reorganisation of the North American press have also been felt on the international scene. Some examples: in the late 60s, Time-Life invested in five publishing houses abroad. This was the period, for example, when they took a minority share (46%) in the publishers, Robert Laffont, a bridgehead of North American publishing in France. The recent launching of a monthly instalment series on Space, for the mass market, and similar contemporary phenomena, only takes up the formula already tried by its parent publisher, which had already been applied in France by the subsidiary of another North American enterprise, Western Publishing Co. The *New York Times* is co-proprietor with the *Washington Post* of the *International Herald Tribune*, whose international penetration over the last three years is unquestionable ('Certain Frenchmen read a second newspaper every day, like 250,000 well-informed Europeans', as a recent advertisement in the Paris newspapers put it).

The owner of the Gannett Co. is also owner of the press agency, AP (Associated Press), and Gannett's criteria of efficiency have prevailed in the reorganisation of the agency's world-wide services. Associated Press has about 10,000 subscribers of whom 4,500 are in the United States, and more than 100 offices in foreign countries or territories. An agreement between AP and Dow Jones gives the latter the means for the world-wide dissemination of its special service of financial, economic and commercial news (AP-Dow Jones Economic Report) which AP distributes in 23 companies and is extensively used by the economic press of the capitalist countries. This network is no more than the first step in a much vaster grouping whose aim is the control of international financial and economic information. Thus the launching in March 1976 of *The Asian Wall Street Journal*, an Asiatic version of Dow Jones's principal publication. In order to achieve this first major operation in the decentralisation of the economic press, which conforms with the United States turning its attention towards the Pacific archipelago, the North American group chose associates from among its clients: four of the largest newspapers in the region (the Japanese *Nihon Keizai Shimbun*, the Hong Kong *South China Morning*, the *Straits Times* of Singapore, and the Malaysian *New Straits Times*).

'Our links with Asia have been forged carefully. Journal coverage of Asia has been an established fact for decades . . . The Journal, in a joint effort with the Associated Press, has served the Asian business community for nine years by providing a high quality economic and business news service, the AP-Dow Jones Economic Report . . . with the assistance of these partners [the four Asian newspapers], we shall go to Asia with the realistic expectation of becoming a vital, integral part of Asian business life'. The London *Financial Times* replied by launching an international edition on 2nd January 1979. Scripps-Howard, fourth largest chain in the United States, owner of 32 newspapers, 8 weeklies, a tv chain, a radio network, and the famous comics syndicate, United Features, is also proprietor of the world's foremost press agency UPI (United Press International). UPI employs more than 10,000 people. It has 6,400 clients in 114 countries; 238 offices in 62 countries. Its releases are translated into 48 languages. By way of comparison, France-Presse employs 2,000 people, and Reuter of Great Britain 1,635.

The growing importance of satellite transmission, and the preferential tariffs the North American agencies enjoy on these systems, dominated by US firms, are new factors which complicate competition for the press agencies of other capitalist countries. As an index of the supremacy of the North American agencies in the countries of the Third World: around 1970, UPI covered 40% of the information reproduced in the 14 principal Latin American newspapers, AP 31%. The rest was divided between Reuter, AFP and other minor agencies.[35]

It is not because the newspapers of the Latin American countries are the surest clients that the flow of information transmitted in their direction by the North American agencies is more abundant. On the contrary, pluralism of information is so much a function of competition in news consuming countries that it's just like any exchange value. AP, for example, transmits on average 100,000 words each day to European teletype machines, and 65,000 to the Far East. But the flow of words to Latin America, Africa, South-East Asia and the Near East does not exceed, 60,000.[36]

Towards the internationalisation of cultural production?

White House spokesmen are scarcely accustomed to being long-winded about the supremacy of the United States in the domains of information and mass culture. 'The whole communications revolution was created by the United States. The technology which is the essence of the communications revolution was created in this country. In the use of that technology for the dissemination of ideas and information and entertainment, we were the world's leaders. We dominated motion pictures and television for years. We still do. 'Madison Avenue' has become a world-wide cliché for referring to the technique of marketing, and that's the dissemination of ideas.'[37]

In 1972, it was estimated that total North American world exports in television series and documentaries ranged between 100,000 and 200,000 programme hours. On Latin American television chains an average of 60% to 70% of the programming came from the North. In Western Europe dependence was around 20%, while in South Korea, North American television programmes filled more than 90% of transmission time.[38] In France, the sale into private hands of what used to be ORTF coincided with increasing dependence of television on foreign programmes and on advertising (in 1977, advertising revenue represented 61.5% of total receipts on the first channel and 50.7% on the second). Denouncing the fall in original production on French television, two documents put out by the Assemblée Nationale in 1976 made the judgement that home production was being replaced by series and programmes of foreign origin, principally North American. According to the terms of article 24 of the law, said one of the reports, the companies had to ensure that 60% of drama transmission (feature films excluded) should be of French origin or of majority French participation. This proportion was no longer achieved during the first half of 1976 on channel one, where 50% of drama production was of foreign origin. And on channel two, 60% of drama production was of foreign origin.[39]

Series like *Bonanza* or *Chaparral* collect an audience of 250 million in almost 85 countries every week. Warner's *FBI* series is shown in 107 countries, series produced by MCA in 115. Between 1958 and 1973, sales of North American series abroad increased from $15 m. to $130 m. As another US Information Agency functionary put it, one of the reasons why North-American TV series distributors have had so much success is that for a long time they were the only ones occupying the field. Until 1960, there was practically no competition from other foreign distributors on the international market. But the North American distributors not only had the chance of beginning on their own but also that of disposing of a stock of programmes which had already gone the round of the US networks and produced enormous profits. An extremely favourable foreign market exists for these programmes. New stations have an urgent need for programmes. After having realised considerable profits thanks to sales within the United States, the North American distributors were able to offer these programmes abroad at very reduced prices. The result was the conquest, from the beginning, of a very strong position on the world market for television series. This predominance of the United States will doubtless be maintained for a long time. As much through the volume of its sales as through the distribution of its products, the North American television industry is firmly established on the international market.[40] *

If this phenomenon of the export of finished products corresponds to the first phase of international diffusion of North American mass culture, it also constitutes the dominant characteristic of the penetration of the US culture industry, and more particularly the television industry, throughout the world. But the export of finished products, essential as it continues to be, reveals only one of the modes of the real dependence of various countries on North American producers. Even within the limits of the export of ready-made programmes, changes can nevertheless be observed. Conversations held by North American representatives at the Cannes MIP TV Fair in 1975, where 68 countries came together to create a television programme exchange, indicate certain lines of attack: 'Foreign markets', said the vice-president of Paramount Television, 'are expanding, and new outlets are appearing—South Africa for example—and we are beginning to work seriously with the countries of the East'.[41] According to general opinion, there is a marked tendency for a set-back in drama, and an increase in reportage and cultural programmes. 'This is not to say that the famous North American series have lost their prestige. The tendency is rather to make less but better, with more important means, artists of greater repute, getting rid of the excess of violence; here too, to the extent that it increases the market, international norms are being formed.'[42] It can be seen that this kind of internationalisation is far from placing essential North American 'norms' in peril.

* British television has also been extending its entry into the world market over the last few years. Overseas receipts by British tv companies (including BBC Radio and ITV) went up from £5 m. in 1966 to £18.4 m. in 1976, although against this, the purchase of foreign programmes, and money spent producing programmes abroad, increased from £3.5 m. to £17.6 m. over the same period. (*Films and TV Material: Overseas Transactions in 1976*, Dept. of Trade and Industry, 26 Aug. 1977) BBC overseas sales in 1976 reached £8.5 m., while Thames Television, which took over New York's channel 9 for a week in September 1976, in a promotional exercise, achieved overseas sales of £3 m. (*Financial Times*, 21.IV.1977, *IBA Annual Report 1977*) A Thames advertisement in *The Times* (27.VII.1977) boasted 'Every night around the world, they're watching Thames Television'. 'Our market', said the advertisement, 'is bigger than the TV entertainment stations of the world. Universities are among our most regular international customers; *The World at War*, now seen in 64 countries, was acquired by the US Army and Navy for their education divisions; and our factual documentary on the French DC10 disaster found buyers among the top world airlines'. At the end of 1976 two other British commercial television companies, Anglia and Trident, formed a new joint company for overseas sales. Even the Open University has been expanding in this direction. OU turnover has increased from £96,000 in 1971

However, what concerns us is to elucidate the consequences which may be involved at the level of the production of information and culture by the process of the internationalisation of culture which can be seen in the various sectors of the economy. Take the adage which the Ford Motor Company erected into a rule of conduct: 'To be a multinational group, it is necessary to be national everywhere.' Is this confirmed in the culture industry? Two sectors of the North American culture industry seem specially to have been forced to move away from classical export norms and to tailor their products instead according to a preoccupation to satisfy the 'needs' of their foreign consumers: publishing and the cinema. One should add that there is no single strategy of internationalisation. Even if these strategies can be grouped according to major tendencies, they vary from company to company. Let us look first at the example of publishing.

The trajectory of international expansion of the Time-Life magazines illustrates a primary tendency, and allows us at the same time to trace the various phases of North American penetration of foreign markets.[43] *Time* was founded in 1923, *Life* in 1936. The first significant steps towards the exterior were made in 1941. The publishers decided in that year to print *Time* on airmail paper for the Latin American countries. What mattered in this period was to counter the influence of the Axis powers in the Southern hemisphere, and most major magazine publishers participated in this offensive. The first foreign language editions of the *Reader's Digest* also date from this period. The major difference with *Time* was that while *Time* was distributed by airmail, *Reader's Digest* took itself right to its Spanish readers' doorsteps. In 1942, *Time* brought out another airmail edition for the GIs stationed abroad. In 1943, Life Overseas was launched for the armed forces. It contained no advertisements, but it was soon transformed into *Life International*, which did carry advertising and was aimed at the general public. The same year, Time-Life launched the Canadian edition of *Time*. For the first time, an edition of *Time* for overseas included a

---

to £576,000 in 1976, including an increase in the proportion of overseas sales from one tenth to one half. ('Moving into the Open market', *The Guardian*, 5.IV.1977) At the same time the BBC is joint owner together with Reuter's (one third each) and the national broadcasting corporations of Australia, New Zealand and Canada, of Visnews, the world's largest television news agency. Visnews has 190 subscribers throughout the world, including the Eastern block, covering, the company claims, 99% of the globe's tv sets. The agency feeds news material (in neatly packaged $2\frac{1}{2}$ minute segments with timed commentary and background information) via satellite to Australia, the Arabian Gulf, and (from Madrid) to Central and South America, as well as participating in the daily Eurovision News Exchange. The company has an annual turnover of £6.5 m., and more satellite services are planned. (Peter Fiddick, 'Open the box, and what do we find? Visnews.) *The Guardian*, 24.I.1977)—(Translator's note.)

special section on the country where it was sold, and advertising adapted to the companies in that country. *Life* in Spanish was launched in 1953. Printed in the US for distribution in Latin America, it never grew beyond 450,000 copies and was closed down in 1969, as a result of a deficit owing to a lack of advertising. (The only magazine not of North American origin to have tried the same experiment in Latin America was the London *Economist* which published a Latin American version between 1967 and 1970; but it also met with failure.)

A primary reorganisation of the foreign correspondents network (435 correspondents in 33 bureaux) took place in 1958. This re-organisation preceded the launching of the first regional edition of *Time*, for the Pacific countries, primarily Australia and New Zealand, printed since 1959 on the Time-Life presses in Melbourne. No special adaptation to the reality of the countries it was aimed at could be seen in this regional edition, which of course was still in English. Meanwhile in 1960, subscription offices were opened in Amsterdam and Mexico, in order to accelerate foreign subscriptions. Four more regional editions were launched in 1961, the Atlantic, Asiatic, Latin American and South Pacific editions. This still only involved geographical de-centralisation of the operations of printing and distribution. The Atlantic edition of *Time* is printed in Holland by the firm Smeets Offset, a company which belongs to the big publishing house of V.N.U., which, like most of the big netherlands printers, has turned detemindedly to production for major foreign publishers. In 1974, for example, 70% of production by this company was being exported.[44] Holland also provides Time-Life with its highly developed dispatch services. (Another company, Proost en Brandt, provides stockholding and distribution for Time-Life books, even though these are printed in Italy.) In 1972, *Life* magazine disappeared after 35 years' publication. By this date, the North American edition of *Time* had achieved a weekly circulation of 4,250,000 copies; the Canadian edition, 480,000, the Atlantic 430,000, the Asiatic 180,000, the Latin American, 115,000 and the South Pacific edition, 155,000. *Time* therefore distributed almost 300 m. copies a year to readers in more than 180 countries.

In 1973, the firm began the decentralisation of the magazine's contents, but as yet only in Europe. In the Atlantic edition, 4 to 6 pages were added containing news and analysis on the European countries. The rest of the magazine was identical to the North American edition. Somewhat curiously, a special section was begun the same year on questions relating to women's emancipation. In a report put out with a view to preparing the changes in the Atlantic edition, one reads: 'Behind Time's ever-evolving presentation of the news were changes in the mechanics of gathering the news. Early in 1972 a new Paris-based "Euroedit" team was established to coordinate the work of all European correspondents and to develop a better perspective on many European stories that transcend national boundaries. In another organisational move, the Time-Life News Service, formerly an independent division of the company, was merged into Time's editorial department. Both of these changes will provide the possibility of more varied careers for editorial staff members, more interchangeability between "home office" and "field" and more opportunity for firsthand inquiry by editors, writers and researchers. These organisational changes will also help generate special editorial material for the new section, Europe, that is scheduled for addition to Time's Atlantic edition in 1973.'[45]

Another magazine, *Newsweek*, owned by the *Washington Post*, adopted a somewhat similar strategy. Without, however, dividing its edition according to the various geographical markets, it launched an international edition, a half of whose contents differed from the North American edition. We can let their own publicity explain the development of this change and its motivations. The day has passed, we are told, when a US news magazine could render itself international by overprinting a logo on its cover which says 'International Edition'. 'If you want to know what's going on the world, you can no longer take Washington as a unique reference point, you have to *think* international. The change which *Newsweek* has undergone has been in the air for 4 years. At that time, *Newsweek International* was absolutely identical—apart from its advertising—to *Newsweek US*. However, our editors have gradually undertaken to insert more and more articles which respond to a genuine international interest in place of those which are of interest only to Americans. Surprisingly, our readers have accepted the change very well. Our circulation—unique among international publications—has increased considerably in the last three years. It was the readers' response—in fact, their demand—which led us to take the logical step. On 1st January 1973, we introduced the first *truly* international news magazine, a news magazine with brains as international as its readers.'[46] The target of this international alliance: 'the men who make the decisions in the business world and the political leaders of all the nations of the globe'.

Reader's Digest represents a second type of international strategy. From the time of its first moves abroad, with the Latin American edition started in 1940, it has preferred the choice of the local language in order to achieve better penetration of the continents. The French edition dates from 1947. Currently *Reader's Digest* is published in 14 languages with 41 editions and circulating in more than 100 countries.

The geographical decentralisation of printing operations even in the same language, is a model of its kind. There are no less than 9 Spanish editions, each printed in the place where it is distributed: one in the Caribbean, one in Central American, one in Mexico, one in the countries of the Rio de la Plata, Peruvian, Columbian, Chilean and Venezuelan editions and finally one in Spain. 400,000 copies are printed and sold in Mexico every month. In Chile, even under Popular Unity, more than 140,000 copies were printed by the State publishing house Quimantú as a result of a contract inherited from the preceding period. In France, the magazine has a circulation of more than 1.2 million (*L'Express* has a circulation of about 600,000). Does this mean that the contents are decentralised? This is what it claimed when it published the words of the President of Coca-Cola: 'Technology isn't the only thing which has produced rapid progress. Language, as a result of its pressures, has had to bring things out into the open. I will offer an example: the word 'multinational' does not yet figure in the dictionaries, and yet it is already current in business language, where it has replaced the word 'international'. Perhaps it is because Coca-Cola operates in 136 countries that I am particularly conscious of the word 'multinational'. Beyond its immediate signification, the word signifies for me something more than foreign commerce; it implies a certain interest in people of other countries, in their customs, in their social structure; it signifies participation in all aspects of life and in the way of life of a particular nation. For several decades we have had in the *Reader's Digest* a magnificent example of 'multinational' interests. Even though it is of North American origin, the *Digest*, thanks to its editions in 14 languages, speaks the language of men in at least 170 countries; furthermore, and perhaps this is the most important thing, it shows great sensibility towards the traditions, the hopes and the interests of the peoples of the whole world.'[47]

But in Latin American countries, themes of local interest scarcely account for more than 10 to 20% of the contents, while in countries like Canada more than half of the magazine differs from the US edition. Obviously the question of the 'nationalisation' of a review cannot be decided on the basis of the percentage of contents of local interest or articles edited nationally. According to ex-members of the *Reader's Digest* editorial teams abroad, a more centralised review does not exist, and it is always Pleasantville, a few miles from New York where it was founded in the 20s, which dictates the terms of the nationalisation of the contents. Within the limits of a liberal doctrine, the Canadian Parliament seems to have understood this well enough since in May 1975 an Act was introduced which affects the status of *Reader's Digest* and other US magazines (notably *Time*). Ottowa even invoked the possibility of closing down the local editions if they did not accept the demands of 'Canadianisation': 80% of the contents of these magazines were to be of national origin, and so too the majority of the proprietors. *Time* decentralised its Canadian edition rapidly. But in addition to this rejection of cultural domination there was the pressure of economic factors: according to the report of the Canadian Parliament, the disproportion between the circulation of North American magazines and Canadian ones could only grow. In 1969, 130 m. copies of North American magazines were sold in Canada, against 34 m. copies of Canadian weeklies. Furthermore, *Time* and *Reader's Digest* carried off more than half the advertising revenues.[48]

Reader's Digest must have felt the change and indeed perceived the limits of its national adaptation when, again through the mouth of a North American businessman, it felt obliged to justify itself: 'The International editions of The Digest carry more or less the same articles as the US editions. The editors have discovered that subjects which are important to people in Iowa, California and New York are equally important to people in France, Tokyo and Rio.' And, betraying itself, it added: 'Thus it comes about that Digest editors have a profound influence on people who are free to read what they want. *This magazine exports the best in American life.* In my opinion, The Digest is doing as much as the United States Information Agency to win the battle for men's minds.' (Italics in the original).[49]

Only well after the *Reader's Digest* did other North American press enterprises internationalise their production by launching foreign editions of magazines of theirs whose original editions were in English. The first to follow the Digest was the Hearst group, but not until after 1965. In 1966 the group launched a Latin American edition of its women's magazine, *Good Housekeeping*, which became *Buen Hogar* in Spanish. Now produced in 7 countries, it defines its target thus: 'We publish for the young, modern, well-bred, well-off Latin American housewife.' The Spanish edition of another of the group's magazines, *Cosmopolitan*, appeared in 1973. The first venture into women's magazines in France by the Hearst group was made only in 1974, with the French editions of *Cosmopolitan*. Analysis of *Cosmopolitan* in French, and in Spanish for Latin America, reveals the same differences as those which exist between the Canadian and Latin American editions of *Reader's Digest*. Apart from that, the fate of *Cosmopolitan* on the two continents is very different. In France, its circulation is scarcely a quarter that of the big women's magazines such as *Marie-Claire* or *Elle*, while in many Latin American countries it manages to compete with the women's magazines published by the local publishing groups. Apart from the international balance of conditions which happens to favour this kind of operation, one of the major factors to facilitate the adaptation of the Hearst publications in Latin America is undoubtedly the presence in Miami of the ex-proprietors of the Cuban press from the days of Batista. From their exile they form the relay the North American groups need to invade the markets of the Southern Hemisphere. The most important Cuban group (De Armas), proprietor of 15 publishing and distribution houses in Latin America' in this way publishes 15 m. copies every month of every type of magazine, from *Mecanica Popular*, another Hearst group magazine, to the picture-novels inherited from the time of the dictatorship.

But it isn't always Latin America which serves as the scene of experimentation in the process of internationalisation. Other groups like the Condé Nast magazines (Newhouse group) have begun in Europe before moving on to the Latin American countries. In April 1975 a local edition of *Vogue* was launched in Brazil, but Condé Nast had installed *Vogue* in Europe well before. Apart from the Latin American edition, *Vogue* has been published for years in Great Britain, France and Italy. *House & Garden* has a French edition, *Maison et Jardin*; there is also *Structures Décoratives*. In Italy, Condé Nast publish 4 magazines.

Playboy, which after 21 years claims 28 m. readers in 156 countries or territories, constitutes a special example of cosmopolitanism. It inaugurated its fourth foreign language edition in July 1975. After German, French and Italian, came the Japanese edition with a print run of 350,000. At the end of the same month came the fifth edition, in Portuguese, aimed primarily at Brazil, renamed *Homem* (120,000 print run). These editions are absolutely identical apart from the advertising. Indeed the magazine's policy is based on this uniformity: ' . . . one of the greatest tributes to the strength, vitality and relevance of *Playboy* is its successful entry into foreign markets. Surprisingly, Playboy has accomplished this almost wholly without changes in either editorial format or content—proof of both the universality of the *Playboy* concept and its uniqueness as a publication. Indeed, the editorial content of *Playboy* has proved eminently translatable—relying as it does on fine graphics, the best in contemporary literature, sophisticated humour, beautiful women, provocative personalities and features of universal interest.'[50]

You only find North American publications giving us this assurance that their material is easily translatable from the moment the big companies decided to internationalise their concept of management. The big business magazine, *Forbes*, whose circulation is pretty well the same as *Business Week* or *Fortune*, is not afraid to say 'We have translated American Business into Arabic' in presenting its Arab language edition, launched in 1975. And to put a signature to this advertisement: *Forbes, capitalist tool*.[51]

One way or another, all the North American press enterprises who have embarked on an aggressive foreign policy have discovered the benefits of geographical decentralisation without at all losing vertical control over foreign production. Even Walt Disney Productions has yielded to this. Some recent statistics reveal the extent of foreign participation in the manufacture of its comics. The Chilean edition, which also serves Peru, Paraguay and Argentina, uses up 4,400 pages of comic strips per year in its four magazines (whose total circulation is 800,000 per month). A third of these comes from the studios in California, a third from the North American Western Publishing Co., about a quarter from Italy and the rest from Brazil and Denmark. The Mexican edition is supplied almost totally by North American material. Brazil, with 5 magazines and 2m. copies a month, gets one-fifth of its material from Italy (1,000 out of 5,000 pages), produces a bit more than a fifth itself, and imports the rest from the US. Italy undoubtedly provides the largest proportion of its own material, half the 5,000 pages published there every year.[52] In France, *le Journal de Mickey* takes half its material from North America.

The local manufacture of the adventures of Donald, Scrooge McDuck and other heroes clearly follows a very strict Disney code. In an imaginary interview with Mickey in France, his business manager makes the little creature say, 'A proper imprimatur must be obtained to use my name and my image. Walt has imposed draconian conditions not only with regard to my drawing but also my personality. And that's precisely the essential element.'[53] And again, the same claim to universality: 'Certainly I have assisted the great wave of Americanism in the world. For I am the image of America, of a certain America, that of the pioneers, of adventure, action, courage. An America sure of itself and of the quality of its mode of life. Conquering. Enterprising. But, far beyond that, and without false pride, I touch the most profoundly constant elements of the human soul, the struggle of the little against the big, David against Goliath. If not, I wouldn't have become what I am: a universal figure.'[54] The relative freedom of action simply allows local editors to adapt the strips so as to place emphasis on certain latent characteristics of the message in particular historical moments. In Popular Chile, for example, a special virulence appeared in stigmatising sympathisers of another order, and ridiculing them with such words as 'bandits', 'delinquents', and so forth.

Cinema coproductions

The internationalisation of film production is a well-known phenomenon, consecrated several years ago.

In October 1956, Paramount celebrated the 35th anniversary of its presence in France. The editor-in-chief of the review *Le Film Français* wrote in a special edition devoted to the event: 'With the perspective of time, one appreciates better the importance of the arrival in 1921 for the first time in our country of a major American film company. In setting up a branch in France, with its own distribution agency, Paramount introduced us to new methods and new ideas, which didn't only help to make their trade mark, their stars and their directors better known, but also stimulated French distribution and exhibition. Was it not Paramount who, for the first time, created a special service in exhibition, effectively giving directors a shoulder up by means of ingenious publicity, thus assuring a maximum return on their films? In the field of French-American collaboration in the cinema, Paramount was equally innovative in producing major French films in our studios from 1923 on, such as *Les Opprimés* with Raquel Meller, and, in 1925, *Madame Sans-gêne* with Gloria Swanson. This policy of Paramount's in favour of French films had its full effect in the 'talkie' revolution, with the films of Maurice Chevalier shot in Hollywood, and above all with the French production at the Paramount studios of Saint-Maurice where, among others, Pagnol's famous *Marius*, with Raimu and Pierre Fresnay, was made ... Extremely useful lessons can be learned from these 35 years—more than a third of a century—of Paramount in France. Indubitably the rise of our industry owes a lot to this company which, in establishing its own trade-mark everywhere, also established cinema.'[55]

Table 23

US Majors' Foreign Film Market Shares: 1972–74

Company	1974* %	1973 %	1972 %
Warner Bros.	22.5	12.5	13.0
Universal	17.0	10.5	9.0
United Artists	16.0	22.5	21.0
Columbia	14.0	10.5	12.0
20th Fox	12.0	16.0	16.5
Paramount	10.0	14.0	14.5
MGM	8.5	14.0	14.0
Total International Sales (in millions of dollars)	**450.0**	**375.0**	**350.0**

Source: *Variety*, 6.VI.1975.
* Portion due to each US film company out of total film rentals realised abroad by all seven. Not including commercial transactions in Canada.

The recent crisis in Hollywood has done no more than hold back this well established process. But it has added a new element. Producers have had to consider the specific needs of each region. At least if you believe what they say on the crest of the wave of recession. 'Meanwhile, moviemakers are getting only 33% of their total revenues from overseas, compared with a time-honored 50%, year after year. To recapture foreign moviegoers, some US companies are starting to make films abroad for specific geographic markets. MGM, for example, will make six movies in Europe to be shown only in Europe. Warner Bros. has made three movies in Italy and three in France for European distribution. When United Artists made *Last Tango in Paris*, it planned distribution only in Europe. Not until the film received rave reviews at French film festivals did UA decide to distribute it worldwide.'[56]

The phenomenon of coproduction therefore tends to become confirmed. During 1973 and 1974, 434 films were produced in France. 200 were the fruits of coproduction.[57] Normally this kind of asso-

Table 24

US Direct Investment Receipts of Fees and Royalities, by Area and Major Industry
(1970–1973)
(en millions de dollars)

Company/region	Petroleum		Manu-facturing		Trade		Films Foreign rental		Other	
	1970	1973	1970	1973	1970	1973	1970	1973	1970	1973
Canada	17	27	225	307	15	24	37	38	63	83
Europe										
EEC*	31	43	287	526	30	55	48	66	17	36
Others	27	39	229	320	41	93	63	67	37	61
Australia, N. Zealand,										
Japan, S. Africa	21	19	117	226	11	31	67	78	19	43
Latin America	38	32	115	135	33	32	54	49	78	114
Others**	82	122	28	57	26	27	30	27	33	64
Total	**216**	**281**	**1,002**	**1,570**	**156**	**263**	**299**	**324**	**247**	**400**

Source: *Survey of Current Business*, August, 1974.
   * Includes Belgium, France, Germany, Italy, Luxemburg and the Netherlands. 'Others' includes G.B.
   ** Includes Africa (apart from S. Africa), Middle East, Asia (apart from Japan) and the Pacific countries (apart from Australia and New Zealand).

Table 25

US Film Industry's Top 15 Foreign Markets in 1976

1976 Rank	Country	Rentals*	1975 Rank
1	Canadax	$60,800,000	1
2	Japan	$52,100,000	2
3	France	$51,900,000	4
4	Italy	$45,000,000	3
5	W. Germany	$41,300,000	5
6	U.K.	$37,100,000	6
7	Spain	$31,100,000	8
8	Australia	$28,700,000	7
9	Brazil	$25,400,000	9
10	Mexico	$21,000,000	11
11	South Africa	$11,200,000	10
12	Netherlands	$ 9,500,000	14
13	Sweden	$ 9,100,000	12
14	Venezuela	$ 9,000,000	15
15	Switzerland	$ 8,000,000	13

Source: *Variety.*
* Includes sales of advertising materials, also rentals from foreign films and/or films from smaller US producers released in limited areas by major American companies.

ciation is concentrated on big budget films. Among the list of French films in the second half of 1974, the four biggest budget films (more than 10 m. francs) were all coproductions: *Les deux missionaires* by Franco Rossi, a French-Italian coproduction (20%–80%); Bertolucci's *1900* (French-Italian-German, 40%–40%–20%); Lucio Fulci's *Le retour de Croc Blanc* (French-Italian-German, 60%–20%–20%); and Duccio Tessari's *Zorro* (Italian-French, 75%–25%). (Only one of these films, Bertolucci's *1900*, was given a release in Great Britain, and that only four years later in 1978 after a long and involved argument between Bertolucci and the North American parent company, United Artists, on the version for English release.) In two of the four films, the producer representing the French participant was the Parisian subsidiary of United Artists (Prod. Artistes Associés). In all four, France was represented by capital, while the directors were all foreigners, and as for the actors only one in each was a French star. Bertolucci's *Last Tango in Paris* was also an Italian-French coproduction, but effectively, through the same United Artists subsidiary, an Italian–US coproduction (60%–40%). By using the French subsidiary, the North American company was able to profit from subsidies granted to the film industry in European countries by the State.*

This stratagem was perfectly explained in an article in the magazine *Le Cinématographe* in January 1975: 'State support has turned cinema into a protected industry. Because if all films which are issued in France contribute to financing the funds used for this support, only French films benefit from the redistribution effected by the funds. It's the same in all countries where such an aid system functions, which explains the growing number of coproductions: a film produced by an Italian and a Frenchman will benefit from aid at the same time in Italy and in France. Why are there no French-American coproductions? Because there is no State aid to the cinema in the US. Furthermore, coproduction is pretty often a piece of fakery: a French-Italian coproduction with majority French participation signifies simply that the film is produced in France and sold in Italy once it's finished; this sale is cheerfully called 'participation in the production'. This kind of trickery well reveals the weaknesses of the producer, always in search of expedients. Without State aid, the whole production system would collapse: it represents almost a quarter of the resources available to producers . . . Cinema once came under the Ministry of Industry: it has now passed to the protection of Cultural Affairs. Sometimes one might ask why.'[58] Film activity is more and more regulated by criteria which are dominant in other sectors of industry. What has been underlined here in relation to film coproduction can be found, with a few differences, in data-processing and nuclear power, where the State has become a partner of multinational groups.

Subsidiaries are also excellent bases for prospecting for new themes

---

* 78 feature films were produced in Britain in 1974. Figures on costs are unavailable. British film production has not yet entered very extensively into European coproduction, but North American companies operating in Britain have still been able to take advantage of subsidies in the form of an automatic aid, known as the Eady Levy, which is a box office levy, redistributed to films qualifying as British productions, in proportion to their box office receipts. The aid system in Britain is currently due for reorganisation. Ex-Prime Minister Harold Wilson, who set up the present institutional structure of the British film industry, which has given the North American producers such advantages, when he was President of the Board of Trade in the late 1940s, is now (1978) chairman of a government committee preparing fresh legislation intended to revitalise the British film industry yet again. It is highly unlikely to succeed in this aim, since the Interim Action Committee Report (HMSO, Cmnd 7071, January 1978) indicates no real attack on the major problems, viz, the domination both culturally and economically of the British film industry by the North American majors and the two British monopolists, Rank and EMI, who are tied in with and obtain the largest part of their films for exhibition, from them. Meanwhile, the Wilson committee also faces the problem that under the terms of the Treaty of Rome, the Eady Levy is illegal as long as it operates as a national preference subsidy. (Translator's note.)

in the cinema which are likely to meet with public success in particular markets. *Emmanuelle II (Emmanuelle l'anti-vierge)* was produced by Parafrance who joined up with the French producer of *Emmanuelle I.* In July 1975 the same company announced that it would coproduce the film version of the memoirs of the famous hooker Madame Claude, with another French producer.[59]

In terms of television, this practice of coproduction with the North Americans is less developed. We may cite a relatively exceptional case, that of BBC coproductions with North American producers. 153 programmes were coproduced in 1972. The year before the figure was 77. Most of these coproductions were bi-party, while others were made in collaboration by a number of organisations.[60] One of the most ambitious projects of this kind, announced in March 1977, is a BBC-Time-Life project, to be spread out over six years at a cost of about £25 m., to record the entire cycle of 37 Shakespeare plays. Time-Life will contribute a little over 40% in return for North American rights, mainly for sale to television companies, but, according to a BBC spokesman, 'Artistic control will be entirely British'.[61] The future of these co-productions may bring surprises. Other European countries are thinking of coproductions with the North Americans as a way into the US market and of extending their international clientéle. Discussions have taken place between the Société Française de Production (SFP) and Paramount.

Defining 'national culture' in the multinational era

But the phenomenon of the internationalisation of cultural production doesn't boil down to a growing penetration of the market by North American enterprises. It is built up to the extent that local ruling classes are persuaded of the efficacy of the schemes and norms of production which have proved themselves in the metropolis. For these local bourgeoisies, modernity, and the North American plan of manufacture and expansion, are equivalent.

When *L'Express* was modified according to transatlantic models, its editor-in-chief declared, defending himself for having followed the North American example: 'Our characteristic is not the American style, but our regard for modernity.'[62] In June 1975, the magazine *Strategies*, itself tailored on a North American model, announced, under the questioning title 'A Second Life for the Press?', the creation of 4 new magazines, three of which responded faithfully to a North American model which had been duly tried on the market. 'Three more new magazines will be placed on the French market in September-October. French nationalists are certainly getting heated about this, but it is now a fact in Europe that the best ideas about the press—the ideas which succeed—have been drawn from the United States. The best example is surely that of the news magazine. *L'Economiste*—the title is still provisional—resulting from the merger between *Entreprise* and *Informations*, does not hide its origins. It is directly inspired by *Business Week*. J. L. Servan–Schreiber, an old hand in the business' since *L'Expansion* is a kind of French *Fortune*, openly acknowledges that it was the success of the *Book Digest* which decided him to launch *Lire* in September with Bernard Pivot . . . Elisabeth Lefèbvre also declared her colours: *Jacinte*, a monthly women's magazine for the young which appears at the end of September, is inspired by formulae which have been highly successful in the United States: *Glamour, Seventeen, Mademoiselle*, which have a total of 4 m. purchasers every month.' The director of the future French *Business Week* gets the last word in the affair: 'If we want to produce a French *Business Week*, this is because if there is a good model we don't see why we shouldn't be inspired by it.'[63]

There is a final observation to be made which in itself suggests the inevitable direction which research would have to take in order to discern the nature and limits of the process of internationalisation of cultural production. One should ask if the effect of North American imperialism will be the disappearance of so-called national cultures, cultures that are elaborated and controlled by the ruling classes of each nation; and if these cultures will now cede their place to a culture which knows no frontiers. It is not possible to answer this question without attaching it to the more general question of the internationalisation of capital and of the national State.[64] In the same way that it is difficult to accept the widespread idea[65] that multinational companies and the internationalisation of capitalist relations are conducive to the decline of nation-states, so it is also difficult to accept this other idea of the disappearance of so-called national cultures. Changes in capitalism do not in any way remove States from the map, but rather give birth to new State practices. New forms and practices also arise in the domain of culture and State apparatus. Take the need of North American publishers and producers to define readers' and viewers' centres of interest in each region more precisely, though this is necessarily tempered by a claim to universality which every imperialist ideology makes for its own particular values. Doesn't this indicate their intuition for the evolution of cultural apparatuses? The need, for example, which the producers of *Sesame Street* experienced to adapt the programme 'to the national reality' and not simply to dub their new educational series into foreign languages—isn't this one index amongst others of the need for cultural imperialism to decentralise?

Everything leads us to believe that in the present phase of accumulation of capital, the internationalisation of business will proceed apace with a wave of 'cultural nationalism', even in countries where the development model is entirely adapted to the needs of the multinationals. The way in which the Brazilian technocracy, for example, is in the process of reformulating the models of the North American technocracy and amalgamating them with elements which come from other kinds of ideology, that is, ideologies which are less dependent on imperialism, merits examination in terms of this perspective for anyone wishing to determine the lines on which these national cultures can develop and still conform with multinational expansion. In a context which privileges the most camouflaged, the most secret forms of the North American invasion, the 'nationalisation' of the models which constitute the axes of North American production is an almost inevitable necessity.

In order to define the concept of cultural imperialism, it is first necessary to try and delimit that of 'national culture'. This notion cannot be specified except by considering the relation of the national (or, in their absence, creole) bourgeoisies to the groupings of the North American Empire. National culture, in the era of the multinationals, has to guarantee the reproduction of the dependence of these bourgeoisies on the United States at the same time as that of their own hegemony as the ruling class in a particular nation; that is to say, it has to continue to sanctify their position as an 'interior bourgeoisie'.[66] Such a perspective would have the merit of removing discussions on cultural imperialism from a 'culturalist' sphere. It would re-establish its historical and its class character, relating it to modifications in the respective roles of these bourgeoisies. On the one hand, cultural imperialism changes form and content according to the phases of the political, economic and military expansion of the Empire, and on the other, it adapts itself to diverse realities and dominant contexts. It is by infiltration through the most porous elements of these so-called national cultures that North American imperialism reproduces the superstructural conditions which allow it to prosper.

Notes

1 To trace the crisis of the film companies see: *Moody's Industrial Manual*, the company reports and various articles on the subject published between 1961 and 1975 in *Business Week, Dun's Review, Wall Street Journal, US News and World Report, Variety, Le Film Français*.

2 *Business Week*, 23.VI.1973.
3 *Redstockings of Women's Liberation Movement*,New York, press release, 9.V.1975.
4 *Business Week*, 8.I.1972.
5 The British television company, Trident, seems to be following these examples in its acquisition of Windsor Safari Park (Translator's note).
6 Gulf & Western Industries, *Annual Reports 1966–73*.
7 Gulf & Western Industries, *Annual Report 1969*.
8 Gulf & Western Industries, *Annual Report 1972*.
9 Tahrir, *Bulletin de liaison entre le monde arabe et l'Amerique Latine*, Rome, 1975, No. 2.
10. In *Le Film Français*, 8.II.1974.
    In 1977, the rhythm of film industry diversification has hardly slowed down. Some examples: Columbia Pictures paid out more than $50 m. for D. Gottlieb & Co., the largest US maker of pinball machines; it has also been looking for another company to purchase, and just broke off talks with Filmways Inc., a film producer and publisher, for a merger. Warner Communications has moved into the video games' field with its acquisition of Atari Inc., and has been making preparations to enter the perfume market with the formation of Warner Fragrances Ltd. It also announced another acquisition: an agreement to purchase the Knickerbocker Toy Co. Warner is also the largest shareholder in the Coca-Cola Bottling Co. of New York (Author's note).
11 *Business Week*, 23.VI.1973.
12 For a comprehensive analysis of the media in Great Britain, see G. Murdock and P. Golding, 'For a political economy of mass communication', *Socialist Register 1973*, Merlin Press, 1974. (See also the same authors, 'Capitalism, Communication and Class Relations' in *Mass Communication and Society*, eds. Curran, Gurevitch and Wollacott, Edward Arnold, 1977, and *passim* (Translator's note).
13 'L'événement: le cinéma français', *Le Monde*, 29.I.1975. For an analysis of the European film industry, see Claude Degand, *Le Cinéma cette industrie*, Paris, Editor's techniques et économiques, 1974.
14 *Le Film Français*, 31.I.1975.
15 For the evolution of EMI and the Rank Organisation, see *Informations Internationales*.
16 Cf. Pekka Gronow, 'The record industry: multinational corporations and national music traditions', International Institute for Music, Dance & Theater in the audio-visual media (IMDT), Vienna, document presented to the Conference in Ottawa, 1.X.1975.
17 Xerox Corporation, *Annual Report 1974*.
18 Murdock and Golding, *op. cit.*
19 Thomas H. Guback, 'Film as International Business', *Journal of Communications*, Winter 1974, Vol. 24, no. 1.
20 'L'événement: le cinéma français', *Le Monde*, 28.I.1975.
21 *Le Film Français*, 18.XII.1974; *Variety*, 16.VII.1975. Pathé-Gaumont also owns a cinema in New York and sixteen in Belgium.
22 *Le Film Français*, 6.XII.1974.
23 Francis Wyle, 'Gannett: where local news is global news', *Finance*, April 1973.
24 *Finance*, April 1973.
25 For the process of concentration in the US press, See *Columbian Journalism Review*, Nov–Dec. 1972; *Atlantic*, July 1969; *Business Week*, 29.VIII.1970, 27.V.1972; *Finance*, March 1972; *Advertising Age*, 6.V.1972, 14.VII.1975.
26 *Business Week*, 27.V.1972.

27 Jacques Sauvegeot, 'Deuz nouvelles alertes', *Le Monde*, 6–7 August 1975; 'La presse écrite en France', *Le Monde-Dossiers et documents*, No. 15, Nov. 1974.
28 J. Richard Elliott, 'The talk about the Times', *Finance*, April 1973.
29 *Broadcasting*, 2.VI.1975.
30 J. Michel Quatrepoint, 'Le papier comme le petrole', *Le Monde*, 26 March 1974.
31 Time Inc., *Annual Report 1972; Advertising Age*, 21.VII.1975. For other North American press enterprises, *Finance*, April 1973.
32 'Reed International *Limited*', *Informations Generales*.
33 J. Michel Quatrepoint, *op.cit.*
34 See A. Mattelart, *Agresión desde el espacio*, Buenos Aires, Mexico, 1973, Editorial Siglo XXI.
35 Cf. the studies of the centre for journalism (CIESPAL) of UNESCO, Quito, Ecuador.
36 Report by USIS in *USIA Appropriations Authorization Fiscal Year 1973*, US Senate, *op.cit.*
37 Interview with Frank Shakespeare, 'Who's Winning the propaganda war', *US News & World Report*, 1 May 1972.
38 Cf. the study by Kaarle Nordenstreng and Tapio Varis, *La télévision circule-t-elle à sens unique, revue et ànalyse de la circulation des programmes de television dans le monde*, Paris, UNESCO, 1974. This study reckoned French and British TV exports at 20,000 programme hours; those of RFA at 6,000.
39 Assemblée Nationale, Commission des affaires culturelles, familiales et sociales (Avis presenté par M. de Préaumont) 1976.
40 Wilson Dizard, *Television: a world view*, Syracuse University Press, 1966.
41 Pierre Girard, 'MIP TV 75: un marche en pleine expansion', *Le Film Français*, 2.V.1975.
42 *Ibid.*
43 Cf. the annual company reports.
44 H. Lottman, 'The Dutch are still strong on the printing scene', *Publishers Weekly*, 28.X.1974. Italy, Spain and Yugoslavia are other countries where the multi-nationalisation of these printing operations are directed.
45 Time Inc., *Annual Report 1972*.
46 *Advertising Age*, 26.III.1973 (Retranslated from French).
47 Published in *Selecciones del Reader's Digest*, Chilean edition, August 1972.
48 Ben Swanskey, 'Monopoly control of Canada's mass media', *Communist Viewpoint*, Toronto, May-June 1971.
49 Words of the President of the Advertising agency Ogilry & Mather, David Ogilvy, Broadcasting, 9.XII.1974.
50 Appeared in *Advertising Age* during the course of 1975.
51 *Ibid.* In the field of book publishing, the phenomenon of multinationalisation is most advanced in the areas of art books and encyclopaedias. These operations have customorily brought together big North American publishers like McGraw-Hill and their European counterparts (Larousse, Robert Lafont, Rizzoli, Mondadori, Noguer). Agreements generally cover co-publication and joint printing arrangements (more rarely joint conception of a project). Cf. *Publishers' Weekly*, 15.IV.1974.
52 Introduction by D. Kunzle to *How to Read Donald Duck* by A. Dorfman and A. Mattelart, International General, New York, 1975.
53 *Réalités*, Paris, December 1974.
54 *Ibid.*
55 Pierre Autré, '35 ans de présence', *Le film francais*, édition spéciale, October 1956.

56 *Business Week*, 23.VI.1973.
57 *Le Film Français*, 18.X.1974, 28.II.1975. In 1974, according to official statistics of the Centre National de Cinema (CNC), the 234 feature-length films produced in France represented a total investment of 637 m. francs. Foreign participation represented 242 m. or 38%. The average cost of a film in 1974 was 2.7 m. francs. (*Le Film Français*, 14.II.1975).
58 'La production française', *le Cinématographe*, January 1975.
59 *Variety*, 16.VII.1975, 23.VII.1975.
60 Thomas Guback, *op. cit.*
61 *The Guardian*, 3.III.1977.
62 Cited by Jean-Claude Texier, 'Métamorphoses d'une industrie de la pensée', *Le Monde Diplomatique*, December 1974.
63 *Strategies*, 16 June–29 June 1975.
64 On this theme cf. Nicos Poulantzas, 'L'internationalisation des rapports capitalistes et l'Etat-nation', *Les Temps Modernes*, February 1973; A. Martinelli and E. Somaini, 'Nation States and Multinational Corporations', *Kapitalistate*, No. 1, 1973; Robin Murray, 'The internationalisation of capital and Nation state', *The Spokesman*, No. 10, 1971.
65 Cf. the works of Raymond Vernon.
66 To use N. Poulantzas's expression. See also the present author's own analysis in *Mass Media, idéologies et mouvement révolutionnaire*, Paris, 1974. English edition forthcoming, The Harvester Press.

CHAPTER VII

WHEN ADVERTISING BECOMES POLITICS

'PUBLIC opinion polls are one of the most powerful and one of the most perfect instruments of modern democracy.' It was in these triumphant terms that the North American George Gallup—founder of a network of public opinion institutes covering 36 countries—justified, some 25 years ago, the rapid development which this kind of research has continued to experience in the Western world. Since then, this conviction has been passed on to Gallup's disciples. Today their motto is 'To the "Know Thyself" of Socrates, the basis of individual life, advertising adds "Know Them", the basis of social action. This isn't demagogy, it's enlightened democracy'.[1] The words of the President of the North American J. Walter Thompson advertising agency are similar in principle though somewhat less sophisticated: 'During the 27-year period of 1946–1972, advertising volume in the US increased from $3.4 billion to $23 billion, or seven times. This coincides with the greatest economic growth period in American history, and not so coincidentally with the period of the greatest advances in social justice in our society. The corollary is in the fact that the growth of other free-world societies seems to run roughly parallel to the growth of their advertising expenditures.'[2] Lastly, the President of Batten, Dunstine & Osborn puts it more aggressively: 'Democracies with high living standards are at the top of the list of countries spending a high per cent of national income on advertising, whereas communist dictatorships with relatively low living standards are at the bottom of the list.'[3] Freedom must have its advertising, he said, or else it will surely run into danger. Thus the same company president-cum-transatlantic marketing theorist concludes his declaration of principles elsewhere with the remark: 'The American Marketing System has as its basis that sudden upsurge of the idea of human freedom.'[4]

The transparency of these declarations enables us to view with some scepticism the remarks of other managers on the supposed neutrality of their scientific methods of assessing the needs, getting to know the attitudes, and predicting the behaviour of their public: 'Fundamentally advertising . . . is neutral; that is to say it can serve very different ends'.[5]

It would be useful briefly to summarise the postulates of the advertising industry which must be questioned in coming to grips with the subject. Firstly, the assumption that advertising is situated outside the mode of production which gave birth to it. It only acquires meaning through its effects, good or evil according to the narrowest of manichean dualisms. The means of production of information is not subject to the 'law of value'. In some way advertising occupies a privileged place, where the market relationship of producer to consumer, broadcaster to receiver, is not reproduced, a place where words and power are handed over to the audience. As J. W. Thompson already wrote in 1909, 'advertising is the shortest route from producer to consumer'; which, when applied to electoral advertising, becomes 'advertising is the shortest route between candidate and voter'. If you follow through even to a limited extent the thesis of the end of ideology and the politics put forward by these technocrats, this becomes 'advertising is the new party, the party of those without party'. As a former Wall Street journalist observed in his book, *The New Politics*,[6] after following the campaigns of the future Governor of California, Ronald Reagan, and of the Rockefeller brothers, campaigns which were planned by electoral management firms: 'I think that these firms are anti-party, because they tend to become substitutes for the regular party apparatus'.

Secondly it is supposed that market research or motivation studies can be in themselves something other in capitalist society than plebiscites. To put it another way, that they can be other than the ratification of programmes pre-established by rampant institutionalism, which introjects tastes and attitudes and sets up its democratic features on this pregiven basis. The sphere of production is governed by the 'dictatorship of the consumers'. The choice between several products is no longer a false choice under the pressure of advertising, but a free choice corresponding to each person's options. After the last presidential elections in France, the director of the country's second largest advertising agency, Publicis, opposed the government's decision to ban publication of the latest opinion polls on the eve of the elections, and spoke in terms of the 'repression of a fundamental right'. 'To defend the complete and total freedom to publish the results of polls during the election period is to defend essential liberties.'[7] Apart from this particular point, the same declaration constituted an apologia for the Institut française de l'opinion publique (French Institute of Public Opinion), Gallup's correspondent in France: 'Placing itself at the service of the public, in a spirit of devotion to common interests, its [research] constitutes an instrument of progress. In politics, it helps to take account of the needs, problems and hopes of the citizen to enable government to take account of him. That's called democracy. In the domain of production, it gives eyes to the creative imagination which would otherwise be blind, and ears to commerce which would otherwise be deaf, and it allows for the needs of the citizen-consumer to be met. For his part, the citizen consumer has the right to vote and it is interesting to know in advance how he is going to use it: the right to buy or not to buy.'

The third and final assumption is that advertising has nothing to do with the sophisms of the theory of public opinion which legitimises the specific form of political regime known as bourgeois democracy. These sophisms allow the class which represents capital to shelter behind the pluralistic appearance which the 'majority vote' confers upon it, in order to establish its dominion both in the representative chamber of Parliament and in the press, where it assumes the right to represent the majority, which is to say, 'public opinion'.

Advertising can indeed serve highly diverse ends, but under one condition: that of guaranteeing the reproduction of existing social relations. Instead of making it sell washing powders, cars and gadgets, it can be made to serve 'non profit making' ends: it can defend 'social causes'; it can promote an educational policy; design an electoral campaign, the fight against pollution, the fight against alcoholism. It can be given a different appearance but it cannot be made to change sides. To ask it to do other than *sell a consumer product*, 'profit-making' or otherwise, is to ask it to liquidate itself as a system—to use the terms of the North American theorist already quoted, who assimilates advertising to the exercise of 'democracy' or 'liberty'. With the disappearance of the market relation between consumer and producer, another form of the determination of power appears which renders the class power of abstract 'public opinion' obsolete, the power which advertising, conceived as an illusion of democratic participation, rests on.

From presidential campaigns to publicity campaigns against nationalisation

Beneath the formulas of a worn-out schematicism, which invariably identifies freedom and the human personality with the freedom and personality of capital, interference by advertising agencies and other services over the last five years has increased. The refinement of these formulas is inversely proportional to the rhythm of growth of fascism in the groups which have recourse to them. Not content to organise the electoral campaigns of the right, to predict the success of their candidates using all the latest computer techniques, and to install them in advance through the influence of the opinion polls, market research firms have become party to the ideological offensive of the ruling classes. Examples abound.

Among Richard Nixon's inner circle were three former top-ranking executives of the J. Walter Thompson organisation: Robert Haldeman, special assistant, one of the first heads to roll in the Watergate affair; Ron Ziegler, White House press secretary; and Harry Treleaven, adviser on political propaganda. The president of J. Walter Thompson, Dan Seymour, is himself one of the most important members of the Council of Foreign Relations (CFR), effectively a parallel State Department which decides on the foreign policy both of the US Government and of the multinationals. Moreover, Nixon's period of office marked a significant increase in the use by the political powers of the ideological apparatus of broadcasting. 'The Nixon Administration, more than any other administration, has been a government by television. Political manipulation of broadcasting by the executive branch is the most visible form of government pressure on electronic journalism. The President's central role in national policy-making has given him access to the network airwaves on short notice. President Nixon and his advisers not only understand the power of television, but also acknowledge the political importance of *control* over communications processes, and do not hesitate to exploit it.'[8]

In spite of this policy, we still find, in November 1970, proprietors of North American advertising agencies criticising 'the inefficiency of the State Department, the CIA and the USIS' (United States Information Service) in creating an image of the United States abroad. The president of Kenyon & Eckhardt—a former military communications expert and one of the organisers of Johnson's 1964 campaign—wrote a letter to Nixon: 'The US Government should turn to the advertising industry for advice and leadership in establishing a propaganda programme that would serve a twofold purpose—improvement of the US image abroad, and subsequently, the creation of a better climate for American companies wishing to do business in foreign countries.'[9] This is not the first time that Kenyon & Eckhardt have entered the political arena. They previously moved one of their directors to the Pentagon to manage its labour policy, and that was in 1967. The same year, the founder of Benton & Bowles—a former under-secretary of State in the Truman administration—taking part in a campaign which brought together all the heads of the advertising agencies, put forward 'a Marshall plan in the field of ideas' in order to demonstrate 'the strength and stability of our economy.'[10] The president of another agency, Arthur Meyerhoff Associates, organiser of the Association of North American advertising agencies, outlined a new foreign policy on ideological matters with the substantial collaboration of USIS: 'US programs abroad are in a 25-year rut of speaking primarily to the intellectual elite. They don't talk to the man in the street as American advertising has proved it knows how to do.'[11]

In 1972, the campaign to promote the myth of the 'Brazilian miracle' was launched from New York, on a world scale, by the Kenyon & Eckhardt agency.[12] Sticking to Latin America, consider first two isolated facts: in 1968, the North American agency Compton Advertising, was given charge of the electoral campaign of the Christian-Democrat candidate in the Venezuelan elections, Rafael Caldera; and in 1972, the Argentinian subsidiary of J. Walter Thompson undertook the presidential campaign of the brother of General Alsogaray, the unsuccessful candidate of a new party supported by the military in power.

Let us now pass to the case of Chile. In the struggle against the Popular Government, the ideological apparatuses of the Empire and of the local bourgeoisie were assigned a new role. In 1970 the Chilean subsidiary of J. Walter Thompson planned the campaign of the traditional rightist candidate Jorge Alessandri. Once Salvador Allende had been elected, the agency decided to quit Chile—although it had been operating in Santiago since 1944, was the most important in the country, and had an annual turnover of $4.5 m.—at the same time as its principal client, the Anaconda mining company, on whose behalf, in July and August 1970, the agency had conducted a campaign of psychological terror aimed at 'blocking the path of the Marxist candidate'. Before leaving, JWT was careful to distribute its 85 experts inside the right-wing media and in the various services of the embassy of the United States in Santiago. It also took care to hand over its budget to the local agency Publicidades Fabres y de Heeckeren, which gave it the advertising for the oldest conservative daily in Santiago, *El Mercurio*, the enthusiastic leader of the ideological offensive against the Popular Government.[13] This agency served as the legal intermediary for the transfer of funds from the North American embassy and multinational companies to the Chilean reactionaries, funds destined to finance press campaigns and to prop up these means of communication controlled by the local bourgeoisie. On 17th September 1970, only two weeks after Allende's victory at the polls and before the Senate had ratified his election, Hal Hendrix and Robert Berrellez, officials of the ITT's public relations department in Latin America, sent a letter to their vice-president, E. J. Gerrity, in which they said:

The Mercurio newspapers are another key factor. Keeping them alive and publishing between now and October 24 is of extreme importance. They are the only remaining outspoken anti-Communist voice in Chile and under severe pressure, especially in Santiago. This may well turn out to be the Achilles heel for the Allende crowd.

And even more explicitly:

We have recommended, apart from direct assistance, the following:

1. We and other US firms in Chile pump some advertising into Mercurio. (This has been started)

2. We help with getting some propagandists working again on radio and television. There are about 20 people that the Matte and Edwards groups[14] were supporting and we should make certain they are revived. Allende now controls two of three TV stations in Santiago and has launched an intensive radio campaign.

3. Assist in support of a 'family relocation' center in Mendoza or Baires for wives and children of key persons involved in the fight. This will involve about 50 families for a period of a month to six weeks, maybe two months.

4. Bring what pressure we can on USIS in Washington to instruct the Santiago USIS to start moving the Mercurio editorials around Latin America and into Europe. Up until I left they were under orders not to move anything out of Chile.

5. Urge the key European press, through our contacts there, to get the story of what disaster could fall on Chile if Allende & Co. win this country.[15]

In 1962, the Chilean subsidiary of the North American Gallup network had begun putting into effect the express request of the Kennecott Copper Company for systematic opinion polls on leaders of opinion (union leaders, parliamentarians, heads of corporations, employers' organisations and the Press), to 'try and assess the reasons for attitudes and behaviour towards the nationalisation of the copper industry and, in more general terms, towards foreign investment in the country'.[16] In the questionnaire which circulated two months before the presidential elections of 1964, there were questions such as the following: 'In your opinion, why was President Joao Goulart removed from office? (a) because he went too far in moves to nationalise the country's national resources; (b) because he did not respect the constitutional principles and traditions of the nation; (c) because he was identified with the parties of the left, especially the Communist Party.'[17]

During the three years of Popular Unity, under the pretence of defending the 'democracy' which allows them to exist, calls made through advertising became calls for sedition. Advertising was transformed into 'subvertising', and prepared 'public opinion', 'the silent majority' to answer its calls and come out onto the streets demanding that the army put an end to marxist 'chaos'. The North American McCann Erickson agency and its research division, Marplan, played a decisive role in this operation: their polls and publicity campaigns tried to put an end to the policy of nationalisation.[18] At the same time, the

Brazilian extreme right, which acted as the CIA's courier and relay service, admitted after the coup that its experts had helped the Chilean right not only to arm and train the anticommunist militia but also to set up bureaux for the development of opinion research and propaganda to back up the women's demonstrations, the strikes of the bosses' organisations, and the 'mass' movement of the bourgeoisie.[19]

After 11th September 1973, the same advertising and marketing agencies provided the military dictatorship with advice and advisers in questions of repression and psycho-political warfare. McCann Erickson experts, in close contact with experts belonging to USIS, found the most efficient ways for Pinochet to 'rout marxism from the minds of the Chilean people' and to fabricate an elementary concensus over the Franco-smelling 'modern organic democracy' they wanted to impose.[20] From November 1973 to February 1974, in spite of an economic situation bordering on catastrophe, the amount of money spent on advertising in Chile increased sevenfold.[21] The Gallup organisation also returned. Enlisted by the Junta's propaganda organisations, troubled by what they described as 'international communist campaigns', Gallup ran an opinion poll in 1975 based on 'two thousand people from different social backgrounds, using the usual research techniques'. 59% thought the new regime a good one, 79% approved of its authoritarian character.[21] And so this technique, which according to Gallup is one of the most perfect instruments of modern democracy, comes to an accommodation with a regime which denies the most elementary freedom of opinion.

The role which several North American advertising agencies operating overseas have been called upon to play, that of a cover for the Empire's intelligence operations, was once again confirmed in January 1975, when an inquiry was conducted by the North American Senate on the activities of the CIA. It was clearly established, for example, that the Washington advertising and marketing agency, Robert Mullen Co., had served as a screen for a North American spy-ring in Europe, the Far East and Mexico. It was also revealed that this small agency concealed another, with which it was closely linked—J. Walter Thompson. The ultimate index of this circularity—State-Industry-Advertising—occurred in January 1974 when the Robert Mullen company closed down and its former president was appointed director of the Summa Corporation, which is owned by Hughes Aircraft and which, a year later, was accused by the same Senators of having undertaken missions on the high seas on behalf of the CIA.[23] In July 1975, the director of the French subsidiary of J. Walter Thompson was obliged to deny—rather unconvincingly—a story carried in an English newspaper that the CIA had used two of the subsidiary's officials for intelligence purposes in France and in Europe generally.[24]

Apart from this last affair, cases of explicitly political interference by North American advertising agencies and other organisations cause less of an outcry in Europe. In countries where class conflict is more disguised, North American influence is a reality, but more highly mediated by the role played by third parties. Technocratic models in the North American style enter the terms of reference of local bourgeoisies to the extent that their systems of alliances are confirmed in the formation of an Atlantic camp. Management and advertising—clearly linking in to the most permeable elements of so-called national cultures—prepare the ground and act as openings for 'changes' which do not simply tolerate but actively support bourgeois politicians. The technocrats' ideology of modernisation cannot actually dispense with management, but henceforth sets out to resolve social conflict which necessarily confront employers just as it confronts their political representatives . . . 'To reply to the ideology of trade unions by means of material arguments is wholly inadequate. It is necessary to put forward an ideology and a philosophy which, it should be said, are at the moment conspicuous by their absence. It is a matter of defining the 'new man' which the big modern company needs: the man who will know how to pilot the enterprise so as to avoid the reefs of disaster . . . This is what lies behind the techniques which must be inculcated into those who will design and use the instruments of management.'[25] This remark was made in the French magazine *Le Management* which at that time was still jointly owned by Servan-Schreiber and the multinational publishers McGraw-Hill.

The last French presidential campaign was pretty symptomatic of the attraction these Atlantic models of modernisation exert on the politicians. The way in which the future head of state's team conceived the electoral battle reflects the arrival to power of the new system of alliances. To organise this campaign a call was put out to the firm which had been responsible for the elections of Kennedy and Johnson, Joseph Napolitan Associated of Springfield, Massachusetts, a firm of professional political managers with an international office in London. Giscard d'Estaing was only its second foreign client, after Carlos Andrés Perez, Venezuelan presidential candidate elected in 1973.[26] In the course of this campaign, which sanctified electoral marketing and opinion polls as 'democratic' instruments, a simulation model—one of those games which imitate a real process in order to predict results, first used systematically by Kennedy when he became President—was employed by the French subsidiary of the Centre for Industrialisation and Marketing (CIM). According to *Le Management*, a magazine which gave its subscribers the results of the job a week prior to the last

Table 26

Public Opinion Studies ordered by USIA (1972)
(US Senate Document)

REA country	Title	Contractor
Africa: Kenya	African Opinion Rider Survey	Associated Business Consultants, Nairobi
South Asia: India	Image of the United States in Urban India	Research and Marketing Services, Bombay, India
East Asia: Japan	Japan Opinion Rider Survey	Central Research Services, Inc., Tokyo
	New Economic Policy Survey	—do—
Australia, Japan, Philippines	Trends in US Standing Abroad	Roy Morgan Research Centre, Melbourne; Central Research Services, Inc., Tokyo; International Research Associates–INRA, Far East
Western Europe:		
Britain	British Opinion Survey	Social Surveys, Ltd; London
Britain, Italy, Belgium, Norway, Netherlands, Spain, Switzerland	Opinion Towards US Investment in Europe	Conrad Jameson Associates, Ltd: London
Britain, Germany, France, Netherlands.	New Economic Policy Survey	Social Survey, Ltd., London; MARPLAN, Offenbach Main; IFOP, Paris; NIPO Amesterdam
Britain, France, West Germany, Italy	Trends in US Standing Abroad	Research Services, London; COFREMCA, Paris; MARPLAN, Offenbach Main; DOXA, Milan
Latin America: Colombia	Colombia Business Study	Adolfo Montanero, Washington, D.C.
Argentina, Brazil, Colombia, Ecuador, Mexico, Venezuela	Image of the United States in Latin America	Mediterranean Research Associates, Washington, D.C.
East Asia: Vietnam	Saigon Public Opinion (September 1970)	Centre for Vietnamese Studies, Saigon
	Qui-Nhon Public Opinion	—do—
	Dalat Public Opinion	—do—
	Saigon Public Opinion (January 1971)	—do—
	Can Tho Public Opinion	—do—
	Quick Response Survey in Saigon	—do—
Indonesia	Indonesian Atitiudinal Survey	International Research Associates, INFA-Far East
Philippines	Philippine Influentials Study	Ateneo de Manila
Western Europe:		
Germany, Britain, France	Attitude Surveys in West Germany, Britain, and France	MARPLAN, IFOP, Offenbach; Main Social Survey, Ltd., London
France, West Germany	Multi-Country Business Image Survey.	Conrad Jameson Associates, Ltd., London
Britain	London Space Standing	Social Surveys, Ltd., London
Greece	Greek Youth Rider	Institute for Research in Communication, Anthens
Greece	Athens Year-Ender Poll Purchase	Institute for Research in Communication, Anthens
Latin America:		
Colombia	Attitudes Toward Foreign Enterprise in Colombia	Inter-America A.C., Bogota
Argentina, Brazil, Colombia, Ecuador, Mexico, Venezuela	Image of the US in Latin America	Inter-American Research, Bogota; Opinion Research Corp., Mexico; Marketing Maxicana, Mexico; Investigadores de Marketing Assoc., Buenos Aires; Instituto IPSA, Buenos Aires; INESE, Rio de Janeiro; Market Research C.A. Caracas; DATOS, Caracas; Org. NORLOP. Guayaquil; IECOP, Quito; Mediterranean Research Associates, Washington, D.C., Mathilda Stephenson, Bethesda, Md., Dr. W. Hazard, Austin, Tex
Near East Israel	PORI Subscription	Public Opinion Research of Israel, Ltd. Tel Aviv

round, it was 'the same model as that used in the United States by CIM in several primaries . . . Its purpose was to assess the efficiency of several campaign themes in terms of votes . . . it was also able to predict election results with a margin of error never greater than 2 or 3 per cent. Of course the level of accuracy was no greater than can ordinarily be obtained through opinion polls, but it is important to point out that this level of accuracy is not obtained here through people's declared voting intentions but by simulating the process that voters' decisions pass through. This model is explanatory, analytic and strategic at the same time.'[27] Judging by the increase in the number of opinion polls during the first year of Giscard d'Estaing's government, the advice of what are known in the US as 'technologists of the new politics' has been heeded.

One final fact. The French Institute of Public Opinion (IFOP—L'Institut français d'opinion publique), a member of Gallup's international network, is responsible for keeping the US Government informed on French attitudes towards the United States. Following an inquiry in 1972, the US Senate Foreign Affairs Committee published a list of firms which periodically produce opinion polls on behalf of USIS.[28] According to the list, in France IFOP and COFREMCA, a subsidiary of the North American firm INRA—International Research Associates—are responsible for the production of the surveys of the attitudes of various social groups in France towards US policy in outer space, the status of foreign investment, foreign policy etc. . . . In Italy, these investigations are produced by Gallup's representative in Milan, the Doxa agency; in Germany by Marplan, a division of McCann Erickson. In every country where Gallup operates, it is the correspondent and confidant of USIS. It could hardly be otherwise, given that George Gallup is one of the five members of the USIS supervisory council. Among his colleagues on the council there are Hobart Lewis, director of *Reader's Digest*, and the former president of CBS, who is now president of Simmons, the commercial research firm. In France, McCann Erickson also has a subsidiary whose administrator is none other than the President's brother, Oliver Giscard d'Estaing. Two representatives of the Hachette group and two of Credit Lyonnais are on the board of COFREMCA.

All this, which must now be placed in a wider context, indicates a new reality: advertising firms, marketing firms, and other 'service companies' are run by the multinationals. They are in the process of becoming their ideological appendages and, in addition, their Home Offices and their Foreign Offices, which are, in their turn, just offices of the imperial State. The next objective will be to uncover the subtleties of this mutation, and to assess its implications for the

Table 27

International Billings of Ten Principal US Advertising Agencies (1974)

Rank	Agency	In millions of dollars	% of total business	No. of foreign subsidiary
1	McCann Erickson	492	70	100
2	J. Walter Thompson	466	53	57
3	SSC & B-Lintas	388	73	42
4	Ted Bates & Co.	311	55	29
5	Ogilvy	300	57	53
6	Young & Rubicam	282	37	30
7	Leo Burnett Co.	212	37	45
8	D'Arcy-McManus-Masius	184	45	20
9	BBDO	152	30	18
10	Norman, Craig, Kummel	130	65	21

Source: Taken from data published in *Advertising Age*, 24.II.1975 and 31.III.1975, plus various annual company reports.

strategies adopted by the Empire and its allies in the sphere of ideology to counteract the rise of popular movements.

Multinationals advertising companies

In 1970, the North American took more than 62% of the world advertising budget. Capitalist countries that year spent $33 billion on advertising: $20.6 billion by the United States (they estimate that in 1980 the figure will be 37 billion), 8 billion by Western Europe (slightly less than 1 billion by France) and 2 billion by Japan. Ten years previously North American advertising turnover was $5.7 billion, Japan $600 m. and France $450 m. A few more figures are enough to give some idea of the place occupied by advertising in these respective economies: in the USA advertising represents 2.11% of the national revenue. In Japan, the figure is 1.14%, and in France 0.72%. In Brazil and Argentina we find the slightly higher figure of 1.25%.[29]

The world's top ten advertising firms are all North American owned.[30] In 1974, McCann Erickson—the most important of a group of six agencies, the Interpublic Group of Cos., whose world revenue is slightly more than one billion dollars—invoiced $492 m. overseas, that is to say, 70% of its total turnover. The second most important agency, J. Walter Thompson, picked up $466 m. overseas, slightly more than 53% of its total revenue. The fifth largest firm, Ogilvy & Mather, made $300 m. on the international market, 37% of its total, while the tenth largest agency, Norman, Craig & Kummel, conducted 65% of its business overseas. For purposes of reference, note that in 1974 France's biggest agency, the Havas Conseil group, recently renamed Eurocom, seventeenth largest advertising agency in the world, made $233 m. at home and abroad. It follows from these figures that most of the personnel employed by the North American firms are stationed overseas. Out of McCann Erickson's total workforce of 4,536, 3,592 live outside the USA. The same goes for 80% of the staff of SSC & B-Lintas.

The profits made by these firms overseas are constantly rising. Over the last ten years McCann Erickson's international turnover has quadrupled, whereas its domestic turnover has merely doubled. It is the same with J. Walter Thompson, which in 1965 drew only 36.5% of its revenue from overseas. This development has a lot to do with the setting up of subsidiaries in advanced capitalist countries which obviously have more advertising agencies susceptible to North American competition than in Third World countries. In 1973, the Ted Bates agency climbed to third place in the list of advertising agencies operating in France: wholly North-American-owned, it was set up in Paris in 1967 and had grown by 18.4% by 1972. Over the same period, Havas-Conseil and Publicis, numbers one and two on the French market, increased their turnovers by 0.12% and 1.93% respectively. The gold medal for 1973 must go to another North American agency, Ogilvy & Mather, which includes American Express among its clients, and which increased its turnover by 133%. Between 1968 and 1973, advertising sales by the two leading French agencies doubled, whereas those by Ted Bates and J. Walter Thompson (which was eighth on the French market in 1973) almost quadrupled. In 1974 it was again a North American agency which proved to be the most dynamic. Young & Rubicam entered the top ten with a growth in its turnover of more than one third, while the same year was marked by the relative decline of Publicis, which lost 9% of its turnover.[31] Young & Rubicam jumped to first place in Italy, while in Britain, McCann Erickson, fourth largest agency on the British market, increased its revenue by 85.2% between 1970 and 1972. In Brazil, where it has been the leading agency for some years, McCann Erickson doubled its receipts from 1971 to 1972. In 1974 in Brazil, the most spectacular progress was recorded by a joint-held company, Mauro Salles Inter-americana, the property of a Brazilian group and of Kenyon & Eckhardt, which went up from $23 m. to 33 m. The Brazilian sub-sidiary of McCann Erickson had a revenue of almost 40 million.

Recently, however, a shadow has been cast over this prosperity. A reduction in publicity budgets by certain clients has reduced the

Table 28

**North American Presence Among the 20 Largest Agencies
in Brazil and France (1973)**

Agency	BRAZIL	Status
	Ranking on national market	
McCann Erickson	1	Subsidiary
J. Walter Thompson	2	Subsidiary
Needham, Harper & S.	3	Representation agreement with Norton de Sao Paulo
Kenyon & Eckardt	5	Minority participation Mauro Salles/Interamericana
Lintas-SSC & B.	8	Subsidiary
Ogilvy & Mather	10	,, (Standard)
Leo Burnett	11	,, (CIN)
Grant Advertising	14	,,
Quadrant	17	,,
	FRANCE	
Needham, Harper & S.	1-22*	Growing participation with Univas (Havas) & minority participation in SIGMA
Ted Bates	3	Subsidiary
BBDO	4-30	Partner in Interplans, holds 30% in CLM/Team
Lintas-SSC & B.	5	Subsidiary
J. Walter Thompson	8	Subsidiary
Compton	9	20% in Dupuy-Compton
McCann Erickson	10	Subsidiary
Grey	11	68% in Dorlond-Grey
Young & Rubicam	12	Subsidiary
Kenyon & Eckardt	13-59*	Agreement with Synergie and Subsidiary (Promos CPV)
Norman Craig & K.	16	Subsidiary
Danger, Fitzgerald, S.	18	International network with Delpire-Advico
Doyle & Bernbach	19	Subsidiary

Source: For Brazil, 'Foreign Agency Billings', *Advertising Age*, 26.III.1974. For France, *Stratégies*, No. 48, 17–30 September 1973 and No. 60, 4–17 March 1974.

*When two figures are given, this refers to the respective positions of the two agencies with which the North American agency is associated.

turnover of several companies. But the crisis has had very different repercussions for each of the ten leading North American firms. In 1974, the world growth of McCann Erickson was a mere 2.9%. Taking inflation into account, this is a drop in business. In France, its turnover declined by 15.8% and the firm dropped from tenth to thirteenth place. There was much the same decline in Argentina, although it remained the top agency. The politically insecure situation led to its returns falling from $16 m. to $10 m. On the other hand, growth in Brazil continued. However, this bad year did not prevent McCann Erickson from expanding its overseas network, as we shall see. The situation of J. Walter Thompson (with a 3.5% growth) was hardly more brilliant. But agencies like Young & Rubicam, Leo Burnett, Ted Bates and BBDO all increased their takings by at least 13% over the previous year. This means that the ten leading companies maintained an average growth rate of 8.5%.[32]

More than ever, internationalisation is the order of the day. The director of Ogilvy & Mather said, in August 1973: 'My major preoccupation is to internationalise advertising. Previously, an agency had only one office in a given country. Now that many clients are becoming international, multinational, the big agencies have to follow suit and set up business wherever their clients need them. It is sometimes difficult: because some countries refuse to allow foreign companies to move in.'[33] Out of the top 25 North American agencies, only two do not have overseas subsidiaries. More recently, internationalisation has also become a preoccupation for a number of Japanese and European agencies. The consequences of this policy—which in many cases didn't just begin yesterday—are already apparent.

In France in 1973 the big North American agencies took 22% of the market. This figure could well be 30% if you take into account not only wholly-owned subsidiaries but the appropriate part of the turnover of companies with North American participation. Out of the twelve leading advertising agencies, which account for more than half the French advertising cake, nine are North American (five subsidiaries and four with varying North American shares). And this isn't even one of the better example, as France is one of the few Western European countries to be relatively protected. As the president of the Havas Agency remarked in 1972: 'Our country is now the only one among the developed non-socialist nations to have its own advertising agencies, especially Havas-Conseil, holding top place, rather than, as everywhere except Japan, North American agencies.'[34] And the president of Publicis added, around the same time: 'Together with Havas we have simply proved that French firms can dominate the French market. This has been our sole aim, and the result is conclusive, as France is the only country where the Anglo-Saxons are not the leaders in advertising.'[35] These statements, however, are on the way to being disproved. The Havas agency, in which the French State took a 67.6% shareholding in 1945, has begun to go private. Some of its shares have recently been sold to new shareholders, such as the Banque de Paris et des Pays-Bas, and it is likely that this process can only attract North American capital and the establishment of alliances with North American companies. On the other hand, without toppling Havas and Publicis from first and second place in the French market, the North Americans are increasingly taking over smaller agencies which find themselves in difficulties. In the course of the last few months of 1974 and the first few months of 1975, the big North American agencies laid claim to no fewer than three French advertising firms. The Impact agency became Impact/Foote, Cone & Belding, and took twelfth place among French agencies. The André Coutau agency relinquished 47% of its shares to its North American partners, Benton & Bowles, who had taken a 20% share in 1965. In a press statement the new partners explained: 'This decision indicates a wish to expand. Firms are finding

Table 29

Leading Advertising Agencies in Great Britain

Agency	Gross Income		Status
	1976	1975	
1. J. Walter Thompson Co. Ltd.	$16,718,000	$13,786,000	US subsidiary
2. Ogilvy, Benson & Mather	$14,212,663	$11,754,871	US subsidiary
3. McCann-Erickson Advertising	$10,922,000	$10,888,000	US subsidiary
4. Masius, Wynne-Williams & D'Arcy-MacManus	$10,600,000	$ 8,211,000	US subsidiary
5. Saatchi & Saatchi	$ 9,440,000	$ 7,650,000	Subsidiary of Compton (US)
6. Charles Barker ABH International	$ 7,500,000	$ 5,800,000	Associated with Ayer Barker Hegemann International (US)
7. Leo Burnett Ltd.	$ 7,156,000	$ 5,800,000	US subsidiary
8. Young & Rubican Holdings	$ 6,738,000	$ 6,704,000	US subsidiary

Source: *Advertising Age*, 18.IV.1977.

increasingly that progress can best be achieved in the conquest of foreign markets. André Coutau (which retains a 33% holding and the presidency of the board of Benton & Bowles S.A.) feels that it is now in a better position to solve the problems faced by French advertisers overseas and by overseas advertisers in France.'[36] In June 1975 the owners of McCann Erickson, the Interpublic Group of Cos., signed an agreement with Schneider Conseil S.A. of Paris incorporating the latter into its Paris subsidiary. To clinch the deal all that was needed was the go-ahead from the French Government.[37] Leo Burnett, one of the latest North American agencies to set up in Paris, established a subsidiary after vainly trying to buy shares in its French partner. Its director justified the move in these terms: 'It was unthinkable that we should not be in on the market, given the mode of our evaluation and the place we occupy as much in the States as in the rest of the world.'[38]

In other countries the North American presence in the advertising industry is more evident. Seven out of the top ten agencies in Belgium are subsidiaries or partners of the North Americans. Belgium's dependency recently deepened—if that were still possible. By acquiring Troost International, the European group of German origin with offices in Dusseldorf, Milan, Amsterdam and Brussels, the Interpublic Group of Cos. took control of the fourth largest Belgian agency in 1975. If we now add together the income of this new property and that of McCann Erickson, the agencies in Brussels belonging to the Interpublic Group come to head of the field, more than ten million dollars in front of their nearest rival, a jointly owned firm (Publicontrol/Benton Bowles) which previously occupied first place with an income of $28 m. Among the ten largest agencies in Italy we find 7 North American companies, one European group, one Euro-American group and a single Italian firm. The six leading agencies in Great Britain are all North American. They include J. Walter Thompson at the head, with a gross income in 1976 of £10 m., and, in fifth place, Saatchi & Saatchi, which was entrusted by the Tory Party in April 1978 with their advertising for the next General Election. In the Scandinavian countries, where McCann Erickson, Ted Bates, Lintas and others all operate, Ogilvy & Mather bought the Swedish agency STB in 1972, one of the country's three largest, which also operates in, among other places, Denmark, Finland and Norway. That was only the beginning. In 1974 Leo Burnett took over a network of four other agencies, with offices in Copenhagen, Oslo, Stockholm, Malmo and Helsinki. In 1975 Benton & Bowles bought an 80% share in one of the biggest Norwegian agencies, Hoydahl Ohme.

Having inherited an advertising apparatus with a strong North

American presence, Portugal, during its revolutionary upsurge, was treated little better than Allende's Chile. The five leading agencies are all foreign, or partners of foreign groups. The leading company is a wholly-owned subsidiary of SSC & B-Lintas, with an income in 1974 of $4.4 (one million down on the previous year). The second largest, Latina-Thompson Associadas, is a member of the J. Walter Thompson network. Unlike Chile, where this organisation left after the Popular Unity Government came to power, it stayed in Lisbon and saw its turnover rise from $1.7 m. to $3.1 m. Norman, Craig & Kummel have two agencies, Ciesa-NCK and Promo Beja, with a total income of $4.1 m., virtually the same as under the Salazar dictatorship. Aside from Leo Burnett, in fourth place, Havas and Publicis are also among the top ten.

In Central America, in countries like Guatemala, Nicaragua and El Salvador, advertising is in the hands of practically only one company, McCann Erickson, though North American hegemony was reinforced in 1975 when J. Walter Thompson entered the area. Among the ten leading agencies in Argentina there are 6 North American subsidiaries, which account for more than 70% of the income of the top ten companies. In 1974, despite financial difficulties, McCann Erickson managed to take over another agency (Gowland). In Brazil, the turnover of the two leading companies, McCann Erickson and J. Walter Thompson, is about twice that of all the major Brazilian agencies put together, which anyway have been penetrated by North America capital. There too McCann Erickson is still expanding. In 1974, the Interpublic Group took over the country's second largest agency (Proeme). In order to fight this all-too-evident supremacy, two of the main supposedly national agencies, (MPM Propaganda and Casabranca) merged in 1975, but this still only put them in fourth place. In Venezuela, the ten leading agencies are either North American or else they are tied in with North American capital. In Africa, where the monopoly represented by Havas's international network is particularly strong in various countries (it counts as a Euro-American company), Lintas nevertheless dominates the market in Ghana, Sierra Leone and Nigeria. Leo Burnett and J. Walter Thompson can be found in Rhodesia. In Asia, McCann Erickson, Burnett, Ogilvy and Lintas totally control the Malaysian market, Lintas that of Indonesia, J. Walter Thompson and McCann Erickson share India and so on.[39]

However, the invasion of the North American advertising agencies does not occur in a uniform manner. The analysis of their movements on the international market enables us to distinguish three major strategies of internationalisation, which sometimes intersect.

The imperial model

Here the most faithful representatives are J. Walter Thompson and McCann Erickson. They are also the oldest, the very instigators of the 'advertising and marketing system'. Indeed, let us once and for all put aside any account of the history of advertising which tries to locate its roots in the patter of the town crier or in information circular; even under the French Consulate! All this ignores the fact that advertising operates within a set of social relations which correspond to a precise stage in the development of the productive forces. J. Walter Thompson was set up in the latter part of the nineteenth century (1864) and McCann Erickson dates from 1912. The rhythm of the setting up of foreign subsidiaries closely follows the successive waves of the Empire's expansion over the last 70 years.[40]

The founder of J. Walter Thompson was a former naval commodore. He recruited his first clients from the detergent industry (Procter & Gamble, Lever Brothers) and cosmetics. The firm's oldest client is Cheseborough-Pond's (dating from 1886). His contemporaries didn't only consider him as a pioneer in advertising, but also as the person who gave women's magazines the prominence they have today. To attract new clients to the firms whose advertising he was handling, he imagined turning the woman into the prototype of the consumer. He was in fact the initiator of what we now know as the 'woman's magazine'. His first step overseas was the setting up of a sales office in London in 1899. For more than 20 years it was closely tied to the history of British colonialism. In 1923, he followed the request of this Chicago client, Libby, McNeill & Libby, to transform the London sales office into a proper subsidiary, primarily to handle the advertising for their jams. This was the foundation stone of the North American advertising empire. In 1927 General Motors asked J. Walter Thompson to represent the company throughout the world and to open an office in every country where General Motors made or assembled vehicles. In this way subsidiaries were born in Canada (1929), India (1929), Australia (1930) and South Africa (1930). The French and Belgian subsidiaries were set up in 1927 and 1928 respectively. By 1929, J. Walter Thompson was operating in Argentina, Brazil and Uruguay. In all these countries, apart from General Motors, it followed the expansion of Ford, Gillette, RCA, Kraft, Kelloggs, J. B. Williams and Procter & Gamble. During the Second World War, the initiative of launching the Advertising Council fell to an expert belonging to this very agency. The Advertising Council is a non-profit-making association supported by North American industrialists from all sectors of the economy, with the purpose of using advertising for 'social causes'. In strict relationship with the Office of Strategic Services (OSS), the predecessor of the CIA, J. Walter Thompson launched recruiting campaigns and propaganda for war production. Several of its employees were promoted to the rank of intelligence officers and filled the posts of directors of planning for OSS 'moral' and psychological operations. After Cairo and Casablanca they became the mentors in subliminal warfare.

It was not until January 1975 that J. Walter Thompson's first covert mission for the North American State was revealed in front of the US Senate. From the beginning of the Second World War, J. Walter Thompson agreed that its representative in Uruguay should combine his advertising functions with the function of being the FBI's principal agent in Latin America.[41] This was also the period when J. Walter Thompson first publicly defined advertising as 'the most modern, streamlined, high-speed means of communication plus persuasion yet invented by man', reasons why they recommended its use 'by governments . . . political parties . . . labour unions . . . farm organisations . . . churches . . . universities . . . It ought to be used to create understanding and reduce friction.'[42]

In the 40s came the second wave: with Anaconda and companies like W. R. Grace, the agency perfected its Latin American network and established subsidiaries in Mexico (1943), Chile (1944), Peru (1957) and finally Venezuela (1964). It deepened its penetration of Asia, successively capturing the Philippines (1956), Japan (1956), Pakistan (1956) and in the same year Ceylon, though it was forced to leave again in 1971. In Europe, during the same years, it set up subsidiaries in Germany, Italy and the Netherlands. One of the latest is the one in Madrid, dating from 1968. In 1975, J. Walter Thompson employed 5,746 persons, spread out in 27 countries with a total of 57 bureaux. It is the foremost agency in 6 countries; in 3 it occupies second place and third place in 4, while in others it is invariably to be found among the top ten. Merely the advertising for the Panam airline and its Hilton International hotel chain—principal clients since 1942—gives it a presence in 121 cities and 84 countries and produces translations of its copy into 36 languages.

This bridge thrown across five continents over geographical and linguistic frontiers allows it to proclaim the arrival of a new internationalism and of the new democracy, where all men are equal because citizens have become consumers habituated to the same appetites. In its annual report to shareholders for 1972, you may read: 'In countries as diverse in political and economic structure as Spain and Switzerland, Sweden and France, Japan and Brazil, advertising has developed in similar ways and to a similar degree. Even the

Russians have been struggling for some years to create a consumer advertising programme. Country after country seems to repeat the same basic discovery: that advertising has a fundamental role to play in modern social systems. In a sense the more things change, the more they remain the same. National differences seem to be most acute when the rate of economic development is low, but as people prosper, their spending patterns tend to parallel those of other affluent societies. The swelling demand for automobiles, processed foods and travel in Europe, South America and Asia is evidence of the universality of consumer interests. This development, perhaps more than any other single factor, accounts for the success of the multinational company with its great potential for translating knowledge and experience from more sophisticated markets to those that are a phase behind them.'[43] In reports prepared by managers and publicists on the situation in Third World countries like Brazil, the level of socio-economic analysis which these remarks produce lead to such statements as 'Sales of cigarettes, automobiles, detergents and cosmetics could be considered good barometers of a country's economic development'.[44]

McCann Erickson has had a very similar trajectory. Its beginnings lay in the public relations department of the Standard Oil Company, which it split off from when anti-trust laws divided up the Rockefeller family's oil cartel into several companies. While it became autonomous it kept all its preferential ties with the enterprises of the same financial group. This explains why in particular it has taken care of its Latin American sales. In fact McCann Erickson is installed in every Latin American country, which brings it more than $65 m. every year, or more than 20% of the company's international turnover. Among the portfolios currently handled by the agency is that of one of its oldest clients, Coca-Cola, which it has made into one of the most everyday and 'natural' symbols of North American imperialism, with a universal presence which not even the Walt Disney characters exceed. In 1963, McCann Erickson had subsidiaries in 31 countries outside the United States. In the course of ten years this increased to 47. Its 4,536 employees conceive advertising copy 'for more than three billion consumers spread out throughout the whole world in 25 languages, for more than 1,600 clients.'[45] This enables them to claim that their professionals 'have the same effect in Bangkok, Buenos Aires or Boston'. McCann Erickson, as already pointed out, is, moreover, only the principal agency in the Interpublic Group of Cos., which is made up of six different agencies. The group's latest North American acquisition is Campbell Ewald, in 1972, which has handled advertising for Chevrolet since 1922. On the international market the most important of the group's other agencies is Quadrant International, fifth largest in

Britain, also established in six other European countries, in South Africa, Australia and Brazil. The latest annexations made by the group outside the United States has transformed it into one of the most balanced multinational advertising associations. A third of its turnover comes from the US, a third from Europe and a third from the other continents.

Abroad, the clients of these agencies—like those of most North American agencies—are by preference of the same nationality. In France, for example, 17 of J. Walter Thompson's official clients are North American companies (such as Holiday Inns, Burroughs, Ford, Kellogg's, Kraft, Panam), together with French companies like Bidegain (chief among the modernist French employers) or other multinationals like Nestlé. In Mexico the proportion is 25 out of 27. Again, in Portugal, J. Walter Thompson includes Reader's Digest, Levi-Strauss and Pfizer among its principal clients. In general, it is the North American companies who spend the largest sums on advertising and thus tend to impose their own model outside the metropolis: big budgets and the use of the most developed means. So the North American agencies tend to impart the dynamic to new kinds of advertising such as television advertising. In fact Ted Bates, Young & Rubicam and Lintas all get more than 52% of their turnover in France from making tv ads, while in the case of Havas the proportion is only 19%. Similarly, the last cry in electronic advertising, the advertisements which cover the walkways in the new airport in Paris, are a monopoly of Publicité Claude, an ITT subsidiary. In 1972, four manufacturers of detergents, Colgate-Palmolive, Lever-Savinneries, Henkel-France and Procter & Gamble, all foreign companies, were among the five foremost advertisers in France. Colgate reinforced its position at the top with investments in advertising which went up 49% in one year. In 1972 they invested 107 m. francs in advertising. Lever, their immediate competitor, invested less than half that.[46] This predominance of North American firms is also found at the level of syndicates or associations of advertisers intended to 'protect the common interests of their members', as the Venezuelan society of advertisers proposed when it was set up, 'as purchasers of advertising, to protect the essential values of advertising as an instrument for increasing or promoting sales and to establish the necessary technical services for the improved orientation and utilisation of investment in advertising'.[47] Among the members of the directorate of the 'Council of Advertisers' in Venezuela are the local directors of General Electric, Sears-Roebuck, Procter & Gamble, Philip Morris, Nestlé and 4 national companies. In France, the director of Colgate-Palmolive presides over the 'Union of Advertisers'. Among the three vice-presidents are representatives of

Harriett Hubbard Ayer, Oréal and Roussel—which was recently taken over by a German group.[48]

This scheme of things tends to be reproduced in all countries where North American-based multinationals, through their advertising expenditures, increasingly constitute a factor of pressure on the media. To give a final example: in Peru in 1969, Colgate-Palmolive and Procter & Gamble between them provided 11% of the advertising receipts on national television. And a global reference: the increase in advertising expenditures by Procter & Gamble, the foremost advertiser in the United States, led to a figure in 1974 of $325 m., or 7% of the company's turnover.

J. Walter Thompson and McCann Erickson are prototypes of the imperial model principally because of the character of their international insertion. Even if 96% of the personnel in the international service of these companies are natives of their own countries, these agencies are in almost all cases full owners of their subsidiaries. It was this classic imperialist style which decided J. Walter Thompson to erect buildings in Paris and Tokyo which were copies of New York skyscrapers. The company swallowed up $8 m. in these symbols of invasion reminiscent of the good old times of colonialism with hardly any concern for what the local people might think. *Veni, Vidi, Vici.* J. Walter Thompson hasn't altered its expansionist behaviour in the slightest since the year of its creation. Already in 1909, in a book which was to become the bible of all self-respecting public relations consultants, Commodore J. Walter Thompson wrote:

> Every period in the world's history has been distinguished by the phrases it creates. The whole history of Roman conquest was summed up in the laconic message of three words, 'Veni, vidi, vici' which Caesar sent back to the senate. The voice of the Revolution became articulated in the name of the great Jehovah and the Continental Congress. The present age is pacific. The splendid energy of the people today is happily expanded in the arts of industry. And the character of our advertising tells the tale. The phrases developed by genius operating in the business field show that the American people are taking a delight in the buying and selling of merchandise. Commerce has passed the sordid age. The American magazine is a national institution. It is progressive. It never tires nor stands still. It commands the services and the energies of the greatest editors, writers, and illustrators of the day. It is a magnificent monument to American enterprise, American genius, and American skill.[49]

As far as they can, the ten foremost North American agencies try not to deviate from the sacrosanct principle of one hundred per cent ownership of their subsidiaries. For some, the international market is a novelty. Ten years ago few of them had overseas operations. In 1963, Ted Bates, founded in 1940 in the shadow of Colgate, had practically no presence on the international market. In 1975, it had 26 offices in 23 foreign countries. It owns 11 European subsidiaries and 12 Asiatic ones. In 1963, Young & Rubicam operated in 7 countries. Now it can be found in 20, 14 European, 4 Latin American, 1 Near East and Canada. In the United States it specialises in advertising aimed at blacks and chicanos. Ogilvy & Mather, founded in 1948, had only one foreign subsidiary in 1964. It now has offices in 12, and owns all its subsidiaries except in Argentina where it has a national group as partner. Leo Burnett, founded in 1935, had no foreign bureaux in 1963 apart from Canada and England. In 1969, through acquiring Britain's second agency, the London Press Exchange, it inherited, in one fell swoop, an international network of 23 offices in 19 countries.

Nationalisation by consent and other subterfuges

As the director of Ogilvy said (see above), many countries resist the entry of foreign companies. In these conditions, the most rapid way of penetrating and progressing in a so-called national market is to acquire a share in a national company. In this way, a new doctrine and a new practice has been born among North American companies: the deliberate 'nationalisation' of their operations, with their consent. Obviously this is only an adaptive process parallel to what is already accepted in the field of counter-insurrection. With the overthrow of Allende in Chile, imperialism clearly indicated that it preferred to choose modes of intervention closer to the evolution of the country and above all to the evolution of the local ruling classes. Returning from a voyage of inspection in Latin America and the Common Market, the President of Kenyon & Eckhardt justified this new policy in these terms:

> From what I've always heard, the thrust of most American agencies in international (*sic*) is for control. Therefore, we have J. Walter Thompson Co., McCann Erickson, Young & Rubicam, and now Ogilvy & Mather beginning to buy out their overseas operations. I categorically think this is wrong. I think the local nationals have an absolute right to control their own destiny. The American affiliate can own up to, say, 49% and put in its technical expertise. If there is anything to the hypothesis that a good American should have a share, why shouldn't the local guy? ... The Common Market is going to make countries more nationalistic than ever. One interesting point is that in countries where nationalism is strong the local companies don't want to affiliate with another company that has a strong American bank, strong American legal firm and other American ties ... Every place I've gone, I've talked to many people, including consul generals and even presidents, and all of them subscribe to this theory. K & E/CPV is interested in buying into or merging with agencies interested in moving ahead. We want to buy into a shop where there is good young talent and not where the management is 65 and ready to retire.[50]

Still in terms of the same philosophy, association with a national agency helps to remedy errors committed by North American agencies: it avoids chauvinist attitudes when they exist; it offers the best of both worlds, which means it is less 'alienated'; it fits the particularities of the national market thanks to the presence of natives who know the ways and customs of their country.[51] This sudden concern to safeguard the heritage of national cultures is all the more unusual on the part of those agencies whose continuing recommendations to their experts for launching campaigns, for example, for beauty products (like those of Helena Rubinstein), considers that 'women are the same the world over'. 'The differences are in the degree of sophistication of distribution and marketing, not in the women . . . In some areas of Latin America, women simply have not been exposed to as many products, but potential heavy users of cosmetics exist everywhere and will respond to the same promise of beauty'.[52]

In 1971, anticipating a possible nationalisation of its Chilean subsidiary by the Popular Unity Government, which however didn't take place, Kenyon & Eckhardt sold 52% of its shares to local nationals. Flagrant proof of the opportunism of this 'nationalist' doctrine, once the Junta was in power the company immediately offered to repurchase the shares at double the value from the straw men they had themselves set up. On 14th September 1973, three days after the coup d'état, the director of the agency in New York said in an interview that 'whichever route Chile's new government takes, it will still present a more receptive climate for foreign companies than the Allende government did'.[53]

Kenyon & Eckhardt, 24th largest agency in the United States now maintains a presence in more than 25 countries. It has applied this policy in the Antilles, in Argentina—where it collaborates with one of the biggest agencies in Buenos Aires, Gomez Ferran Interamericana—and in Brazil, where it is associated with the country's fifth largest agency, Mauro Salles. In France, where it already owned CPV Promos with a British partner, it established a tie-up with the third largest French agency, Synergie, in 1974. For some years, six months have not gone by without Kenyon & Eckhardt announcing some collaboration agreement or acquisition of shares. Towards the middle of 1975, it increased its shareholding in a Cologne agency (CPV-GFA), merged with another in Munich and signed a cooperation agreement with an agency in Lyon. In July 1975 it achieved a masterstroke in acquiring majority participation in another North American agency, Grant International. It thus added 12 offices to the 35 it already possessed, but more than that, entered markets it had not previously succeeded in infiltrating, in Asia: Bombay, Madras, New Delhi, Bangkok, Kuala Lumpur, Singapore, Taiwan, Hong Kong, Djakarta, Manilla and Tokyo.

The same policy of capturing an international network was applied in 1970 by SSC & B—founded in New York in 1946—which acquired a 49% share in Lintas, the property of the multinational Anglo-Dutch firm Unilever. In 1963, when it didn't have a single foreign subsidiary, SSC & B had a turnover of scarcely $88 m. Eleven years later, thanks to this operation, it shared $532 m.—73% from the international market—with its partner. It now has 42 offices in 29 countries. The strength of this network can be understood in relation to its association with one of the most dynamic of non-US multinationals. In 1974, under Unilever's aegis—Unilever is one of the oldest colonial companies—the first seminar on advertising communications took place in Johannesburg. Its main object was the adaptation of advertising to 'the black mentality'. 'The fact is: of recent years coverage by conventional media has been vastly extended, and advertisers have applied in African-directed media the format of European-style advertising, with its emphasis on the written as opposed to the spoken word. In short, it would appear that because we do not talk to our audience face-to-face we may have lost the ability to talk to them through Black reasoning, Black frames of reference and Black idiom, with a consequent loss in comprehension of the message . . . And no understanding, no message. Money and sales opportunities are lost.'[54] Apart from its association with the North American agency, Unilever set up a network of 30 research and marketing institutes to satisfy its international expansion. Most of them are not identifiable as its properties and shelter under more academic names. In France, SECED, Société d'Etudes Commerciales et Documentaires is an institute of this type.

During the last few years, most North American agencies have resorted to minority participations to introduce themselves to different national markets, and since the epoch of complete networks has obviously passed, it seems that this policy will now prevail. In 1973, Young & Rubicam acquired a 50% share in a new Mexican agency. In the same way, Ogilvy & Mather entered the Venezuelan market, becoming a minority partner in the country's largest agency, CORFA; and in 1973, it acquired between 20 and 30% of the shares in a Spanish advertising agency (Publicidad y Marketing Fernandez). Other agencies have systematically applied the same policy for some time. This is the case with Compton Advertising, which has 37 offices abroad and scarcely owns as much as 40% of its affiliates. In France, for example, employees were able, in May 1974, to acquire a share in the capital of

Dupuy-Compton, of which the North Americans own 20%. This is also the case with such agencies as Grey Advertising, which owns about 55% of its affiliates. The biggest agencies like J. Walter Thompson are also adopting this new line of action. This is the way it installed itself in Portugal, a little more than a year before Caetano's fall. It also entered the markets of Central America in 1975 by acquiring participation in a local agency in Guatemala (Agencias Publicitarias Centroamericanas Unidas). Apart from its offices in Guatemala, this agency also operates in Cost Rica, Honduras and Nicaragua, J. Walter Thompson dispatched a Colombian employee of theirs, who had worked in their head offices in New York for seven years, to become codirector of this new joint subsidiary.

Often this acquisition of minority participation in local agencies is only an initial step. Because sooner or later the problem of power and control poses itself. This at any rate is the conclusion suggested by an analysis of the expansion of firms like Benton & Bowles, which is in the height of its ascent in the international market. After having purchased the majority of shareholding in its Norwegian and French partner, the director of Benton & Bowles presented the reasons for this move: 'Within the laws of a particular country and with the support of local management, we want to become the majority partner in our overseas agencies. The key to our desire . . . is that we don't want to be just an investor. We do believe in foreign nationals running a company. On the other hand, we want those companies to operate within the framework of serving our clients. To do that, we must be a strong voice in the operation.'[55] Benton & Bowles now has this kind of majority power in six of its twelve foreign agencies (those in Norway, Great Britain, the Netherlands, France, Canada and Trinidad). It still has to conquer in Italy, Belgium, Germany, Austria, Spain and Argentina.

In Canada, on the other hand, under the nationalist tendency of the Government, North American agencies have been seriously handicapped in these intentions. In January 1975, Norman, Craig & Kummel ceded 55% of the shares in its subsidiary, of which it had been the full owner, to a Canadian partner, and its colleagues Ogilvy & Mather and J. Walter Thompson announced that they were facing the same situation. This constraint involves only disadvantages. In obliging the North Americans to cede the majority of shares to nationals, thus 'nationalising' their subsidiaries, the Canadian Government offers them to their clients, and opens the market in public administration to them. Through an annual investment of $7.4 m., the Federal Government reveals itself to be one of the country's principal users of advertising. Parallel to this, expenditure by US industrial firms continues and constitutes the most obvious part of the business of these

Canadian agencies. Among these North American companies operating in Canada, Procter & Gamble is the foremost consumer of advertising, with an annual expenditure which reaches almost $10 m.[56]

Around 1970, to complete the internal changes produced within the big North American agencies, multinational advertising conglomerates of a kind previously unknown began to develop. The big European agencies began to cross their international networks with those of the North American giants. The most important creation of this kind succeeded in bringing together a French agency, a British agency and a North American agency. The history of this drawing together illustrates very well the movement which has been going on at the base in the world of advertising for some years.

Let us trace this history. In 1970, an agreement was signed by the fourteenth largest North American agency, Needham, Harper & Steers, a British agency called Benson, and the Havas-Conseil international network, set up in 1968 under the name UNIVAS. This triplicate, baptised BNU, represented a total sales figure of $300 m. and totalled 21 affiliates in 13 countries. In 1971, Benson was bought up by the Rothschild investment fund who then sold it to Ogilvy & Mather, who considered the union at variance with a North American agency. Univas and Needham therefore signed an agreement with a new partner, the British agency KMPH Ltd (property of the giant Pemberton group). In 1973, the billings of the international advertising front had already reached a total of $457 m., which is to say it had overtaken the international billings of J. Walter Thompson. It operated in Europe, the Near East and Africa, and in 1973 Needham extended its overseas network through another agreement with Norton Publicidade of Sao Paulo, the sixth largest agency in the Brazilian market and one of the country's foremost national agencies.

There are a number of other cases—not all of them successful—which reveal this pressure and this desire to establish vast international complexes. Also in 1970, two North American agencies, d'Arcy Advertising & McManus, and John & Adams, joined with Intermarco, which has its head office in Amsterdam and owns a network of agencies in 12 European countries (in 1965, on another tack, d'Arcy had set up a 'European agency', Multi-National Partners, which was dissolved a short while ago). The association with Intermarco came to end in 1972. At this date the French agency Publicis took over Intermarco, bought the foremost Swiss agency Dr Rudolf Färner and thus set up the first 'entirely European' international network, Publicis-Intermarco-Färner (billings of 220 millions in 1973). For its part, d'Arcy reached an agreement with a London agency to reconstitute its European network. A final indication of the importance of this model of the invasion of advertising: in 1974 two further international networks were set up in France. The Delpire-Advice agency now has a holding company which brings together an English, a German and a North American agency, and the Moors-Warot-Hardy agency has come together with agencies in New York, London and Hamburg.

The Japanese are also moving insofar as their multinational companies are increasing their penetration. In 1973 the Dentsu agency (which has a turnover of more than one billion dollars, half of which, however, come from its other activities including administration, publishing and the press) set up its first international subsidiary in London where it decided to take the business of its compatriots Toyota, Honda, Nissan, Sony, etc., away from the big North American agencies.

Shortly, according to North American experts, if this phenomenon of concentration and mergers is pursued (and there is nothing that suggests that it won't be) it is more than probable that only ten or fifteen large agencies will remain on the international market.[57]

Diversification of production

In addition to extending themselves in terms of territories, the North American advertising agencies are increasingly interesting themselves in diversifying their production. This policy, which has only really got under way in the last five or six years, takes on two directions. On the one hand, there is the creation of a complete chain of services relating to modernised advertising work. Clients are offered everything from the conception of a television advert and its production, to studies of public motivation, by way of advisory services in investment, Public Relations, recruitment and organisation of personnel, market investigation and so on. On the other hand, the process of diversification has very little to do with the original area of advertising production and research, since new acquisitions can include supermarkets or drugstores just as easily as the management of insurance companies. It should be said that this second form of expansion is scarcely yet typical of all agencies. Some of them are still concerned above all to consolidate their advertising empire itself. Let us look at some examples of these policies of diversification.[58]

Advertising agencies specialise. They set up or absorb firms adapted to the promotion of products demanding a particular approach from the client, corresponding to the most dynamic sector of the market. The most important area for this specialisation is that of medical and pharmaceutical products. There are no less than 6 pharmaceutical firms among the 20 leading North American advertisers, and the growing importance of promotional campaigns to sell medicines is well known. The scandals they involve have already been frequently noted. In a recent inquiry into the French pharmaceutical industry—which is dominated by foreign companies—an analyst in *Le Monde* explained the phenomenon of overpromotion, which is inversely proportional to the therapeutic value of the new medicine. The more that interest stagnates, the more the pharmaceutical industry pumps money into advertising to achieve success. 'They begin to promote a medicine in as vulgar a manner as a dog or cat food. With crafty ideas and money, lots of money. At least, to be sure, with the exception of an essential discovery, in which case there is no need for advertising. Unfortunately such discoveries are rare. The medical authorities agree among themselves not to classify within this category more than four or five, at most ten, of the two or three hundred 'novelties' which appear on the French market every year.'[59] J. Walter Thompson set up a medical and scientific division called Deltakos in 1967 to overcome this problem. In 1975 they appointed no less a person than the present under-secretary of the US Department of Public Health. Among Deltakos's clients are all the big companies in the pharmaceutical industry and the manufacture of medical instruments, Parke-Davis, Bausch & Lomb, Smith-Kline Instruments. In 1973, J. Walter Thompson's Paris subsidiary decided to increase its capital from 2.7 m. to 10.7 m. francs and included among the five main points of this new strategy, the 'creation of a pharmaceutical advertising agency, and of a financial advertising agency'.[60] In 1974, Young & Rubicam embarked on the same process by taking over a North American firm which specialised in medical promotion. Remarks by the president of Young & Rubicam about this new annexation tell us how these new properties are made profitable, by expanding their sphere of activity, which until now has scarcely moved beyond the frontiers of the United States: 'Synergism may be an overworked word, but it's valid in this case. Sudler & Hennessey, for example, was a one-office agency in the US. With their name on the door, and our know-how in overseas operations, we can go all over the world with expert medical campaigns. We've already opened in Australia, Mexico and Canada.'[61]

Public relations are another field of diversification. Agencies like J. Walter Thompson, McCann Erickson, Ted Bates, Young & Rubicam and Burson-Marsteller all now have independent divisions which offer clients this kind of advise and appropriate specialists. They now compete with traditional firms in this area (like Hill & Knowlton, which is still at the head of the list). J. Walter Thompson's Public Relations division, Dialog (independent since 1973) already the fifth position in the list, and employs 271 persons, 170 of them abroad. Their job is to serve the public relations departments of the big multinationals and certain government institutions. The job is clearly defined in the *Public Relations Journal*, their professional organ: 'U.S. multinationals aren't all bad, but the very word or term "multinational" has taken on a severly negative meaning in many foreign nations. With less government regulation and a climate that would permit the operation of the basic laws of supply and demand, the world economy would be better . . . While these US companies see a growth in their overseas markets, they see a diminishing US corporate profile overseas in favour of an emergence of their local interests as part of the local business scene. Even greater involvement as responsible corporate citizens is likely. In this regard, these large companies intend to use overseas public relations counselling firms increasingly for guidance in connection with overseas population likes and dislikes.'[62] Officially, the function of Public Relations covers a number of services: relations with the press, writing speeches for the senior personnel, advice in financial matters and accounting, administration of philanthropic relations with schools, hospitals, etc., advice in anti-pollution matters. Dialog's clients include, for example, Eastman-Kodak, Kraft, Sears-Roebuck, and . . . *the U.S. Marines!* J. Walter Thompson in fact has charge of all public relations for this famous elite corps. It designs recruiting campaigns and campaigns replying to tensions with so-called public opinion. Infoplan Inc., which belongs to a group which forms part of McCann Erickson, includes the Ministry of Tourism of the Bahamas and Lockheed Aircraft among its clients. The Chilean dictatorship turned to Dialog in August 1974 to cleanse its international image. A team from North America took a month-long trip to Santiago, and since then the replies made by members of the Junta's Interior Ministry to protest letters against torture and arbitrary detention have become a model of courtesy. Strange coincidence. Dialog's director had signed the same kind of contract with the Greek Colonels in Athens in December 1967.[63] Have we forgotten that the whole ITT conspiracy plot against Allende was hatched by ITT's own public relations division? All these firms habitually engage former journalists or functionaries of North American propaganda agencies. Thus Hal Hendrix, head of ITT public relation for Latin America, used to be a journalist with the Scripps-Howard chain, owners of the Press Agency UPI. In 1962 he received the Pullitzer prize for revealing the existence of Soviet rockets in Cuba at the time of the October crisis. As for Kennecott's public relations chief, Lester Ziffren, responsible for the 'psychological terror campaigns' during the presidential campaigns of

1964 and 1970, he had been press attaché to the US Embassy in Siantiago de Chile during the 40s, after covering the Spanish Civil War as a UPI reporter.

A third area which these advertising firms have adopted for diversification is that of commercial research, which involves a spread of interdisciplinary knowledge, especially economics and psychology. Marplan Research International's research bureaux are just as able to investigate the attitudes of housewives towards a washing powder as the effect of a campaign of rumours against a popular government. J. Walter Thompson's American Market Research Bureau periodically publishes the results of investigations into consumer use of major products, the characteristics of the various media, and makes its own census counts, into order to sell them to advertising agencies, media owners and other more official customers. These 'back-room' research bureaux now compete directly with specialist firms in the field, who monopolised this kind of study a short while ago, such as Simmons and Nielsen. The various research needs have prompted the creation of ever-more specialised service within the advertising agencies. McCann's Perception Research Inc. studies consumer responses to subliminal messages with the aid of an electronic eye. The same agency's 'Strategy Workshop' is a real box of surprises. It aims to deal with any kind of unusual problem which major companies are posed with. Among its most immediate projects are the discovery of a system to measure the consequences on the environment of the installation of a new chemical factory, and the invention of new packing systems. All these divisions, in addition to carrying out these researches, serve as centres of professional training. McCann's Varicom Inc. offers a group of courses and seminars on closed circuit television programming, the organisation of televised meetings and the production of educational programmes. J. Walter Thompson's Communispond division likewise. If a multinational firm or government needs a communications expert, it can always turn to 'Communications Counselors Network Inc.', again a member of the McCann group. In July 1975 the Australian opposition parties protested against an official decision of the New South Wales Government to give J. Walter Thompson the job of setting up a new communications centre to be responsible for official relations with the press, the carrying out of public opinion polls, and the stocking of a library.

Only a little while ago, although on a small scale, the big North American agencies tried approaching the owners of the mass media with the idea of buying them. In 1972 J. Walter Thompson acquired a share in a television programme production company in London 'with the intention of exercising creative control over the final product'. The McCann Erickson group owns a publishing house (Ceco Publishing Co.) which produces specialised magazines for big companies. Foote, Cone & Belding has acquired cable tv systems. This kind of penetration into the media is much more advanced in countries like France, where Havas, for example, has a 45% holding in 'Usine Publications' (*l'Usine Nouvelle, Les Informations*) and, as with Publicis, where there is now a growth in interest in the market for new audio-visual media, like video-cassettes and cable tv. In the United States, electronics and aerospace firms are the leading competitors in this race for the media. Advertising agencies come up against the same competition when they try to sell data processing by offering their clients computerised services. But some have succeeded in setting up in this way, like McCann Erickson's Dataplan Inc.

Finally, non-advertising acquisitions. There is every reason to believe that in 1980, 35 to 50% of the profits of the ten largest North American advertising agencies will be provided by sales which have nothing to do with advertising.[64] Yet in fact only one firm has so far moved into areas which break with its origins. In 1973, J. Walter Thompson drew 11% of its revenue and 19% of its profits from extra-advertising operations. Among these is a company hiring vehicles and equipment to major industrial enterprises (Interlease Corp), dating from 1972. They have also had a 50% participation since 1970 in a tourism and credit card company, the famous Diners/Fugazy Travel & Incentive, which operates in most of the big cities of Europe, Latin America, Africa and Asia, a competitor of American Express. Leo Burnett followed the same path through buying up a Canadian travel agency in 1974, after already buying up art galleries. J. Walter Thompson also owned a large insurance company in Puerto Rico until 1973, when they disposed of it in order to buy an advertising agency in the US. One last example in this area of diversification, Kenyon & Eckhardt, together with the Chemical Bank of New York, set up a financial management service company in 1968, which offers its services in obtaining loans. The recent reduction in advertising budgets on the part of the principal clients and the agencies' wish to reduce their dependency on the fluctuation of these budgets will undoubtedly accelerate this double process of diversification. The need to desist in the promotion of potential needs which an economy of wastage requires, and on the contrary, to consider a hierarchy of real needs on the part of various publics in an economy of scarcity, can only accelerate and deepen the process of mutation in the advertising industry.

A new research complex

The advertising industry is now encroaching on various servicing areas which until recently were closely guarded by specialist firms: Public Relations, Management Consultants, Auditing, Market Research, Employment Agencies. But in the course of the last few years, these other servicing companies have in their turn undergone a process of multinationalisation and diversification. They have often changed hands and taken hold of areas which were not their original concerns. This double process of redefinition, by advertising agencies and by other servicing companies, which tends to lead them both to operate in a rather grey area in between, contributes in fact to formation of an immense complex of precisely adjusted research services, which becomes the bureaucracy needed by the big multinational companies. The 'ideas factories' which these research bureaux consist in, offer the technical expertise which is increasingly needed in this period of crisis.

As the major ideologue of North American management, Peter Drucker, remarks, suggesting that marketing and management techniques have been applied till now badly or hardly at all, 'What is happening now is very healthy. Managers are now going to have to apply what they have learnt. We are going to see what they have retained . . . ' Yet paradoxically, this new phase in the ideological offensive is marked by a belief in the end of ideology: 'It is the end of ideology. We may be getting to the idea of "does it work" instead of "is it right". It may be all we have. We may have a better idea of not the good society but the tolerable society—based on avoiding the negatives we don't want. We may need to be looking for the acceptable ranges of imperfection.'[65] It is the utopia of the bourgeoisie which is dying. The 'Know Them' of our public opinion polls theoretician is becoming 'Know the limits of their universe.' After all the circumlocutions, here is the principle of the need to maximise social control. As another North American management type ingenuously remarked, pleading in favour of the urgency that existed to understand the behaviour and hopes of consumers faced with the crisis: 'The very same unpredictability of the world that we live in has made it necessary for new types of management approaches . . . Even in the political field, conclusions can be drawn from the success of such films as *The Godfather* and *Godfather II*. One of the most crucial dilemmas that we are likely going to be faced with in the future and which will have immediate consequences for marketing and advertising will be the dilemma of the authoritarian vs. democratic approaches. There is a growing desire for what we euphemistically call strong leadership.

Millions of people go to see and enjoy *The Godfather* because we, without admitting it, admire this kind of a much more "fail safe" organisation of the world.' It isn't necessary to go to New York to find such shrewd suggestions about the crisis of the capitalist economy and the parables which accompany it within the world of entertainment spectacle. The film critic of a French economic magazine (*Valeurs actuelles*) recently saw, in catastrophe films (*The Towering Inferno, Earthquake*, etc.), 'a shaking up of Western values ... These fables preach a kind of revaluation of values. They underline, in particular, the impotence of the crowd alone to govern itself, the necessity of hierarchies and masculine supremacy. These heroic films in fact exalt essentially virile values'.

To pursue the exploration of these new research complexes: in the last 5 years, 20 of the most important commercial research companies in the United States have changed hands, several of them even twice. The nature of the companies which have bought them shows us the new profile of the power structure in this sector. The largest number of new owners are outsiders, those coming from a branch of activity foreign to the profession. The result was that in 1971, more than 45% of the research industry in this field escaped the firms originally employed in this work. It can be reckoned that in two or three years this share will increase beyond 60%. Who are the new owners?[66]

At the head of the list come the data-processing companies who see an excellent outlet for their computers and information services in the field of applied research. Thus, Control Data took control in 1967 of the American Research Bureau, after capturing another research company, CEIR Inc. In 1969, Leasco Data Processing Equipment Corp. bought the firm of Daniel Yankelovich Inc. Among other purchasers in data processing are firms like Computer Applications, Computing and Software, which bought the famous W. R. Simmons & Associates in 1971.

The second type of purchaser consists of mass media owners. In 1968, the textbook and commercial publishing giant McGraw-Hill bought up Opinion Market Research Corp. The same year the film company Columbia Pictures Industries Inc. bought two commercial research companies, Grudin/Appel Research Corp. which specialises in attitude research, and N. T. Fouriezos & Associates, which is given over to opinion polls among consumers and small traders. These two companies joined another Columbia property, Audience Studies Inc., a logical extension of film and television production, since it specialised in audio-visual advertisement testing. At the same time and yet again in the same direction, Columbia set up two further companies, Comlab Inc., a veritable mass communications laboratory, and a data processing company, Computer Advisory Services. In 1969, all these pieces were assembled to form Columbia's Inmarco Inc., which is now one of the largest commercial research companies in the United States. Finally, a last example, in 1969 the Cowles press group, publisher of the defunct *Look* and numerous other magazines and newspapers, shareholder in the *New York Times* and owner of radio and television stations, bought Oliver Quayle & Co. After 1966, since setting up a division specialising in commercial research (Sami-Selling Areas Marketing Inc.) and buying up minor data processing companies, the Time-Life group has turned to the most modern computer equipment. This division is now among the first five in the list of North American companies in this area.

The most important firms in the Advisory industry, who take over small and medium commercial and market research companies, constitute the third type of purchaser. The firm Booz, Allen & Hamilton acquired National Analysts Inc., one of the oldest companies in the field, in 1971. In 1975, another notable firm of consultants, Arthur D. Little, took over McGraw-Hill's New York subsidiary, Opinion Research Corp.

The international expansion of these research bureaux is directly related to the policy of multinationalisation of the firms which buy them and which use them as much to supply themselves with their services as in order to sell them to other companies. You only have to remember the case of McGraw-Hill to get an idea of the power of penetration these 'outsiders' wield. The year it bought the Opinion Market Research Corp. in the United States, it set up an international bureau in London, Market and Opinion Research International. Among the studies they produced in 1972 was an inquiry into the public image of large multinational companies throughout the world. Inmarco draws 31% of its turnover from abroad, and possesses offices in 5 Asiatic countries and in Germany. But this is only the least of its resources since it is accompanied by the vast network of film and television circuits which its owners, Columbia Pictures, possesses. And even if the activities of Time-Life's research firm are mostly limited to clients of the metropolis, it is nonetheless at the service of the whole group of international weeklies, books and other audio-visual products wielded by its parent firm.

The equivalent of McCann Erickson and J. Walter Thompson in the field of advertising, the majors within this sector continue to prosper alongside the new arrivals. The foremost of them, topping the commercial research list ahead of Columbia's Inmarco in second place, is the company of A. C. Nielsen, established in 1923, with a presence in 21 countries including all the European countries as well as Japan,

Australia and New Zealand, Canada and Mexico. Its two most recent establishments were set up in Brazil in 1970 and Argentina in 1973, where it purchased a local company. The firm's gross income in 1972 was $128 m. (against J. Walter Thompson's $133 m.). 80% of this figure came from research business in marketing or on the mass-media. The other 20% were already the result of a deliberate policy of diversification: an information service relating to exploration for oil reserves and other energy sources, a subscription service, etc. Studies undertaken by Nielsen cover all fields: television audience research according to age, sex and social category, market research in preparation for the launching of new products, known as test-marketing, and comparative product testing in supermarkets, known as mini-tests. One of its world specialities, market studies are based on the technique of a panel of retailers, an inquiry which is conducted at sales points in order to evaluate product sales rhythms (Nielsen Food Index, etc.). Sticking to Europe, the only continent where they have begun to experience competition from other firms, Nielsen shares this kind of study with Europanel, a group which brings together British, German, Austrian, Swiss, Danish, Belgian, Italian, French and Dutch companies.[67]

On the international market apart from Nielsen there is INRA, which has already been mentioned, which operates in all the European countries and several in Latin America. IMS International Inc., the leading specialist firm in medical and pharmaceutical products marketing, has set-ups in 41 countries and its international work brings in 67% of its turnover. Burke International Research (with 26% of its turnover coming from the international market) has offices in Mexico, Italy, France, Brazil, Argentina, Germany and Canada. This is the kind of advertising it surrounds itself with: 'What's the fastest way to get dependable data from Mexican Markets or Hamburg Hausfraus? Burke International gives you a single, reliable source for market information from strategic operating bases in both hemispheres. And the information you get reflects a single uniform standard of excellence. Burke interviews everywhere speak the local language, but they deliver research that speaks yours—information that makes sense both logically and economically. When you need information from markets, foreign or domestic, find out how much Burke's standardised procedures and quality controls can contribute to the timeliness and accuracy of your marketing decisions.'[68]

Gallup International, with its network through 36 countries, is by no means last in the line to increase the services it offers to its clients. Among studies produced by its French correspondent, IFOP, for example, 'Number one specialist in human behaviour study' as it calls itself, there is a study on problems of advertising, promotion, public relations, communication and 'image' for clients as diverse as industrial companies and political parties; international studies, thus: 'IFOP and its division Etmar, thanks to technical agreements with members of the international Gallup chain, is in a position to conduct and coordinate studies on an international level: for multinational companies, French enterprises wishing to install themselves abroad, foreign companies wanting to approach the French market';[69] and also entire studies on the information media (contents, audiences, etc.).

New think tanks

The Advisory industry is another strategic sector of commercial research and forecasting. It has also undergone profound changes. But it is difficult to fill in the contours of the map. The North American firms of consultants guard most jealously the secrets of the kind of activities they are engaged in. Even their national competitors complain about this secretiveness and have gone as far as to claim that 'The iron curtain behind which most of the American based companies hide, hinders a study of the whole sector'.[70] On the other hand, consultants themselves legitimate their attitude by claiming that their semi-clandestinity is based on the same thing as the secret confessional. They are dedicated to preserve their sphere of activities by making it into an uncontaminated area, a neutral space: 'Because he is outside the enterprise, the consultant is free from the constraints of the structure'. This enables him 'to make judgements about everything concerning the enterprise with complete freedom'.[71]

The four biggest North American firms in the counselling industry are in the process of extending their network abroad, on the international market, precisely where competition is much less than in the United States. The sector comprises some 3,000 firms which share an annual revenue of almost $2 billion. Following competition from big companies, their own former clientele, who have set up their own consultancy departments, these firms entered a period of recession around 1970.

McKinsey should be distinguished among the four major firms, because it already conducts more than half its operations in some 15 foreign countries. It has been in Paris since 1964. In Britain, the BBC has been one of its clients. Booz, Allen & Hamilton has a dozen branch offices abroad. A. T. Kearney owns 5 agencies in Europe, 6 in the USA and one in Japan. Arthur D. Little, whose chief executive is General James Gavin, has a dozen subsidiaries abroad and works or has worked in the last few years in 85 countries.

Among this last company's notable projects in 1971 were: the development of the defence industry in India; harbour installations in Iran; the expansion of the chemical industry (evidently in the hands of the multinational Dow Chemical company) in Chile; the development of small industry in Mexico (the same company produced an inquiry on attitudes towards North American investment in the same country earlier, around 1968); of export industries in Colombia, food production in Greece, the paper industry in New Zealand; the reorganisation of the police force in Surinam, and of the Irish airline; and planning for tourism in 12 countries. In 1970, one of its biggest projects in Brazil, where it has a permanent subsidiary as in Venezuela and Mexico, set up quite recently, was to draw up the industrial development plan for the state of Minas Gerais. Its other giant project was a study on potential economic development in 7 countries of South East Asia.

One way or another all these consultancy firms were involved in the Vietnam war. In 1968, for example, Arthur D. Little was responsible for a study on the possible use of psycho-drugs in counter-insurrectional warfare.[72] All four major firms have done planning and research work on chemical and bacteriological warfare. In 1974, without relinquishing contracts with the industrial-military complex, these firms were fully involved in the process of conversion to civil use, where peace-time counter-insurrection research occupies an important place.

The big Think Tanks like the Rand Corporation, MITRE, the Hudson Institute, the System Development Corporation and ABT Associates, who planned the war in South-East Asia and discovered the first models for counter-insurrectional struggle, are also undergoing the same process of redefinition. In 1974, for example, the Rand Corporation not only tried to characterise the Peruvian regime in one of its reports but also, with experts from the Ford Foundation, developed a plan for cable television exploitation. We have seen that the new models of mass communication and the institutionalisation of new audio-visual media have become a concern for firms operating in this grey area. At the same time, all of them continue their work in 'peace-time' counter-insurrection.

For example, in 1973, the 400 young specialists of all disciplines employed by ABT Associates, at the same time produced studies on educational policies in European countries for the OECD, and, at the bidding of the Pentagon, daily added to the puzzle of conspiracy in Chile by playing games with the simulation model Politica, making moves on the table with fictional actors to represent the roles likely to be adopted by various social groups such as the organisations of the lorry-owners, small businessmen, and doctors.[73]

MITRE, set up in 1958 by the Massachusetts Institute of Technology (MIT) at the express request of the USAF, works for the Defense Department on tactical military satellites and naval communications systems, exploits telephoto data from ERTS satellites for NASA, and is trying to rationalise urban traffic problems for the Transport Ministry. Its report on activities for 1973 says: 'The basic technologies of information systems, pioneered by the Air Force and MIT for air defense, proved to have widespread application to many other problems. As a consequence, MITRE's have expanded slowly and steadily ever since its formation. Our client list now numbers more than 60, and we were involved in some 160 projects during the year. In addition to our well-established sites located in the United States, Europe, and Asia, we have as clients government-related entities in Canada, England, France, Singapore, and the European Economic Community at Brussels . . . We foresee continued dedication to defense programme as MITRE's major task, but with a substantial number of civil programs as an essential element of its overall activity.'[74] In France, among the European clients of this particular Think Tank in the civil field, there is the Direction d'aménagement du territoire et des activités régionales (DATAR). In military matters, MITRE was put in charge in 1972 of designing the modernisation of the Spanish air defense network (Project GAMBIT Grande) and coordinated this job with the similar French air force programme (STRIDA II). MITRE, which over the years has become progressively more independent of the university which founded it, is said by mischief-makers to stand for MIT Rejects, because all the projects MITRE habitually accepts were previously refused by other academic centres because they were considered too compromising. MITRE is also one of the top of the list of cable television programmers in the United States.

Conflict of the new arrivals

The big certified public accounting firms in the United States are also no longer content with their traditional activities. They now employ management experts. In 1972, no less than 20% of the fees paid out to North American consultants went to firms of this kind.[75]

Set up in the beginning to counsel and audit the accounts of major companies, the Audit firms have gone beyond the specific task and are henceforth offering their clients such diverse services as work evaluation and manpower planning, executive recruiting, mergers and the acquisition of multinational companies for other enterprises. In the last five years, the fees they have received have doubled, and their services have been called upon not only by industrialists but also by governments, unions, professional corporations, the European and Latin American Common Markets, religious institutions, educational foundations and universities.

Just like the consultancy firms, they have access to a fabulous amount of confidential information. For example, the public accountancy firms Peat, Marwick, Mitchell & Co., with offices in most Latin American and European countries simultaneously holds information on the national and international activities of General Electric, Singer, Xerox, First National City Bank, Chase Manhatten and 326 other major companies which are its exclusive clients. Interference by these firms is such that they are in general the referees of the rise in compensation awarded when various Third World countries carry out a kind of nationalisation of their natural resources which can be called 'negotiated nationalisation'. That is what happened in Chile, under Frei, where Price Waterhouse & Co. was responsible for arranging the terms and conditions of the 'Chileanisation policy' for copper. In April 1974, *Business Week* reported that the Algerian Government had decided to engage Peat, Marwick, Mitchell & Co. together with Arthur D. Little, the Hudson Institute, McKinsey and Booz Allen & Hamilton, to rationalise the working of various sectors of the Algerian economy. 'We are all at work on confidential projects', said a North American consultant, and to justify the new practice, a Peat & Marwick expert added: 'We are not there to question their system but to make it work.'[76]

The North American audit industry is undoubtedly the branch among servicing companies which has registered the greatest degree of concentration. 8 firms hold in their hands the business of more than 2,100 North American enterprises. Apart from the two already named, there is Arthur Andersen of Chicago, with 380 clients, and 190 million in annual fees; Ernst of Cleveland (265 clients); Lybrand, Ross Bros. of New York (260 clients); Arthur Young of New York (160 clients); and also of New York, Touche Ross (150 clients). The foremost, Peat, Marwick, Mitchell & Co., makes more than $255 m. a year and operates 106 offices in the US with 660 partners.

These same oligopolies take themselves wherever the big companies they advise go. In Venezuela recently, the Faculty of Economics of the University of Caracas denounced the negative activity of these Audit firms in the country: 8 North American companies ruled practically 95% of the country's market and advised institutions and private national and multinational enterprises alike.[77]

The violent polemic which, in 1974, divided French accountants and North American audit firms operating in Paris, says something about the extent and limits of a certain kind of resistance to the penetration of models which United States servicing companies impose both at home and abroad. The disquiet is well based: Price Waterhouse, Arthur Andersen and Lybrand have succeeded in capturing such pillars of the French economy to place beside their multinational clientele as Rhône-Poulenc and Saint-Gibain. In this way, foreign audit firms pick up almost a quarter of the profession's fees.

In 1974, in the name of a principle of defense which is more than corporatist, the president of the professional accountants' associations in Paris called for control of North American firms operating in this field by French nationals. He also demanded the expulsion from the profession of 70 French employees of Price Waterhouse, regarded by the corporation as being guilty of combining the functions of accountancy and consultancy. Contrary to legislation in force in the United States, the French commercial code forbids the joint practice of these two professions. Paradoxically, the proceedings against North American professional accountancy shows up one of the things which explains the superiority of the transatlantic firms over their French cousins. The North Americans do not stop at indicating to their clients doubtful items in the accounts, but thanks to the use of sophisticated techniques which employ a multitude of data, they are in a position to present their clients with a diagnosis of the whole company situation, and, at the same time, if need be, advise on the measures which can be taken to reorganise and remove weakspots.

The representative of the French accountants limited the conflict by saying that 'There is no question of stopping them from working in France. But there is no question, either, of letting them do as they please'. Nevertheless, from the moment the transatlantic model enters a country which till then has had neither need nor experience of it, one may well ask if there's any way the match could be an equal one. This is the way a more modernist representative of French capital seems to have understood it: 'We're going through the pain of transition from family-held companies to publicly-held companies. It is undeniable that the Anglo-Saxon accountants are bringing benefits to French companies and the French economy. It would be ridiculous to exclude them.'[78]

The North American invasion is just as strong in all the other servicing branches. It would take too long to cover all the various areas they are involved in exhaustively, from temporary employment agencies to public relations. Let us simply take a few haphazard examples.

Manpower, whose worldwide network comprises more than 630 branches and which also owns Parker pens, is one of the three principal temporary employment agencies in France (and together with Bis and Ecco covers more than a third of the total business). Recently it took over Europe-Secrétariat and Europe-Industrie and has launched into subcontracting. Here it is worth remembering that during the postal workers' strike of November-December 1974, 600 (out of 800) Manpower employees ran 'parallel' sorting offices around Paris. In 1972 the North American public relations giant, Hill & Knowlton, which operates in more than 20 countries, took a 55% controlling interest in the French agency G.B.S. Conseil, which had been set up in 1967. They told their French director: 'This agreement should allow G.B.S. to acquire an international dimension which it lacks. On the other hand, it should open up to us the doors of a number of sectors, such as financial information, in which Hill & Knowlton has considerable experience, and in any case, it will assist us in unproblematically resolving the concerns of multinational companies with information. Our long term aim is to enlarge the area of activity of public relations to the maximum.'[79] The rush of petrodollars in the countries of the Near East has demonstrated once again the promptitude with which North American public relations firms move in on new markets. 'The Arabs . . . are not without know-how. They have, however, a great desire for a more rapid achievement of their objectives, and these can only be attained by what is magic to their ears—"transfer of technology". They also seek tried and true public relations techniques, effective advertising and management savvy, and the entire successful spectrum of service industry development. They know that with huge amounts of money, they can buy the best and they want only the best.[80] North American public relations firms have an annual turnover of more than $2 billion. Let us finally note the flowering of consultancy firms in human investment, the 'executive search' bureaux, where experts are management specialists rather than psychologists. In 1973, more than 20% of the executives recruited by French enterprises came through these specialised bureaux.[81]

Neither should we forget the considerable development of Wall Street-type lawyers' practices, which are increasingly involved as mediators for the multinationals. Moreover, they offer good schooling. Take one of the most famous of New York law firms, Nixon, Mudge, Rose, Guthrie, Alexander & Mitchell. It supplied the United States with a President, Richard Nixon, and one of his principal counsellors, one of the first to be accused in the Watergate affair, John Mitchell. Around 1965 the film served as a cover for the future presidential candidate in the receipt of substantial assistance from Pepsi Cola, their major client, who financed Nixon's trips abroad when he was losing steam in the metropolis. Once Nixon was elected, the roles were reversed, and the president of Pepsi, Donald Kendall, became the new President's principal economic adviser. Another episode: the first to speak with the Brazilian putschists after the coup against Goulart in 1964 was another firm of lawyers (Millbank, Tweed, Hadbey & McCloy) whose experts escorted the North American ambassador, Lincoln Gordon, to Castelo Branco to demand the restoration of the mining concessions nationalised by the Goulart regime as a precondition of US financial aid. Like most other US service companies, these firms recruit former functionaries, ambassadors and officials as counsellors, who thus have the chance on retirement of a new career fitting to their knowledge of the area where they previously represented the Government.

The same phenomenon can be observed with Peace Corps veterans, as we already noticed when examining developments in tele-education such as new series of the *Sesame Street* kind. The example can be extended convincingly. In March 1976, *Business Week* published a report on what happens to the young volunteers. It may be offered in evidence so that we can avoid being branded as partisan: 'It may not always be clear what Peace Corps volunteers do for the countries they serve in. What is clear is that the Peace Corps today rivals the most prestigious business schools as a training ground for international managers—a fact that has not been lost on multinational companies and banks ... No one knows exactly how many of the 65,000 volunteers who have graduated from the Peace Corps since its beginning in 1961 have ended up in overseas management jobs. But South America probably has more volunteers-turned-manager than anywhere else because the continent has big countries like Brazil that have vast underdeveloped lands as well as big international companies. In Colombia, Peace Corps director Manuel Villalobos estimates that 10% of the 300 volunteers arriving annually have stayed on in corporations or government jobs. Banks in particular seem to be attracted to Peace Corps veterans. Bank of America has hired about three dozen former members. Morgan Guaranty Trust in 1973 tapped Robert H. Barbour Jnr. to be its chief representative in Brazil; he had helped set up fishing cooperatives at Sâo Joâo da Barra, a small town north of Rio de Janeiro.'

It is therefore hardly astonishing to find that the staff officer of the North American embassy in Santiago during the Allende Government had been the chief of the Peace Corps in Chile in the mid-60s.

'Global University' managers

To complete this survey of the business culture which accompanies the invasion of the multinationals by reproducing the ideological conditions which allow them to be accepted as natural, one should pay attention to the other agents of socialisation which go to make up the training centres of future representatives and employees of these enterprises. We can bring together abundant and varied documentation on this theme. It illustrates first the real cycles of training organised by these firms and the agreements for instruction of pupils reached between the local business and administration schools and the subsidiaries of North American companies. It touches in passing on the matter of the 'brain drain' through which big US companies literally pump the meagre resources of the proletarian countries in technicians and researchers into their own pools of profit. In more than one faculty of medicine, engineering or economics in countries like the Dominican Republic more than half the graduates end up in the United States. The investigation brings to our attention, among other things, the decisive importance of university exchanges in establishing the conformity of neo-colonial mentality. The recent history of Chile offers a sad example of the inauspicious results of this cooperation. The dictatorship's economic team, appropriately known as the 'Chicago Boys' descends directly from an assistance plan provided to the Catholic University of Chile by the school of economics of the University of Chicago in the early 60s. Finally we touch upon the scholarship programmes set up by the big multinationals. Here it is enough to remember that in 1975, ITT's international scholarship programme permitted 184 students from 40 countries to pursue their university studies abroad—the programme's avowed aim is 'to promote international understanding among those who tomorrow will be among the first ranks in business, public administration and the arts'. Financed by the company itself, the programme is directly administered by the Institute of International Education which also handles a good number of other projects of scholarships by North American educational foundations.

As the present book was nearing completion, the author discovered a report produced by experts belonging to the Chemical Bank in May 1976. Its title was provocative and evocative: *US-Style MBA programs catch on in Europe*. To reproduce this report can say more than any individual analysis of the problem. Here, in their own words, is how the multinational managers record the victory of the North American style in the business schools of the European countries:

American-style management training, with its interdisciplinary approach and its emphasis on interaction between the manager and his environment, is becoming more and more common in Europe. The trend is most noticeable in the specialised management schools, like the European Institute of Business Administration (INSEAD) at Fountainebleau or the Cranfield (UK) School of Management, which have become prominent in the last ten years.

But even traditional university-affiliated business faculties such as the one at the Catholic University of Louvain (Belgium) or the prestigious Ecole des Hautes Etudes Commerciales in Paris, have introduced US teaching methods, which are characterized by the use of the Harvard-pioneered case approach for teaching management skills.

As the number of graduates of such programs increases, American companies located in Europe will have a larger pool of local managerial talent to draw on. If current trends continue, such executives are likely to be less expensive to hire than either Americans with successful multicountry management experience, or Europeans trained in the top American business schools. According to a study recently published by the Swiss management consultants Egon Zehnder and Associates, Harvard graduates command 'significantly greater' remuneration than do their peers from a comparable European institute such as INSEAD.

'Modern' business education was first introduced in Europe in the early 1960s, partly as a result of concern that European businesses were not as productive, in real terms, as their American and Japanese competitors. Government-sponsored reports in France and the U.K. concluded that one of the reasons for the low productivity was that managers' performance was less than adequate, and this in turn might be due to the fact that very few managers had any formal training in their profession. With official encouragement, a growing number of young Europeans, led by the French, went to American business schools such as Harvard, M.I.T., and Stanford. On returning to Europe, they moved right into major jobs and quick careers, especially with the American companies that were beginning to establish headquarters in Europe. Other MBAs immediately got important teaching posts in the commercial schools and universities that were starting to adopt the American methods of teaching. This, of course, led to an even wider use of the US-style education.

Now there are a number of independent management schools in Europe. The top ones, according to management consultants here, include INSEAD in France; Cranfield School of Management, the London Business School and the Manchester Business School in the United Kingdom; and IMEDE in Switzerland. All offer programs that are similar in structure to the ones offered by American schools. The study sequence at Cranfield, for example, includes the familiar range of courses on Finance, Accounting, Marketing, Operating Management, and Personnel Management. One difference from American schools, though, is that most of the European programs run for only one academic year, compared to the two years that is normal in the US.

In addition to these specialised schools, there are a growing number of 'traditional' university faculties that incorporate the case method in at least some of their business courses. Many non-degree granting institutes like the Center for Education in International Management (CEI), Geneva, conduct short seminars for working managers. It is interesting to note that CEI was founded by the Canadian-based Alcan Aluminium Ltd., to help train its European managers. And in 1972 the Management School of Boston University inaugurated an evening degree program in Brussels. The transition to American-style education, with its implicit cultural assumptions, has not been easy. Gerard E. Watzke, the Director of Boston University's MBA Program in Brussels, thinks that this is because the case method runs counter to the

Table 30

Remuneration of Business Graduates by Age, Country and Business School Attended

Ages		Harvard				INSEAD			
		U.K.	France	W. Germ.	Belgium	U.K.	France	W. Germ.	Belgium
25–29	Mean	17,200	18,350	22,000		9,750	15,650	18,500	15,000
	Median	16,500	18,500	23,000		11,800	17,300	21,000	16,500
30–34	Mean	22,000	25,500	29,000	20,000	17,450	17,500	21,400	19,500
	Median	22,500	25,600	27,500	22,500	18,300	15,000	22,400	22,200
35–39	Mean	30,000	31,000	60,000	30,000	17,500	24,200	29,000	33,600
	Median	31,700	33,500	60,000	30,000	16,500	26,650	31,000	30,000

Salaries in thousands of US $'s.   **Sources:** Egon Zehnder, *Survey of Business School Graduates in Europe,* 1975.
Medians approximate.

grain of European culture. It forces the neophyte manager to recognise problems, formulate solutions to them, and, significantly, test his ideas against a critical peer group audience. 'Europeans tend to be more reticent and reserved than Americans are,' says Watzke, 'and they often find this a traumatic experience.' What's more, the typical MBA program cultivates a certain type of aggressiveness in its graduates that doesn't always sit well with strongly hierarchical European companies. 'There is a sort of "don't rock the boat" attitude that makes some companies view these managers with suspicion,' says Watzke.

*   *   *

Certainly, American-style management training differs radically from the kind of education that Europe's top managers have received in the past.

In France, Belgium, the U.K. and Germany, the way to the top has traditionally been rigidly controlled by a sort of 'broad-based elitism', as Jean-Philippe Deschamps of Arthur D. Little describes it. 'All the top positions in France go to people who were mathematicians,' he says—referring to graduates of France's big three finishing schools for future managers, the Ecole Polytechnique, the Ecole des Mines, and the Ecole Nationale de l'Administration. These schools offer top quality education in mathematics and the physical sciences, but little or no training in management subjects. Deschamps estimates that about 70 per cent of the Presidents/General Managers of French companies come from these schools. In addition, many get to the top through family ties, and probably 10 to 15 per cent are US-style professional managers.

The same elitism is essentially true in Germany, where schools like the Mannheim Geschaeftshochschule educate future managers.

Critics of this type of management education say that in such a traditional university environment there is no give and take between the students and the professor, let alone among the students. They claim that the teaching method encourages passivity among the students. Courses are given in lecture form by a professor, and any questions the student may have are answered in separate sessions with an assistant. Once out of the university environment, the student tends to adopt the rigid attitude of the professor in dealing with his own subordinates. D. F. Berry, the Dean of INSEAD, says that such schools tend to produce 'small armies of industrial civil servants' instead of the entrepreneurial managers needed by European business in a changing economic climate.

Another difference is that such education generally doesn't offer the inter-disciplinary approach to management training characteristic of the US style. Having grown out of university economics departments, such traditional business faculties may offer courses in economics and finance—interspersed with studies of geology, or mathematics, or engineering. Courses in subjects like marketing or operations management are generally not offered. The emphasis is on acquiring theoretical knowledge, rather than on developing the skills needed in a decision-making position.

*   *   *

Despite the conflicts between the European and American style of management, even relatively conservative European companies are now trying to attract the flexible, aggressive managers produced by schools like INSEAD or IMEDE. Luc Hanssens, a partner in the Brussels office of Egon Zehnder, thinks that this shift is mainly due to external factors like the difficult business climate which has resulted from the energy crisis and the recession. 'The market punishes companies that keep a man on the staff because he is a friend of some uncle, or because he is charming, if he doesn't perform,' he says. Hanssens cites Société Générale de Belgique, the country's largest holding company, as one traditionally conservative company that has sharply increased its efforts to hire MBAs in the last few years. These graduates are specially in demand for the group's overseas activities, which require flexible, mobile managers.

In general, there seems to be a growing conviction in Europe that it is possible to teach people to be good managers. But not everyone agrees, of course. Those who believe that special education is not crucial in determining a manager's success like to point out that the Germans have as a whole been uninterested in most forms of advanced management training. 'I guess they're too busy learning how to run their companies,' said one observer.

Notes

1 Denis Lindon, 'Le marketing sans but lucratif', *Le Management*, Paris, No. 46, April 1974, p. 55.
2 Dan Seymour (President of J. Walter Thompson) in *Advertising Age* (the national newspaper of marketing), Chicago, 21 November 1973, p. 218. The weekly *Advertising Age* is the most important organ of the US advertising agencies.
3 Tom Dillon, *Advertising Age*, 21 November 1973, p. 204.
4 Tom Dillon, *Never Boil an Alarm Clock*, the Batten, Burton, Durstine agency, 1968.
5 Denis Lindon, *op.cit.*, p. 50.
6 James M. Perry, *The New Politics, The Expanding Technology of Political Manipulation*, Weidenfeld & Nicolson, 1968.
7 M. Blenstein-Blanchet, 'Supprimer les sondages', *Le Monde*, 23.V.1974.
8 Henry Smith, 'Goebbels in space, government use of telecommunications', *Cinéaste*, New York, 1973, Vol. V, No. 4.
9 *Advertising Age*, 9.XI.1970.
10 *Advertising Age*, 17.VII.1967.
11 *Advertising Age*, 9.XI.1970.
12 *Visão*, Sao Paulo, 1.VIII.1972.
13 *Advertising Age*, 17.I.1972.
14 Owners of *Mercurio* and 68 industrial and commercial enterprises (Author's note).
15 Complete edition of the *Secret Documents of ITT (Documentos Secretos de la ITT)* (in English and Spanish), Ediciones Quimantú, Santiago, Chile, 1972.
16 'Las encuestas antichilenas', *Mayoria*, Santiago, Chile, 16.II.1972 (cf. also 'El archivo secreto de la Braden' in the same magazine, 5.I.1972). In March 1973, the ex-director of the CIA admitted, before the Senate Foreign Affairs Committee, that the CIA had assigned $400,000 to the Chilean right 'to cover propaganda activities against Allende during the election period of 1970'. Cf. 'A $400,000 Chile Fund Reported', *Washington Post*, 28.III.1973. Since the 1964 presidential campaign, the Christian Democrats received almost $20 m. through the agency of German foundations which served as intermediaries for North American in-

telligence services. On funds directed by the CIA to opposition forces to overthrow Allende, cf. Colby's revelations in *International Herald Tribune*, 9.IX.1974.

17 *Ibid.*

18 cf. Mattelart, *Mass Media, idéologies et mouvement révolutionnaire, op. cit.*

19 Marlise Simons, 'The Brazilian Connection' *Washington Post*, 6.I.1974.

20 cf. Dossier on the Chilean Junta, *Le Monde Diplomatique*, July 1974.

21 See the magazine *Ercilla*, Santiago, Chile, February 1974. Between 1973 and 1974 the turnover of the principal Chilean advertising agency—Publicidad Fabres y de Heeckeren—increased from $274,000 to almost 2.5 m., that of Kenyon & Eckhardt's subsidiary from $24,000 to 400,000 (*Advertising Age*, 31.III.1975).

22 *Résistance, bulletin d'information*, Algiers, 12–19 May 1975.

23 Ramona Bechtos, 'Undercover admen: JNT linked to CIA front', *Advertising Age*, 3.II.1975.

24 *L'echo de la Presse et de la Publicité*, Paris, 21.VII.1975.

25 Bruno Lussato, 'Des concepts démodés', *Le Management*, Paris, January, 1971.

26 *Advertising Age*, 11.VIII.1975. On the strategy of the firms of political consultants, cf. James M. Perry, *op.cit.*

27 Duplicated letter circulated by *Le Management*, 15.V.1974.

28 *USIA Appropriation Authorization, Fiscal Year 1973, op. cit.*

29 *Advertising Age*, 24.IV.1972.

30 Most of the figures on North American agencies are taken from *Advertising Age*, 21.XI.1973, 25.II.1974, 24.II.1975 and 31.III.1975.

31 On the situation in France, cf. the organ of French publicity companies, *Stratégies*.

32 Some figures on the slackening off of certain companies' publicity budgets: Exxon's budget in 1973 amounted to $28 m., $24 m. in 1974. During the same period. Coca-Cola's budget was reduced from $76 m. to $74 m. that of Chrysler from $96 m. to $86 m. (*Advertising Age*, 18.VIII.1975).

33 'Ou va la publicité'? *Entreprise*, Paris, 24.VIII.1973.

34 M. Chavanon, polemic with M. Duverger in *Le Monde*, June 1972.

35 M. Bleustein-Blanchet, cited by Francis Legal, 'La publicité, rôle économique et social', *Economie et Politique*, Paris, March 1974. On the evolution of Havas, see *Le Monde*, 10.V.1975, *Stratégies*, Nos. 24 & 59.

36 *Le Monde*, December 1974.

37 *Advertising Age*, 30.VI.1975.

38 *Stratégies*, No. 47, 1973.

39 The analysis of the expansion of the North American agencies is based on data published in *Advertising Age* over the last five years.

40 For the official history of North American advertising agencies, cf. the annual company reports and the special edition of *Advertising Age* published on 7th December 1964 on the occasion of J. Walter Thompson's centenary. For a critical analysis within a marxist perspective cf. Stuart B. Ewen, 'Advertising as social production', *Radical America*, May–June 1969.

41 Ramona Bechtos, 'Undercover admen: JWT linked to CIA front', *op.cit.*

42 *Advertising Age*, 21.XI.1973. It may be mentioned, among other things, that under the Johnson administration, the proprietor of J. Walter Thompson, Stanley Resor, who had been president of the agency for 40 years (1916–55), was nominated Secretary of the Army.

43 J. Walter Thompson, *Annual Report 1972.*

44 Ramona Bechtos, 'Key consumer goods growing fast in Brazil', *Advertising Age*, 5.III.1973.

45 Interpublic Group of Cos. Inc., *Annual Report 1972.*

46 Secodip data published in *Stratégies*, No. 40, 7–13 May 1973.
47 Antonio Pasquali, *Communicacion y cultura de masas*, Caracas, 1972, Monteavila Editores.
48 *Annuaire de la Presse et de la Publicité*, Paris, 1973.
49 J. Walter Thompson, *Advertising as a Selling Force*, Thomson Blue Book on Advertising, 1909–1910.
50 *Advertising Age*, 29.X.1971.
51 *Advertising Age*, 26.VI.1967.
52 *Advertising Age*, 13.I.1969.
53 *Advertising Age*, 17.IX.1973.
54 *Unilever Magazine*, No. 9, November-December 1974.
55 *Advertising Age*, 23.VI.1975.
56 *Business Week*, 27.I.1975.
57 *Advertising Age*, 21.X.1973.
58 The analysis of this policy of diversification is based on the annual company reports as well as the annuals published by *Advertising Age*.
59 P. M. Doutrelant, 'Le médicament malade du profit', *Le Monde*, 16.V.1975.
60 *Stratégies*, No. 13, 18 June–1 July 1973.
61 *Business Week*, 1.VI.1974.
62 James B. Strenski, 'Problems in International Public Relations', *Public Relation's Journal*, May 1975.
63 Ramona Bechtos, 'Undercover Adment: JWT linked to CIA front', *op. cit.*
64 Forecast by E. B. Weiss, *Advertising Age*, 21.X.1973.
65 The first statement of Peter Drucker comes from an article by J. Grapin, *Le Monde*, 12.XII.1975; the second from *Business Week*, 9.II.1974. The third statement is by Ernest Dichter, *Advertising Age*, 5.I.1976. the film criticism from *Valeurs actuelles* is cited by S. Sorel in *Teleciné*, Paris, May 1975.
66 Jack. J. Honomichl, 'Big Business Snaps Up 22 Top Research Firms', *Advertising Age*, 20.IX.1971, and same author, *Advertising Age*, 11.V.1970 and 15.VII.1974.
67 For Nielsen, cf. *Les Dossiers d'Entreprise*, February 1974; 'Sociétés de service', *Le Management*, special number, 1974; *Advertising Age*, 16.IV.1973 in particular.
68 Advertisement in the specialised press.
69 *Les Dossiers d'entreprise*, February 1974.
70 *Ibid.*
71 'Les Conseillers d'entreprise, pour quoi faire?', *Le Management*, Special number, 1974.
72 Cf. Paul Dickson, *Think Tanks*, Ballantine Books, New York, 1971; 'AAAs in Mexico. Science and Technology in Latin America', *Science for the people*, December 1972; *Subliminal Warfare, The Role of Latin American Studies*, NACLA, 1970. Mention may also be made that in the committee set up by the US Government and the multinational companies to fix the policy of 'invisible blocs' against Popular Chile, alongside bankers and other business men, were the former president of McCann Erickson and a consultant from Arthur D. Little. Cf. *NACLA's Latin America & Empire Report*, Vol. VII, No. 1, January 1973.
73 Cf. Armand Mattelart, Firmes multinationals et syndicats jaunes dans la contre-insurrection', *op. cit.*
74 The Mitre Corporation, *Annual Report 1972*.
75 For an analysis of these Audit firms, cf. the report in *Business Week*, 22.IV.1972.
76 *Business Week*, 20.IV.1974.
77 Manuel Rodriquez, 'Intergracion economica capitalista y empresas multinacionales', *Supplemento Cuadernos*, Carcas, July–August 1972.

78 *Business Week*, 1.VI.1974.
79 *Strategies*, No. 28.
80 Edward Burke, 'The practitioner's role in tapping Arab markets', *Public Relations Journal*, February 1975.
81 on 'Exeucutive search' bureaux, cf. *Le Monde*, 1.VI. 1974, p. 25. On law firms, see *Le Management*, January 1971, pp. 31–37; *NACLA's Latin American & Empire Report*, vol. VII, No. 9, Nov. 1973, pp. 5–14.

CHAPTER VIII

REDEFINING THE TARGETS

Parallel espionage networks

JEALOUS of their autonomy, the big industrial multinationals today dispute their fields of activity with the big service companies. They have sometimes created specialised departments which not only conduct their activities within the company but also beyond it. About 300 companies are now working for other enterprises after having created their own management consultant divisions. General Electric, for example, operates an office of 150 consultants who devote 10% of their activity to outside jobs.[1] Moreover, it has for several years maintained a centre of advanced studies in California called TEMPO (Technical Military Planning Operation). This veritable Think Tank, tailored to the same model as the better known Rand institutions (MITRE, etc.) was the first to study in depth 'the secondary education system in Popular China as an instrument of power'. This is the title carried by one of its confidential reports published in the 60s. One of the founders of TEMPO was Thomas Paine, ex-supreme chief of NASA, promoted in the meantime to the Vice Presidency of General Electric, invariably the space agency's second or third largest client.

The development of the US electronics and aerospace industry in the field of information and pedagogy will undoubtedly make its effects felt increasingly on all the service companies. Many North American experts, for example, are coming round to asking themselves if by 1980 the proprietors of the new audio-visual technologies should not have replaced and absorbed the numerous publicity agencies. According to one of these visionaries: 'I must point out that the science of communications obviously finds itself in a stage of extraordinarily creative explosion. The traditional function of the advertising agency is but a spectator confronted with the increasingly more ample definitions of mass communications, such as are formulated by the incredible and surprising advances of technological communication, that is not produced around the corner but is produced here. General Electric is intimately involved in the technological development of these technological advances and, likewise, with their commercialisation. This link could confer on the advertising services affiliated with GE a road of reconversion, which would consist of conceiving and implementing advertising programmes for future innovations in mass electronic communications . . . What is true for GE may also be equally valid for RCA and the other giants of electronic communications . . .'[2]

The same type of evolution seems to project itself in the larger field of information systems. Those in data-processing who have experience of time-sharing (the sale of facilities to various subscribers on a time-sharing basis) occupy a strategic position in setting up new types of alliances with certain clients. Once again, General Electric figures among the pioneers of this new kind of activity. In 1974, 360 towns in the United States, Canada, Western Europe, Japan and Australia were connected to its international data-processing network MARK III. To establish the growing time-sharing industry in Japan, General Electric found that it was able to do no better than form an association with the largest Japanese advertising agency, Dentsu. The Japanese subscribers to its network could pick up a telephone at the terminal, dial the number of the Dentsu central relay station and be automatically connected by satellite to the General Electric computer bank situated in the State of Ohio. In taking this decision which, among other things, overcomes problems which arise from restrictions on the import of computers, General Electric demonstrated uncommon knowledge of the rivalries between different members of the groups which dominate the economy (Zaibatsu). Thus the terms in which it justified the alliance with Dentsu in 1973: 'From GE's standpoint . . . Dentsu has one large advantage: not only has the big agency access to countless boardrooms through its advertising business, but it has no direct ties to any single member of the powerful Zaibatsu, such as Mitsui or Mitsubishi. Thus, Dentsu can approach all of Japan's giants without fear of prejudicing established relations—a rare forte in Japanese business.'[3] Once again, the function of foreign ministry which the giants of advertising like Dentsu are called upon to fulfil for the multinational companies is confirmed.

Such an analysis of the power structure in a country where a multinational wishes to install itself is clearly possible only because there is an intelligence network behind the company working for it. Even if at the same time it always has recourse to the services of a company of consultants in order to know more about its competitors, the biggest of these companies tend increasingly to delegate to their own management and marketing departments what is actually a job of espionage. In fact these big companies possess their own intelligence systems. The businessmen themselves are beginning to recognise this:

'Corporations, no less than countries, have been gathering information about one another for years. Among nations, it is called spying and may involve sophisticated techniques, lots of money, specially trained personnel, and covert methods. Companies are more likely to call it market research or commercial analysis, and until recently their efforts have been mostly fragmented and loosely planned, more tactical than strategic. Now, with business more complex and the economic climate so uncertain, corporations are becoming far more sophisticated at scrutinising the competition. They seek out more information, spend more time and effort analysing it, and some even have full-time executives who specialise in ferreting out and interpreting nuggets about their rivals.'[4] These operations imitate all aspects of government intelligence activities. They are, in operation, clandestine and semi-clandestine. They exploit open sources (annual reports, economic and scientific publications); they have their computer networks (salesmen, researchers). When necessary they infiltrate their competitors' with informants and entice away their personnel. As in all clandestine political work, certain companies even practise a very wily compartmentalisation in order to protect their researches against leaks. As the Marketing Director of a major electronics firm put it, 'Tactics for keeping track of the competition are at times sneaky, may be even immoral or unethical. The line is drawn only when something might be illegal.'[5] In order to devote itself to this kind of work IBM, which is very much a model of industrial intelligence, operates a specialised instrument, its Department of Commercial Analysis, which forms part of its Data Processing Division. The latest Anti-Trust accusations which it incurred before the Ministry of Justice revealed that hundreds of its employees reported information daily on its competitors' installations (IBM's competitors such as Sperry Rand have confessed to playing the same kind of game).

When the enemy is no longer exclusively an industrial competitor, the intelligence system moves to a new level. This enemy is habitually identified by the term 'terrorism' or 'extremism'. Once it has been diagnosed, it is a question of neutralising it with adequate means. A private security system comes to superimpose itself on a private intelligence system, a programme of counter-intelligence. Ties are woven with specialist firms in this kind of surveillance. The multinational companies can call on firms which are devoted to the protection of property and persons, such as William J. Burns International Security Service or the Wachenhut Corporation. This last, for example, has private militia services in Brazil, Colombia, Ecuador, Venezuela and Santo Domingo, and offers protection to North American businessmen travelling abroad. Other companies such as Hughes Aircraft turn to private intelligence organisations such as Intertel (International Intelligence Inc.). Finally, the most important envisage setting up their own network for Defence and Intelligence on their own account, calling upon the experience of Police Associations. Thus IBM engaged the International Association of Police Chiefs (IACP), which we already saw was courted by Northrop who offered it its latest alarm circuits. The results of this co-operation between IBM and IACP are contained in a course which is run for the company officials, which carries the title *Security: A Management Style. A Course of Instruction in Corporate Protective Services. IBM as a Target for Terrorists*. This course was revealed at the time of the scandal of the IBM Papers in November 1974.[6] The following paragraphs may be presented without commentary:

> Simply because it operates overseas, IBM will have some vulnerability to terror or violence there. Add to this simple fact of location the fact that IBM is identified with Western technological supremacy and, to some degree with so-called 'American Imperialism', and the overall assessment of IBM's future overseas vulnerability must be placed relatively high on a scale of judgements. South America is probably the most important single source of the theory now influencing terrorist violence around the world. Marighela's *Minimanual* is a minor classic, widely read in the Western Hemisphere. As one bibliographic source for this Block emphasises, however, there is a possibly critical conceptual difference between the urban guerilla and the terrorist: . . . Urban guerilla warfare can be defined as criminal conduct for revolutionary purposes. Terrorism, on the other hand, is violent criminal activity designed to intimidate for political purposes. The distinction is in goals sought and sometimes in methods used. The guerilla is working toward revolution. The terrorist acts of violence focus attention on a particular grievance. (US Federal Bureau of Intelligence, 'Trends in Urban Guerilla Tactics'. *FBI Law Enforcement Bulletin*, July 1973, p. 2.) In practice, the line between terrorism and the urban guerilla is not as neat. In fact, many little terrorist groups love to preen themselves with the thought that they are 'urban guerillas'; part of their nourishment comes from this fantasy. Indeed, the whole thrust of Symbionese rhetoric was *they were urban guerillas*, and for a long time during the late Winter and early Spring of 1974, American institutions were responding as if they were. On the other hand, urban guerillas fully recognise the value of indiscriminate terror tactics. The kidnapping of Victor Samuelson [Director of Exxon in Argentina, kidnapped by the ERP and released against a ransom of $14.2 million—author's note] has become a classic in the use of a hostage to achieve political ends. Assume that IBM, on strictly humanitarian grounds, insists that it must always keep open the possibility of ransoming any of its kidnapped personnel. Consider now the profoundly destabilising effects of over $14 million in the hands of the ERP—if, indeed, they used part of the money to fund a 'Revolutionary Coordination Board'. Under these conditions, what is the tradeoff between the need to save an executive and the need to arrest the long term assault on the whole structure of the capitalist system? A tough question, at best.

Passing on to review some of the orientations which the company's intelligence and security services should take, the course underlines the importance revealed by the previous experience of the company which involved working with military organisations.

> The range of possible terrorist and extremist actions is potentially broad. This dictates an intelligence system adequate for monitoring the entire threat spectrum. But, there will be substantial resistance to anything that smacks of 'intelligence gathering'—and even more to anything covert or 'spooky'. IBM at CHQ and Site levels, thus will face some hard decisions about how to define and institutionalise this very necessary intelligence capability. An important element of a counter-terror intelligence system will be its ability to generate analyses of incident data. Deriving from these analyses should be projected response scenarios. IBM is unusually well qualified to develop such scenarios. In doing so it can draw upon accumulated expertise within the Defense research and development community ... Even with effective intelligence and analysis, an organisation's response may be slow and uncoordinated, thus conferring crucial advantages on terrorists. A centralised action directorate, close to top management and with the ability to reach quickly to Site, would offer critical managerial capabilities in mounting timely, flexible responses ... The Seven Sins reveal the tremendous psychological pressures under which terrorists and 'urban guerillas' operate. Security specialists should realise that not only do the Seven Sins suggest general psychological and strategic vulnerabilities which they might exploit, but they offer clues about ways in which to force the tactical hands of terrorists. This can lead to projecting potential covert counter-terror operations. Under what circumstances would IBM be justified in covertly exploiting Marghella's Seven Sins? If there were certain circumstances, how would they be defined, and what would be the nature of the cover operation(s)?

IBM seems already to have been to school. At the end of November 1974 Business International, the firm of consultants, organised a seminar on security programmes for large companies with the same Association of Police Chiefs. In a letter of invitation sent to senior officials of these large companies one reads:

> Reorganizing the very real threat to their corporate assets and personnel which kidnapping and international terrorism present—and the huge corporate losses already being incurred—a growing number of firms are creating a new management function—risk management—to develop and implement a program to protect the company's plant, equipment and people. If your company has not yet taken this step, the time to do it is now.[7]

In July of the same year, Business International, which specialises, among other things, in financial research, represented the interests of foreign investors in Chile at a meeting where it was decided, with Pinochet, to violate the Carthaginia agreements containing the statute covering foreign companies in the countries of the Andean Pact.[8]

Imperialism makes its first 'class analysis'

'The market is not made up of demographic groups, but of psychological groups: do executives have the same style, the same conceptions of life? Can they all be assimilated to what is still called the bourgeoisie?

These questions are becoming more and more important. You cannot advertise in the same way for hippies and for farmers.'[9] This significant passage was uttered in 1973 by David Ogilvy, Chairman of the Ogilvy & Mather Agency. While it appears banal, the modern advertising industry has taken more than 20 years to discover it. As one of the directors of Kenyon & Eckhardt confessed in 1967: 'It has been an age old axiom of the advertising business that a writer should talk to one person, and the trouble up to now has been that the writer never knew who that one person was. He never knew what he was like and what he wanted from a product and a product class. So instead of talking to a person, he found himself talking to a bunch of mythical averages; in effect, pieces of people, but not a real person with real wants and likes.'[10] The same year Kenyon & Eckhardt held an international seminar in Mexico with the exclusive aim of questioning this unreal approach to the public through advertising. At the end of the seminar, the company announced that it would explain the application of its new method 'target attitude group' (TAG). 'We will be looking at specific groups of consumers with common attitudes, wants and beliefs. We will not be looking at the 'average' consumer who has never existed anywhere except in the mind of the mathematician.' In justifying why advertising had not previously made any progress Kenyon & Eckhardt spokesmen themselves explained the factors which made this transcendental innovation possible. 'We are only now able to do it because the advent of the computer has given us the capacity to handle the vast quantities of information required to really get a good picture of the psychological profiles of consumers in relation to product categories.'[11]

Here finally the problem is posed. The advertising men link up in their own way with those who have conceived the new tele-education series with a concern to 'sectoralise' their audience. It is no longer possible to embark on mass marketing with an inert definition of the concept of the mass. Now that the economic situation demands, and the application of new technologies allows, the dissection of this amorphous conglomeration—this vast, indistinct and coarse object which until now has formed the basis for the majority of the messages of mass culture—it is possible to discern the 'needs and interests' of each category of consumers and respond to them in a proper fashion. It is enough to recall the sophisms which provide the foundations for the study of attitudes and behaviour in capitalist society to get at least an inkling of a qualitative jump that has been made in the ideological offensive of the ruling classes, or in 'the battle for the conquest of spirits' in the words of the same Ogilvy in the *Reader's Digest* propaganda.

In this readjustment of the target, however, the advertising agencies are more than 15 years behind the Pentagon. But it is not the computer which, within the limitations of technological determinism, allowed the military to discover that the mass is made up of different social categories. The development of computer models applied to the analysis of the population has only followed the development of an approach which was already apparent in certain political situations involving class relations. If we go back to the 1960s, we see that Kennedy's campaign against Nixon indicated no more than the arrival of data processing in the political world. But it revealed a different social approach from Kennedy's own. And this approach to different sectors of the electorate was demonstrated by the still rudimentary simulation models of the period, developed in the course of the electoral campaign by academic sociologists Ithiel de Sola Pool of MIT, William McPhee of the University of Columbia and Robert P. Ableson of Yale. This was only the beginning. Since 1961 a crew of military analysts, specialists of the Rand Corporation, of the President and of his Defense Secretary McNamara, undertook to modify the style of Pentagon strategies, which were over-accustomed to making politics a by-product of the armed forces. In Asia, Africa and Latin America, said McNamara, "there has come into prominence, in the last year or two, a kind of war which Mr Khrushchev calls "wars of national liberation" or "popular revolts" but which we know as insurrection, subversion, and covert armed aggression . . . We have a long way to go in devising and implementing effective countermeasures against these Communist techniques.'[12]

According to Kennedy and McNamara, the decade of the 60's was going to be marked by this kind of war and the increase of these wars would impede the United States in the defense of their interests uniquely by military means. The Kennedy doctrine survived the Dallas assassination. As a result of having paid attention only to its military counsellors, the United States experienced its first defeats in 1964 in Vietnam. Following these defeats and its experience of the guerillas who began to make their presence felt in Latin America, the establishment within the armed forces was forced to take account of the fact that in the last resort it is not only fire-power and other technological factors which necessarily determine the victory. In its offensive against popular movements they learned to reckon on the importance of political factors and glimpsed the necessity of working more with the civil sectors of the population. They would have to incline more towards the diversity of social reality, exploit internal contradictions, discover less direct, more surreptitious modes of intervention. The epoch of a latter-day gun-boat diplomacy, unannounced landings of marines as in Santo Domingo and the Bay of Pigs, had reached its end.

In order to resolve the enigma of these new struggles, the Pentagon now posed new kinds of question. Who are our friends? Who are our enemies? What is happening to internal conflicts? How can we discover the best Party? Who can help neutralise whom? What are the interests each group is inclined to defend? How are the various hierarchies set up? What social resentments motivate the different sectors of the population and are susceptible to making one rise up against the others? Who are the leaders of the workers' and peasants' movements? Do any of them shelter communist influence? What position do the armed forces occupy? What is its social position? In short, the Pentagon discovered that society is divided into classes and for the first time undertook to analyse this. The science of counter-insurrectional war, social systems engineering, generated by the university-industrial-military complex, began to elaborate the first analytic models of social change, and what was euphemistically called social control, in the Third World. In order to study the attitudes and behaviour of various groups, anthropologists and sociologists were called upon to collaborate and the Department of Defense equipped itself with an appropriate division. The first public manifestation of these researches carried the name of the Camelot Plan. It was unmasked in Chile in April 1964. It was discovered with amazement that under cover of a sociological inquiry this vast plan provided the Pentagon with an assembly of elements which would serve for the construction of a social model of the country, a country which clearly had no experience of guerillas but where social tensions had become so strong that the Pentagon brains trust had diagnosed a pre-revolutionary situation. President Johnson himself had to cancel Project Camelot which dealt not only with Chile, but also with Peru, Bolivia, Colombia, Venezuela and countries such as Iran and Thailand. The apparatus of sociological research in the service of the Pentagon became more diffuse from them on.[13]

It was also in this period that simulation models were developed to be applied to counter-insurrectional struggle. Latin America and South-East Asia offered themselves up afresh as possible terrains. ABT Associates designed successively a model for anti-guerilla struggle (Agile-Coin), where once again we find one of the sociologist authors of the simulation model for Kennedy's presidential campaign, Ithiel de Sola Pool; secondly an urban counter-insurrection model; and lastly a more specific model of political and international realities of the Chilean kind, the Politica model. For the first time in this representational game, highly diversified sectors made an appearance because it was a matter of predicting behaviour and attitudes in a revolutionary crisis: the models show the evolution of different parties, landowners, foreign capitalists, middle classes, students, the urban oligarchy, the proletariat. One of the project's designers—who had abandoned it, however—revealed its existence two months before the coup in Chile, and underlined the coincidence of methods (national strikes, paralysis of communications, terrorism, etc.) which reactionary forces and the North American intelligence agencies were in the process of employing in Chile, and those which constituted the elements of the fictional model. According to this same ex-collaborator, this was a fiction which was continually revised, beginning in 1965, and fed with new information, as a substitute for the Camelot Plan.[14]

The growing concern to discover the class contradictions in society and insert them into a perspective within a scheme of intervention, is no longer a monopoly of the Pentagon. The coup in Santiago revealed that the 'indirect' strategy of national security adopted by the North American State had been adapted by the multinationals. As Allende himself put it in his speech to the General Assembly of the United Nations: 'The aggression is not overt and has not been openly declared to the world; on the contrary, it is an oblique, underhand, indirect form of aggression, although this does not make it any less damaging to Chile. We are having to face forces that operate in the half-light . . . ' The group of strategic researchers of the Pentagon's National School of War, after conducting a study which came to the conclusion that 'the phenomenon of the growth of multinational enterprises, mostly North American, can play a major role in the amelioration of our political, military and economic global strength', underlined the need for the civil and military apparatuses to draw closer together in a secret document, saying that it was necessary in order effectively to guarantee the security of the Empire. This document recognised the importance of ideological battle, considering how important it was to preserve North American values and assure the propagation of the transatlantic mode of life: 'on this ever-smaller globe of ours, all societies, all cultures are engaged in an inevitable competition for predominance and survival. Those who will fashion tomorrow's world are those who are able to project their image (to exercise the predominant influence and a long range influence) . . . If we want our values and our life style to be triumphant we are forced to enter a competition with other cultures and other centres of power. For this purpose, the multinational company offers considerable leverage. Its growing business arsenal with its foreign bases works for us 24 hours a day. It is a fact of osmosis which does not only transmit and implant entrepreneurial methods, banking techniques and North American commercial relations, but also our judicial systems and concepts, our political philosophy, our mode of communication, our ideas of mobility, and a way of contemplating literature and art appropriate to our civilisation.'[15]

Kennedy and McNamara recommended the officers of the Pentagon and their students in the School of War works on popular war and guerilla warfare by Mao Tse-tung and Che Guevara. Fifteen years later one should not be surprised to discover that IBM's top management has encouraged its functionaries to submerge themselves in the writings of Carlos Marighella, *The Seven Errors of the Urban Guerilla*. According to an investigation made in 1974 by the Magazine *Fortune* among 600 senior officials of North American based multi-national companies, 58% of the businessmen interviewed thought that the kind of external action which the United States should conduct in the next ten years belonged to the domain of counter-insurrection (only 9% reckoned that it would be involved in a war using tactical nuclear arms).[16]

What happens to the propaganda apparatus in a period of so-called détente?

'If the definition of the cold war is a struggle of ideologies—a war carried on by means other than military conflict—then the cold war evidently still exists, in terms of a struggle for men's minds (. . .) one answer is: we've got to stay strong. But the other answer is we've got to recognise the nature of the enemy, that we are in a psycho-political war—and we'd better shape up.'[17] These aims were stated in May 1972 by Frank Shakespeare, head of the USIA (US Information Agency), which is known abroad as USIS (US Information Service). If the year 1974 was marked by the explosion of revelations and charges against the CIA, in 1972 it was the USIA which took its place in front of the Senate committee. And this statement by its director is just one of the numerous answers to the attacks directed at the official propaganda institution of the US government during that year. Most of the charges were very often contradictory. But these contradictions confirm once again the difficulty the whole ideological apparatus of the imperialist State found in identifying its target, which in the case of USIS, was the foreign addressee of its propaganda operations. The new conditions of the international class struggle changed the nature of the enemy, as well as the forces in charge of fighting it. The necessity of adhering to a new type of strategy, the so-called 'low-profile' strategy, demanded from organisations such as USIS that they abandon the open, necessarily provocative style of action in order to follow the lines of the new diplomacy.

In March 1972, during the debates in front of the Foreign Affairs Committee of the United States Senate, a number of senators came to suggest, and even to demand, that the USIA be suppressed, or that its statutes, which openly supported the cause of the cold war and the world distribution of clear anticommunist catchwords, be radically revised, for the USIA was evidently unable to react to the new political context created by détente. Senator Fulbright, President of the Committee, wasn't using rhetorical formulas to characterise the ideological line followed by USIA during the whole preceding period when he said:[18] 'The public reached by its messages cannot but believe in the old monolithic model of a conspirator communism, the image of the communist society must be that of a world in which men risk their lives daily to escape to freedom. From Czechoslovakia to Austria, from China to Hong Kong, from Cuba to the sea. The whole system is made up of walls, guardians, sub-machine guns and terror.' And this was actually the way the USIA mounted its campaigns. If any further proof is needed after Senator Fulbright's declaration, a glance through the catalogue of programmes offered by this agency to the radio and TV of the world and the sub-capitalist world is enough to convince us:

The Vicissitudes of 091 (17 programs of 30 minutes each) Adaptation of a book written by Ku Ken Chung, who describes the authentic tragedy of a merchant in the province of Canton, China. He describes the methods introduced in China by the reds when they seized the government. *The Trap* (52 programs of 30 minutes each) Each program tells the story of a naive person who falls into a communist trap. The program can be shown in any order, for each is autonomous with respect to the rest. Half of the series has been produced in Mexico, the other half in Bogota. *New Horizon* (39 programs, 25 minutes each) A North American worker in an automobile factory marries a Latin American woman. He is a very active member of his union. His brother-in-law comes from South America and starts spelling out extremist ideas. Two neighbours, refugees from Cuba and East Germany, reject his ideas for they know the communist system very well. The theoretician brother-in-law finally realizes the truth about communism and the dictatorship it exerts over the trade unions. It gives a perspective on the daily life in the United States and a good analysis of North American trade unionism.'

In order to point out the incompatibility of this propaganda with the new demands of American diplomacy, Fulbright cunningly recalled the tone of the official communiqué sent by Nixon to Mao before travelling to Peking:

The United States supports individual freedom and social progress for all of the people of the world, free of outside pressures or intervention. The United States believes that the effort to reduce tensions is served by improving communication between countries that have different ideologies so as to lessen the risks of confrontation through accident, miscalculation or misunderstanding. Countries should treat each other with mutual respect and be willing to compete peacefully, letting performance be the ultimate judge. No country should claim infallibility and each country should be prepared to reexamine its own attitudes for the common goal.'

In fact the USIA inherited a wartime conception of psychological operations. After the Second World War, the US refused to demobilize the diverse psychological war units which, throughout the whole conflict and by means of the air waves, pamphlets, and other propaganda activities, tried to weaken the morale and attitudes of the enemy, as well as stimulating the combative spirit of the population and the allied forces. After the First World War the US had founded a propaganda bureau (The Creel Committee on Public Information), but this bureau was abolished as soon as the armistice was signed. On account of isolationism, there was no special foreign-directed propaganda in the interwar years. In 1945 the US had four organisations whose main job was to 'persuade world opinion' of the good foundations of the North American policy. The Office of War Information (OWI) had been created in 1942, with the purpose of coordinating the cultural and informational activities of the government. From the very beginning this office was provided with a powerful instrument, the 'Voice of America' radio network. The second organisation was created in 1938 and was the first answer of the American government to Nazi propaganda in Latin America. This was the Office of Interamerican Affairs (OIAA). Headed by Nelson Rockefeller, it mobilized the whole American media against the power of the Axis. In this period, for instance, big magazines such as *Time, Life,* and the *Reader's Digest,* were recruited for the official campaigns of the government. And it was also under its protection that, somewhat later, Walt Disney comics and films appeared there, with the sole purpose of convincing the Latin American population of the good will of Uncle Sam. Popular characters of the Andean countries, Brazil and Argentina appeared in these films and comics, and they were naturally integrated into the witty community of the traditional heroes, Donald Duck and his friend Goofy. The US Office of Strategic Services (OSS) and the various Navy and Army groups in charge of psychological operations were also active in the field of propaganda.

The Korean war definitively precipitated the formation of the USIA. After a period of indefinition and waiting, during which some groups demanded a return to peace propaganda while others insisted on systematic campaigns against what they called 'the big Soviet lie', civil propaganda operations were entrusted to a new organisation which took the name of USIA and absorbed the tasks formerly developed by the OWI and the OSS (which meanwhile became the CIA). The USIA

Table 31

USIA Budget and Personnel by Geographical Region (1973)

Region	Budget 1973 (in millions of dollars	Personnel (1972)	
		N. American	Local
Eastern Asia & Pacific	22,574	183	1,056
Africa	12,943	95	365
N. East/N. Africa	7,045	50	298
S. Asia	15,164	79	850
Latin America	19,828	196	660
W. Europe	19,217	153	795
USSR/E. Europe	5,951	55	172
Special Program (Berlin)	4,421	6	28
World Programs	87,856	3,635	1,201
Total	**194,999**	**4,452**	**5,425**

Source: *USIA appropriations authorization, fiscal year 1973.*

Table 32

USIA in Vietnam-JUSPAO Programme (1970–73)

Organisations	Financial aid (in millions of dollars)			
	1970	1971	1972	1973
USIA	6,436	5,812	5,048	3,662
AID	1,668	1,238	741	30
Saigon Govt. Funds	1,013	1,116	949	—
Defense Dept.*	1,414	602	—	—
Total	**10,531**	**8,768**	**6,738**	**3,692**

Source: as Table 30.
* Does not include military wages.

came under the jurisdiction of the Department of Coordination and Operations, an annex to the Security Council. This department was composed of three other sections: the CIA, the State Department and the Defense Department. In a memorandum written after his accession to power, Kennedy characterised the actions which the USIA was to carry out in the following way: 'The mission of the US Information Agency is to help achieve US foreign policy objectives by

(a) influencing public attitudes in other nations, and (b) advising the President, his representatives abroad, and the various departments and agencies, on the implications of foreign opinion for present and contemplated US policies, programs and official statements. The influencing of attitudes is to be carried out by the overt use of the various techniques of communication—personal contact, radio broadcasting, libraries, book publication and distribution, press, motion pictures, television, exhibits, English language instruction and others . . .;' and he added: 'It is necessary . . . to give the USA the image of a strong, democratic and dynamic nation, qualified for leading the efforts made by the world in order to fulfil this purpose.'[19] To carry out this task, in 1972, the USIA spent more than $200 million, and operated 9,885 agents spread over 109 countries, two-thirds of which are overseas stations. Not all the agents are North Americans. The USIA has practised a policy of 'nationalising' its employees, which makes 5,400 of them 'local' agents, as the USIA calls them. In 1972, the staff of the USIA in Latin America included 196 US employees and 660 local agents. For purposes of comparison, at that time the official French information service had 108 French officials and 37 local employees, while the equivalent services of the Federal Republic of Germany and of Great Britain had 81 (25 of which were local employees) and 83 (30 of which were local employees), respectively. But the USIA does not only employ 'locals' and its own nationals. It also employs a number of stateless persons, refugees from Cuba and Eastern countries, who have so far been the most valuable recruits, thanks to their knowledge of the language and idiosyncracy of the countries in which they work, combatting ideology; and who have very often contributed to transform the struggle of propaganda at the heart of the cold war into a holy war. On the other hand, they are an element which makes the adaptation of the organisations specialising in psychological warfare to the particular conditions of détente more complicated. And it goes without saying that these elements serve as a screen for the real authors of psychological aggression.

Among the material resources held by the USIA we can count the radio network, 'The Voice of America', which broadcasts in 35 languages through 123 stations spread over the world; 35 magazines and 4 newspapers ranging from the French publication *Informations et Documents*, to the Italian magazine *Mondo Occidentale*; 3 big publishing centres in Mexico, Manila and Beirut which print pamphlets, posters, magazines and other publications issued not only by USIA but also by the majority of the organisations of US foreign policy; 127 cultural and information centres in 31 countries, which are self-financed up to 85 per cent, thanks to admission fees. These so-called binational centres organise exhibitions, offer English lectures, open their libraries and develop various sorts of cultural programmes In 1972, 210,000 Latin American students learnt English in these centres, and another 2 million have followed their cultural programmes regularly. As a continent, Latin America shows the biggest concentration of this kind: 100 out of 127 bi-national centres are in Latin America. In Brazil alone there are 29, 13 in Argentina, 9 in Mexico, Colombia and Peru, 7 in Chile which survived during the Popular Unity period. In the rest of the world, the distribution of USIA centres is very uneven: four in Iran, three in Indonesia, four in Turkey, five in Germany, two in India, one in Greece and one in Italy.

In 1970, amidst the Vietnamese offensive, President Nixon added a new mission to the civic one assigned by the Congress and confirmed by Kennedy, though in fact he only gave official recognition to a task that USIA had already performed for a long time: 'to give an adequate support in all that concerns psychological warfare, the military leadership in the field of active military operations, and to provide daily advice and materials of basic information'. Actually, the USIA did not wait until this date to start collaborating with the US troops in Saigon. In conjunction with the high military commanders in Vietnam, the USIA created the well-known JUSPAO (Joint US Public Affairs Office) in 1965, in which USIA officials had the decisive mission of 'winning the hearts and minds of the Vietnamese people to support the efforts of the American war, by influencing journalists favourably, learning the tactics of psychological war used by the enemy and weakening its moral strength'.[20] The most efficient contribution of JUSPAO to the so-called 'pacification' campaigns was undoubtedly the notorious 'Operation Phoenix', which made possible the elimination of over 20,000 opponents of the Thieu regime. Also, from their permanent office in the Ministry of Information in Saigon, USIA officials directed the installation of a publishing centre, a whole TV system (four stations giving coverage to 65 per cent of the country), and a radio network (four stations covering 95 per cent of the country); and they developed a news agency with correspondents all over the country. Incapable themselves of supplying the demands of these new networks, they resorted to the services of a film company, Hearst-Metrotone News, a joint subsidiary of Metro Goldwyn Mayer and the Hearst newspaper chain.[21]

The essential aspects of this history became known when the intrigues of the USIA were unravelled in front of the Commission of Inquiry of the US Senate. During the debates some senators denounced it not for being a weak instrument, but on the contrary, for having overtaken events and in several cases refined itself without the legislature's knowledge, quite apart from public ignorance about the propaganda activities both of this organisation and of the CIA, whose secrets were to become known two years later. Those responsible finally admitted the too-intimate relations that this organisation kept with certain of the country's multinational corporations. In Colombia, the USIA had produced—with the logistic support of the American firms installed in that country—a series of 43 TV programmes on the theme 'Private Investment–Public Profits'. In Mexico, with Procter and Gamble, it organised several visits to the metropolitan installations of this firm in order so they said to convince Mexican businessmen of the efficiency of the struggle against pollution which they were carrying out. Earlier, the USIA had organised a colloquim at the University of Texas between Mexican media officials and proprietors, functionaries of General Electric and CBS, and various professors, on 'the revolution of communications and its national and international consequences'. In Ecuador, when new and considerable oil deposits were discovered, the USIA produced pamphlets for Texaco and Gulf Oil, aiming at 'influencing the attitudes of the leaders and local population in the face of the eventual North American exploitation of the deposits'. In 1975, the President of Gulf Oil admitted before a Senate sub-committee on multinationals, that his company had paid out, between 1966 and 1970, $4 million to the Republican Party in power in S. Korea, $460,000 to Bolivian political operatives, and gifts of some $50,000, through the intermediary of a bank in Beirut, for a programme of information released in the US on the Israel-Arab conflict. Most of the legislators claimed that the USIA had acted in too clandestine a fashion in producing and distributing in ten Latin American countries between 1969–1970, for example, unsigned printed material specially developed for the purpose of discrediting urban guerillas and praising the new pacifist heroes of the 'communal development' kind. Not that *guerilleros* are well thought of in Washington, but the statutes of the USIA, which Kennedy mentioned when speaking of the use of overt communication techniques, obliged them henceforth to sign all publications directed to the public.

It was also discovered that the USIA had published, again without signature, tourist guides, manuals for English teachers, and special pamphlets for the local transport trade unions, a particularly strategic sector—as in Chile—when the aim was to stimulate bosses' strikes directed at challenging popular regimes. All this had been done in Ecuador, Paraguay and Mexico. It is interesting to note that the budget of the USIA in countries like Iran and Indonesia—the USIA is just one section within the American Embassies—was as large as that allocated to the whole diplomatic mission. The budget of the American Embassy in Teheran reached $1.8 million, while that of the local USIA reached $15 million.

Despite these revelations, the US Congress renewed the USIA's annual budget of $200 m. But a commission was appointed to present a plan for the reorganisation of the agency. Its members, headed by Frank Stanton, former director of CBS, were Howard Lewis, from *Reader's Digest*, James A. Mitchener, author of several successful novels, and the inevitable George Gallup. Several reports had already been tabled. In one of the first, produced after the resignation of Frank Shakespeare, who left his post in December 1972 to join Westinghouse, it was already possible to notice acquiescence with the observations of the senators, as well as adhesion to something like the certainty of the old days: 'In a period of détente, communications must help to preserve and reinforce this climate, because they place the accent on the most pacific means of resolving bitterness and political and economic international conflicts, sweeping obstacles and psychological barriers away, reducing hostilities that have been accumulated during these years. In the same way as crisis tends to feed crisis, détente can generate détente, without creating the exaggerated euphoria which is built on not very realistic hopes and ignores the indispensible necessity of a strong security structure. USIA should assume command and take the initiative in all that concerns the explanation of the praiseworthy objectives of Presidential policy, in order to contribute to its entire success.' For the first time in an official document, there appeared the need of identifying the interlocutor. Should the USIA activities be oriented to chosen and selective publics? Must they be concentrated on the 200, 2000 or 20,000 most important persons in a country? Or must it be a mass information agency serving the common citizen? One conclusion seems to appear in a quite definitive manner: the so-called general public was very often unattainable.

Above all, this commission, responsible for the reorganisation of USIA, demonstrated the greatest lucidity on the problem of the destination of the message (what Frank Shakespeare called 'on the nature of the enemy') in relation to the use of television and cinema. 'The USIA must proceed to a complete revision of its films and of the objectives it wishes to attain with its television material. The cinema and television products of the USIA have been of an unequal quality in spite of the number of Oscars which they have been able to win in Hollywood and despite the zeal of the directors and their artistic colleagues, both outside and within the agency. There is in the first place a general tendency of North American directors and producers to take the customs and interests of the North American public as a primary reference point when producing films for the foreign consumer. Frequently the message which is effective and loaded with significance for the United States public cannot serve for foreign publics, given that interests differ considerably according to regions and countries. These interests can only be aligned with their pre-occupations and their present problems and must deal with specific events and national affairs. It is therefore necessary to make a periodic analysis and research concerning the public. Without this the best creative work, the most refined production technique remains in an impasse, because its message is without value for a particular foreign public.'[22]

The definitive report of the Stanton Commission was placed before the White House at the beginning of 1975. It did not fail to provoke violent reactions. It proposed, among other things, that the Department of State should create its own Information Bureau Office of Policy Information, and that an autonomous agency should be created, the Agency for Information and Cultural Affairs, which would be in charge of various cultural and educational programmes which until then had been scattered among the Department of State, the USIA and a multitude of other organisations. Finally it recommended that the Voice of America should become an independent agency. All these organisations would answer directly to the head of the North

Table 33

US Propaganda Priority Targets*

1st rank	Popular China, Federal Republic of Germany, Japan, USSR
2nd rank	Brazil, India, Indonesia, Italy, S. Vietnam, Yugoslavia
3rd rank	Egypt, Argentina, Chile, Cuba, France, Democratic Republic of Germany, Greece, Iran, S. Korea, Mexico, Nigeria, Pakistan, Philippines, Poland, Romania, Spain, Thailand, Turkey, Great Briatain, NATO
4th rank	Colombia, Czochoslovakia, Ethiopia, Hungary, Israel, N. Korea, Marocco, Peru, Venezuela, N. Vietnam, Zaire
5th rank	Australia, Canada, Laos, Lebanon, Panama, Sweden, Tunisia
6th rnak	Algeria, Austria, Belgium, Taiwan, Ghana, Cambodia, Libya, Netherlands, Saudi Arabia, S. Africa
7th rank	Afghanistan, Bolivia, Ceylon, Cyprus, Denmark, Finland, Guatemala, Hong Kong, Iraq, Ivory Coast, Jordon, Kenya, Kuwait, Malaysia, New Zealand, Norway, Portugal, Singapore, Sudan, Tanzania, Uruguay
8th rank	Albania, Bulgaria, Burma, Cameroon, Costa Rica, Santa Domiugo, Ecuador, Ireland, Liberia, Malta, Zambia

Source: As Table 30.

* Priorities established according to 'the global importance of the country to US interests (political, strategic, economic, geographical)'.

American diplomatic service. This would have lent itself to a concentration of the official armaments of ideological battle in the hands of Henry Kissinger who would thus have been able to imprint his own personal style on them, substituting for the crusading tone of their campaigns, the voice of a well-informed technocracy.

Does this mean that crude anti-communist campaigns are a thing of the past? We need only think of the reactionary ideological offensive in Portugal to know that this is not so. Similarly, the creation of neo-colonial states in the southern cone of Latin America, which announces a return to the virulent anticommunism of the worst years of the cold war, is just one more daily confirmation of imperialist aggression.

Notes

1 Cf. 'Les consultants américains cherchent leur second souffle', *Le Figaro*, 30–31 March 1974, p. 7. On the G.E. Think Tank (TEMPO), cf. 'G.E.: Profile of a corporation', *Dissent*, July–August 1967.
2 E. B. Waiss, 'The shape of the agency business beyond 1980', *Advertising Age*, 26 June 1972, p. 62.
3 *Business Week*, 15.IX.1973.
4 *Business Week* 5.VIII.1975; on espionage in the electronics industries. cf. Judith Curtis 'Theft of Secrets: Headache Continues', *Electronics* 15.V.1975.
5 *Ibid.*
6 'The IBM Papers' *Berkley Barb*, 22–28 November 1974.
7 Reproduced in *NACLA's Latin America and Empire Report*, December 1974.
8 *Que Pasa*, Santiago, Chile, 28.VI.1974.
9 'Où va la publicité?' *op.cit.*
10 *Advertising Age*, 4.IV.1967, 5.VI.1967.
11 *Advertising Age*, 24.IV.1967.
12 Cited by Michael T. Klare *War Without End, op.cit.*
13 On the Camelot Plan, cf. Gregorio Selser, *Espionaje en América Latina, El Pentagono, y las Técnicas sociologicas*. Buenos Aires 1966, Ed. Iguazu; Jorge Unsumza 'El proyecto Camelot: producto genuino de la politica exterior norte-americana' *Principios*, Santiago, Chile, August 1965.
14 *Berkeley Barb*, 14–20 September 1973.
15 Reproduced in Josehph Collins' 'Etats-Unis et Transnationale américaines: retour à l'envoyeur', *Politique Aujourd'hui*, numbers 1–2 January–February 1975.
16 *Fortune*, May 1974.
17 Interview with Frank Shakespeare, *US News and World Report*, I.V.1972.
18 'USIA Appropriations Authorization, Fiscal Year 1973', *op.cit.*
19 Reproduced in the audience reports.
20 *The New York Times*, 13.VI.1972.
21 ON USIA action in S.E. Asia, cf. the interview with an ex-official of the organisation in *Communicacion y Cultura*, Buenos Aires, 1975, no. 4.
22 26th Report on the Information, Educational and Cultural Progress of USIS, submitted to the US Congress on 27 January 1973. Published by the Committee of Surveillance of Information (duplicated) (retranslated from the French—See Translators foreword).